THE STATE AND
ECONOMIC GROWTH

Papers of a Conference
Held on October 11-13, 1956,
under the Auspices of the
Committee on Economic Growth

Edited by

HUGH G. J. AITKEN

SOCIAL SCIENCE RESEARCH COUNCIL
NEW YORK   1959

The Social Science Research Council was organized in 1923 and formally incorporated in 1924 for the purpose of advancing research in the social sciences. Its members are chosen from seven associated professional organizations in the social sciences and from related fields.

ASSOCIATED ORGANIZATIONS

American Anthropological Association

American Economic Association

American Historical Association

American Political Science Association

American Psychological Association

American Sociological Society

American Statistical Association

FOREWORD

The Committee on Economic Growth of the Social Science Research Council is attempting to find ways of stimulating research on the major factors that influence the long-run growth of national states and other major geographic units. It is concerned alike with furthering more rigorous empirical study and with encouraging clearer formulation of intellectual frameworks for such study. It is aware that many of the problems of economic growth cannot be examined adequately within the traditional boundaries of economics but must attract the active collaboration of scholars in the other social sciences.

One of the means used to pursue the committee's purposes has been a thoughtfully selected and planned series of research conferences, focused on areas of work that the committee has regarded as strategic in its own discussion of problems in the analysis of economic growth. The conferences have been designed to precipitate around selected questions the thinking of groups of scholars who have demonstrated prior interest, and a readiness to share in the planning of a next stage of research. The conference that gave rise to the present volume resulted from prolonged discussions within the committee regarding the feasibility of establishing an adequate basis for empirical study of the influence of the state on economic growth. It will be evident from the contents of the volume that this basis is not yet established; but it is the committee's hope that the papers that follow will stimulate increasing interest in this subject and will lead scholars to make further progress toward understanding the causes of and obstacles to economic growth.

The Conference on the State and Economic Growth was the seventh of the conferences sponsored by the committee either under its own auspices or jointly with interested research organizations. Previous conferences included one in 1951 on the quantitative description of technological change; one in 1952 on comparisons of economic growth in Brazil, India, and Japan; and four in 1954, on strategic factors in periods of rapid economic growth, on cities and their role in economic growth, on investment criteria in planning development programs, and

v

on entrepreneurship and economic growth. Each conference was intended primarily to promote effective interchange of research experience and knowledge among the participants. However, formal publications resulted in three instances: *Economic Growth: Brazil, India, Japan* was published by the Duke University Press in 1955; a series of papers on the role of cities in economic development appeared in *Economic Development and Cultural Change,* in October 1954, January 1955, and April 1955; and *Investment Criteria and Economic Growth* was issued in December 1955 by the Massachusetts Institute of Technology Center for International Studies. An eighth conference, held in 1958, is expected to result in publication by the Council late in 1959 of a volume on labor commitment and social change.

The Committee on Economic Growth is currently initiating a second series of research conferences to be held in 1960 and subsequent years, with the aim of directing attention to additional significant aspects of the problem of economic growth and extending the committee's relations with other students in its field.

SIMON KUZNETS

CONTENTS

INTRODUCTION

THIS volume is the outcome of a Conference on the State and Economic Growth, held in New York, October 11–13, 1956, under the auspices of the Committee on Economic Growth of the Social Science Research Council. The initial versions of the papers comprising this volume were distributed to participants in the conference some weeks in advance and were critically discussed at the conference. In the light of this discussion most of the papers were revised by their authors, for inclusion in this volume.

The committee responsible for planning the conference—Richard Hartshorne, Bert F. Hoselitz, and Joseph J. Spengler—faced a number of problems, the chief of which was devising a schema that would give some unity to the treatment of the main subject while allowing adequate scope for comparative analysis. A schema with which Hoselitz was then experimenting seemed to meet the needs of the planning committee.[1] According to this schema, countries might be distinguished in terms of three significant continua, and intercountry differences in position on these continua might be expected to be associated with notable differences in the countries' patterns of growth. For convenience of classification and discussion, it was decided to confine attention to countries situated at relatively extreme points on each of the three continua. The committee was thus provided, in theory, with eight types of countries, at least one representative of which, if identifiable, might be the subject of analysis.

The three continua, in the somewhat polar ranges where our interest lies, may be described as follows:

1. Countries might be classified in terms of the degree to which land and other relevant resources had been exploited by the beginning of the period under study. In practice, however, for purposes of the conference, the most utilizable measure of exploitation proved to be extent of land use. Accordingly, a country, whether new or old, was described as *expansionist* if it included a considerable amount of land that had been used very little or not at all; for as this land was brought into use, gross product would grow whether or not cultivation increased in in-

[1] This schema is described by Hoselitz in his "Patterns of Economic Growth," *Canadian Journal of Economics and Political Science*, 21:416–431 (November 1955).

tensity and efficiency per land unit as well as in extent. If, on the contrary, a country could augment gross production only by increasing the intensity and the efficiency with which it cultivated its land, it was said to be undergoing *intrinsic* development. *Ex hypothesi,* of course, degree of use of any or all other natural resources is also available as a criterion in terms of which countries might be classified as undergoing either expansionist or intrinsic development. In practice, however, this criterion is much less suitable than land use in respect to the nineteenth century; for even in Western Europe the exploitation of important resources other than land was still in the expansionist stage in the second half of the century. It may be relevant, furthermore, to inquire how areal expansion affects the intensity with which resources other than land are exploited.

2. Countries might be classified in terms of the extent to which they were self-contained and not dependent upon externally situated markets and sources of merchandise, capital, etc. A comparatively autarkic country that found most of its sinews of growth within its own boundaries might then be described as a *dominant* type, whereas one that was significantly dependent upon foreign sources might be described as a satellite or *nondominant* type.

3. Countries might be classified in terms of the kind of decision that determined how resources were allocated. Decisions concerning resource allocation, especially the allocation of capital for investment, may be made by the same agency (or person, or persons) that makes political decisions, or by an agency separate and distinct from it. A country in which decisions about resource use and capital allocation are made predominantly by an agency distinct from that making political decisions might be described as undergoing *autonomous* growth. A country in which the former decisions were made largely by an agency that also made political decisions might be described as undergoing *induced* growth.

Eight countries were selected for treatment, since their development over a particular period seemed to warrant placing them respectively in the eight categories of this schema. The United States was considered representative of the expansionist, dominant, autonomous category; Australia and Canada, of the expansionist, nondominant, autonomous. Russia was found representative of the expansionist, dominant, induced category; Manchuria, of the expansionist, nondominant, induced. Nineteenth-century France and Germany were considered representative of the intrinsic, dominant, autonomous type; Switzerland, of the intrinsic, nondominant, autonomous. Representative of the intrinsic, dominant, induced type was Turkey after World War I; and of the intrinsic, nondominant, induced type, the "peoples' democracies" of Eastern Europe after World War II. Whether the countries were found to be truly representative of the categories in which they were tentatively placed, or whether the schema employed is analytically and empirically useful, is not indicated in this introduction. The answers to these questions are supplied in part in the following papers on specific countries, and in part in the general papers, particularly that by Hoselitz.

The schema on the basis of which countries were selected was outlined in communications with the authors, but with an indication that it was to be viewed merely as a selective and organizing device. It was explicitly recognized, moreover, that governmental activities had tended to be important even in countries described as *autonomous*. It was suggested that authors might inquire whether a country's dominance or nondominance, or its expansionist or intrinsic development, tended significantly to affect the degree of state intervention, the extent to which decisions governing growth in land settlement or internal improvements or other aspects were made under public or private auspices, and so on. It was suggested, also, that the specific objectives of the growth policies of given states might be identified, together with the circumstances that encouraged the choice of these objectives. Finally, the suggestions to the authors proposed that a common definition of growth be adopted (specifically, increase in production per capita) and that some attention be given to the states' methods of fostering growth—to whether they consisted largely in the creation of a milieu favorable to growth, or in the introduction of measures designed to accomplish specific purposes.

1 THE ROLE OF THE STATE

IN AMERICAN ECONOMIC

DEVELOPMENT, 1820–1890

Henry W. Broude

Economic change in the United States during the nineteenth century followed a pattern which, although set at an early stage by Great Britain, soon became distinctly American in characteristics and timing. The rate of growth increased with an impetus stemming from the simultaneous emergence of new technology and expansion of the domain under the aegis of the United States. The period has been described as typifying extensive and independent growth. Hoselitz has characterized the American setting as expansionist (almost unlimited natural resources), dominant (relatively self-sufficient, self-reliant approach to economic development), and autonomous (minimal intervention by the state in economic activity).[1] The appropriateness of the characterization as expansionist is evident not only as reflected in the advance of the frontier,[2] but also in the burgeoning "American system of manufacturing," unique in itself.[3]

Categorizing the United States of the nineteenth century as dominant may be acceptable, but certain remarks should accompany this designation. Dominance, in the sense used, is open to the qualification that insofar as European capital was used throughout the century American economic development did receive stimulus from abroad.[4] Also,

[1] Bert F. Hoselitz, "Patterns of Economic Growth," *Canadian Journal of Economics and Political Science*, 21:416–431 (November 1955).

[2] From Turner's vantage point (in 1893), "The fall line marked the frontier of the seventeenth century; the Alleghanies that of the eighteenth; the Mississippi that of the first quarter of the nineteenth; the Missouri that of the middle of this century (omitting the California movement); and the belt of the Rocky Mountains and the arid tract, the present frontier."—Frederick J. Turner, *The Frontier in American History* (New York: Henry Holt and Company, 1921), p. 9.

[3] John E. Sawyer, "The Social Basis of the American System of Manufacturing," *Journal of Economic History*, 14(4):361–379 (1954), especially 368ff.

[4] The test would be in whether potential existed internally to generate investment funds sufficient to satisfy demand for them, and whether these funds would have caused the rate of expansion that occurred (if such a rate is regarded as having been desirable).

questions arise concerning the pace of development in the absence of such immigration (and movement of goods to European markets) as took place. In particular, the critical period in the early decades of the century, when the country was evolving from a nondominant status, should not be overlooked.

It is to the third classificatory term, autonomous, that attention is given in this paper. Is the term appropriate when applied to American growth from 1820 to 1890? Rather than a complete catalogue of state activity in the economic sphere, we present material which, it is suggested, should temper the characterization of American growth in the nineteenth century as autonomous. Although one may well be wary of assigning weights to the "evidence" (and thereby appearing to tilt with the image of the American economy of that century), it seems worth while to attempt an appraisal of the role of the state in American development. The contemporary vogue in "economics of growth" of recommending policy based on analogy with past experience justifies detailed research on an example so frequently cited in present-day studies of underdeveloped areas. The more we relate the specific and detailed aspects of American economic development to each other and to the context of the period, the more sensitive and operationally significant any attempts to use this historical material may be.

The strategic location in the economy of governmentally induced activity may prove to have leverage implications for development well in excess of what highly aggregative studies may indicate. This may be true not only in the sense of specific impact at spatially and temporally strategic points, but also in the sense that the mere *presence* of government gives rise to activity that appears in history as purely autonomous; in actuality the effects of government may be cloaked in the data left behind.

The first part of the discussion below is concerned with the character and degree of governmental intervention in the economy. Next we present evidence on what might be termed positive aspects of the state's role. Finally, observations are made regarding the validity of the characterization and the potential usefulness of the American example in a framework of typical growth patterns.

CHARACTER AND DEGREE OF INTERVENTION

An appraisal of the degree of private enterprise in the development of a given economy might begin with specification of its industry sectors and estimates of each sector's share of output originating under the control of private establishments. For America in the nineteenth century, this would give a picture of overwhelming proportionate dominance of the private sphere. It might be desirable to supplement such an appraisal with a more qualitatively oriented survey of the sources of initiative in innovational activity. Both approaches would be needed to support the picture of America (undoubted here) as a society geared to individual enterprise, to general conformity to the profit maximization model, and to a growth pattern attuned to adopting new techniques as they emerge.[5] But what of the additional attribute of a minimal *role* for government? [6]

It is on this question that the evidence becomes less clear, and it is on the interpretation of what constitutes "government intervention" in economic life that the outcome of a judgment will depend. Hoselitz, for example, states: "Governmental practice may not coincide with the norms stipulated for the conduct of the political authorities. In other words, the relations between government and private individuals in the economic sphere may be so conceived as to leave, ideally, all significant decisions to the private individuals, yet government may impose narrow limits within which private initiative may be exercised or may use various forms of subsidies, so that, in practice, the process of growth depends primarily upon the government's 'inducements' rather than upon autonomous private decisions." He goes on to conclude, however: "If, therefore, we draw our line of distinction between induced and autonomous patterns of growth in such a way as to include in the former only those types of governmental action which have the aim of consciously allocating productive factors in a specified direction, the

---

[5] Hoselitz indicates (see pp. 325 ff. infra) that economic growth means a rise in the output of an economy and specifies that an increase in real product per worker signifies growth. In this connection Leontief has pointed out that if some assessment were made of the relative "importance" of (1) the extensive application of capital-using techniques as economic societies expand, as opposed to (2) the introduction of new methods leading to higher productivity of the capital that is either in use or is introduced, the latter—i.e., the changing production function—would be credited with the more far-reaching significance. Thus study of economic change should reveal technological innovation rather than capital accumulation as the motive force where these alternatives, as categories, are compared. For present purposes, however, it is worth noting that inducement to investment as a consequence of expanding markets is an aspect of "growth" that may not initially involve technological change, but nevertheless has the requisite significant effects on output.

[6] Government here refers to both state and national government. The differing influence of state versus federal intervention is discussed on pp. 12–14 infra.

policies of almost all governments in the period before 1914 should be regarded as permitting an autonomous process of growth." [7]

Definition of the limits within which governmental intervention is considered to be passive and minimal plays an important part in evaluating the American situation, for the really significant role may be found to lie outside the defined function of "consciously allocating productive factors in a specified direction." One finds in aggregated data on governmental shares of national wealth (Table 1) or income realized from the government sector (Table 2) that the proportionate shares of government were relatively low, although on the rise during the nineteenth century.[8] An examination of federal finances shows federal expenditures to be a small portion of gross national product, and years in which budgetary surpluses existed were frequent in the earlier part of the century.[9]

TABLE 1. PERCENTAGE SHARES OF GOVERNMENT IN TOTAL REPRODUCIBLE WEALTH, UNITED STATES *

	Structures		Equipment	
Year	Current prices	1929 prices	Current prices	1929 prices
1805	3.4	3.9	–	–
1850	2.9	3.1	–	–
1880	2.4	2.7	0.8	0.6
1890	2.8	2.8	0.9	1.0
1900	3.5	3.5	1.2	1.2

Source: Raymond W. Goldsmith, "The Growth of Reproducible Wealth of the United States of America from 1805 to 1950," Table I, pp. 306–307, in International Association for Research in Income and Wealth, *Income and Wealth of the United States: Trends and Structure*, Income and Wealth Series II (Cambridge, England: Bowes & Bowes, 1952).

* Including nonprofit institutions, but excluding military; inventory data not available.

All of this substantiates the assertion of an autonomous climate. Yet even at the outset of the period there are signs of conflict regarding the

[7] "Patterns of Economic Growth, *op. cit.*, p. 425.

[8] Limitations of the data available for periods before 1880 are well known; nevertheless, reference to early series for an indication of relative magnitudes is useful for our purposes.

[9] Cf. Albert S. Bolles, *The Financial History of the United States from 1789 to 1860* (New York: D. Appleton and Company, 1883), especially pp. 203–216, 538–566, 576–609.

TABLE 2. REALIZED INCOME FROM GOVERNMENT, BY KIND, UNITED STATES, 1799–1900

Year	Realized income from government (million $)	Percentage of total realized national income	Production income from government (million $)	Other income from government (million $)
1799	6	0.9	6	–
1809	11	1.2	11	–
1819	17	1.9	15	2
1829	21	2.2	20	1
1839	39	2.4	37	2
1849	58	2.4	57	1
1859	101	2.3	100	1
1869	290	4.2	271	19
1879	322	4.5	284	38
1889	558	5.2	486	72
1899	1,005	6.5	910	95
1900	1,052	6.5	957	95

Source: Robert F. Martin, *National Income in the United States, 1799–1938* (New York: National Industrial Conference Board, 1939), p. 87.

assumed ideological basis of this pattern. Jefferson and Jackson were clear about federal intervention, and there is a record of relative absence of "federalism" in fiscal matters in the United States up to and after the Civil War.[10] The patterns of minimal expenditure, however, during the administrations of Madison, Monroe, and John Quincy Adams obscure what was in reality a period of conflict in defining the *intended* role of government in the American economy in terms of both degree and level. These presidents, although in favor of federal expenditures for internal improvements, for example, were constrained either by their own doubts as to constitutionality or, in the case of Adams, by the impossibility of getting measures through Congress.[11]

[10] Cf. James A. Maxwell, *The Fiscal Impact of Federalism in the United States* (Cambridge: Harvard University Press, 1946).

[11] Fabricant writes of a later period: "Even a Democratic president, vetoing the appropriation for seed corn . . . could state: 'I can find no warrant for such an appropriation in the Constitution, and I do not believe that the power and duty of the general government ought to be extended to the relief of individual suffering which is in no manner properly related to the public service or benefit. A prevalent tendency to disregard the limited mission of this power and duty should, I think, be steadfastly resisted, to the end that the lesson should be constantly enforced that,

From the early differences regarding governmental intervention there emerges a picture of men with ideological appetites for a laissez-faire menu, but one highly seasoned with selective exceptions. The record shows that up to the end of the nineteenth century the wage and price system, usage of resources, credit creation, and provision of capital,[12] as well as other elements of the entrepreneurial function were kept within and held to be within the province of the private sector of the economy. Government effected a land tenure policy for the country, controlled immigration policy (conditioning the supply of labor), maintained intervention in the banking system (varied over the period),[13] established protection of trade through tariff and patent legislation, performed the roster of services "rightfully" governmental, and represented and strengthened the particular legal framework within

---

though the people support the government, the government should not support the people.' [His citation: "Veto of the Texas Seed Bill, Feb. 16, 1887, *The Writings and Speeches of Grover Cleveland,* edited by G. F. Parker (Cassel Publishing Co., 1892)."] He goes on to state: "Yet efforts were constantly being made by every group 'seriously dissatisfied with the results of private enterprise, or of private enterprise as regulated by local or state governments,' to use the federal government as an agency for attaining what it desired."—Solomon Fabricant, *The Trend of Government Activity in the United States since 1900* (New York: National Bureau of Economic Research, 1952), pp. 6–7.

[12] As to facilitating the availability of capital, Spengler has noted: "The state can contribute to the augmentation of equipment per worker by preventing waste of resources, by creating a milieu favorable to saving and capital formation, by facilitating the provision of an efficient banking system, by emphasizing investment rather than consumption expenditures in its anticyclical policies, and in general by fostering the increase of per capita output and of the fraction of this output devoted to capital formation. It should be noted that, for technical and economic reasons, a state's power to increase equipment through the importation of capital is quite limited."—Joseph J. Spengler, "The Role of the State in Shaping Things Economic," *Journal of Economic History,* Vol. 7, Suppl. (1947), p. 135.

[13] Early discussion of government intervention in this sphere is cited by Victor S. Clark: "After the War of 1812, when other means to promote manufacturing than the tariff were under discussion, attention was drawn mainly to the difficulty of procuring capital for their support. 'Some thought it would be best for the Government to establish manufacturers and carry them on at public expense by managers and superintendents to be appointed by the Executive.' [Quoted from the *Aurora* undated, in Carey Clippings, VI, 281.] The Secretary of the Treasury suggested the expedient of a Government circulating capital, to be loaned without interest to manufacturers and to be repaid by them as conditions admitted [*American State Papers, Finance,* II, 430, 431]."—*History of Manufactures in the United States, Vol. I, 1607–1860* (Washington: Carnegie Institution, 1916), p. 369.

which private business was organized.[14] Despite the acknowledged dominance of the autonomous sector of the economy, however, the record does indicate that at the end of the century calls for governmental aid had resulted in the holding by government of approximately 7 percent of the nation's capital assets and the employment by government of approximately 4 percent of the national labor force.[15]

Although the intent of this paper is to comment on the actual manifestations of state intervention rather than to discuss history of doctrine, one point regarding the intellectual climate of the period may be emphasized. There was tacit acceptance of an ideology; yet within it there were notable internal paradoxes and there were extensive departures from it in practice on a "selective" basis. This perhaps stresses the obvious but indicates the linked relationship, typically traced in discussions of economic growth, between investment (as the focal point in a dynamic industrial economy) and entrepreneurial action (responsive to expectations and the accessibility of usable funds).[16] Interwoven in such analysis is a link between ideology and growth and, hence, between the attitude of the entrepreneur toward the political climate and the state's role as it relates to the economic sphere. The pertinent question is whether the internal paradoxes and departures from the ideal that existed in the nineteenth century were at variance with the American entrepreneur's economic objectives or supplemental to them. Departure from a laissez-faire ideology means, of course, intervention of government. What must be established is whether intervention left the "representative" entrepreneur hostile, neutral, or perhaps with positive sentiments. If it appears that most "interventions" were compatible with the goals of the entrepreneur, it may be suggested that in evaluating the role of the state in economic

[14] Fabricant classifies government services "in terms of their ultimate objectives: (1) maintenance of order; (2) promotion of economic activity; (3) production to meet current needs; (4) development of the nation's capacity to defend itself and satisfy its needs; and (5) distribution of the nation's income."—*Op. cit.*, p. 48.

[15] *Ibid.*, p. 7. Assets cited are "exclusive of roads and streets and most military and naval equipment."

[16] "Further analysis seems to be called for, at least so far as American capitalism is concerned, analysis that will come to closer grips with the special features of American social structure and the various influences which made for a strong entrepreneurial bias in the 'social character' of the nineteenth-century American."— Leland H. Jenks, "Railroads as an Economic Force in American Development," in Frederic C. Lane and Jelle C. Riemersma, eds. *Enterprise and Secular Change* (Homewood, Ill.: Richard D. Irwin, 1953), p. 179.

growth we cannot consider only (or merely) the amount of income generated in the government sector of the economy, or the cases where impediments to activity in the private sector had been removed by government. Rather we must consider what the entrepreneur saw as the accommodation potential of the political structure in aiding him in his pursuit of his "special" needs along an uncertain and hazardous course.[17]

The next section presents examples of three aspects of government's positive role: giving specific and direct support to industry in the private sector; taking initial risks, leading the way, and removing bottlenecks; and creating a favorable climate which had salutory effects on expectations in the private sector.

POSITIVE ASPECTS OF THE STATE'S ROLE

The range of possible government actions affecting the economy is so wide that any discussion could become a mere exercise in cataloguing. It seems preferable, therefore, to consider particular episodes that illustrate "positive" action. Positive is here contrasted with passive or minimal, and a complete roster of such positive action in the nineteenth century would include attempts to modify the physical environment and the level and skill of the labor force, the introduction of new techniques, and the direct undertaking of business ventures, as well as support of industry in the private sector.[18]

A survey of the many dimensions of economic participation open to political units in the nineteenth century impresses one with the ex-

[17] Spengler has provided a basis for examining governmental effect on national income aggregates, dividing the range of state action into three subcategories. He states that distribution of income "is governed (a) by the functional division of net output among the co-operating productive agents, which depends, under simple competition, upon the comparative rates of growth of the several classes of human and nonhuman productive agents, and upon the elasticity of substitution of each type of productive agent for other agents; (b) by the distribution of the ownership of economically significant talents, output-creating factors, and income-generating institutional relations not otherwise covered; and (c) by the changes produced, by gifts and taxation, in income distribution as determined by (a) and (b) alone."— *Op. cit.,* p. 132.

[18] A condensed survey of government activity in business (1789–1932) was made by Warren Persons, who was concerned with evaluating the relative "success" of undertakings (he found them unsuccessful); in the course of this evaluation he surveyed the range of activity. See his *Government Experimentation in Business* (New York: John Wiley & Sons, 1934).

tensive functional range of these activities at all levels of government. Yet discussions of governmental intervention often implicitly emphasize government at the federal level. It is advisable, therefore, to differentiate explicitly between state and federal action as their effects were felt during the century.

Before the Civil War, government intervention in economic life was widespread but it was concentrated at the state level. The recent studies by the Handlins, Hartz, Heath, Pierce, and Primm [19] all present evidence not only of the extent of government intervention but of the fact that respective states held the center of the stage.[20] In his study of expenditures on railroads in the South, Heath concludes that public investment should be credited with more than 55 percent of total investment in that area (based on the total value of its railroads in the Census of 1860). He indicates that 4.7 percent of total public expenditures were federal, 56.7 percent were state, 26.0 percent municipal, and 12.6 percent county. In addition to direct expenditures, there was aid in the form of services of public officials and property, grants of rights of way, public lands and building sites, materials, tax exemptions, banking facilities, and other privileges.[21] There was activity at the local level also. Martin, in his study of living standards in 1860, points

[19] Oscar and Mary F. Handlin, *Commonwealth: A Study of the Role of Government in the American Economy: Massachusetts, 1774–1861* (New York: New York University Press, 1947); Louis Hartz, *Economic Policy and Democratic Thought: Pennsylvania, 1776–1860* (Cambridge: Harvard University Press, 1948); Bray Hammond, "Banking in the Early West: Monopoly, Prohibition, and Laissez Faire," *Journal of Economic History,* 8:1–25 (May 1948); Milton S. Heath, "Public Railroad Construction and the Development of Private Enterprise in the South Before 1861," *Journal of Economic History,* Vol. 10, Suppl. (1950), pp. 40–53, and *Constructive Liberalism: The Role of the State in Economic Development in Georgia to 1860* (Cambridge: Harvard University Press, 1954); Harry H. Pierce, *Railroads of New York: A Study of Government Aid, 1826–1875* (Cambridge: Harvard University Press, 1953); James N. Primm, *Economic Policy in the Development of a Western State: Missouri 1820–1860* (Cambridge: Harvard University Press, 1954). Material presented in Pierce's study shows intervention well after the Civil War. Cf. Howard R. Lamar, *Dakota Territory, 1861–1889: A Study of Frontier Politics* (New Haven: Yale University Press, 1956).

[20] For a nineteenth-century perspective on the relative success of state aid to early railroad development (and of attempts at internal improvements by the states), see John L. Ringwalt, *Development of Transportation Systems in the United States* (Philadelphia: published by the author, 1888), pp. 79–82.

[21] Heath, "Public Railroad Construction and the Development of Private Enterprise in the South Before 1861," *op. cit.,* pp. 40–43.

out that before 1860 local government expenditures were called forth, in part at least, by increased needs for goods and services.[22]

The nature and scope of the role of the respective states in the earlier part of the century is reflected in conclusions by Hartz:

. . . the mixed enterprise program . . . , embracing both profit and control objectives, . . . had more than simply a promotional significance. Originating in the banking field in the late eighteenth century, it flourished with increasing strength for half a century, eventually being extended to transportation and embracing various types of enterprise there. In 1844 over one hundred and fifty mixed corporations were currently listed in the official records of Pennsylvania, with public investments ranging from a few shares of stock to several thousand. It is hard to view such a policy as an incidental phase of state action worthy of only marginal notice.

Nor is it easy to regard as incidental the role of the state as entrepreneur exclusively in its own right. . . . It was with the inception of the public works in the 1820's, where a process of steady expansion and increasing investment was premised at the outset, that the entrepreneurial function of the state assumed major proportions.[23]

Writing of government action at the various levels in unlocking the reservoirs of national wealth, Potter calls attention to the rejection of "public capitalization of a great economic asset" in favor of "widespread access to wealth." Yet, as he notes, the potential for economic development depended not only on the now available land, but also on access to markets. Government participation in providing such access was extensive, taking the form of furthering internal improvements to facilitate communication with markets. Sometimes the federal government directly undertook projects, such as construction of the Cumberland Pike; sometimes the state government took responsibility, as New York did with the Erie Canal; and there were many cases of indirect participation, through offers of public credit or the power of eminent domain, as well as direct financial support of entrepreneurs.[24]

---

[22] "The old voluntary fire and police departments were totally inadequate. A municipal water supply was essential to a crowded population, and sewers had to be provided. Greater distances and heavier traffic called for better streets and sidewalks, bridges, and (in other local divisions) roads."—Edgar W. Martin, *The Standard of Living in 1860: American Consumption Levels on the Eve of the Civil War* (Chicago: University of Chicago Press, 1942), pp. 280–281.

[23] Hartz, *op. cit.*, p. 290.

[24] Cf. David M. Potter, *People of Plenty: Economic Abundance and the American Character* (Chicago: University of Chicago Press, 1954), p. 124; also Carter Goodrich, "American Development Policy," *Journal of Economic History*, 16:449–460 (1956).

Hibbard has pointed out that land grants as part of a program of internal improvements were "a major part of the whole episode of conscious development of the nation through public action. It was believed that private action was likely to be too uncertain and too slow." [25] Indeed there was an approach to conscious economic planning, which is reflected in President Fillmore's assertion, on signing the Land Grant Act in 1850, that it could be "expected to help undeveloped regions of West and South."

Controversy has long existed over how to evaluate a policy that transferred the disposal of resources to one industrial sector at the expense of alternative uses. Welfare criteria brought to bear on this discussion would have to weigh against the rapid expansion of a transportation system and the unifying effects on the nation such considerations as the episodes of waste, mismanagement, and erratic growth patterns.[26]

[25] He continues: "Beginning with wagon road and canal grants in the twenties, followed closely by river improvement grants, the plan of granting the land to the states was devised. These specific grants extended over a period of about forty-five years, from 1823 to 1869. A more general plan was embodied in the half-million acre grants, mainly for the same, or at least similar, purposes in the act of 1841. . . . The grants for railroads, the most liberal donations ever made for the encouragement of private enterprise, reached the figure of 129,000,000 acres, and even this is somewhat short since other lands granted to states, not specifically for railroads, were turned over to them nevertheless. Minor grants, and grants to states for miscellaneous purposes, run well into the millions."—Benjamin H. Hibbard, *A History of the Public Land Policies* (New York: P. Smith, 1939), p. 267. Cf. James A. Maxwell, *Federal Grants and the Business Cycle* (New York: National Bureau of Economic Research, 1952).

[26] Gates makes the point: "At the very moment when Congress was promising free land to settlers, it was enacting measures which gave to railroads, in order to aid in their construction, an area three times the size of New York State. Congress was also giving lands to states as subsidies for education in universities, vocational, and grade schools. These lands were not to be given to settlers but instead were to be sold at the highest possible price. Furthermore, despite the advent of free homesteads in 1862 Congress neglected to repeal measures providing for unrestricted sale of public lands. Consequently, many million acres continued to be sold to speculators, lumber barons, cattle kings, and land companies, who secured the profits in rising land values that the Homestead Act had intended to assure the small man. In keeping old policies and superimposing upon them the new and more generous policies, Congress was moving away from the well-organized, consistent, and coherent policies of the past into a complex maze of inconsistent and inharmonious measures that minimized greatly the benevolent character of the new program."—Paul W. Gates, *Fifty Million Acres: Conflicts over Kansas Land Policy, 1854–1890* (Ithaca: Cornell University Press, 1954), pp. 13–14. Cf. also his "The Homestead Act in an In-

Characterization of specific activities and policies in an appraisal of the state's role must take account of continuing governmental action to make resources and areas more readily accessible as the economy developed. Initially, reference was made to internal improvements with emphasis on communication. However, as changing technology brought new resources (coal, iron, waterpower, oil) and new methods of production into use, government's role in "facilitating growth" covered the range of activities typically discussed in a survey of American developmental history: a legal structure conducive to corporate ownership of production units with guarantees of equal advantage in internal competition and, through tariff barriers, protection against competition from abroad.[27] Aitken has suggested that the temptation to minimize the role of tariffs in this respect should be resisted for two significant reasons: they have the effect of redistributing income among sectors of the economy and serve as means of reducing the uninsurable risks for private investment. Inclusion of these considerations in the American picture would depend on whether tariff protection effectively blocked sources of competition for American producers, whether entrepreneurial willingness to undertake certain amounts of production would have been affected at the margin by a risk element removed by the existence of the tariff barrier, and whether protection did not insulate enterprise from stimuli to greater growth than took place. The last possibility appears to be the one on which the firmest assertion can be made: it seems reasonable to say that stimulus to growth was not wanting and that, unlike France for example, the existence of protection did not result in stifling the dynamic potential of the period. Also, assurance of domination of domestic markets and the ensuing reduction of risk and promise of increased returns affected the rate of capital formation and the areas of the economy to which it was directed. However, in these latter developments one would be reluctant to assign a weight to the "importance" of protection. It does seem appropriate to say, with Aitken, that tariff protection deserves to be considered as among the "nonminimal" functions of government.

To fill out the picture, two other "types" of intervention should be examined. Manufacturing, commerce, and agriculture continually faced bottlenecks. Use of this term denotes short-run, "isolated" bar-

---

congruous Land System," *American Historical Review,* 41:652–681 (July 1939); Thomas C. Cochran, "Land Grants and Railroad Entrepreneurship," *Journal of Economic History,* Vol. 10, Suppl. (1950), especially pp. 55, 64, 67; and Jenks, *op. cit.*
    [27] Cf. Potter, *op. cit.,* pp. 124–125.

riers to or inhibitors of development, as contrasted with continuing problems on a broad front of economic change. Removal of such barriers by government should be treated separately because, as in any bottleneck situation, coping with the critically placed obstacle may call for expenditure of relatively insignificant amounts with consequences of major importance.[28] Where government is the only source of initiative and action to remove such obstacles, assessment of the "importance" of this aspect of government's role is essential.

Examples range from the literal bottleneck to the psychological. On one hand, the raft of the Red River might be cited; on the other, the "presence effect" of government—i.e., the effect of government activity in an area, giving moral support to undertakings in the wilderness (geographic and technological) that would be too risky in the absence of nearby recourse to aid. We have an indication of one of many such literal bottlenecks:

At the date of the report just cited, the accumulations of drift at the head of the raft in the main river had been multiplied to such an extent that the navigation was rendered impracticable nearly to the head of Red bayou, which then had become the only channel or outlet through which the entire navigation of the river must be conducted, and fears were entertained that a few more accumulations of drift would effactually and entirely destroy the navigation of the entire river in its passage through the district of the present raft.

Agreeably to the latest information received concerning the raft, this catastrophe, if it has not already occurred, is likely to take place on the occurrence of the next considerable river freshet, when the abundant and valuable commerce of this important river will unavoidably be incommoded and obstructed by a difficult and expensive land portage of many miles in extent.

In view of what has already been stated on numerous occasions, in reference

[28] Aubrey comments on this problem in regard to European experience: "Time was of the essence, partly to cope with existing or threatened shortages, partly to 'catch up and keep up' in competitive trade. It was, therefore, important that a few fortunate or shrewd individuals who managed to smuggle information out of England should not hold a monopoly. Thus, in many instances, the government set up foreign technicians in the business of making the new machines and paid them premiums or subsidies for each machine they sold. By such means a fairly wide distribution was achieved in a relatively short time. In other cases, the government needed only to make a gift of prototypes of new machines. In this manner the state assumed risks and cost beyond the capacity of many entrepreneurs. It made, thus, an important contribution toward the private investment decision."—Henry G. Aubrey, "The Role of the State in Economic Development," *American Economic Review*, 41:268 (May 1951).

to the importance of keeping open a navigable channel through the district of the Red river raft, it is manifest that the fostering aid of Congress should be again extended to this object in the way of continued appropriations for its accomplishment.[29]

Government records give abundant evidence of the part played in removal of such obstacles as those in the Red River. Examples of providing links and easing the way are easy to find. The following items are typical: [30]

Constructing two piers and improving the navigation at the mouth of Vermilion river, Ohio	$10,777 (1839)
Improving navigation of the Arkansas river	17,452 (1839)
Road from Milwaukie [sic] by way of Madison, to Mississippi river opposite Dubuque	10,000 (1839)
Improving the harbor of Mobile	52,184 (1840)

There is evidence also in the sponsorship by Congress of scientific expeditions and surveys throughout the period. This pathfinding was certainly motivated in part by military needs,[31] but also by the desire to open areas for settlement and to increase communication and commerce. In these efforts should be included river surveying, well digging, resource surveying, wagon-road building, as well as cartography and other aspects of scientific exploration.[32] Congress approved a survey, largely under Army leadership, of a possible railroad route between the Mississippi and the West Coast; and during 1853–55 five surveys were made between the 32nd and the 49th parallels. The resulting empirical material was not only useful for railroad building but also added much to scientific knowledge of the area.[33]

[29] "Annual report of Lieutenant Colonel S. H. Long, topographical engineers, for the year ending June 30, 1859, and continued till the 5th October following," Appendix C to *Report of the Secretary of War*, U. S. Senate, 36th Congress, 1st Session, Ex. Doc. No. 2, Vol. 2 (1860), p. 749.

[30] Reports of the Secretary of the Treasury of the United States, for the respective years.

[31] Cf. William A. Ganoe, *The History of the United States Army* (rev. ed.; New York: D. Appleton-Century Company, 1942).

[32] Cf. William H. Goetzmann, "The Corps of Topographical Engineers in the Exploration and Development of the Trans-Mississippi West," unpublished Ph.D. dissertation, Yale University, 1957.

[33] "Payments from the Treasury, expenditures on account of public lands, surveys, administration, salaries, &c. from January 1, 1785, to June 30, 1880, were (estimated) $46,563,302.07. . . . The expenses of the Indian Department, on account

In an attempt to gauge the pattern of government expenditures with reference not only to internal improvements but also to other outlays of specific significance in the growth of the economy, the Reports on the Finances of the respective Secretaries of the Treasury, 1821–45, have been examined.[34] Listings of so-called "selected" expenditures have been made for each of the years containing those items of federal expenditure that appeared to have particularly direct impact on the facilitation of economic activity. A summary of the relation of the selected items to total federal outlays is shown in Table 3. Because of the arbitrariness of selection, the lists should perhaps be characterized as impressionistic. All items covering pay and subsistence as well as most ordnance, arsenals, and armories, are excluded from the expenditures for the military establishment. The resulting figures should understate the extent of expenditures.[35] The breakdown is useful in indicating lower limits on the share of expenditures that affected the aspects of intervention under discussion here. The percentage figures indicate the extent of governmental involvement in economic pathbreaking and in activity which may have resulted, though only as a by-product, in positive contributions to development. The years 1836–38 show outlays greater than the trend would suggest. These can be explained largely by expenditures incurred in dealing with the Indians as is indicated, for example, in this item for 1837: "Carrying into effect treaty with Cherokees of 29th Dec., 1835 – act 2d July, 1836 . . .

---

of holding treaties, &c. and including yearly payments for annuities and other charges, which are, in fact, in consideration for surrender of occupancy-title of lands to the Government, from July 4, 1876, to June 30, 1880, was $187,328,903.91."— Thomas C. Donaldson, *The Public Domain: Its History, with Statistics* (Public Land Commission, 1881), pp. 18, 20. Cf. Forest G. Hill, "Government Engineering Aid to Railroads before the Civil War," *Journal of Economic History*, 11:235–246 (Summer 1951).

[34] Federal expenditures on internal improvements amounted to approximately $15,000,000 over the period 1791–1820 and rose to $54,400,000 during 1820–40.

[35] Heath refers to a similar problem in his discussion of the effects of land grants: "The estimates on public land grants are tentative, and other items are subject to further refinements through additional studies. It does not represent the total of the public effort, since no account is taken in this summary of the investment values of the many important public and quasi-public contributions in services, the uses of public streets and other properties, tax exemptions, and banking privileges. An adequate appraisal of these must await further research."—"Public Railroad Construction . . . ," *op. cit.*, p. 40.

1,132,834.81." In the same year, $4,010,162 was listed for "Preventing
and suppressing Indian hostilities." [36] These items are included in the
selected expenditures since efforts to remove hostile Indians were
significant in making an area safe for economic development. The lands
taken through treaties, of course, became part of the resources made
available in the government land and settlement programs.

Finally, there is the somewhat elusive factor—the psychological impact of government's presence. Fleeting references in historical material
acknowledge that this influence was of critical importance in conditioning the rate of growth. Part of the effect was due to the "credit
standing" of the government. For example, commenting on the inability of private corporations to command a supply of capital in the
years before 1840, Callender pointed out that "There was no body of
private individuals in the country well enough known and with sufficient influence in the business world to establish the credit of a corporation so that it could command the confidence of both these classes of
investors. The only securities that could do this were public securities,
or the securities of corporations which were guaranteed or assisted by
the government. American public credit had been raised to the highest
pitch by the debt-paying policy of the federal government; and it was
inevitable that the American people should turn to the only means in
their power to provide for their needs." [37]

The psychological factor affected entrepreneurial expectations. The
individual investor was reluctant to venture into the West alone; but
his attitude was different with the government at his side, or more
likely ahead of him. The effect was to encourage more and larger
entrepreneurial undertakings. Many of the ventures that preceded the
government into "uncharted" territory were unsuccessful, and this
lesson was heeded by the entrepreneur. Certainly at early stages in
American economic expansion, the presence of the government, usually
in the form of the army, meant a tie with less primitive aspects of
society. This tie was evidenced through the exchange of physical goods
with governmental outposts, but it had a psychological impact as well
in sustaining those who had moved to remote areas. This is reflected,

[36] Report of the Secretary of the Treasury of the United States on the Finances,
September 1837.

[37] Guy S. Callender, "The Early Transportation and Banking Enterprises of the
States in Relation to the Growth of Corporations," *Quarterly Journal of Economics,*
17:45 (November 1902).

TABLE 3. FEDERAL EXPENDITURES: COMPARISON OF TOTALS WITH SELECTED EXPENDITURES FACILITATING ECONOMIC ACTIVITY, UNITED STATES, 1821–45

In thousands of dollars

	Civil, foreign, miscellaneous			Military establishment		
	Expenditures		Selected as % of total	Expenditures		Selected as % of total
Year	Total	Selected		Total	Selected	
1821	2,241.9	440.2	19.6	5,162.4	537.8	10.4
1822	1,968.0	180.1	9.2	5,635.2	797.8	14.2
1823	2,022.1	197.8	9.8	5,258.3	904.3	17.2
1824	7,155.3	221.8	3.1	5,270.3	1,011.2	19.2
1825	2,748.5	419.4 *	15.3	5,692.8	1,602.0	28.1
1826	2,600.2	406.7 *	15.6	6,243.2	1,768.9	28.3
1827	2,713.5	150.5 *	3.7	5,675.7	1,824.2	32.1
1828	3,676.1	203.3 *	5.5	5,719.6	1,821.1	31.8
1829	3,101.5	563.0 *	18.2	6,250.2	2,219.6	35.5
1830	3,237.4	403.5 *	12.5	6,752.7	2,427.9	36.0
1831	3,064.7	206.1 *	6.7	6,943.2	2,542.4	36.6
1832	4,577.2	473.5 *	10.3	7,982.9	2,841.5	35.6
1833	5,716.3	831.6	14.5	13,096.2	3,690.3	28.2
1834 †	3,584.1	222.7	6.2	8,349.4	2,115.7	25.3
1835	3,705.4			9,507.6		
1836 ‡	3,850.1	714.8	18.6	13,010.1	6,878.2	52.9
1837 ‡	4,024.8	736.5	18.3	16,310.2	8,554.6	52.4
1838 ‡	4,029.7	414.8	10.3	15,731.3	7,779.9	49.5
1839 ‡	3,649.4	470.9	12.9	10,791.8	3,545.3	32.9
1840 ‡	4,175.8	315.6	7.6	8,750.8	2,333.4	26.7
1841 ‡	4,615.4	222.6	4.8	10,834.1	3,756.5	34.7
1842 ‡	4,372.0	233.8	5.3	7,065.0	1,764.8	25.0
1843 §	2,867.3	96.5 ‖	3.4	4,158.4	974.9 ‖	23.4
1844 ♯	5,231.8	320.6 ‖	6.1	8,231.3	2,064.3 ‖	24.9
1845 **	5,618.2	281.3 ‖	5.0	9,533.2	2,555.7 ‖	26.8

Source: Reports of the Secretary of the Treasury of the United States, for the respective years. See pp. 18–19 supra for elaboration of "selected expenditures" category.

  * The "selected expenditures" shown for the years 1825–32 include amounts subscribed to stock in various canal companies, such as the Chesapeake & Delaware, the Dismal Swamp, the Louisville & Portland, and the Chesapeake & Ohio.

  † Three quarters, January 1 – September 30. Aggregate figures for the year were: civil, foreign, miscellaneous, 4,404.7; military, 10,064.4; navy, 3,956.3; total federal expenditures, 24,602.0.

  ‡ Three quarters, January 1 – September 30.

  § Six months, January 1 – June 30.

  ‖ Selection based on less disaggregated data.

  ♯ Fiscal year, July 1, 1843 – June 30, 1844.

  ** Fiscal year, July 1, 1844 – June 30, 1845.

TABLE 3—*Continued*

Year	Navy establishment			Total ††		
	Expenditures		Selected as % of total	Expenditures		Selected as % of total
	Total	Selected		Total	Selected	
1821	3,319.2	.2	.01	19,090.6	978.2	5.1
1822	2,224.5			17,676.6	977.9	5.5
1823	2,503.8	6.0	.2	15,314.2	1,108.1	7.2
1824	2,904.6	4.4	.2	31,898.5	1,237.4	3.9
1825	3,049.1	1.9	.1	23,585.8	2,023.3	8.6
1826	4,218.9	1.3	.03	24,103.4	2,178.2	9.0
1827	4,263.9	6.8	.2	22,656.8	1,981.5	8.7
1828	3,925.9	1.1	.02	25,485.3	2,025.5	7.9
1829	3,308.7			25,044.4	2,782.6	11.1
1830	3,239.4			24,585.3	2,831.4	11.5
1831	3,856.2			30,038.4	2,748.5	9.1
1832	3,956.4	3.8	.1	34,356.7	3,315.0	9.1
1833	3,901.4	1.2	.03	24,257.3	4,521.9	18.6
1834 †	2,913.2			16,545.3	2,338.4	14.1
1835	4,917.0			18,189.2		
1836 ‡	3,931.2			20,791.4	7,593.0	36.5
1837 ‡	5,061.9			25,418.9	9,291.1	36.6
1938 ‡	4,325.6			28,427.2	8,194.7	28.8
1839 ‡	4,713.7			29,061.4	4,016.2	13.8
1840 ‡	4,620.3			21,188.1	2,649.0	12.5
1841 ‡	4,230.0	8.7	.2	24,734.4	3,987.8	16.1
1842 ‡	6,717.1	10.7	.2	26,264.9	2,009.3	7.7
1843 §	3,672.7	4.0 ‖	.1	11,560.0	1,075.4 ‖	9.3
1844 ♯	6,497.0			32,958.8	2,366.9 ‖	7.2
1845 **	6,228.6			29,968.2	2,837.0 ‖	9.5

† Three quarters, January 1 – September 30. Aggregate figures for the year were: civil, foreign, miscellaneous, 4,404.7; military, 10,064.4; navy, 3.956.3; total federal expenditures, 24,602.0.

‡ Three quarters, January 1 – September 30.

§ Six months, January 1 – June 30.

‖ Selection based on less disaggregated data.

♯ Fiscal year, July 1, 1843 – June 30, 1844.

** Fiscal year, July 1, 1844 – June 30, 1845.

†† Including expenditures related to the public debt.

for example, in the diary of a Minnesota farmer, William R. Brown, who wrote in 1845:

Friday 26th   Haskell & I went to Fort Snelling   took my pork   Brot home my Flour 4 Barrels, 4 Barrels Beans 7 Bushels Corn   Bot. a Buffaloe Robe at $2.50   bot 40 lbs of Harness leather for Charley at (Henry H.) Sibleys. learned of Steel that the Black & White cow of the Doe (?) Cattle that I sold to F. Steel weighed lighter than 400 lbs.   Bot 7 Bushels Beans of Lieutenant (Robert S.) Granger   paid $1.50 per Bushel   took a Receipt of him arrived at home at about 7 oclock. . . .

Saturday 24th   I borrowed J. A. Fords train and went to Fort Snelling bot. 1 Barrel Beans @ 3.50   Bot Cloth for 2 Vests   one for myself & 1 for Harrison   Bot ⅔ of a Bushel fine salt . . .

. . . March 2nd . . . I went up to the Fort & carried up 40⅓ bushels of Oats Steel was well pleased with them   they were Clean & the grain well filled.[38]

LEVERAGE EFFECTS OF GOVERNMENTAL INTERVENTION

Several observations on the general nature of American economic development seem important within the context of the present discussion; and in discussion of comparative development one must say something about *uniqueness*—particularity, rather than generality, emerges from a survey of the nineteenth-century American scene.[39] The word "pattern" should perhaps be avoided. As must be clear from preceding sections, the West, the revolution in transportation, and the continuing flow of new techniques in production dominate the picture. In the literature various hypotheses provide general developmental frameworks and direct special attention to a particular aspect or factor, for example, the frontier and abundance.[40] Taken separately or looked on as parts of a "total explanation," they provide a basis for illustrating the uniqueness of the American situation. They delineate development of a country with an expanding geographical area, in a position to use the know-how gained through the pathbreaking of another country, and to do so in an environment with a growing labor force and a growing market—all in what appears to be nearly optimal concomi-

[38] "The Diary of William R. Brown, 1845–46," in Rodney C. Loehr, ed., *Minnesota Farmers' Diaries*, Minnesota Historical Society Narratives and Documents, Vol. 3 (St. Paul, 1939), pp. 52, 59, 64–65.

[39] Cf. Simon Kuznets, "Measurement of Economic Growth," *Journal of Economic History*, Vol. 7, Suppl. (1947), pp. 29–30; and Warren C. Scoville, "Discussion— Factors in Modern Industrial Development," *American Economic Review*, 41:275 (May 1951).

[40] Turner, *op. cit.;* Potter, *op. cit.*

tance. The highly special set of circumstances that existed over the period should make one hesitant to generalize from the American experience. The constraint becomes all the more forbidding when, to these contextual factors, a series of specific *events* unique in character and having immediate impact on the course of economic change in America are added. These events include, of course, the conflicts arising from regional tensions (East vs. West, as well as Civil War and reconstruction), the pattern of settlement of the West, the role of foreign capital, the emergence of combinations in business, and the events conditioning the social and political milieu. These episodes and factors affected the attitudes of the entrepreneur and resulted in a conception of his social role quite different from that in other cultures. These ramifications reinforce the aspect of uniqueness.[41]

After reference to the role of the state in the development of the American West, there remains the task of pulling together the characterization of the West's impact on the East and hence on national economic growth. This can be done without re-evaluating the issues in the Turner controversy.[42] Nevertheless, in the literature on the Turner thesis there is implicit acknowledgment of the accelerator impact of the West on the East, with little recognition of what might be called the leverage effects of Eastern expenditures on the Western border and in areas newly opened to settlement.[43] Ready availability of land and the emergence of markets did act as stimuli to expansion of plant in the East, but more than this was involved: as Duesenberry has pointed out, it is likely that the *extension* of national economic activity over a wide and geographically remote area resulted in the need to duplicate as well as enlarge capacity.[44] Thus there were induced increments to national wealth. Along with the activity that generated

---

[41] Sawyer, *op. cit.*

[42] See bibliography in Oscar Handlin and others, *Harvard Guide to American History* (Cambridge: Harvard University Press, 1954), p. 21.

[43] For an exception to this see Clarence H. Danhof, "Economic Validity of the Safety-Valve Doctrine," *Journal of Economic History*, Vol. 1, Suppl. (1941), p. 106.

[44] "It is to be emphasized that the services in question [specialized medical, legal, and personal] cannot be imported. The facilities for producing them have to exist in the region in which the demand exists. The existence of such facilities in the East was of no use to the farmers of the Midwest. In consequence of this situation trading communities sprang up in strategic locations throughout the developing area. The people of these communities provided services to their agricultural hinterland."—James S. Duesenberry, "Some Aspects of the Theory of Economic Development," *Explorations in Entrepreneurial History*, 3:98–99 (December 1950).

income in areas that had been dormant (the West), there was stimulus for the already active areas with associated multiplier effects throughout —all as a result of the regionally focused expansion.[45]

Martin states that "to introduce the question of whether additional expenditures for military purposes would have 'raised' the level of living is futile." [46] This seems somewhat harsh; if the raw data were available and if the multiplier effects seemed conceptually useful enough to warrant a quantitative indication of the force of new expenditures in the area,[47] available analytical tools could aid in this research.

In more descriptive terms, evidence can be found in the multiplier effects of various governmental undertakings (in addition to railroad building and land policy): for example, in exploration and survey; in the use of local facilities to sustain governmental operations, as in the purchase of forage and subsistence items for the Army from farmers in the vicinity of a post; and in sutlers' activities.[48] All these were responsible to some degree for the introduction of new money into the remoter areas, giving rise to higher expectations and to subsequent investment activity.

In the light of the foregoing discussion and in conclusion, it may be well to return to the appropriateness of the designation "autonomous." The question does arise whether the factor so central to our discussion, i.e., the presence of the West, the advancing frontier, and its impact on the American experience, may not be the very condition that contributed most to the aptness of the general and ultimate characterization of the American pattern as one of autonomous growth. It is the view of some, for example, that because of the particular circumstances of expansionism in America (the open frontier combined with the ideological biases that were part of nineteenth-century America), the

[45] Aitken suggests that perhaps the very act of acquisition of new territory constituted "the most important single contribution of the government to economic growth."

[46] Martin, *The Standard of Living in 1860*, pp. 280–281.

[47] ". . . the multiplier for any sector is the ratio of the final change in its receipts to the initial disturbance. If each sector's marginal propensity to spend to every sector is known, it is possible, mathematically, to calculate the value of the multiplier."—John S. Chipman, *The Theory of Inter-Sectoral Money Flows and Income Formation* (Baltimore: Johns Hopkins Press, 1951), p. 22.

[48] For a description of the extent of sutlers' operations, see William N. Davis, Jr., "Post Trading in the West," *Explorations in Entrepreneurial History*, 6:30–40 (1953–54), especially p. 31.

role of the central government was smaller than it might otherwise have been. They would argue that the very factors that placed America in the expansionist category were functionally linked in the case of the United States with placing it in the autonomous category. This suggests that the expansionist attribute in itself might contribute to minimization of the government's positive role in the economic life of the country. There is need for further study of this question.

There is, of course, need for detailed analysis of the functional role of government at different periods, not only of the various aspects of a positive role, but also in terms of changing functions and possible negative effects on development. Further study may show that the effects on allocation were more significant than the leverage effects.

Nevertheless, and even in the light of the argument referred to above, there appears to be good reason to hesitate before allowing the United States experience for the period 1820–90 to be placed, without qualification, in the autonomous category. For reasons suggested in this paper, it seems advisable to use caution in applying the American experience in analogies of growth; to emphasize the need for qualitative interpretation of governmental activity at both the state and federal levels, particularly because of the possible leverage effects of government action; and finally, to assert that the role of the state in American economic development in the nineteenth century was surely more than minimal. The effects of the action and presence of government on growth were significant and were manifested throughout the period.

2 COLONIAL SOCIALISM IN AUSTRALIA, 1860–1900

Noel G. Butlin *

"The Government has provided, free of cost," said the Queensland Treasurer, surveying his depleted coffers in 1879, "passages from Europe to our shores for 106,000 people—more than half the present population of the colony; it subsidises our charitable institutions on a scale of liberality rarely equalled in older countries; it drills, clothes and pays the Volunteers; it bears the entire cost of the education of the young, and heavily subsidises the more advanced pupils in our grammar schools and in foreign universities; it maintains reserves and parks for public recreation in the principal towns of the colony; it provides roads and bridges everywhere, while a toll is a thing unknown; it supplies railway communication to some districts at a price which does not pay the working expenses of the lines, to the great enhancement of the value of the private lands, and the general benefit of their owners and occupiers; at the same time it pays large subsidies for both land and sea services, which enable travellers to reach their destinations partly at Government expense; it carries all our newspapers gratuitously to and from the utmost limits of the colony, and defrays one-half the cost of conveying every posted letter and of transmitting every telegraphic message; and it even relieves the Queenslander of one moiety of the cost of killing his own marsupials." [1]

Intent on his pruning knife, the Treasurer conveniently overlooked other important government activities which he, as a landholder, hesitated to reduce: capital grants to sugar mills and farms; assistance for the importation of Polynesian farm workers; government outlays on artesian bores and rabbit-proof fencing; extremely heavy capital expenditures on the construction of railways, telegraphs, river and harbor works, water and sewerage facilities, including reservoirs, together with the normal government paraphernalia of administrative buildings and defense works. He omitted to mention, too, government activities

---

* In preparing basic statistical data, I have been assisted by Ruth Inall and Garry Pursell.

[1] Financial Statement, June 4, 1879, in *Queensland, Official Record of the Debates of the Legislative Assembly*, Vol. 29, p. 289.

that yielded revenue rather than required expenditure: protective tariffs to assist local industry and agriculture; Crown land sales which transferred government lands to private use; and, perhaps above all, the introduction of large sums of British capital through government agencies.[2]

With few amendments, this list applied throughout the Australian colonies. Victoria was strongly protective in tariff policy and gave other aids to local manufacture. New South Wales, on the other hand, professed a strong adherence to free trade. It was the common pattern of positive government intervention, with the central feature of large-scale outlays for capital formation, which earned the contemporary title—sometimes the epithet—of colonial socialism,[3] and defines a particular (though not unchanging) pattern of partnership between government and private institutions to which the Australian economy was subject for most of the second half of the nineteenth century.

NATURE OF AUSTRALIAN ECONOMIC GROWTH

Conventional impressions invite suspicion. But any attempt to classify Australian economic growth as either autonomous or induced is quite untenable.[4] The belief, which is also common, that this expansion concentrated on rural settlement or the pastoral industry is as difficult to accept as is the sunburnt bushman as the typical Australian (and for precisely the same reasons). Satellitic the economy has usually been regarded, on external tests; but the path of the satellite was so independent as to make one doubt the value of these external tests.

[2] For a more formal list, see N. G. Butlin and H. de Meel, *Public Capital Formation in Australia, Estimates 1860–1900* (Canberra: Australian National University, 1954).

[3] Alternatively the phrase "state socialism in the colonies" was common. See, e.g., Henry de R. Walker, *Australasian Democracy* (London: T. F. Unwin, 1897); Edward Jenks, *A History of the Australasian Colonies* (Cambridge: The University Press, 1896).

[4] Hoselitz's classification of Australian economic development as extensive, nondominant, and autonomous is an accurate reflection of the usual view ("Patterns of Economic Growth," *Canadian Journal of Economics and Political Science*, 21:426). Contemporaries tended to be unduly conscious of government intervention in the nineteenth century, and later historians have gone in the opposite direction in virtually ignoring it. Lack of information on the building industry has helped to obscure the importance of the growth of cities. The somewhat esoteric statistics of Cairncross, Imlah, and other recent writers have not yet entered the general literature of Australian economic history.

There were, perhaps, two bursts of sustained growth [5] in Australian economic history in the nineteenth century. With the first, the original pastoral exodus from the overgrown jail and the Nineteen Counties, we are not concerned.[6] Perhaps for two brief decades something like a frontier existed in Australia. This preliminary expansion during the 1830's and 1840's was checked and disrupted by the social and economic upheaval that followed the discovery of gold in 1851. After the peak of alluvial mining, a new phase of growth occurred, dated roughly from 1860. The succeeding expansion reached its climax for Australia as a whole in 1889. Then followed a long period of deep depression, which may have continued until as late as 1897 and which was part of the background for basic economic, social, and political readjustments in the closing years of the century.

The crowded years of the 1850's left the Australian colonies in 1860 in a position strikingly different from that of ten years before. The passage of the Australian Colonies Government Act in 1850 paved the way for the separation from New South Wales of Victoria in 1851 and of Queensland in 1859. Responsible government in 1856, followed by manhood suffrage, radically altered the political balance of social groups and went far toward eliminating the autocratic character of Australian government. The birth of new colonial administrations was accompanied by a modest but important spawning of local and semi-governmental authorities, particularly during the years 1858–60.[7] Demographic changes were also marked. Population rose threefold from 400,000 in 1850 to 1,150,000 in 1860. This increased population was drawn from Great Britain, Ireland, China, and North America and flowed largely into Victoria. In 1860, Victoria was bursting at the seams, with over 100,000 people living in tents. As a result of the gold discoveries a great internal migration to the gold fields occurred, denuding pastoral and agricultural activity, industrial crafts, and service occupations of labor and contributing to a distortion of wages and prices which was still apparent in 1860. The pastoral industry responded to this situation partly by realizing assets through the conversion of output

[5] The period of the gold discoveries has not been properly studied. Proper investigation will possibly reduce the distinction, which I have retained, between these two periods of growth.

[6] The best account is by Stephen H. Roberts, *The Squatting Age in Australia, 1835–47* (Melbourne: Melbourne University Press, 1935).

[7] Butlin and de Meel, *op. cit.;* and George H. Knibbs, *Local Government in Australia, 1835–1847* (Melbourne, 1918).

from wool to meat, partly by initiating far-reaching technological changes which were destined to reduce greatly the rural demand for labor. The growth of population and wealth encouraged an expansion of commercial activity and the promotion of trading and financial enterprises which placed Melbourne in a position of financial leadership in the Australian colonies.

Subsequent economic growth occurred in a continent that was isolated from world trading and population centers and, with available technology, not well-endowed with resources. A large part of the area was desert; much of the occupied plains lay in regions of low rainfall subject to severe droughts, poorly served by rivers and primitive transport systems. Moreover, the greater part of the usable land was already occupied, though not properly utilized, by pastoral lessees who in the main had obtained security of tenure as leaseholders under Orders in Council of 1847.

In structural terms, the growth of the Australian economy after 1860 did not depend essentially on pastoral production but centered around four related fields of activity: the pastoral industry, transport, building, and service occupations. In all these fields, growth was extremely rapid until the end of the 1880's. It was led by pastoral activity in which the production of wool for export from New South Wales increased elevenfold between 1860 and its peak in 1892. So great was this expansion that the peak of flock population was not again matched until the end of the 1920's. Railways, which first appeared during the 1850's, quickly superseded other forms of transport, with trunk lines fanning from the major ports into the interior. The building industry expanded primarily in the principal cities in response to a growing population, which was becoming predominantly urban.[8] Quantitatively, it was the building of cities and interurban railways, rather than the extension of rural settlement, that absorbed Australian resources. This reflected the concentration of settlement on the southern and eastern fringe of the continent. Partly in response to urbanization, partly as a reaction to pastoral expansion, there was a great increase of employment in service occupations of all sorts, financial, commercial, personal and governmental, all chiefly in the main port cities.

[8] An indication of the urban growth is given by New South Wales population data:

	1861	1871	1881	1891
Urban	159,800	234,800	426,900	730,000
Rural	189,100	266,800	321,300	388,200

By contrast, other activities lagged and some actually declined. Mining as a whole dwindled steadily, although there was a steady growth of coal and nonferrous metal mining. After a modest burst of growth, chiefly in the late 1870's and early 1880's, agriculture languished. Manufacturing, largely confined to Sydney and Melbourne, followed a gradual but unsteady upward course.

The expansion that occurred until 1889 was remarkably stable for Australia as a whole. Recessions in 1866, 1871, 1878, and 1886 were only slight checks in a strong upward movement. Expansion led, however, into a highly speculative boom in the second half of the 1880's and ended in a crisis with severe monetary difficulties and disorders in balance of payments during 1890–93. The recovery which began haltingly in the closing years of the century was related to important structural change—gold production in Western Australia, agricultural rather than pastoral expansion, the development of nonauriferous mining, and a critical diversification of export commodities.[9]

Australian expansion was associated with several important domestic features. First, pastoral growth was achieved not primarily by the extension of settlement but by the more intensive use of lands already occupied. It was based on important technological changes, partly mechanical, such as spout washing, but essentially through heavy capital outlays on fencing and water conservation schemes. Because of this labor-saving investment, wool output increased with a declining labor force. Second, the growth of transport systems and the development of cities implied heavy capital outlays. Something of the urban concentration is suggested by Table 1. Third, growth was achieved in very many fields in conditions of falling prices. Import and export prices fell heavily and more or less continuously; domestic retail prices were inclined to sag throughout the whole period. Fourth, there was a steady rise in money wage rates, with a more definite upward movement in real wages. Finally, while the population became predominantly urban, the rural workforce provided a geographically highly mobile labor supply, moving readily between and within colonies in response to fluctuations in rural activities and construction projects.

In the domestic economy, the basic condition of economic growth was a high and sustained process of capital formation. The equipment of the pastoral industry and the building of railways and cities meant

[9] W. A. Sinclair, *Economic Recovery in Victoria, 1894–1899* (Canberra: Australian National University, 1956).

TABLE 1. PRIVATE CAPITAL FORMATION IN MELBOURNE, 1870–90 *

In thousands of pounds

Year	Melbourne			Total Melbourne	Melbourne as % of total Victoria
	Industrial	Residential	Commercial		
1870	66	911	151	1,128	46.8
1871	—21	256	–	235	26.6
1872	117	1,169	261	1,547	52.8
1873	214	988	31	1,233	37.0
1874	592	595	190	1,377	49.6
1875	499	657	—6	1,150	30.3
1876	334	723	—91	966	32.4
1877	452	642	—114	980	27.3
1878	571	526	19	1,116	83.5
1879	208	782	140	1,130	37.5
1880	163	700	246	1,109	45.6
1881	163	874	417	1,454	48.5
1882	398	888	831	2,117	56.3
1883	66	1,084	—37	1,113	34.6
1884	597	1,817	—202	2,212	65.2
1885	33	2,378	748	3,159	56.1
1886	316	2,704	1,202	4,222	60.5
1887	645	778	1,197	2,620	36.2
1888	890	3,023	2,211	6,124	74.1
1889	—547	4,436	—13	3,876	80.4
1890	1,139	978	470	2,587	60.4

* Based on data collected for N. G. Butlin, *Private Capital Formation in Australia, Estimates 1861–1900* (Canberra: Australian National University, 1955). These data understate the importance of Melbourne.

a relatively simple construction activity, without any great demand for skill. The main economic problem of the Australian colonies was, therefore, to provide an army of unskilled laborers and to secure savings which would sustain them. Despite the growth of population during the "gold period" and subsequent population expansion and changes in age composition, local supplies of both labor and capital were inadequate.[10] A formal satellitic relationship was established in that the scale of Australian activity and the rate of growth were limited, in the aggregate, by the supply of British capital and migrants.

[10] The size of fortunes earned in the goldfields is unknown. These fortunes were probably important in private capital formation in the early 1860's.

The Australian economy undoubtedly has a satellitic appearance, as Table 2 shows. Possibly two thirds of total new Australian capital formation during the period was financed by British capital. Migrants, most of them British, accounted for between a quarter and a third of successive intercensal increases between 1861 and 1891. A high proportion of total Australian output passed through international trade, symptomatic of a close dependence on overseas markets and of a high propensity to import. Roughly three quarters of Australian imports were obtained, and three quarters of Australian exports sold, in Great Britain. In particular, key equipment for the production of durable assets was almost entirely obtained there.

Despite this satellitic appearance, Australian experience *until 1890* in relation to Great Britain seems to have been very different from that of other countries, some of which had similar connections with it. The point is important in determining the character of Australian economic development; it is fundamental to an understanding of the role of government in Australian economic growth.

By 1900, some 350 million pounds sterling of British capital had been invested in Australia, mostly since 1860. Unfortunately, most of our detailed knowledge of overseas borrowing by Australian individuals begins only with 1871. After 1870, British foreign and domestic investment went through the now familiar cyclical pattern shown by Cairncross,[11] a pronounced inverse movement between the two series. Excluding short-run movements, the two massive peaks of British foreign investment in 1872 and 1890 surround a deep trough, bottomed in 1877, while home investment rose to a high plateau during the years 1874–82. As far as it goes, the information available on American and Canadian experience suggests a definite pattern of relationship with the British economy. American building [12] and Canadian borrowing [13] seem to have conformed quite closely, in the long run, with movements in British overseas investment and hence to have behaved inversely with British home investment, but this does not seem to have been the case with Australia, up to 1890. Until then, the flow of British capital

[11] A. K. Cairncross, *Home and Foreign Investment, 1870–1914* (Cambridge, England: Cambridge University Press, 1953).

[12] Clarence D. Long, Jr., *Building Cycles and the Theory of Investment* (Princeton: Princeton University Press, 1940).

[13] Penelope Hartland, "The Canadian Balance of Payments since 1868," in National Bureau of Economic Research, *Trends in the American Economy in the Nineteenth Century* (Studies in Income and Wealth, Vol. 24, in preparation).

TABLE 2. MEASURES OF AUSTRALIAN EXTERNAL DEPENDENCE

Year	Total capital formation *	Overseas borrowing †	Population ‡ Annual increase	Population ‡ Net immigration	Exports Total§	Exports To Gt. Britain‖	Imports Total§	Imports From Gt. Britain‖
	Thousands of pounds				*Thousands of pounds*			
1861	6,213		21,974	—6,545	17.4	11.6	17.7	12.4
1862	5,682		37,029	6,959	18.1	11.0	20.6	14.0
1863	6,418		50,638	20,936	19.3	10.0	21.2	15.4
1864	6,810		64,940	31,033	19.0	9.4	20.5	13.9
1865	7,124		63,842	29,598	19.7	12.6	20.7	14.1
1866	6,446		52,923	23,339	19.0	11.7	21.3	14.1
1867	7,032		39,116	7,169	18.4	13.6	16.0	10.4
1868	8,962		54,559	17,203	21.7	16.9	18.4	11.3
1869	8,351		52,244	15,100	20.1	13.4	19.9	13.2
1870	7,368		55,117	15,909	18.0	10.8	17.8	11.3
1871	6,572	—2	51,820	11,798	21.7	15.5	17.0	10.2
1872	10,450	756	41,550	3,098	22.5	16.6	18.8	12.7
1873	11,568	2,894	51,577	11,663	26.4	20.5	24.6	16.7
1874	13,304	3,781	54,369	17,007	25.6	19.2	24.6	17.4
1875	16,619	4,875	48,284	18,194	25.0	17.4	24.9	20.0
1876	17,072	6,264	59,785	24,946	23.5	17.3	24.0	17.1
1877	22,255	8,769	71,882	34,294	23.1	16.9	25.8	19.2
1878	19,454	8,160	60,664	21,709	23.8	16.6	26.2	18.8
1879	17,117	8,896	69,652	25,339	21.2	15.3	24.2	16.6
1880	19,950	1,491	68,766	23,903	27.3	21.9	22.9	16.5
1881	25,763	8,807	74,610	28,529	27.5	19.7	29.1	20.9
1882	21,934	16,292	80,486	37,655	27.3	19.8	36.1	26.0
1883	25,724	13,705	116,584	69,293	30.1	22.1	35.5	26.2
1884	27,338	16,114	98,529	49,994	28.7	21.6	37.0	26.6
1885	26,517	17,669	86,380	34,911	26.7	19.6	36.9	27.1
1886	31,203	24,577	88,887	34,717	21.7	16.7	34.2	24.6
1887	31,816	18,098	90,096	31,461	23.4	17.8	29.6	21.0
1888	34,478	20,085	100,321	39,778	28.9	22.6	36.9	26.1
1889	30,472	19,624	78,954	21,743	29.6	22.2	37.6	25.5
1890	28,574	17,510	86,036	22,823	29.3	20.5	36.2	23.5

Note: Western Australia is excluded from series of total capital formation, annual population increase, and exports and imports from Great Britain.

* N. G. Butlin, *Private Capital Formation in Australia, Estimates 1861–1900.*

† Roland Wilson, *Capital Imports and the Terms of Trade, Examined in the Light of Sixty Years of Australian Borrowings* (Melbourne: Melbourne University Press, 1931).

‡ *Commonwealth Demography Bulletins.*

§ *Commonwealth Year Book, 1910.*

‖ Computed from *Statistical Registers* of individual colonies.

to Australia seems to have occurred almost regardless of both long- and short-term fluctuations. Australian borrowing from Great Britain and Australian domestic capital formation follow each other closely in a sustained expansion until 1889–90, bearing little resemblance to the movements in British home or foreign investment, American building, or Canadian borrowing. This was the case, despite the fact that by far the greater part of Australian domestic capital formation was financed by British capital while Australia—as perhaps Great Britain's biggest customer, especially during the years 1874–83—absorbed a high proportion, of the order of a third to a half, of total net British lending overseas.[14]

A similar contrast existed in population movements. Migration from Great Britain was closely linked with British foreign investment, while immigration to the United States followed the course of American building.[15] In Australia, immigration and domestic capital formation behaved similarly, so that the flow of migrants into Australia bore little resemblance to the outflow from Britain. In this case, however, Australian immigration accounted for a much smaller proportion of the total British outflow than did the Australian share of British overseas investment.

Much the same pattern of contrast can be seen in series of exports and imports. The basic fact about all the Australian series is the sustained, stable growth, without pronounced cyclical movement before 1889. This stability is the special characteristic of the expanding Australian series until 1889, indicative of the highly independent orbit traced by the Australian satellite.

Undoubtedly certain British conditions were necessary for Australian growth, and these conditions were being fulfilled throughout the 1850's and 1860's. Although before 1850 the overgrown jail of New South Wales may have been a source of spasmodic annoyance and little profit to the Imperial Government, the six Australian colonies of 1860 were endowed with considerable graces. Not only had gold been produced in quantity; here, now, was an important market for British goods and a promising source of industrial raw materials. The British investor, with his stake in India still insecure after the events of 1857 and his fingers burnt in the Canadian Grand Trunk, became less unwilling to

---

[14] For a series in real terms, I have relied on Brinley Thomas, *Migration and Economic Growth: A Study of Great Britain and the Atlantic Economy* (Cambridge: Cambridge University Press, 1954) for British foreign investment.

[15] Thomas, *op. cit.*

contemplate the antipodes as a source of profit. The British textile manufacturer, engaged in technological innovation to permit the more extensive use of short-fiber wool,[16] was looking increasingly to Australia as the rising merino producer. And more Britishers were willing, with the way paved for them by the migrants of the 1850's, to brave the long southern voyage in place of the shorter Atlantic crossing.[17]

The initiative for Australian development lay with none of these, however. The inflow of British funds must be regarded essentially as a response to the demand from two groups, of roughly equal quantitative importance in the Australian colonies: government authorities and private Australian individuals. So, too, the inflow of migrants fell into two groups, roughly equal in size, each linked to separate sectors of the Australian economy: assisted migrants, arriving in response to government aid; and unassisted migrants, partly influenced by conditions and personal inducements of private Australian employers and acquaintances.

These funds and migrants were deployed in two distinct sectors of the economy. The government sector, apart from service functions in education, health, justice, etc., concentrated on the growth of land transport and communications, water and sewerage, harbor and defense works and administrative buildings, and the operation of the enterprises involved, to the virtual exclusion of private individuals. The private sector covered pastoral and building industries, and commercial and financial enterprises, as key fields; less important were mining, manufacturing, and agriculture. Table 3 indicates, at the level of capital formation, how broadly similar in size these two sectors were.

This partnership of private and government institutions was not based on doctrinaire attitudes; it represented rather an ad hoc solution to the problem of developing local resources in the face of considerable physical difficulties. Until crisis conditions in the 1890's forced a reorientation of government policy towards stabilization, this partnership was not based on government regulation of private activity. Ostensibly, governments were concerned with the development of private enterprise by means of a sustained program of government capital formation and a less substantial scheme of assisted immigration. Governments did, however, intervene to influence private activity in two other ways: (1) by the adoption, in some colonies, of tariff protection; (2) by the

16 J. Alan Barnard, *The Australian Wool Market, 1840–1900* (Melbourne, 1958).
17 Frank Crowley, "The British Contribution to the Australian Population, 1860–1919," *University Studies in History and Economics* (Perth, W. A.), July 1954.

TABLE 3. COMPOSITION OF AUSTRALIAN CAPITAL FORMATION
In thousands of pounds

Year	Private capital formation			Government capital formation			
	Residential	Agricultural and pastoral	Other	Railways	Other communication	Local authorities	Other
1861	1,506	1,198	449	1,252	880	387	541
1862	1,767	593	259	1,552	561	454	495
1863	1,928	1,068	688	1,120	666	464	1,084
1864	3,080	1,010	225	1,007	623	593	270
1865	2,861	601	1,288	698	648	682	344
1866	2,311	438	1,114	670	704	650	558
1867	2,812	8	672	1,210	606	777	945
1868	2,371	2,056	1,383	1,317	446	776	613
1869	2,984	602	1,892	972	589	834	475
1870	2,792	1,205	659	857	473	901	484
1871	2,345	59	1,235	753	646	941	595
1872	3,616	2,702	1,230	1,008	609	921	363
1873	3,643	2,415	1,940	1,106	826	920	719
1874	3,568	3,729	1,394	1,691	952	1,076	893
1875	3,790	5,859	1,481	2,565	1,102	947	875
1876	5,348	5,498	1,121	1,783	1,167	1,065	1,089
1877	3,837	10,656	2,063	1,955	1,333	1,104	1,307
1878	3,565	6,844	1,532	3,294	1,442	1,300	1,476
1879	3,959	4,344	267	4,052	1,540	1,358	1,587
1880	3,595	6,054	2,370	3,785	1,455	1,362	1,329
1881	5,941	8,408	2,802	4,367	1,304	1,456	1,486
1882	6,177	1,709	3,787	5,088	1,636	1,639	1,899
1883	9,854	2,663	1,183	5,830	1,671	1,873	2,681
1884	9,339	2,860	2,745	5,897	2,064	2,130	2,302
1885	8,088	3,396	2,135	6,447	1,826	2,161	2,464
1886	6,959	8,793	2,060	6,697	1,567	2,352	2,776
1887	9,285	7,541	3,398	5,291	1,797	2,381	2,132
1888	10,203	7,880	4,598	5,661	1,544	2,466	2,147
1889	6,250	8,154	2,699	5,887	1,601	3,051	2,829
1890	7,726	2,965	3,816	5,775	1,776	3,813	2,703
1891	5,633	9,116	3,323	6,077	2,089	3,523	2,486
1892	4,393	1,610	−487	3,300	1,625	3,503	1,802
1893	3,001	58	−1,565	2,084	1,130	2,920	1,367
1894	3,709	1,033	411	1,303	871	2,276	1,010
1895	2,907	−1,228	−672	978	1,019	3,075	1,294
1896	3,087	1,385	1,840	1,218	1,193	2,468	1,329
1897	1,169	−1,643	24	1,421	1,190	2,443	1,427
1898	3,318	1,434	1,704	1,681	1,346	2,422	1,762
1899	1,160	1,490	2,826	2,158	1,498	2,434	2,001
1900	851	1,725	714	2,371	1,631	2,948	2,027

Source: N. G. Butlin, *Private Capital Formation in Australia, Estimates, 1861–1900* (calculated from data in pp. 4–15).

introduction of land legislation for the disposal and occupation of Crown lands. In the end, these two influences became closely linked with government capital formation for its own sake.

PURPOSE OF GOVERNMENT ACTION TO 1890

It was the orientation, not the fact, of extensive government intervention in the Australian economy after 1860 that was new. Prior to the gold discoveries in 1851, the Australian and Imperial Governments had, traditionally, occupied key roles in Australian history. As the importance of the original penal settlement declined, particularly from the 1820's, the significance of the British Government and its representative, the local governor, was reduced. Colonial government authorities assumed an increasing direct responsibility, largely by an extension of attitudes appropriate to prison supervision to the slowly growing free society.

In practice, for the first quarter of the nineteenth century, official behavior tended to work in two conflicting directions. Official positions were used to establish private enterprise and to distort the disciplined penal structure. On the other hand, formal authority tended to emphasize control and limitation of extra-prison activity, in attempts to fix wages, prices, conditions of employment, trading activity, the geographical area of settlement, etc., and to limit access to land to government grantees. Before 1830, some positive steps to aid private enterprise were taken in the establishment of banking,[18] the chartering of two major settlement companies (the Australian Agricultural Company, and Van Diemen's Land Company), and faltering measures to provide for land sales in a more regular way.

It was not, however, until the pastoral eruption of the 1830's that serious inroads were made by private entrepreneurs into the position of colonial governors.[19] Then, as the interior of the continent was occupied during the two succeeding decades, strong pressures were exerted by private individuals to induce governments to provide the conditions suitable to the growth of free enterprise. The introduction of regular land sales and of government assistance to immigration under the influence of E. G. Wakefield,[20] the cessation of convict transportation,

---

[18] Sydney J. Butlin, *Foundations of the Australian Monetary System, 1788–1851* (Melbourne: Melbourne University Press, 1953).

[19] Roberts, *op. cit.*

[20] Richard C. Mills, *The Colonization of Australia, 1829–42* (London: Sedgwick & Jackson, 1915).

and the provisions of leasehold land tenure outside the settled counties to give legal security to pastoral "squatters" were all designed as government aids to private enterprise. In addition, aid was forthcoming through government expenditure, traditional from Macquarie's time, on such physical assets as roads and bridges needed in a geographically expanding economy.

A number of important changes occurred during the 1850's. The fragmentation of New South Wales through the separation of Victoria and Queensland, the appearance of responsible government, elective parliaments, and the sudden growth of local and semigovernmental organizations led to a redivision of government functions and a change in the character of government activity. As the old autocratic elements disappeared, the social upheaval due to the gold discoveries, particularly the big population increase, brought fundamental changes in the content as well as form of government activity. With the disappearance of restrictive policies and the emergence of new conditions requiring positive policies to facilitate the development of economic activity on a much larger scale than before, the stage was set for a reorientation of policy.

The outstanding change to be explained is the fact that between 1860 and 1890 governments came to be as important, quantitatively, as private entrepreneurs in Australian capital formation. Some traditional features of government activity persisted after 1860 and throughout the remainder of the century. Construction of roads, bridges, harbor and river works, and defense works was carried on without question as a normal government responsibility. Within this traditional area, however, a redistribution of responsibility occurred, with the transfer to local and semigovernmental authorities of the main construction activities. It was because of these tasks, supplemented during the 1880's by water and sewerage projects, that local authorities assumed such quantitative significance in government capital formation.[21] However, the division between local and colonial governments was a shadowy one. Except in the main cities, neither population nor wealth was adequate to support these local organizations, and all tended to rely heavily on the colonial government for financial aid. Until the closing years of the century, these bodies were essentially local and regional agencies of the colonial government.

The main departure from tradition occurred when the colonial

[21] Butlin and de Meel, *op. cit.*

governments began the construction and operation of railways and tele-graph systems, to the virtual exclusion of private entrepreneurs. It was this step that brought governments on a par with private enterprise as a whole in the provision of durable assets, made government officials leading entrepreneurs and the principal employers of labor in the colonies, prompted the extension of government-assisted schemes of immigration, and brought governments into the London capital market as the leading Australian borrowers. As the construction of these com-munications facilities grew, slowly during the 1860's and with increas-ing tempo after 1870, traditional areas of government capital formation shrank into insignificance. Explanation of the origins and extension of government railway-building also substantially explains the rise of government capital formation to a level matching that of private capital formation.

The entry of the colonial governments into railway construction occurred in conditions broadly similar in all colonies. Railway (and telegraph) projects were initiated just before the gold discoveries, in almost every case by private entrepreneurs. In New South Wales pastoralists who were anxious to improve interior transport (1849), and in Victoria merchants who were interested mainly in port and short interurban lines first attempted railway construction. Although a Vic-torian company prospered, the projectors did not extend their opera-tions and left to government the task of more extensive building. In New South Wales the government gradually accepted increasing in-terest, financial responsibility, and executive control and finally, in 1854, ownership of the assets. From this time, with some exceptions, government responsibility for railway construction and operation was substantially complete.[22]

No obvious security motive prompted the government decision to enter this field.[23] Also, except in South Australia, there was no clear

[22] In Australia practically no use was made of the device, which was common in Canada, of government guarantee of interest or capital as a means of assisting private enterprise. This was tried in the 1850's in New South Wales and Victoria, without success, and much later, briefly, in Tasmania. Also, there was very little interest in land grant railways. Queensland occasionally professed some interest in land grants, and Western Australia actually began a land-grant railway, without much success. The lack of interest in these devices possibly turned mainly on the absence of entrepreneurial ability and organization by private individuals.

[23] This is contrary to the interesting findings of W. Thomas Easterbrook in *Change and the Entrepreneur* (Cambridge: Harvard University Press, 1949).

link with the tradition of government intervention. In fact, opinion was originally strongly opposed to government entry into railway building.

The failure of private enterprise was, in a sense, accidental. The discovery of gold, two years after the first railway project was promoted, completely altered construction conditions. Wages rose rapidly, labor became unprocurable, and capital was diverted to gold mining and commercial ventures. These unforeseeable changes brought private construction to a standstill. It was the belief in the superior ability of the government to raise capital, particularly in London, and to secure navvies through assisted immigration that prompted the original transfer. This belief was reinforced by a sense of urgency in providing railway transport between the main ports and the gold fields.[24]

These were, however, short-run difficulties. Indeed, one of the striking features in this context is that railway enterprise in the hands of governments was profitable, even though government policies of rate concessions and rapid construction deliberately operated to limit profits.[25] The basic facts seem to be that, at a critical time, private individuals were unable to develop adequate business organizations for railway operation; and that governments with access to capital were able to overcome the immediate obstacles that checked private promoters. The point may be illustrated by the successful flotation in London of the £8,000,000 debentures authorized by the Victorian Government in 1858 —a feat beyond imagination a few years earlier and still far beyond the power of private interests in 1858.[26]

Just as the original government entry into railway construction represented a nondoctrinaire ad hoc solution of an immediate problem, so the continuation of government railways to the exclusion of private is to be explained mainly in ad hoc terms. Attempts have been made to justify the private abdication of the railway field in terms of long distances, sparse settlement, and an underlying poverty of Australian resources. The financial results of government railway operation do

[24] John Rae, *Report on the Origins of Railways in New South Wales to 1865* (Sydney: Government Printer, 1866).

[25] John Rae, *Report on the Construction and Progress of the Railways of New South Wales from 1866 to 1871 inclusive* (Sydney: Government Printer, 1873). See also numerous parliamentary statements, e.g., *Victoria Parliamentary Debates, 1871,* Vol. 12, p. 194; *1889,* Vol. 60, p. 769.

[26] Debate on Berry's speech at Geelong, *Victoria Parliamentary Debates, 1871,* Vol. 12, pp. 948–950. The debentures were sold during 1859–64.

not square with this interpretation. Undoubtedly, private railways could have operated profitably.

Indeed, to some extent, the occasional moves toward private railway enterprise after 1860 were based on this knowledge.[27] Several reasons for the absence of private railway promotion and the persistence of government railways can be suggested. During the 1860's the intense shortage of physical capital meant that private individuals were preoccupied with the provision of residential, commercial, and industrial assets. Pastoralists, the main source of local savings during the 1860's and 1870's, were intent on the much more lucrative equipment of pastoral estates. The proposals for private railways appear to have foundered regularly, not only on questions of access to capital but perhaps mainly on the lack of entrepreneurial ability. Queensland ideas on the possibility and value of attracting American railway men to Australia were symptomatic of this basic weakness. On the other hand, colonial governments did have access to capital, they could devise an adequate administrative structure, and they were free from other construction tasks once the short-term problem of providing government buildings for new and expanding administrations had been met.

It is indicative of the approach to the division of responsibility between government and private institutions that in the first decade railway building was undertaken with fairly strict attention to the prospect for profits. Moreover, factors in the absorption of private lines into the growing government systems rested not so much on social considerations as on whether absorption was "good business."[28] Subsequently, in the early 1870's, a social purpose in railway construction and operation crystallized: limitation though not disregard of profits, progressive rate reductions, and the planning of construction to aid general economic development. The initial favorable reaction of private individuals to this policy clinched the place of governments in the field, and the early success of the policy left little prospect of private intervention. When this social policy was distorted later to permit railway building for political ends, rate concessions for highly sectional interests and the operation of railways in direct competition with private

[27] Sir F. Dillon Bell, "The Indebtedness of the Australian Colonies in Relation to Their Resources," *Proceedings of the Royal Colonial Institute, 1882–83*, Vol. 14 (London, 1883).

[28] *Victoria Parliamentary Debates, 1878*, Vol. 28, p. 134.

interests, particularly in shipping, protests could produce a political crisis but not a change in economic organization.[29] By the 1880's, the private sector was committed to government railways.

In two other lines of government intervention, tariff policy and land legislation, this gradual shift of government purpose is again reflected. In these cases the shift seems to have been linked with a growing awareness of the importance of land and tariff policy for government capital formation.

Both tariff and land policy after 1860 have been explained conventionally in terms of immediate "postgold" problems. Land legislation initiated in New South Wales in 1861 was followed generally by other colonies; tariff policy aimed at protection dates from the Victorian schedules of 1866. In both cases it has been suggested that policy was designed to provide employment for surplus gold-miners and for an expanding population by encouraging manufacturers and small-scale agriculture.[30] The trouble with this explanation is that the problem of surplus miners was soon dealt with by internal and external migration. Though this problem played a part, it was not a significant element in the policies pursued in the 1870's and 1880's and much less important in original legislation than has been thought by some historians.[31]

The importance of tariff protection varied among the different colonies. Victoria was ardently protective after 1871. New South Wales remained staunchly free trade until the 1890's. The other colonies included some protective features in their tariff schedules. The way to the introduction of protective tariffs was opened by the separation of Victoria and Queensland from New South Wales and by Imperial approval in 1850 for the imposition of nondiscriminatory colonial tariffs.

Victoria took over the New South Wales tariff structure in 1851. Pressure to alter this structure to a protective tariff seems to have originated in Geelong and was directed mainly toward agricultural protection.[32] The arguments were widened to include manufactures, which soon became the primary basis for protectionist arguments.

[29] Timothy A. Coghlan, *Labour and Industry in Australia* (London: Humphrey Milford, 1918), pp. 1417ff.

[30] See any standard work, e.g., Edward O. G. Shann, *An Economic History of Australia* (Cambridge, England: Cambridge University Press, 1930).

[31] David Packer, "Victorian Population Data, 1851–61," *Historical Studies: Australia and New Zealand,* 5(20):307–323 (May 1958).

[32] I am grateful to Professor John La Nauze for access to certain of his notes on tariff history.

Although conceived as protection for manufacturing during the gold period, the arguments for protection became associated at the end of the 1850's with proposals for radical social policy: manufacturing was to be encouraged in order to provide employment for surplus miners. This was the immediate purpose behind the 1866 tariff in Victoria—a tariff which went only a very small distance toward meeting protectionist demands.

In much the same way, preliminary proposals for land policy were made part of a wider plan for the re-employment of surplus miners. The basic conditions under which land was occupied in the main eastern colonies were prescribed in the 1847 Orders in Council. These represented a degree of security for large pastoral occupiers who controlled access to usable land, particularly in New South Wales. Although attempts were made in the 1850's to revise the 1847 Orders, these attempts were channeled in the end into the radical demand to "unlock the land" for small-scale agriculture.[33] In this tone the New South Wales legislation of 1861 was passed to provide for land sales to small selectors and revised leasehold tenure with rights of pre-emption for pastoralists. This legislation was followed in a general way by the other eastern colonies and remained the basis of land policy until the mid 1880's.

Neither the New South Wales land legislation of 1861 nor the Victorian tariff schedules of 1866 met the radical demands. The former failed to provide financial conditions to permit sales of much land, and the latter could scarcely be regarded as protective. It was not accidental that revisions in both cases came in 1871, in the one case to ease credit purchase of land and in the other to provide effective protection for Victorian manufacturing; for the purpose of both forms of intervention had changed. It was financial difficulty that prompted the timing of both changes, broke down the free trade opposition in the Victorian parliament,[34] and opened the gates to large land sales in New South Wales.

In a situation in which neither transport, technology, climate, nor capital was adapted to small agricultural farms, it is perhaps not surprising that this part of government policy had limited if any success. The New South Wales legislation was notable mostly for the ensuing struggle between selectors and pastoralists for access to land, which

[33] Stephen H. Roberts, *History of Australian Land Settlement, 1788–1920* (Melbourne: Macmillan and Co., in association with Melbourne University Press, 1924).
[34] *Victoria Parliamentary Debates, 1871*, Vol. 12, p. 200.

ended in the acquisition of large areas of freehold by pastoralists and confirmed pastoral control of available land. On the other hand, tariff legislation, which was altered substantially on only four occasions between 1866 and 1890 (1871, 1878, 1879, and 1899), was an inefficient means of sheltering manufacturing when the prices of imported manufactured goods fell heavily and continuously throughout the whole period, while wages tended to rise steadily. Attempts to assess the actual effects of tariffs are questionable mainly because major tariff changes were made during recessions and it is impossible to separate the structural from the cyclical changes.[35] Indeed, the chief visible results seem to have been the growth of friction between the colonies over the collection of duties, and the addition of a major obstacle to the federation of the colonies.[36]

Whatever may have been the original purpose of policy in both cases, and despite the enthusiasm for protection as such in Victoria, the financial significance for government activity was increasingly recognized. Limited land assets made customs revenue much more important in Victoria than in New South Wales. Whereas, in periods of recession and budgetary difficulties, Victorian governments were forced to rely largely on increased customs duties, New South Wales was able to act administratively to increase land offerings, without legislative action. In fact, both Victorian tariff increases and New South Wales land sales came to be linked with government capital formation, as we shall see later. It was not until the unwisdom of lavish land sales was recognized in the mid 1880's that policy was revised, to introduce conditional leases instead of outright sales and to attempt to break up large holdings by large-scale resumptions. By then, however, the major factor influencing the government budgetary situation was neither customs revenue nor land sales; it was fear of risking the flood of British capital that made the New South Wales governments less willing to alienate Crown lands.

[35] W. A. Sinclair, "The Tariff and Manufacturing Employment in Victoria, 1860–1900," *Economic Record,* 31:100 (1955). One other difficulty has usually been overlooked, namely, that Victorian tariffs, by reducing the freedom of entry of goods into Victoria, made the whole of Australia less attractive to British exporters. Hence it is impossible to unscramble the effects of free trade and tariff policies in each colony.

[36] Cephas D. Allin, *A History of the Tariff Relations of the Australian Colonies,* University of Minnesota Studies in the Social Sciences, No. 7 (Minneapolis, 1918).

SHORT-TERM INTERACTION OF GOVERNMENT
AND PRIVATE SECTORS, 1860–90

The striking feature of the Australian economy between 1860 and 1890 is the rapid and highly stable growth in aggregate indexes—whether we refer to movements in the value or volume of imports or exports, the level of total capital formation, total overseas borrowing, or financial and monetary activity. I have already pointed to the contrast with Britain, the United States, and Canada in movements in capital formation, international capital flows, and international migration.

It may be tempting to explain this stability in long-run terms of the steady upward pressure of government capital formation. Government outlays for capital formation did not rise greatly during the 1860's, but after 1870 a highly stable expansion is apparent (see Table 3). Actual outlays between 1870 and 1890 diverge only slightly from a straight line trend, representing a constant absolute annual increase in capital expenditures, without much regard for fluctuations in the rest of the economy or in the outside world.

Private capital formation, on the other hand, was not nearly so stable, following a much more cyclical path with the bottoms of troughs of activity in 1867, 1871, 1879, 1882, and 1885. These fluctuations in private capital formation can be explained by a number of influences that operated mainly on residential and pastoral investment.[37] The injection of relatively stable government outlays meant, arithmetically, that the movement of total Australian capital formation was a smoothed version of the fluctuating private series. It seems certain that the character of government action was such as to force on its own expenditures a high degree of stability. The whole departmental and parliamentary process depended on long-term planning of expenditures and the approval of construction commitments several years ahead.[38] Parliamentary approval included also the adoption of finan-

[37] For more detailed references, see my *Private Capital Formation in Australia, Estimates 1861–1900*. The aggregation of data for Australian colonies can be misleading. There are important contrasts in behavior and some impediments to factor movements between the colonies. These impediments can, I think, be greatly overrated. The mobility of capital and labor between the colonies was extremely high, sufficiently high to justify an approach provisionally treating the colonies as one economy.

[38] William Thompson, Financial Statement, February 9, 1871, *The Financial Statements of the Colonial Treasurers of New South Wales* (Sydney, 1881), p. 265.

cial proposals on a long-term basis. Partly for mechanical reasons such as the transfer of large funds to field officers, partly because of the need for positive action in Parliament to reduce expenditures, but mainly because of increasing political and national pressures for railway expansion, it became increasingly difficult to reduce expenditures below planned levels. On the other hand, increases in expenditures could be voted without much trouble and actual expenditures could rise if funds were available.

A steadily growing government capital outlay undoubtedly introduced a stable sector into the economy, but whether this was a stabilizing influence is another matter. When we turn from long-run to short-run characteristics in government and private capital outlays, the striking thing is the short-run inverse relationship between the two series. This inverse relationship cannot be explained in terms of deliberate antidepression spending by governments, nor in terms of a lagged or leading response of private entrepreneurs to the provision of government transport and communications facilities.[39] In mechanical terms, the inverse movement offset declines in private capital formation on five occasions (1866–67, 1878–79, 1882, 1885, and 1889–91) and possibly on a sixth (1870); it helped to dampen the effects of private expansion on five occasions (1863–65, 1868, 1876, 1880, and 1887); and it was responsible for smooth growth in the aggregate during 1877–83, and for the recovery in total capital formation after 1895. Throughout the whole period, government and private capital formation moved in the same direction in, at most, 12 years. Generally, when private capital formation was falling, public capital formation was rising and vice versa. Moreover, on no occasion did the two series have a common peak or trough. Only during two very brief episodes did the two sectors move together.

By itself, the interrelation of public and private capital formation might be suspect. But when we consider the relations of capital formation, overseas borrowing, and immigration, a definite pattern emerges. Government and private borrowing overseas moved, in the short run, in a very striking and consistent inverse fashion. Here, it was two highly unstable series, moving inversely, that produced a very stable aggregate. Although somewhat less marked, there was a persistent inverse

[39] Spending to relieve unemployment was undertaken on a limited scale mainly in 1878 and 1886. As for the response of private entrepreneurs to railway construction, there is little evidence that Australian entrepreneurs responded in the manner of American entrepreneurs. Cf. pp. 70–74 infra.

relationship between government and private capital formation. Finally, there was a much less definite tendency for assisted and unassisted immigration to move in opposite directions in the short run.

This general pattern cannot be ignored. The question of a persistent functional relationship between the two sectors requires investigation.

General Government Impediments to Private Enterprise

Throughout the period of expansion to 1889, we are dealing with an economy in process of rapid growth. It moved from the beginning fairly quickly to a position approximating full employment; government and private capital formation concentrated on fairly simple projects with a high labor content; there was a very high rate of importing and, possibly, a high marginal propensity to import; there were steadily falling import prices and rising domestic wage rates. Although not necessary in suggesting the general lines of government impediments to private enterprise, it may be useful to remind readers that these features were accompanied by a rapidly rising inflow of British capital as the main source of investible funds and by a continuous, more variable inflow of migrants.

In these circumstances an increase in government capital formation had a very limited expansive influence on the private sector in terms of either multiplier processes or direct demand for materials and equipment. In the absence of any strong response in private investment to the prospect of enlarged or improved government transport services (cf. pp. 72–73 infra), government capital formation cannot have been a major direct determinant of the level of private activity. An increase in government capital formation meant, basically, an increased demand for labor and investible funds.

Under these conditions, an increase in government capital formation may have impeded private capital formation by outright poaching of resources of labor and investible funds, or by exerting pressure on wage and interest costs for the private sector.

Poaching of labor from private activity implied a direct reduction in private capital formation. Pressure on private wage or interest costs may have operated more subtly in the same direction. Increased costs in the private sector would mean reduced incentive to invest, particularly in those export industries where prices were declining or in import-replacing industries (virtually the whole range of consumption goods) exposed to competition of foreign goods whose prices were falling. Both direct poaching and increased wage costs reduced private capital formation and reduced output of traded goods.

These effects on the domestic economy may have been reinforced by influences on the balance of payments that induced further reduction of private capital formation. Expansion of government capital formation led to increased imports. Where this expansion was financed by government absorption of local investible funds, the combination of reduced output of traded goods and increased import on government account could have had serious consequences for the balance of payments and hence could have made further inroads into private capital formation. With increased government borrowing abroad, however, the decline in production of traded goods could imply some reduction in private capital formation as a result of the worsening of the balance of payments. This effect might be greatly intensified if government capital formation was expanding when a recession in private activity was threatening because of overseas depression and reduced private Australian exports. Then while preference for safe securities by overseas investors might help to stabilize the economy as a whole by permitting the growth of government capital formation, this might make further inroads into private investible funds and hence into the distribution of labor between the government and private sectors.

Whereas governments might exert pressure on private labor supply fairly directly, either through outright competition or by the emergence of wage leadership of government institutions, the methods by which governments might poach on private supplies of investible funds were much more complicated. The colonial governments were able to divert private investible funds to government use by customs taxation, land sales, local debenture sales, banking transactions, and *possibly* by direct competition in the London capital market.

Insofar as the colonial government poached funds *and actually spent them* on construction projects, the same process occurred as in labor poaching. This process was reversible. It implied that private expansion would tend to concentrate in those industries able to convert to capital-intensive production in which the return on capital was high. These conditions fitted basically the pastoral industry with its ancillary services of banking and commerce. Moreover, it should be noted that, formally, a growth of private capital formation could make just as many inroads into government resources as did an expansion of public capital formation into private resources. As we shall see, private individuals were able on occasion to make some inroads. But the private sector was in a very much weaker position than the government sector, which had a relatively centralized machinery for decision making in each colony, an unquestioned dominance in the field of employment, and an administrative and budgetary organization which was able to curb private activity directly. Since the private sector was not normally in a position to exert great pressure on the government sector, we cannot avoid giving priority to government action.

Further, the manipulation of flows of investible funds, whether by private or government institutions, did not necessarily have the same effect as manipulation of labor supplies. Funds raised and spent by governments were largely lost to the private sector by leakage abroad. But insofar as funds were not immediately spent they could be made available to the private sector. In this way, governments were in a position to accelerate the growth of the private sector. Such a growth, however, was highly unstable since governments could recover these funds by administrative act and force an even more drastic curtailment of private activity. This particular complexity forces us to be wary in examining related movements in private and government borrowing.

The Demand for Investible Funds

Largely because of the various methods by which governments could draw on supplies of investible funds, government behavior could lead to quite sharp changes in the distribution of funds between the two sectors. Because both sectors depended heavily on supplies of British capital, it is useful to concentrate discussion on overseas borrowing by private institutions and by governments. In particular, we have to explain the marked inverse movements in the overseas borrowing of the two sectors.

Government capital formation perhaps could fairly be described as a smoothed version of government borrowing overseas. The connection derives from the underlying interrelationship of the two series: the chief rationale of overseas borrowing was government capital formation, while the supply of overseas funds could affect the course of capital formation. In fact, however, government borrowing overseas could behave in a manner highly independent of *current* government capital formation, *in the short run*. The fact that this short-term divorce could occur is fundamental to an understanding of the inverse movements of government and private borrowing overseas, and to the ability of governments to use several methods of poaching on private investible funds.

Long-term planning of government capital formation and long-term authorization of expenditures, combined with the possession of cash balances adequate for immediate purposes, made it possible for governments to manipulate their calls on different sources of funds, in order to secure the best short-term position on the London capital market while using local Australian investible funds to the best advantage.[40] Through this position governments were able to use their administrative control to poach on private supplies of investible funds, by customs taxation, land sales, the issue of local debentures, or banking transactions. These forms of influence on the private demand for overseas funds and to a less extent on local Australian funds contributed to a systematic relationship between government and private borrowing overseas, and partly through this to a systematic relationship between private and government capital formation. A rise in private borrowing overseas could induce a fall in government demand for overseas funds; a rise in government demand for overseas funds could produce a fall in private demand.

This systematic relationship was intensified by the fact that for institutional reasons private investment was short-term (mainly by bank overdraft), while governments followed the short-term movements in the London capital market even though their borrowing was for long-term purposes. The result was the sharp inverse swings in government and private borrowing from Great Britain.

It is important that these swings were based on a systematic relationship, and it is worth noting that Australian experience does not seem to have been isolated. Canadian government and private borrowing overseas seem to have experienced similar sharp inverse swings, possibly due to the same basic circumstance: substantial government capital outlays, financed in part by overseas funds, accompanied by similar substantial outlays of private capital, in an open economy with a high rate of importing.[41]

---

[40] There are some exceptions to this statement, particularly in the timing of conversion loans (see pp. 60–61 infra). We have used, basically, Roland Wilson's figures of capital imports into Australia (*Capital Imports and the Terms of Trade,* Melbourne: Melbourne University Press, 1931) after a partial independent check. This check supported Wilson's estimates and confirmed that both public and private borrowing data include only long-term investment and do not include any automatic compensating factors.

[41] Hartland, *op. cit.*

(1) *Customs Taxation and the Demand for Funds*. As may be seen from Table 4, the sources of Australian revenue were three: railway receipts, customs and excise, and land revenue. Excluding railway revenue as committed to operating expenses and interest payments, two remained as significant sources. Variations in both were intimately linked with government and private overseas borrowing.

These two sources of revenue should first be discussed separately. In an economy with a high marginal propensity to import, an inflow of privately borrowed funds, leading to an increase in private capital formation, implied increased imports and a rise in customs revenue. With a given rate of government capital and current expenditure, there was a tendency toward creation of a budget surplus (reduction of deficit) [42] and hence a fall in government demand for loans. There was no similar connection, of a purely monetary sort, operating through an increase in government borrowing. But a rise in government capital formation, with or without overseas borrowing, could be financed in part by increased customs taxation, thereby putting a brake on private capital formation and private demand for overseas funds. This brake could operate partly through the absorption of private funds in customs receipts, and partly through the added costs to private projects from higher duties on imported goods (higher equipment costs or, indirectly, higher wage rates).

This relationship was well understood, particularly in Victoria and Queensland (to which customs revenue was much the most important source of ordinary revenue), as shown by the following remarks in a budget debate: ". . . we are aware that, if people have full employment, their consumption of dutiable articles will be correspondingly plentiful. That is the case just now. Through the influx of wealth an enormous expenditure in every direction is going on. People who cannot get good interest for their money in other ways have gone in for building all round the city, and the consequence is full employment and good wages for a vast number of artisans and labourers—a class who usually spend their money lavishly on articles of luxury—the result being revenue returns of a most flourishing kind." [43]

Perhaps more significantly, the tariff alterations that were made before 1890, especially in Victoria, had a basic and explicit justification

[42] In Australian usage, a budget surplus referred only to the balance of ordinary revenue and expenditure, excluding all operations in respect to the loan market or short-term transactions with banks.

[43] Sir John O'Shanassy, Budget Debate, *Victoria Parliamentary Debates, 1882*, Vol. 39, p. 499.

in plans for government capital formation and associated budget difficulties arising from commitments for construction. The early steps
toward effectively protective tariffs, particularly in Queensland in
1870 and Victoria in 1871, were taken in response to just these diffi-

TABLE 4. SOURCES OF REVENUE, NEW SOUTH WALES, VICTORIA, AND QUEENSLAND

In thousands of pounds

Year	Customs	Land	Railways
1861	2,166	1,567	262
1862	1,906	1,801	399
1863	2,057	1,333	568
1864	1,997	1,360	657
1865	2,179	1,656	764
1866	2,279	1,687	792
1867	2,564	1,591	758
1868	2,469	1,660	884
1869	2,627	1,669	966
1870	2,470	1,641	941
1871	2,718	1,672	1,040
1872	3,057	2,103	1,184
1873	3,370	2,205	1,368
1874	3,268	2,559	1,538
1875	3,147	3,423	1,682
1876	3,213	4,259	1,879
1877	3,389	4,706	2,131
1878	3,357	3,696	2,344
1879	3,200	2,894	2,406
1880	3,412	2,923	2,965
1881	4,083	4,390	3,439
1882	4,498	4,354	4,056
1883	4,524	3,081	4,564
1884	4,956	3,106	5,099
1885	5,127	3,096	5,424
1886	5,587	2,817	5,463
1887	5,804	3,544	5,860
1888	6,554	3,609	6,550
1889	6,867	3,368	6,738
1890	6,382	3,411	7,011

Note: These data are from the *Public Accounts* and *Government Gazette* of each
colony. The different financial years in each case have required some splicing to
convert the data to calendar years. Land revenue includes income from leases in
addition to sales.

culties and explicitly in preference to overseas borrowing and increases in land revenue. There was good reason for this preference: Victoria had a large distributing trade and could tax a fairly high turnover, whereas her land resources were limited. Queensland was attempting to attract population by offers of free land and, on the assumption of an inelastic demand for imports, considered increased customs taxation to be a lesser irritant than increased land revenue.[44] Major tariff adjustments in Victoria in 1878, 1879, and 1889 were all made (as was the tariff of 1871) in recessions associated with declining private capital formation and budget difficulties, and as precursors to expanding government capital formation. Before discussing the statistical evidence, it is necessary to deal with land sales and the demand for loans.

(2) *Land Sales and the Demand for Investible Funds.* New South Wales relied much more heavily on land revenue than did the other colonies and had a much more spectacular method of checking private capital formation and of diverting private investible funds to government use, through the sale of Crown lands to private individuals. The capital transaction involved appears historically to have been financed by overseas borrowing on private account,[45] and insofar as this was the case, a definite sequence was possible: increased private borrowing abroad, increased land sales by governments, higher budget surpluses and reduced demand for government loans, especially overseas borrowing. Although increased land sales may have been spontaneous during 1871–73, later sales were largely the result of planned increases in government capital formation that governments financed by the sale of land, which entailed diversion of privately borrowed British capital or of local investible funds.[46] This continued until 1884.

Sale of land was substantially equivalent to the local issue of debentures. The main difference was that there were considerable pressures on pastoralists to buy or at any rate to "peacock" land (i.e., to attempt to purchase key portions of a holding, thereby rendering surrounding areas unusable by others) over the first 25 years of our period, particularly during 1871–84. The New South Wales land legislation of 1861,

---

[44] Treasurer's Budget Statement, *Victoria Parliamentary Debates, 1871,* Vol. 12, p. 200; *Queensland, Official Record of the Debates of the Legislative Assembly, 1870,* Vol. 23, pp. 53–58.

[45] See, for example, George Dibbs, Financial Statement, February 7, 1883, *The Financial Statements of the Colonial Treasurers of New South Wales,* 2nd ed., p. 484.

[46] See New South Wales Financial Statements during 1875–80.

ostensibly to encourage agriculture and reduce pastoral leaseholds, resulted in a strenuous struggle between pastoralists and selectors, in
which pastoralists acquired title to very considerable areas. Alterations
in credit conditions in 1871 intensified this struggle. Moreover, pastoralists had a strong incentive to buy key areas since freehold title
implied complete legal title to improvements, not merely rights of com-
pensation. As a result, Crown land sales rose steeply between 1871 and
1884, and land revenue consequently increased. New South Wales government budgets were generally overflowing during these years, and
this was not accidentally linked with rising government capital formation, a very tepid interest on the part of New South Wales Treasurers
in the London capital market, and rising private borrowing overseas.
Illustrating the fact that government absorption of private funds did
not necessarily imply inverse movements of government and private
capital formation, these two series moved together during 1873–74 and
1876. But the tendency to inverse movement in both borrowing and
capital formation was very noticeable.

The process of poaching by means of land sales and using them as
an alternative to overseas borrowing was soon recognized. For example,
after commenting on increased land sales, the New South Wales
Treasurer in 1874 reported: "Practically we have been employing for
some time past a large portion of the cash balance at the credit of the
Consolidated Revenue Fund on public works of a reproductive character, for pending the sale of debentures we have temporarily transferred to the Railway Loan Fund 36 Vic. No. 17, £215,000 and to the
Public Works Loan Fund, 38 Vic. No. 2, £150,000." [47]

His successor was fully aware of the underlying process and more
concerned about the swapping of one public asset for another: "We
cannot shut our eyes to the fact that all the money drawn from such
a source as this [land] . . . is part of the capital of the country, and it
behoves us . . . to endeavor as far as possible to apply at least a portion of it, if not a considerable portion, to the improvement of the
land of the Colony itself." [48]

As land revenues rose and budget surpluses snowballed, scruples
diminished. The full implication for government borrowing came to be
seen, and Treasurers found themselves increasingly independent of

[47] George A. Lloyd, Financial Statement, November 19, 1874, *The Financial Statements of the Colonial Treasurers of New South Wales*, p. 321. Examples similar to
this and to the two following quotations could be multiplied.
[48] William Forster, Financial Statement, April 2, 1875, *ibid.*, pp. 333–334.

London: "... notwithstanding the market is highly favourable for the purpose [borrowing], as the securities of this Colony were never in greater demand or stood higher in the estimation of the public. ... I am glad to say that there is no immediate urgency now, as we have a balance at the bank at the present time sufficient to enable us to meet not only all the requirements of the Consolidated Revenue Fund, but also to make such further advances to the general loan fund as may be found necessary." [49]

Three years later, the government became concerned that the disposal of its land assets diminished the attractiveness of the colonial securities in the London market, and a halt was called in the form of a revision of land legislation in 1884. The immediate results were a budget deficit and much greater reliance on borrowing from London. For this the Treasurer's justification was simply, "We have saved the land of the country." [50]

(3) *Budget Deficits and Surpluses and the Demand for Funds.* Since our data on overseas borrowing are for Australia as a whole, we cannot demonstrate the influence of each main source of revenue on the relations between government and private borrowing. Movements in government and private overseas borrowing, in budget surpluses or deficits in New South Wales, Victoria, and Queensland, and in bank deposits by their governments suggest the character of the process and its timing. Throughout the whole period, with the single exception of 1886, a fall in private overseas borrowing and a worsening of the budgetary situation went together. A rise in government overseas borrowing and a budgetary deficit were also normally associated. Finally, a rise in private overseas borrowing, an improvement in the budget, and a fall in government overseas borrowing usually accompanied each other.

The successive budget surpluses during the 1870's were matched by relatively limited government borrowing overseas, while fluctuations in the size of the surplus were generally associated with opposite movements in government borrowing overseas. The sharp movement into deficits in 1878–79, matching a sagging private sector, brought a big increase in government borrowing overseas. The improved budgetary situation of 1880–82 brought a trough in government borrowing, while subsequent deficits until 1886 encouraged large government issues in London. These issues slackened throughout 1887–88 as budgets im-

---

[49] James Watson, Financial Statement, February 9, 1881, *ibid.*, pp. 477–478.
[50] Dibbs, Financial Statement, December 11, 1885, *ibid.*, p. 572.

proved. The first moves into the depression of the 1890's were accompanied by a worsening of the budgetary situation and a resumption of high overseas government borrowing during 1889–91. Thereafter, the profound depression left little opportunity for this inverse pattern to operate, chiefly because of the drying-up of supplies of British capital.

Reduced overseas borrowing was not the only possible government reaction to a budget surplus, nor was increased overseas borrowing the only response to a deficit, even given government current and capital outlays. The other main response lay in the manipulation of government cash balances, particularly in the form of government deposits with commercial banks. This requires separate consideration, along with general government banking transactions.

(4) *Banking Transactions, Interest Rates, and the Demand for Funds.* For most of the period, Australian colonial governments held large cash balances, almost entirely in the form of deposits—some current, some fixed—with Australian and British banks. These balances represented a combination of unspent loan proceeds and accumulated unspent surpluses on account of ordinary revenue funds. Table 5, comparing movements in banking advances and general deposits with government deposits and "British" deposits, i.e., fixed deposits of British investors with Australian banks, shows the importance of changes in government bank deposits for the operation of the banking system.

As bankers to the governments, the Australian banks undertook important functions. Not only did they hold government balances; they served as advisers or intermediaries for government security issues in London and in the colonies and as suppliers of short-term credit to governments. But the links of the banks with the private sector made them a key channel of influence between governments and private institutions. The Australian banks were the primary institutions concerned in private overseas borrowing. Institutionally, private borrowing abroad took the form of company calls, debenture issues, immigrant funds, direct investments, and British deposits. Table 5 shows how important changes in British deposits were in the banking system and in the total inflow of British capital to Australia. With these deposits and with government cash balances at their disposal, the Australian banks dominated the supply of investible funds. But their dominance exposed them, and the private sector, to peculiar risks.

Because of the importance of British and government deposits in banking activity, rates of interest on deposits tended to be a basic in-

TABLE 5. CHANGES IN BANKING ACTIVITY, NEW SOUTH WALES, VICTORIA, AND
QUEENSLAND COMBINED, COMPARED WITH CHANGES IN BRITISH
DEPOSITS IN AUSTRALIA

In thousands of pounds

Year	Changes			Changes in British deposits (Australia)
	In bank deposits	In bank advances	In government deposits	
1861–62	501	680	681	–
1862–63	354	1,721	—489	–
1863–64	361	723	—326	–
1864–65	752	1,204	144	–
1865–66	1,113	2,313	—165	–
1866–67	—112	—1,745	388	–
1867–68	2,419	279	—281	—647
1868–69	—423	1,644	387	184
1869–70	604	982	1,208	239
1870–71	177	—1,160	403	—114
1871–72	3,156	—357	346	315
1872–73	2,587	4,350	114	—138
1873–74	988	2,433	—1,066	—37
1874–75	3,274	2,576	1,247	993
1875–76	3,029	2,745	—22	967
1876–77	4,733	6,113	1,111	1,244
1877–78	—20	3,759	—476	—552
1878–79	669	—498	458	137
1879–80	830	—3,270	—1,447	1,176
1880–81	6,141	2,521	2,304	737
1881–82	4,751	11,266	—1,201	582
1882–83	4,205	5,539	—893	3,749
1883–84	4,225	3,285	1,230	3,086
1884–85	6,303	9,465	—233	160
1885–86	2,029	6,999	805	3,233
1886–87	4,529	2,205	1,348	3,958
1887–88	8,135	11,285	—1,128	—26
1888–89	3,109	13,278	769	5,835
1889–90	3,924	2,489	—938	3,574
1890–91	78	4,192	—3,804	2,765
1891–92	650	2,771	1,031	539

Sources: Changes in bank deposits and advances are calculated from *Commonwealth Finance Bulletin* (any year to 1918). Changes in government bank deposits are estimated from data in the *Public Accounts* of New South Wales, giving cash balances held in Australian banks in Australia, and the Finance Statements of Victoria, which show only cash balances. Changes in British deposits have been calculated from comparison of Australian banking returns (see appropriate *Statistical Registers*) and of balance sheet data (*Sydney Morning Herald* and *Australasian Insurance and Banking Record*). Bank advances, in the classifications of the day, were something of a hotchpotch, including a lot of bank credits that would not now normally be included in bank advances; also included are bank holdings of government and local authorities debentures. British deposits must be calculated for Australia as a whole.

dicator for banking and the local capital market in Australia. In particular, a basic determinant of government financial policy emerged from comparison of local deposit rates with security yields in London. In dealing with the loan market, this comparison was influential in determining whether to borrow in London, borrow on the local market, secure short-term overdrafts from banks, or draw down bank deposits (cash balances). Reducing government deposits in banks was important as a stopgap measure, to provide for expenditures while deferring action to raise funds or awaiting the right moment in the loan market. In fact, the government's desire to make the most businesslike decision often required the short-term reduction of cash balances. This was also necessary, largely for administrative or physical reasons, while preparing for new security issues in London in response to government budget deficits.

Rising deposit rates, with given yields in London, might be associated with a diminishing inflow of British deposits (declining private capital formation, tendency to government budget deficit) or with falling government deposits (to meet immediate cash needs of an unbalanced budget), or both. Falling deposit rates, with given security yields in London, might be associated with rising British deposits or the accumulation of government deposits, with pressure to reduce government borrowing overseas.

The data suggest a very close connection between falling private borrowing overseas, declining government bank deposits, budget deficits, and rising government borrowing overseas. There were substantial declines in government deposits in 1874, 1878–80, 1882–83, and 1890–91, and minor declines in 1885 and 1888. These reductions in government bank deposits entailed quite drastic variations in banking activity, at times that were exceedingly inconvenient for the private sector. The very heavy withdrawals in 1890–91 must have seriously affected the course of the downswing after 1889. At other times, however, government withdrawals coincided with the onset of private recession, which might have been offset by government *support* to the banks.

Banks were not unwilling to protest at this treatment. The complaint of the Bank of New South Wales in 1885, when a rather slight withdrawal occurred, may not have been as justified as the language suggests, but indicates the character of the problem created: "You have postponed and postponed a settlement until your loan has been floated. You have meanwhile gone on overdrawing your account with us, contrary to all agreement terms, to the extent of £1,300,000 in Sydney, without previous arrangement with us of any kind; and we cannot now consent (it is strangely unreasonable that you should ask us to consent) to further disorganise and tear about in this huge and spasmodic fashion all our financial strength and weakness. . . . You seem to be unaware that, whilst you are using provocative language to us of dictation and threat, you are and have been for sometime past absolutely dependent upon our self-sacrificing willingness to pay your daily cheques." [51]

In the colonies agreements between governments and some (not all) banks fixed, among other things, the terms on which government deposits would be held, limited the maximum interest-bearing deposits of governments, and prescribed the minimum deposit. In the beginning the maximum interest-bearing deposit was very low, and the growth of government cash balances and the scale of government borrowing prompted repeated raising of the maximum. By the mid 1870's governments had become adept at playing the London against the Australian banks and contracting Australian banks against noncontracting banks to such effect that governments normally could expect to place the greater part, if not all, of their cash balances in interest-bearing deposits. The prospect of investing cash balances became increasingly important to governments,[52] particularly since a year's interest on loan receipts deposited could often equal or exceed the costs of flotation plus the discount on loans.

This consideration, although probably not as significant as the immediate cash requirements of an unbalanced budget, did contribute to the inverse relations between government and private borrowing overseas. An increase in the latter, by reducing the deposit rate, could have several repercussions. Local investors would find local debenture issues attractive; banks would be more willing to offer special overdraft facilities to government; and with given security yields in London, colonial governments would find it harder to induce banks to offer an adequate rate of interest on deposited loans. A fall in private borrowing overseas, by raising deposit rates, would work in the opposite direction. On the other hand, an inflow of government borrowing, by swelling bank deposits, tended to reduce deposit rates and to discourage

[51] Dibbs, *ibid.*, p. 559, Bank of New South Wales to the Colonial Treasurer of New South Wales, October 21, 1885.

[52] *Victoria Parliamentary Debates, 1871,* Vol. 12, p. 950; Lloyd, Financial Statement, October 16, 1873, *The Financial Statements of the Colonial Treasurers of New South Wales,* p. 302.

the inflow of British deposits. A government decision to abstain from the London market similarly induced a rise in deposit rates and in bank demand for British deposits.

The problem of investing budget surpluses or unspent loan proceeds was continuous. The following statements typify the attitude of the Treasurers:

It was the intention of the Government last year to have launched a loan in the London market during the present year; and debentures were accordingly prepared for the purpose, but since then money has become so plentiful in Sydney that the proceeds of such a loan, if brought out to the Colony, could not be invested with the banks (if indeed any of it would be taken by them) at rates other than what would create a serious loss to the country.[53]

Indeed I would have declined to borrow more than was indispensably necessary, unless I was in a position to place another £1,000,000 at deposit with the banks on advantageous terms—on terms which would preserve us from any loss in connexion with the transaction.[54]

I made up my mind that, unless we could get a certain price for our debentures, it would be more profitable for the colony . . . to enter into some arrangement [with the banks] for a temporary loan.[55]

A rise in local deposit rates does seem to have been associated, until the mid 1880's, with increased government borrowing and reduced private borrowing and private capital formation. This was particularly the case in 1866, 1870, 1874, 1878–79, and 1882–83. On the other hand, a relative rise in security yields in London tended to be connected with reduced government borrowing and high private borrowing overseas.

(5) *Timing of Conversion Loans.* The systematic inverse relationships between government and private borrowing could have been intensified or offset by fortuitous conditions associated with government borrowing, particularly in the timing of conversion loans. Fixed conversion dates forced governments onto the London market, except where loans were actually repatriated. Our data on government borrowing exclude conversion loans as such. But because conversion loans were required at certain dates, securities might be issued in excess of conversion needs merely for the convenience of having one bite at the London market. In fact, this does not seem to have happened very often. The problem of conversion loans did not arise significantly dur-

---

[53] Watson, Financial Statement, February 9, 1881, *ibid.*, pp. 477–478.
[54] John Gillies, The Budget, *Victoria Parliamentary Debates, 1887*, Vol. 54, p. 534.
[55] James Service, The Budget, *ibid., 1885*, Vol. 48, p. 421.

ing the 1880's, while during the 1870's several loans were repatriated, not converted.[56] Nevertheless, conversion dates may have produced some exceptional peak in government borrowing.

(6) *Influence of British Supply Conditions.* It is possible that British supply conditions might have intensified or reduced the characteristics of Australian demand for overseas loans. Unfortunately, the institutional history of the London capital market is poorly explored and no very definite suggestion is possible.

We have seen that a definite connection between the supply of or demand for British deposits and the demand for government loans operated through the Australian bank deposit rate. Apart from this, we have to be very tentative. First, total Australian borrowing, particularly from 1872 to 1883, absorbed a very high proportion of total net British lending overseas. Australian private and government borrowers may have found it difficult to operate simultaneously in the British market because of direct competition for funds. The significance of this point turns largely on the sources of British funds for investment in Australia, about which virtually nothing is known. Possibly there was a progressive widening of the scope of investors in Australian government securities, to include those investors who supplied funds to private Australian borrowers. In the 1860's Australian government securities appear to have been taken up by only about half a dozen institutional borrowers. Despite British law on the subject, and despite the difficulties of holding government debentures securely, willingness to accept Australian government securities seems to have increased steadily among trustee investors. By the end of the 1870's, the tenderers for these securities were considerably more numerous. Largely to meet the needs of this type of borrower, the Australian governments changed from debentures to inscribed stock at the end of the decade. This step greatly widened the clientele; by the end of the 1880's subscribers to Australian government issues were numbered in thousands.[57] Since this enlarged clientele probably handled trust funds that found their way also into bank deposits with Australian banks, the pressures to

---

[56] Hon. John Robertson, Financial Statement, December 8, 1875, *The Financial Statements of the Colonial Treasurers of New South Wales*, pp. 344–345; Service, The Budget, *loc. cit.*

[57] Dibbs, Financial Statement, December 11, 1885; *New South Wales Parliamentary Debates, First Series, Sessions 1885–86*, Vol. 18, p. 465; Debate on Address-in-Reply, *Queensland, Official Record of the Debates of the Legislative Assembly, 1888*, Vol. 55, p. 121.

inverse movements in overseas borrowing arising from government and private demand conditions would not be checked, but may well have been encouraged.

Second, there is some indication that in periods of private recession British investors had some preference for safe Australian government securities, first in 1878–79, later in 1885: "It is not more than three years ago that we had to make the most extraordinary efforts to get our debentures sold in London. Better times have come for us now; not that we have bettered our condition to any extent, because that has not been so, but circumstances have changed in England, and the misfortunes and depressions in her trade have not afforded her opportunities for investing her wealth; and we have benefited by that. Let changed times come again to England—let those times come again in England when every man there was busy, and she supplied the world with commodities—and I hope that they will come; and then we shall see that, instead of having money-lenders running after us to lend us money, they will probably give us the cold shoulder." [58]

Immigration and the Demand for Labor

Although some of the inverse relations between government and private borrowing overseas and the poaching of funds may have existed regardless of the level of employment, any influences that changes in the level of government capital formation may have had on the supply of labor to the private sector and on wage rates depended essentially on the scarcity of labor. Although localized labor shortages may have existed before 1870, we are mainly confined to the period 1871–90 in discussing the interaction of the government and private sectors in the labor market.

There were two brief episodes of relatively slight unemployment—in 1878–79 and in 1885–86. Neither episode was simultaneous in the different colonies: in the first, unemployment appears to have spread originally from Victoria northwards and to have reached Queensland when disappearing in Victoria; the second spread from New South Wales in 1885 and reached Victoria in 1886.

Apart from these episodes, there is abundant evidence of a high level of employment throughout the colonies. The growing power of the trade unions, the relative ease of securing wage increases, the steady

[58] Sir Thomas McIlwraith, August 25, 1885, *Queensland, Official Record, 1885,* Vol. 46, p. 428.

rise in real wage rates throughout the 1870's, and the retention of a high plateau of wages during the 1880's despite the large influx of immigrants in 1882–84 are all indirect indications of a sellers' market for labor. Only one official estimate exists, the return of 3 percent unemployed in New South Wales in the Census of 1881. Other official data in Queensland immigration reports and Victoria local government returns on labor requirements testify to a persistently high level of employment. Coghlan's record [59] for all the colonies provides a running commentary in much the same vein.

Contemporary comment is also abundant. At the most conservative level, successive Treasurers of New South Wales recognized the problem of labor shortage. Parkes in 1873 foresaw an "almost certain want" of labor as the great difficulty for government works,[60] and his successors had similar complaints in 1875 and 1876. The 1881 Census estimate mentioned above was supported in 1882 by Watson, who admitted "injurious competition" with private enterprise;[61] and his successor, Dibbs, in 1883 casually observed that the existing difficulty of labor shortage was "no new one." [62]

Complaints in Victoria struck a bitter note. Throughout the 1870's, the allegation was frequent: "our crops are being lost because there is no one to get them in;" [63] or "a complete stop is put to improvements in the interior owing to a shortage of labour." [64] In 1882 there was "full employment and good wages for a vast number of artisans and labourers"; [65] and in 1887 the Victoria Public Works Department felt called upon to state that work would be done in seasonal slacks and not maintained throughout the year.[66]

By 1871 the colonial governments had come to be recognized as the most important employers of labor and had been accorded a degree of wage leadership. The subsequent growth of employment in government construction and in service left no doubt about the direct and

[59] *Labour and Industry in Australia;* see chapters on wages and prices.

[60] Henry Parkes, Financial Statement, November 21, 1873, *The Financial Statements,* pp. 292–293.

[61] Watson, Financial Statement, November 1, 1882, *ibid.,* p. 472.

[62] Dibbs, Financial Statement, February 7, 1883, *The Financial Statements,* 2nd ed., p. 485.

[63] *Victoria Parliamentary Debates,* August 11, 1874, p. 37.

[64] *Ibid.,* p. 938; also *1882,* Vol. 43, pp. 394, 801, etc.

[65] *Ibid., 1882,* Vol. 49, p. 499.

[66] Alfred Deakin, Debate on Labour Bureau, July 13, 1887, *ibid., 1887,* Vol. 54, p. 368.

indirect position of governments as employers. There was a resulting tendency not only toward establishment of a platform of wage rates on which private employers might operate, but also toward accretion of government functions in the labor market. At least as early as 1875 the government of Victoria assumed responsibility for labor bureaus, though in a somewhat haphazard manner.[67] Very unwillingly, in 1878–79, governments accepted some obligations to provide works for unemployed, an obligation which was to be pressed increasingly on them: "Considering that the Government in this Colony undertook works which were usually carried out by private enterprise—that it was the largest employer of labour in the Colony—admitting the abstract right of the able and willing worker to live, there ought to be no difficulty about setting the whole of the unemployed to profitable labour."[68] Full expression of the eight-hours movement was sought through legislative action during the 1880's;[69] government factory legislation was begun in 1873;[70] and trade union bargaining (especially in the skilled crafts) tended to be directed above all at government employers,[71] though it was not until 1892 that positive steps were taken to provide for government intervention in labor disputes.[72]

With the policy of long-term planning of a rapidly rising government investment program, the solution to persistent labor shortages lay in the introduction of labor through immigration. All colonies received a fairly substantial supply of immigrants in almost every year between 1860 and 1890. These were more or less evenly divided between unassisted immigrants and immigrants assisted by colonial governments.

For all practical purposes, the British government played no part in migration to Australia during this period; and some of the colonial governments, particularly in Victoria, were not prepared to continue

[67] *Ibid., 1882,* Vol. 39, p. 499.

[68] *Ibid., 1889,* Vol. 60, p. 518.

[69] For example, New South Wales Debate on Eight Hours System of Labour, February 8, 1881, *New South Wales Parliamentary Debates, 1881,* Vol. 4, p. 276: "But it must be recollected that in this country the State is the largest employer of labour, and that the State is regarded by private employers as a pattern for themselves."

[70] Eric Fry, "The Conditions of the Urban Wage Earning Class in Australia in the 1880's," unpublished Ph.D. thesis, Australian National University, 1955, p. 166.

[71] N. G. Butlin, "Collective Bargaining in the Sydney Printing Industry, 1880–1900," *Economic Record,* 23:206–226 (December 1947).

[72] James T. Sutcliffe, *A History of Trade Unionism in Australia* (Melbourne: Macmillan and Co., 1921), p. 122.

schemes of assisted immigration. It was mainly Queensland, with some assistance on a limited scale from New South Wales and South Australia, that accounted for the influx of assisted immigrants. Queensland alone helped to bring out about two thirds of all those assisted during the period. All the colonies were closely tied together, through the high mobility of immigrant labor. Assisted immigrants entered Queensland and many moved without much delay into the seasonal ebb and flow of labor between Queensland, New South Wales, and Victoria; many, too, seem to have moved out of Queensland into the southern colonies. This movement in part forced Queensland governments to enlarge assistance to migration and may help to explain the lack of similar effort on the part of Victoria. This intercolonial mobility justifies treating (as we must) immigration into Australia as a whole in relation to total Australian capital formation.[73]

Unassisted migration conformed extraordinarily closely to movements in private capital formation and hence, presumably, to the general level of private activity. Any proper attempt to explain satisfactorily this lagless relationship must await another occasion. The type of explanation proposed by Brinley Thomas in another connection [74] does not seem to be very probable in the Australian case. It is reasonably certain that changes in the level of private activity did not produce such an accurate and prompt response in unassisted migration. The reverse is much more likely: unassisted migrants almost certainly, as possessors of fairly substantial funds,[75] influenced short-run changes in the demand for housing. Their possession of funds, together with some speculative building in anticipation of an influx of migrants, may have geared changes in house construction to changes in unassisted immigration. In view of the importance of residential building in total private capital formation, fluctuations in the latter could be expected to follow closely fluctuations in unassisted immigration.

On the other hand, immigrants assisted by governments—farm and general laborers, navvies, domestic servants—neither possessed the funds to make effective demands on residential facilities nor did they generally appear to create a further demand for housing: Absorption

[73] I am indebted to my colleague, W. D. Borrie, for access to certain migration statistics. I have used annual estimates, although they may be more suspect than intercensal figures. These estimates are not at all satisfactory for individual colonies.

[74] Brinley Thomas, *op. cit.*

[75] Timothy A. Coghlan, *Seven Colonies of Australasia 1901–02* (Sydney: G. S. Chapman [1903]), and *New South Wales Parliamentary Debates, 1880,* Vol. 2, p. 1805.

of domestic servants and farm laborers into existing structures, and the housing of considerable numbers of construction workers and their families in tents at the site of projects greatly reduced the influence of assisted immigration on housing needs in the short run.

Assisted immigration was almost entirely financed by government loan funds, not by ordinary revenue. Planning of assisted immigration was tied partly to long-term works proposals, partly to overseas borrowing policy. Since unassisted immigration, on the other hand, seems to have been a significant factor producing changes in private capital formation and hence to have moved directly with private overseas borrowing, there was a definite tendency for assisted and unassisted immigration to move inversely in the short run. This tendency was particularly apparent over the years 1870–82 and 1886–88.

While these modest inverse movements undoubtedly helped to smooth the total inflow of migrants, especially during the 1870's, the tendency to inverse movement was offset by a number of important factors. First, only a small proportion of total loan funds was absorbed by assisted migration, and variations in assistance that did not have much connection with overseas government borrowing were possible. Second, the onset of periods of private recession, with brief periods of unemployment, produced outcries against immigration, to which governments bowed. Third, because of the quantitative importance of assisted immigration and the scale of government overseas propaganda, government assistance programs may have encouraged unassisted migrants to move to Australia. Fourth, whatever plans governments may have made, the actual rates of assisted and unassisted immigration depended on the willingness of people to leave Great Britain and Ireland.

Nevertheless, to the extent that inverse movements occurred, the decline in assisted immigration during periods of rising private capital formation almost certainly aggravated the labor situation, particularly in 1875 and 1880–81 when probably the bitterest attacks were made on government inroads into private labor supplies. Also, when governments bowed to wage earners' demands to reduce assisted immigration in private recessions, as in 1879, this helped to preserve wage levels established during periods of labor shortage.

Underlying this situation, however, was another feature of assisted immigration, namely, the trend element. Except in the years 1882–84, it seems probable that government attempts to ease the labor situation by assisted immigration lagged increasingly far behind government capital formation. Government pressure on the labor market increased steadily during the 1870's, relaxed briefly during 1882–84, and then became intense as government construction continued to rise until 1890.

The remarkably steady expansion of government capital formation between 1871 and 1890 meant in general terms a constant absolute annual increase in capital formation.[76] In this situation and with the assumption of given techniques, an unchanged pattern of construction projects, and perfect mobility of labor between projects, such a rate of increase implied (for construction purposes only) a constant annual intake of additional labor into government projects. Employment on government construction projects rose from perhaps 15,000 in 1871 to about 75,000 in 1890, implying the need for a constant annual intake of about 3,000 to meet expanding government construction after 1871. In other words, government construction could go on expanding at this rate, with these ideal assumptions, provided there was a constant annual inflow of adult male migrant laborers at this level.[77]

Even if these were all the conditions involved, it would seem very unlikely that assisted immigration, disregarding the occupations of the migrants, was adequate during 1867–81. Assisted male immigrants over 12 years of age arrived in numbers ranging from 1,500 to an exceptional peak of about 8,000 per year. Whereas the total number was inadequate in many years, the occupational distribution of assisted male migrants cannot be ignored. Unfortunately, occupational data are not very satisfactory and no firm conclusions can be drawn. Many adult males were equipped only for service occupations; many preferred to remain in the cities rather than accept rural construction jobs. It seems certain that the assisted migrant laborers willing to accept such jobs were far below requirements throughout the 1870's. Furthermore, the assumption of perfect mobility between construction jobs is contrary to fact. The enormous geographical spread of government projects was only partially offset by the high mobility of construction workers. Positive inducements were often held out to construction workers to settle in and around areas in which they were first employed.

A constant annual addition to the construction workforce, however, did not exhaust the labor demands of an expanding government pro-

---

[76] Our series of capital formation are in current prices, but price changes were too limited to affect this conclusion. Again, note that this aggregation obscures some differences of behavior between colonies.

[77] This calculation is based on detailed data on New South Wales railways generalized to other assets.

gram. Assets not only had to be produced; they had to be used. The demand for labor to make use of assets led to a rising total annual intake of new labor on account of construction and operation of facilities. The rate of increase is given by the ratio of (a) the increment of labor required, in combination with an increment of capital, for the achievement of a planned increase in output, to (b) the increment of labor needed to produce the increment of capital. This ratio we call simply the ratio of annual to initial labor.

In some cases this ratio must have approximated zero. For example, reservoirs or defense works required annual labor sufficient only for very low rates of maintenance. But in the main types of government assets, particularly railways, the ratio of annual to initial labor seems to have been fairly constant and relatively high, certainly not less than 1 to 5. Under these conditions the government construction program required a steadily rising intake of additional labor, at a rate considerably above the trend of assisted male immigration during the 1870's.[78]

The program seems to have reached a peak in 1880–81, when intense pressure was exerted on the Queensland and New South Wales governments to increase their assistance to migration. The result was an upsurge of immigration during 1882–84, when the governments undoubtedly provided sufficient labor. A sharp reaction followed, because of the difficulty of absorbing so many migrants in such a brief period and also, to some extent, the failure to persuade many migrants to accept rural construction employment. This failure brought a turning in the history of assisted immigration to Australia. New South Wales virtually abandoned assistance, and Queensland greatly contracted the numbers assisted after 1884. Assisted immigration consequently dwindled rapidly during the rest of the decade, in the face of a continued growth of government capital formation.

Something of the outcome is suggested by price and wage statistics, which indicate a general tendency toward worsening of the Australian cost situation in relation to overseas prices of both exports and imported goods. Not even the migration peaks of 1877 and 1883 seem to have made much impression on the conflicting trend of wage costs and prices of traded goods. In the circumstances the marked tendency toward stagnation in manufacturing in New South Wales and the languishing of agriculture throughout most of Australia during the

---

[78] This calculation is based on New South Wales railway data.

second half of the 1880's may not be surprising. The point was adequately made at the Royal Colonial Institute in London in 1884: "We are importing English capital to a large extent in the promotion of public works, but those who dictate the policy of the country object to the introduction by State assistance of labour to aid in the expenditure of that capital. The manufacturers, however, found that the dearth of labour was operating most prejudicially to the interests of the Colony." [79]

The development of this situation throughout the 1870's and 1880's brought complaints from employers and their representatives and even from members of governments, to the effect that government activity, especially construction, was eating into private labor supplies during periods of government expansion and affecting wage costs. In the early stages these complaints came from farmers, wheat growers, and graziers in Victoria and sugar growers in Queensland. Later, while graziers dropped out, the complaints became more general:

Here we are with a small population, carrying on public works that absorb all the labour of the colony, and will continue to do so for the next two years, and in the meantime our crops are being lost because there is no one to get them in. . . . And with all this staring us in the face, we are told that tenders for fresh public works will shortly be accepted. In view of the railways now going on, and those that are to be begun shortly, and the fact that the public buildings now being erected in Melbourne absorb nearly all the artisans in it, and totally prevent private work from being undertaken, I don't know what the country is to do without immigration.[80]

Similar complaints persisted:

. . . the Government cannot draw more than a certain number of men from the labour market, especially in years of prosperity, such as I hope we are about to enjoy. If they do, they will find themselves in a short time in the position of building railways for districts where the farmers are not able to gather in their harvests.[81]

Queensland officials pointed to the crux of the problem as early as 1877:

There can, I think, be little doubt that to attempt to force their construction [railways] and let a large number of contracts at once, without some scheme of immigration being undertaken simultaneously for the introduction of the

[79] *Proceedings of the Royal Colonial Institute, 1883–84*, Vol. 15, p. 127.
[80] *Victoria Parliamentary Debates, 1874*, p. 37.
[81] *Ibid., 1881*, p. 1223; *1883*, Vol. 43, pp. 384–385.

necessary navvy labour, would inevitably result in a serious disturbance of the labour market, and consequent rise in wages.[82]

The Premier's reply to this report had an air of desperation in expressing a well-worn nineteenth century theme in Australia:

> We do not intend . . . unnecessarily to raise the price of wages. . . . but I hope we shall lose no time . . . in taking the proper steps to secure their [the railways'] formation.[83]

> I have not the slightest wish to rush any railways to the detriment of private enterprise. . . . [but] at present we have neither population nor capital within ourselves and we must hold out inducements [railways] to people from afar. . . . I want people; and people bring money.[84]

So ineffective were these disclaimers that the problem became increasingly acute in Queensland:

> The price of labour, owing to its great scarcity, had gone up to an almost prohibitive figure. . . . In the interior men could not be obtained to shepherd sheep, erect fences and do the ordinary work on stations. A similar situation prevailed on the tinfields, the sugar lands and the goldfields.[85]

Colonial Treasurers in New South Wales recognized the problem in a rather formal manner, at least from the date of Parkes' reference in 1873.[86] In 1882 the Treasurer's statement was classic:

> The Government being such large employers of labour, feel that they are competing injuriously with private enterprise, thereby increasing the cost of buildings and other works not only to private capitalists but to the public, for whom they are trustees.[87]

LONG-TERM INTERACTION OF GOVERNMENT AND PRIVATE SECTORS

It would be a mistake to read into Australian experience the circumstances of North American railway building. Similarly, to conclude that the successful completion by Australian governments of thousands of miles of railway track and other physical assets contributed to Australian economic growth would obscure a basic issue. The mere provision of assets designed to cope with obstacles to growth did not neces-

---

[82] "Mr. Stanley's Report," *Queensland, Official Record of the Debates of the Legislative Assembly, 1877*, Vol. 23, p. 754.

[83] *Ibid.*, p. 762.

[84] *Ibid.*

[85] Debate on Immigration Bill, July 18, 1882, *ibid., 1882*, Vol. 37, p. 113.

[86] See note 60, p. 63 supra.

[87] See note 61, p. 63.

sarily mean that these were overcome. The period during which a complicated economic and social process produced the fruits of economic progress by means of these assets was extremely long.

In many respects the depression of the 1890's left Australian governments with unfinished business, most visible in the railway field. A trunk line system had been laid down in most colonies; the characteristic pattern was established—from each capital city (other than Brisbane) on the coast a fan system of trunk lines radiated to the margins of settlement. Thirty years later, in the 1920's, this trunk skeleton was turned to substantial advantage when a network of branch lines crisscrossed the main agricultural and mixed farming areas. Then, with related changes in irrigation, closer settlement policy, and technical improvements, especially in farm mechanization and wheat strains, the government capital formation of the second half of the nineteenth century began to yield handsome social dividends.

Before 1900 no such return was visible. The effort of the construction workers during 1860–90 was not primarily for their own benefit but that of their descendants. In examining the long-run relations between government and private sectors, we are not concerned with this secular development in which the contribution of government was unanticipated and inseparable from that of many other elements. We concentrate, rather, on the long-run interrelations *during the second half of the nineteenth century*. The statistical contrast with short-term experience is clear: government and private capital formation moved in the long run over very similar paths. This suggestion of sympathy of movement and the possibility of a strong positive contribution of government capital formation to the private sector needs cautious inspection.[88]

Formally, government capital formation and the operation of government enterprises may have influenced private economic activity through the cost of such activity, the demand for its output, or the climate within which it operated. Private costs may have been altered through changes in physical assets and related services or in the availability of factors used by the private sector. The demand for its output may have been affected by government demands for equipment or by multiplier effects of government capital outlays. Government behavior may have influenced the climate of enterprise in several ways, including

[88] For more detailed discussion, see Noel G. Butlin, "Public Enterprise in Australian Economic Development, 1860–90," *Explorations in Entrepreneurial History*, 2:141–158 (March 1950).

the assurance of sustained prosperity over a long period, business leadership by government authorities in certain fields, and the exclusion of private entrepreneurs from major fields of activity.

In reality, the conclusion suggested here is that the limited positive stimulus to private activity from government capital formation was offset. Whether one chooses to treat these as social costs of government action or merely as channels of influence without such significance, the main long-run implications for the private sector are three:

(1) Government pressure to confine the economy within a specialized pastoral mould, particularly by impediments to agricultural and industrial growth;

(2) The establishment of a sellers' market for labor, contributing greatly to the relatively high real wages of the Australian worker and the evolution of a powerful unionism;

(3) The emergence of a government monopoly of the major means of land transport.

The long-run stimulus to private activity from government capital outlays was exceedingly small. The long-sustained rising expenditures undoubtedly encouraged some general development in response to long-term multiplier influences. But with an open economy and the extremely high rate of importing by the Australian colonies during this period, the greater part of any potential multiplier stimulus leaked abroad into imports. The consequent stimulus to local private industry was slow and modest.

Much the same is true of government orders for equipment. Barely 10 percent of government demand for equipment in railway building, for example, was placed in the colonies. Indeed, the significant increase in local production occurred not in response to *new* government capital formation but because of maintenance commitments. The continuing nature of these demands prompted the establishment of local repair shops which eventually grew into substantial undertakings—but as government, not as private, enterprises.

Through the operation of government enterprises, definite but modest contributions were made to private expansion in certain narrow fields. The aid to coal mining is the clearest case. The location of the main fields close to coastal ports made simple the task of providing very short railway lines to them and contributed to the growth of a substantial export trade in coal to North and South America. Also, the locomotive consumption of coal opened a stable and steadily rising domestic market.

In the pastoral industry the contribution was much less definite. Growth was encouraged in some areas and to a limited degree. But the ambitious and monopolistic railway structure stultified the potential value of Australian railways. The fan design was to channel interior freights into the coastal capitals, without regard to alternative port outlets. The railways followed settlement and did not precede it. They did not cut across established lines of communication to any great extent. No reorientation of trade routes was involved, as in the United States, since no important waterway provided alternative means of transport. The railways followed existing trunk roads and the beds of the uncertain rivers. Duplication of transport facilities led to a marked deterioration of main roads and spelled ruin for road haulers along the trunk routes.

For those lucky enough to have settled along the lines of the railways, rail transport meant reduced costs of wool transport and lower actual or imputed interest costs in the speedier delivery of produce to market. Reductions in time of transport along the trunk routes were not great, however. The few weeks saved by rail transport was generally a very small part of the long delay between production and sale of wool. Moreover, as long as climatic conditions were favorable, pastoral production was so lucrative during most of the period that reductions in transport costs meant comparatively little.

For those not close to the railway lines, these modest advantages did not apply, and for very many, the railways might as well never have existed. Even near capital cities, the distances between the fanned routes were soon so great that freight was better transported to the city by road than drawn to railhead and shipped by rail. In other cases, especially on the western slopes of northern New South Wales, the railways merely offered a long cumbersome route down to Newcastle and Sydney instead of short road hauls to other coastal ports. The farther west, the more the transport difficulties related not to the trunk carriage but to the movement over areas between trunk roads. Moreover, the problem of distance in Australia was usually not one of time but of the availability of water. For those whose products had to move on the hoof or to be hauled long distances by bullocks, the question was whether stock could be kept alive until the trunk lines were reached. Without a local network, the Australian railways meant little in time of drought, the ever-present menace of the pastoral industry.

In contrast with these modest possibilities, the influence on the economy by way of the sustained and rising demand for labor was very definite. Perhaps two-thirds of all government capital outlays were absorbed in on-site wages, providing powerful support to the labor market. This sustained pressure, particularly in conjunction with the short-term inverse relations between government and private capital formation, was a major factor supporting the high standard of living of the Australian worker. In this factor we have much of the explanation of the growth of Australian unionism; of the emphasis during the period not on wage increases (which were relatively easy to secure) but on reduction of hours; and of the attempts by wage earners to use government authorities to achieve general social gains.

While Australian working-class standards gained and equality of income was emphasized, economic expansion and industrial diversification were retarded. Continuously rising government capital outlays meant sustained pressure on both interest and wage rates. Money and real wage rates moved steadily upward over a long period; for much of the period, local interest rates failed to match the definite downward trend of overseas interest rates.

In these circumstances escape from the pressure of government action was possible only in those industries where the marginal efficiency of capital was high and rising and where output was progressively less labor-intensive. Only the pastoral industry, with its extremely lucrative returns and rapid increases in productivity and labor-saving equipment (especially fences), was in a position to expand continuously in the face of sustained government pressure. In less fortunate industries— such as agriculture, where returns were falling as production spread, and manufacturing, where small concerns serving local markets were common—the rising trend of wage rates and the relatively high local interest rates operated as restrictive forces. Hence it is not surprising to find both agriculture and manufacturing languishing as government outlays rose to the high plateau of the 1890's. This internal pressure acquired increasing significance with the strong downward movement of import prices, to whose effects both agriculture and manufacturing were exposed. This was an element in the increasing instability that led to the crisis of 1889–90, in which government behavior played a major part.

CRISIS AND THE REFORMULATION OF POLICY, 1889–1900

Discussion of the course of the crisis and depression of the 1890's is outside the scope of this paper, but a few points must be made to explain the reformulation of government policy during the decade, which with other things led to the federation of the colonies into the Commonwealth of Australia in 1901.

Recession seems to have occurred first in the private sector, in 1889. Government capital formation continued to rise until 1890. This reversal of government expenditure was directly connected with the Baring crisis and the drying up of British funds. Australian government securities came to be not merely at a heavy discount; they were unsalable. Government works were temporarily maintained by heavy withdrawal of government bank deposits. But, beginning in 1891, public capital formation followed the private sector into the most severe depression in Australia in the nineteenth century.

No detailed study of the crisis and downswing has been made. Undoubtedly, Australia's satellitic connection with Britain suddenly became vital. Borrowing on government and private account rose rapidly during the 1880's, leading to boom excesses in both government and private sectors. Government extravagance [89] was accompanied by rapid growth of bank advances and the multiplication of mushroom land and finance companies, which led to an intensely speculative land boom, concentrated in Victoria. This boom began to crack in 1889, shortly before the Baring crisis.[90]

This is by no means the whole story. The steady rise of domestic wage rates in the face of a more definite decline in export and import prices pointed to a process of stagnation and eventual crisis in Australia's external trade. Another important element of instability lay in the rising burden of overseas interest commitments on government and private accounts. By the late 1880's these commitments were absorbing a large proportion of Australia's exports. The significance of this burden depended partly on the growth of overseas borrowing, partly on movements in Australian export prices. In particular, either a reduction in British capital or a sharp fall in export prices could produce a severe balance-of-payments crisis by the late 1880's. The combination of both these difficulties in 1889–91 was a crucial part of the

[89] Coghlan, *Labour and Industry in Australia*, p. 1411: "from 1884 onwards Governmental expenditure became a riot, limited only in its violence by the amount of accommodation obtainable in London."

[90] *Ibid.*, p. 1417: "there was more or less wild speculation, an arrest of industry and the withdrawal of large bodies of men from productive pursuits, followed later by a derangement of the labour market, with strikes, lock-outs and industrial unrest." See also N. G. Butlin, "The Shape of the Australian Economy, 1861–1900," *Economic Record*, 34:10ff. (April 1958).

crisis and downswing. The response of the pastoral industry to the growing instability was a definite one. Efforts to reduce shearing wages during 1889–90 led to the maritime strike in 1890, the herald of a period of violent industrial upheavals. The attempt to reduce costs was so successful that it led directly and indirectly to widespread destruction of union organization and of the conditions built up by unions in the preceding expansion. At the same time, pastoral interest in refrigerated meat exports quickened, leading to effective establishment of the refrigerated export industries. This timing is important in view of the fact that technical knowledge and some plant and equipment had existed for a decade. With the onset of the crisis, refrigeration offered an alternative pastoral product; it also opened up the means of destruction of rural assets and their conversion into cash, particularly into badly needed foreign exchange.[91]

The downswing that followed was accompanied by a number of features which subsequently influenced government action. First, caught between the fires of heavy withdrawals by governments, attempts of British depositors to recover deposits, and pressure from local finance companies to sustain the collapsing boom, the entire Australian banking system cracked, leading to liquidations, amalgamations, and a gradual reconstruction extending into the twentieth century. Second, hundreds of mushroom finance companies were swept out of existence. Third, trade unions responded to the downswing by ill-fated attempts to maintain their standards despite rising unemployment. Fourth, unemployment increased very sharply, reaching a peak in 1893. Fifth, governments confronted with financial crisis competed with each other in the London market to obtain urgently needed funds. This intercolonial competition in that market stimulated interest in federation.

The events of the 1890's brought a rapid reorientation of government policy. Before 1890, governments professed to be concerned with general social and economic development, without giving much attention either to questions of stability or to problems of private activity. While the fall in supply of British overseas investment funds reduced government capital formation, the importance of governments in this respect did not shrink in comparison with the private sector during the 1890's. The reorientation that occurred concentrated on the development of a stabilization policy by the colonial governments, and ap-

[91] On the general point raised here, see N. G. Butlin, *Private Capital Formation*, Chapter II.

peared at several levels, from recognition of the financial instability of governments to adoption of detailed principles for carrying on private businesses.

The collapse of expansion confronted the Australian governments with novel problems: general economic instability; explosive industrial relations; balance-of-payments disequilibrium; social distress through heavy unemployment; financial competition between colonies for access to the London market; and competition from imports. Revision of policy to restore the shattered banking system through schemes of reconstruction, writing down of assets, conversion of some deposits to share capital, and reduction of bank advances was taken up by the governments, especially in Victoria and New South Wales. Direct intervention in industrial relations was forced by the 1890 maritime strike and subsequent upheavals, and led to the establishment of government machinery for conciliation and arbitration (New South Wales, 1892). Government aid to the unemployed was initiated in the form of depression works, labor villages, and the provision of travel expenses to help in the search for work. In addition, partly to aid the unemployed, partly to encourage production of exports, government began to take much more interest in detailed problems of agriculture as distinct from the mere land sales and land occupation policy before 1890: types of intervention included planning for closer settlement, individual treatment of land areas in making subdivisions, and the establishment of government agricultural banks to finance agricultural growth.

In New South Wales, the opposition to protective tariffs was greatly weakened as manufacturing unemployment rose. This helped to reduce an important obstacle to colonial federation, as did the recognition of damaging competition between colonies in loan flotations. Before 1890, intermittent discussions looking toward federation had been held between the colonies. These discussions foundered largely on rivalry and disagreement between New South Wales and Victoria. After 1890, the need to rationalize colonial borrowing in London, the importance of measures to deal with intercolonial labor disputes, and the problems of protecting local manufacturing were among the factors speeding up the movement toward federation.

The Commonwealth Constitution was framed in crisis conditions in which attention was concentrated on stabilization, not development. Although phases of major developmental action by governments occurred in the twentieth century, the problem of stabilization came increasingly to the fore. Moreover, government action came to deal increasingly with aids to private enterprise rather than with independent development. It would be meaningless to attempt a judgment as to whether government intervention increased or declined. A basic reorientation—a change in the nature rather than the scope of government policy—was one of the important characteristics of the Australian economy in the twentieth century.

3 DEFENSIVE EXPANSIONISM: THE STATE AND ECONOMIC GROWTH IN CANADA

Hugh G. J. Aitken

I know of no difference in the machinery of government in the old and new world that strikes a European more forcibly than the apparently undue importance which the business of constructing public works appears to occupy in American legislation. . . . The provision which in Europe, the State makes for the protection of its citizens against foreign enemies, is in America required for . . . the "war with the wilderness." The defence of an important fortress, or the maintenance of a sufficient army or navy in exposed spots, is not more a matter of common concern to the European, than is the construction of the great communications to the American settler; and the State, very naturally, takes on itself the making of the works, which are a matter of concern to all alike.—Lord Durham, *Report on the Affairs of British North America* (1839).

In the statement quoted, Lord Durham contrasted the role of the state in the development of North America with its role in Europe. A modern historian would probably not accept Durham's generalization without question, though he might admit that in 1839 the contrast had some validity. The British provinces in North America—particularly Upper Canada, or what is now Ontario—at the time Durham became Governor General had brought themselves to the verge of bankruptcy by undertaking capital investments for development on a greater scale than their slim fiscal resources could support. Their situation, as Durham saw it, was analogous to that of a European nation whose government had bankrupted itself by undertaking a military effort beyond its means. The responsibility for this failure to maintain a satisfactory rate of growth lay, in Durham's view, with the state, just as in the case of a European country that had failed to provide for its own external security.

Durham's opinion that in Europe the primary function of the state was defense while in North America it was development reflected his reaction to the wave of internal improvements that had swept over most of the states and provinces of North America in the 1820's and

1830's. Historians have long recognized that governments played an important role in promoting and financing these early internal improvements. After 1840, however, according to the conventional interpretation, the federal and state governments in the United States tended increasingly to follow a laissez-faire policy. This tendency is alleged to have continued until the 1890's, when the growth of industrialism and public resentment against the trust movement led again to a policy of government intervention.

No analogous interpretation of Canadian development has ever found acceptance among economic historians. On the contrary, the standard interpretation of the entire history of the Canadian economy assigns to the state a major role in guiding and stimulating development: on any reading of the historical record, government policies and decisions stand out as the key factors. The creation of a national economy in Canada and, even more clearly, of a transcontinental economy was as much a political as an economic achievement.

The system of concepts suggested by Hoselitz [1] has one major advantage for the student of Canadian economic history: it enables him to put the Canadian experience in perspective, by comparison with the experience of other national economies. This is, of course, the characteristic virtue of the "ideal type" method. Therefore, if in the following discussion I appear to be emphasizing the discrepancies between the actual course of events in Canada and the pattern suggested by Hoselitz, this should be taken not as an implicit criticism of the schema but as the implementation of the remaining steps in the method.

As a preliminary step, several points should be noted in the case of Canada. First, the relevant area changed significantly over time, as a result of the expansion of settlement and also of constitutional changes. The nation state that today we call Canada dates only from 1867. Before that date we are dealing with a number of distinct and very different regional economies which, in respect to the role played by the state in economic development, cannot be classed together without serious distortion. To find a single pattern in the experiences of these different regions, which faced different problems and opportunities, is difficult. The role of the state in the Maritime Provinces, seeking their development in maritime trade and the fisheries, was poles apart from its role in central Canada, where development was

[1] "Patterns of Economic Growth," *Canadian Journal of Economics and Political Science*, 21:416–431.

considered to depend on the perfection of a transportation artery between the midwest and the Atlantic.

All the colonies were of course within the general sphere of control of the British government in London. This to some extent offsets the heterogeneity of separate legislatures and varying situations, but only at the cost of introducing further complexity. We must bear in mind that the locus of the "state" was neither single at any one time nor constant over time. For example, financial assistance to railroad construction in Canada was provided by governments at all levels— municipal, provincial, federal, and imperial. There was no single locus of decision making, nor even a single hierarchy. Each level of government operated within its particular limitations to achieve its own objectives, and these did not always coincide in all respects. Much the same could be said of banking legislation and fiscal policy.

Thus a plurality of government bodies influenced the direction and rate of economic development in Canada. All these bodies might well be included in our concept of the state, and discussion of its role in Canadian development would then involve the activities of all levels of government in the "direct line of sovereignty" from the British Crown and parliament down to the municipality. The difficulty with this procedure is that at several points in Canadian history a government outside this line of sovereignty—that of the United States—has exercised an influence on Canadian development certainly no less than that of any British government. Throughout its history Canada has been an economic satellite of both Great Britain and the United States.

These difficulties do not make it impossible to apply the Hoselitz schema to the case of Canada, but they do remind us that any theoretical framework involves some degree of oversimplification. The classification of Canada as expansionist, satellitic, and autonomous, however, raises other problems which are more serious and call for careful scrutiny.

THE PERIOD BEFORE CONFEDERATION

The Canadian provinces in the period before Confederation fall into two general groups: the Maritime Provinces of New Brunswick, Nova Scotia, and Prince Edward Island; and Canada proper, which included under a single legislature after the Act of Union of 1840 the two earlier provinces of Upper and Lower Canada (roughly present-day Ontario and Quebec). In addition there was the territory under the control of the Hudson's Bay Company. This included not only the drainage basin of Hudson Bay but also the entire prairie region, the Rocky Mountains, and the Pacific Coast, including until 1846 part of what is now the state of Oregon, and the territory that became the province of British Columbia in 1858.

The Maritime Provinces

Development in this region in the period from 1783 to 1840 depended on fishing, shipbuilding, maritime trade, and lumbering.[2] In terms of the general economic organization of the British colonial empire, these provinces performed the functions that the New England colonies had performed before the American Revolution. The Maritimes were a source of agricultural produce, dried fish, and lumber for Newfoundland and the British West Indies; they served as a base for the coastal and Banks fisheries, exporting their catch—as New England had done—partly to the West Indies and partly to southern Europe; their magnificent stands of white pine provided timber for civil and naval construction in Great Britain; and their shipbuilding industry not only served as a valuable supplement to the output of English shipyards but also furnished ships for a multilateral maritime trading system based on Halifax and Saint John.

As far as Nova Scotia was concerned, the important frontiers of development were those of maritime trade and the fisheries. In agriculture progress was disappointing. Prince Edward Island alone achieved self-sufficiency in foodstuffs. In neither Nova Scotia nor New Brunswick was there a continuous frontier of agricultural settlement in the classic American sense. Immigration into these two provinces from the United Kingdom was insignificant before 1815, reached a peak in the 1840's, and declined in the 1850's; at all times the volume was smaller than the influx into the St. Lawrence colonies and considerably smaller than

---

[2] See W. Thomas Easterbrook and Hugh G. J. Aitken, *Canadian Economic History* (Toronto: Macmillan Company, 1956), Chapters 7, 9, 11; Harold A. Innis, *The Cod Fisheries* (New Haven: Yale University Press, 1940); Arthur R. M. Lower, *The North American Assault on the Canadian Forest* (Toronto: Ryerson Press, 1938); Donald G. Creighton, *British North America at Confederation: A Study Prepared for the Royal Commission on Dominion-Provincial Relations* (Ottawa, 1939); F. Lee Benns, *The American Struggle for the British West India Carrying-Trade*, Indiana University Studies, No. 56 (Bloomington, 1923); and Stanley A. Saunders, *Economic History of the Maritime Provinces: A Study Prepared for the Royal Commission on Dominion-Provincial Relations* (Ottawa, 1939).

that into New England. Immigrants into Nova Scotia—mostly Highland Scots and southern Irish—tended to cluster in the small fishing villages scattered along the Atlantic Coast. When immigrants ventured into agriculture, they were inclined to concentrate on livestock and dairy farming, where the competition of imports from the United States was less severe than in breadstuffs. Partly because of the intrinsic poverty of the area's arable land, partly because of the competing employment opportunities in the fisheries, agricultural development in Nova Scotia was slow and haphazard. Nothing that can be described as a continuous expansion of the frontier of settlement can be discerned.

New Brunswick differed from Nova Scotia in the important role played by the lumber industry in the provincial economy. Nova Scotia after 1815 retained sufficient forest resources to support a prosperous shipbuilding industry, but exports of native timber to Great Britain and the West Indies were insignificant. In New Brunswick, on the other hand, lumbering was the major industry from the American Revolution to the 1850's, surpassing the fisheries and agriculture in numbers employed and in export earnings.

In encouraging the development of the New Brunswick timber industry—and later that of Upper and Lower Canada also—the state, in this case the British government, played a major role. Without preferential tariff protection, the only variety of New Brunswick timber that could be marketed profitably in England was high-quality white pine, used for the masts and spars of naval and commercial vessels. Freight costs from New Brunswick to England in the early nineteenth century were on the average three times as high as from the Baltic ports. Labor costs in the North American colony were very much higher than in northern Europe. And the timber trade of the Baltic ports had been brought to a high degree of organization and efficiency. In these circumstances New Brunswick timber other than large masts could not be sold at a profit in England.

Dependence on Baltic timber supplies was the Achilles' heel of British naval power throughout the seventeenth and eighteenth centuries, but little was done to remedy matters. The outbreak of the Napoleonic Wars, however, compelled a sudden change in policy and led the British government to encourage by tariff protection a general export trade in timber from the North American colonies. Duties on foreign timber were sharply increased from 10 shillings a load in 1795 to 25s. in 1805, 34s.8d. in 1810, and 65s. in 1814. Reduced to 55s. in

1821, they remained at that figure until 1842. Colonial timber entered Great Britain duty free, except for a nominal registration duty between 1821 and 1842.

On the foundation provided by these preferential duties there developed the North American trade in square timber—the economic mainstay of New Brunswick, and to a large extent of Upper and Lower Canada also, from 1810 to the early 1850's. Rapid industrialization in Great Britain provided a growing demand for timber, the universal construction material for factories and residential buildings; the rich forest resources of the St. Lawrence, Ottawa, and St. John Rivers furnished an ample supply; and the British consumer paid in the form of higher prices the difference between freight costs from the Baltic and from North America.

The frontier of the lumber industry in New Brunswick was also a frontier of settlement. In this colony there was no sharp division between natural forest land and natural farm land, as there is in some areas. The rivers, particularly the St. John, by which the lumberman floated his rafts down to the sea also gave the settler easy access to the fertile valleys of the interior. The lumber camps provided both markets for agricultural produce and opportunities for the farmer to obtain part-time employment during the winter and early fall. This close connection between the lumber industry and agricultural settlement produced an approximation to an advancing frontier of settlement, and in this sense the tariff preferences granted by the British government to colonial lumber contributed to the formation of an "expansionist" pattern of development in New Brunswick.

Let us turn to maritime trade and the fisheries. In both these fields development depended on active support from the state, primarily the British government. The central issue in maritime trade after 1783 was whether the United States should be permitted to trade directly with the British West Indies. The merchant capitalists of Nova Scotia and New Brunswick wished the ports of the British West Indies closed to all but British and colonial shipping, hoping that in this way they could monopolize the lucrative carrying trade in breadstuffs, livestock, staves, dried cod, molasses, and rum. The owners of the sugar plantations in the British islands—still a powerful group in British politics, although their influence was not as great as before 1776—wished to obtain their necessary imports as cheaply as possible, and consequently to have the British West Indies thrown open to the shipping of all nations. New England merchants, in their turn, regarded access to the

British islands as a prize worth fighting for, and exerted effective pressure on Congress and the President to retaliate in kind against any attempt on the part of the British government to discriminate against American shipping.

No one, I think, can analyze the tangled history of the retaliatory legislation that this conflict of interests produced (the American Tonnage Act of 1816 and Navigation Acts of 1817, 1818, and 1820, the British Free Port Act of 1818 and Trade Acts of 1822 and 1826) without wondering whether the prize was worth all the complicated maneuvering that it occasioned. Certainly the policies that the British government pursued—if such a series of expedients can be called a policy—were influenced by considerations of more general import than the political pressures that the Maritime Provinces and the West Indies planters could exert. Chief among these I would place the still influential mercantilist doctrine that the carrying trade of the empire should be restricted to British and colonial shipping, combined with an overall strategy of restraining American expansionism in the Caribbean. On the American side, of course, the struggle to secure access to the British West Indies was the last major issue on which the New England mercantile oligarchy was able to use the federal government as its instrument. The election of Andrew Jackson as President ended this phase and made possible the compromise solution in the so-called "reciprocity agreement of 1830." By this time New England merchants had found other fields for their enterprise: South America, the Pacific Coast, and the Orient.

Throughout this period of bitter economic warfare, the mercantile interests of the Maritime Provinces looked to the British government to represent and safeguard what they regarded as their rights as citizens of the empire. They realized clearly that they labored under serious handicaps in open competition with American shippers—greater distance from markets, smaller capital resources, and inadequate sources of agricultural produce—and therefore sought to induce the British government to preserve intact the code of navigation that had been the heart of the old empire. In this they were finally unsuccessful; the American government was a much more formidable adversary to the consolidation of the new imperial system than Holland or France had been to the old. In both Nova Scotia and New Brunswick the concessions that the United States forced from the British government in 1830 were felt as serious economic reversals. The Maritime Provinces had relied on the state to aid them, and the state—necessarily concerned with wider interests than those of the North American colonies —had failed them.

An analogous pattern of state action may be seen in regard to the fisheries. Here expansionism certainly entailed establishing control over the country's resources, but in rather a particular sense. The point in dispute was what in fact and in law were the country's resources, and to decide this question the intervention of the state was required. The Treaty of Paris which ended the American Revolution stated that citizens of the United States were to continue to enjoy unmolested the right to fish in the inshore waters of British possessions in North America as well as on the Banks and in the Gulf of St. Lawrence; and that they should be permitted to dry and cure fish on any unsettled parts of the coasts of Nova Scotia, the Magdalen Islands, and Labrador. On the conclusion of the War of 1812, the British government took the position that by declaring war the United States had forfeited these treaty rights and that the inshore fishing privileges had been automatically cancelled. The United States government, on the other hand, argued that the Treaty of Paris had not granted a privilege but merely recognized a right that could not be cancelled unilaterally. Internal dissension prevented the American delegation from taking a firm stand on the issue, however, and the Treaty of Ghent did not mention the fisheries.

This controversy over the inshore fisheries bedevilled Anglo-American relations for the next half-century. As far as Nova Scotia and New Brunswick were concerned, the issue was one of establishing control over resources that were rightfully theirs. To make good this claim they relied on the power of the state, in the form of the British government. A brief review of later developments will illustrate how this power was exercised.

Immediately after 1815, the British government reinforced its naval squadron in Nova Scotian waters and issued instructions that American vessels were to be warned from fishing within the three-mile limit or using Nova Scotian ports for any purpose connected with the fisheries. Seizure of several American ships produced an attempt to settle the issue by diplomacy. This culminated in the signing of a Convention in 1818 by which, in return for concessions in other areas, the United States renounced any liberty which had previously been enjoyed to take, dry, or cure fish "within three marine miles of any of the coasts, bays, creeks, or harbors" of the British provinces in North America.

Unfortunately for the prospects of a permanent settlement, the Convention of 1818 suffered from the characteristic diplomatic vice of ambiguity. Was the Bay of Fundy a bay within the meaning of the Convention, or was it part of the open sea? Were American fishing ships entitled to pass through the convenient alleyway of the Gut of Canso, even though this brought them within three miles of the shore, or were they not? American fishing captains, as might be expected, adopted a loose construction of the Convention; the Nova Scotia government insisted on a strict interpretation. The dispute was a minor matter in the whole range of Anglo-American relationships but, as is sometimes the case with minor diplomatic frictions which are not alleviated, became a focus of strong feelings on the part of the interests immediately concerned.

For more than three decades the issue was allowed to smolder, principally because neither Great Britain nor the United States felt that much was to be gained by forcing a decision. This situation changed abruptly in the early 1850's when Great Britain opened negotiations in Washington for reciprocal free trade in natural products between the United States and the British North American colonies. Particularly in central Canada the attainment of reciprocity was regarded at this time as of prime importance. In the Maritimes opinion was divided. In the United States there was little strong feeling on the subject either way. The principal obstacle that the British and Canadian negotiators in Washington had to surmount was simply the indifference of the American Congress. Attempts to secure the abolition of duties on natural produce by parallel legislation were abandoned as hopeless in 1852; thereafter efforts were directed toward securing action by treaty. To this end the British government looked around for some issue that could be used to force decisive action, and found the still unresolved controversy over the inshore fisheries. Late in 1852 the British government announced that it intended to enforce its interpretation of the Convention of 1818; the British naval squadron in Nova Scotian waters would be reinforced, and American ships would thenceforth be strictly excluded from the Bay of Fundy.

Whether Great Britain was actually prepared to go to war over the fisheries issue may well be doubted. The threat of armed force, however, provided the diplomatic gambit necessary for securing prompt and favorable action on reciprocity. The President was now assured of Congressional support for a settlement that would include both reciprocity and the inshore fisheries, and in June 1854 the Reciprocity Treaty became law. Import duties were abolished on a wide range of natural products passing between the United States and the British North American colonies, and American shipping was admitted to the use of the St. Lawrence canals on the same terms as British and colonial vessels. American ships were permitted free access to all the coastal fisheries of the British colonies and were allowed to land on the shores of the colonies to dry their nets and cure their fish. Fishing ships from the British colonies received corresponding privileges in the American coastal fisheries north of the 36th parallel.

Throughout this protracted and often acrimonious dispute, the hopes of Nova Scotians of establishing control over what they regarded as their resources depended on the actions of the British government. The power of the state, exercised through diplomacy and on occasion the threat of armed force, was the primary instrument of development. It cannot be argued that this power was always exercised in the best interests of the colonies concerned. In the Convention of 1818, the Reciprocity Treaty of 1854, and the Washington Treaty of 1871, the Maritime Provinces believed—with some justification—that their interests were being sacrificed as "a burnt offering on the altar of Anglo-American friendship." [3] Throughout this period the British government was the state, as far as the relations of the North American colonies with foreign nations were concerned. But the interests of the British government transcended those of the colonies, and British policy could not be directed exclusively or even principally to advancing colonial economic interests. Business and political opinion in the colonies inclined increasingly toward a greater measure of local control over the secular decisions that determined the course of development.

Central Canada

Meanwhile in central Canada events were following a very different course. By the Constitutional Act of 1791 the old province of Quebec had been divided into two provinces, Upper and Lower Canada, each with its own legislature. The hope was that this would enable Upper Canada, in which English-speaking people were in the majority, to work out its development independently of French-speaking Lower Canada. Montreal, the seaport of both provinces, was included in Lower Canada—an act that contained the seeds of much later conflict, as the policies that the English-speaking merchant capitalists of the

[3] Donald G. Creighton, *Dominion of the North* (Boston: Houghton Mifflin Company, 1944), p. 319.

port wished to pursue, such as improvement of the navigation of the St. Lawrence, came to be opposed by the highly unsympathetic French-Canadian Assembly. The division of the provinces also led to a series of disputes over the division of the customs revenue. Import duties levied at Montreal provided both provincial governments with their principal source of revenue. The rates could not be altered without the consent of both legislatures, and the total had to be divided in some ratio set by arbitration. The ability of the government of Upper Canada to expend moneys for internal improvement was therefore limited by the willingness of that of Lower Canada to raise import duties and agree on the way in which revenues should be divided.

The administrative inconveniences that resulted from the separation of the provinces, it can be argued, were the price that had to be paid for enabling Upper Canada to attract British immigrants and British capital, for neither of these necessary resources would have been attracted to the province had it not been free from the encumbrances of French land law and a French-dominated legislature. Whether the price was not too high may well be asked, for Upper Canada was not insulated from the conflicts of Lower Canada. Politically the provinces might be divided, but economically they were a unit. No constitutional act could obscure the fact that the St. Lawrence River bound the provinces together in a single commercial system. The whole development of Upper Canada hinged on free access to the ocean via the St. Lawrence and the port of Montreal. The division of the provinces divorced the merchants of Montreal from the political support they would otherwise have received from their commercial hinterland and hamstrung their efforts to improve the navigation of the river by government financing. Upper Canada alone could not remove or bypass the obstacles to navigation and her access to the ocean, for the most serious of these—the rapids in the St. Lawrence below Cornwall—were in Lower Canada. The merchants of Montreal could not overcome the inertia and hostility of the Lower Canada Assembly once the lines of political conflict between the French- and English-speaking elements in the province had been irrevocably drawn.

In any evaluation of the role of the state in the development of central Canada, the adverse repercussions of the division of the provinces by the Act of 1791 must be weighed against any positive aid that was provided later. The delay in undertaking improvement of the navigation of the St. Lawrence was not the only unfortunate result;

there is also evidence that political separation impeded the flow of capital from Montreal to its commercial hinterland in Upper Canada.[4] Certainly in the construction of the Welland and Cornwall Canals, the two major improvements in navigation undertaken in Upper Canada before the provinces were reunited in 1840, Montreal capital played only a minor role. Montreal's relationship to its hinterland was subtly different from that of Boston or New York or Philadelphia.

Until 1821 the commercial life of Montreal was dominated by the fur trade. The trade in agricultural exports and manufactured imports that developed along with the expansion of settlement in Upper Canada and the American Old Northwest was at first merely a modest adjunct to the trade in furs. In 1821, however, the North West Company of Montreal was absorbed by the Hudson's Bay Company and within a few years the fur trade had deserted Montreal entirely, to be carried on thenceforth from bases on Hudson Bay and the Pacific Coast. This reversal drove several of the leading commercial houses of Montreal into bankruptcy; those that survived did so by switching their capital into the entrepôt trade between England and the settlements of the interior. In future Montreal's commercial prosperity was to depend entirely on how effectively it could compete with the other metropolitan centers on the Atlantic seaboard and the Gulf of Mexico— Boston, New York, Philadelphia, Baltimore, and New Orleans—for the trade of the hinterland. Success in this endeavor depended on the construction and maintenance of a low-cost transport route from the interior settlements to tidewater.[5]

Montreal's commercial aspirations extended far beyond the political boundaries of the British North American colonies. There were only three natural water gateways to the interior of the continent: the Mississippi, the St. Lawrence, and Hudson Bay. The St. Lawrence provided the shortest route from England to the interior, and Montreal commanded the St. Lawrence. During the French regime and until 1821 the natural advantages of the St. Lawrence route had enabled Montreal to monopolize the whole fur trade of the trans-Appalachian region, save only what the Hudson's Bay Company could garner from its northern bases, and a trickle of low-quality pelts to New Orleans.

[4] Hugh G. J. Aitken, "A Note on the Capital Resources of Upper Canada," *Canadian Journal of Economics and Political Science,* 18:525–533 (November 1952).

[5] See Donald G. Creighton, *The Commercial Empire of the St. Lawrence, 1760–1850* (Toronto: Ryerson Press, 1937); Easterbrook and Aitken, *op. cit.,* Chapters 12, 14, 16.

The fur trade had now disappeared, thanks to the superior capital resources of the Hudson's Bay Company; but for Montreal the grand strategy of commercial expansion remained essentially unchanged. The objective of this strategy was the control of trade of the North American hinterland, including not only those areas north of the international boundary but also the rapidly growing settlements between the Alleghenies and the Mississippi—an ambitious design but, in an age as yet ignorant of the railroad, not unrealistic.

The expansion of settlement in Upper Canada was an important component in this over-all strategy. The export and import trade of Upper Canada at least would pass down the St. Lawrence corridor and through the warehouses of Montreal, no matter what happened to the trade of the American Old Northwest. In encouraging immigration into Upper Canada, however, neither Montreal capital nor any government played a major role. Before 1812 most of the immigrants came from the United States—some of them "late Loyalists," others frontier settlers and land speculators of the familiar type. After 1815 restrictions were placed on American immigration. For a few years immigration declined seriously, but in the early 1820's arrivals from Great Britain began to climb, stimulated by the low passage rates which the timber ships, returning empty, offered for the transatlantic voyage. Large numbers of immigrants arrived in each year from 1826 to 1832. Epidemics of cholera and disturbed political conditions in Canada caused a slump in arrivals in the middle and late 1830's, but in the 1840's the influx again increased, stimulated by famine in Ireland. The population of Upper Canada, estimated at 157,923 in 1825, reached 791,000 in 1850, by which date most of the good agricultural land in the province had been occupied.[6]

Until 1825 not only Upper Canada but the whole basin of the lower Lakes, including the American Old Northwest, was tributary to Montreal. The natural advantages of the St. Lawrence River as an export-import route were sufficient to neutralize the international boundary, in an economic sense, despite the fact that the route was almost wholly unimproved (it was interrupted by geographical obstacles at Niagara and between Kingston and Montreal). When De Witt Clinton reminded

---

[6] Gilbert Patterson, *Land Settlement in Upper Canada, 1783–1840* (Toronto: Ontario Bureau of Archives, 1921); Robert L. Jones, *History of Agriculture in Ontario, 1613–1880* (Toronto: University of Toronto Press, 1946); Helen I. Cowan, *British Emigration to British North America, 1783–1837* (Toronto: University of Toronto Library, 1928).

the New York Legislature in 1819 that it cost a Buffalo merchant four times as much to send a ton of produce to Albany as it did to Montreal, he stated only what was common knowledge: the Old Northwest, the political development of which had been so carefully mapped by Congress in the Ordinance of 1787, was economically tributary to a British colony. Commercial control of the interior went to the cities that commanded the water gateways: Montreal and New Orleans.

Within a few years of its completion in 1825, the Erie Canal had completely undermined Montreal's position. New York now controlled a route to the interior which was far cheaper than the unimproved St. Lawrence. Montreal's commercial hinterland was now confined strictly to the area that could be protected by British and colonial tariffs, that is, to Upper Canada, an area in which expansion of settlement to the north and west would always be shut off by the vast wall of pre-Cambrian granite so that nothing like a continuous westward-moving frontier was possible. And even this limited hinterland could not be monopolized by Montreal, for Upper Canada farmers had always the option of shipping their produce across the Lakes to Buffalo or Oswego and thence to New York, whenever the price differential was larger than the American tariff. Montreal's commercial future depended on recapturing Upper Canada and invading the American midwest; and this in turn depended on the improvement of the St. Lawrence route. This was the challenge that faced the economy of central Canada. It was to call for a continuous series of capital expenditures for canals, harbors, and railroads which for the next half-century set the pace for Canadian development.

In these transport improvements the state played a major role. To be sure, the first Welland Canal, between Lakes Erie and Ontario, was constructed by a private company, but extensive financial aid was received from the provincial and imperial governments.[7] In 1841 the private stockholders were bought out, and the Canal was rebuilt and enlarged at government expense. The other canals on the St. Lawrence —the Cornwall, Williamsburg, Beauharnois, and Lachine—were constructed by the government of the province of Canada between 1841 and 1848, while the Rideau Canal between the Ottawa River and Lake Ontario was built by the British government.

Early railroad building followed a different pattern, in which the initial promotion and construction were generally the work of private

[7] Hugh G. J. Aitken, *The Welland Canal Company: A Study in Canadian Enterprise* (Cambridge: Harvard University Press, 1954).

entrepreneurs. But here, too, the government provided essential financial assistance.[8] The Guarantee Act, passed by the Canadian legislature in 1849, provided a government guarantee for half the bonds of any railroad over 75 miles in length, if half the line had already been built. In 1851 the provisions of this Act were restricted to the three major railroads then under construction—the Northern, Great Western, and St. Lawrence and Atlantic—and to roads forming part of the projected trunk line system from southwestern Ontario to the Maritime Provinces. Financial aid extended by the provincial government under this Act and later acts to assist the Grand Trunk Railway totaled approximately $33,000,000. Considerable sums were also disbursed by municipal governments under the Municipal Loan Fund Act of 1852, a measure designed to make it easier for municipalities to float bond issues in London by pooling their credit in a single fund. The debt incurred under this Act, amounting to some $12,000,000, was assumed by the provincial government in 1859.

The extensive financial obligations undertaken by the Canadian provincial government in this period reflected partly the scarcity of large pools of private capital in Canada at this time and the difficulty experienced by Canadian canal and railroad companies in raising capital in London, and partly a conviction that the improvement of internal transportation was the key to the future development of the Canadian economy and therefore a suitable sphere of government action. In this connection it should be pointed out that the pattern of development in central Canada in this period can be called "expansionist" in two quite different senses. In the first place, there was the expansion of settlement in Upper Canada, a process characterized by a moving frontier, large immigration, and a gradual extension of control over the province's resources. Terminal dates are of course rather arbitrary, but in general the process may be said to have begun around 1800 and to have spent its force by 1850. This is expansionist development in the sense most clearly indicated by Hoselitz's definition. Government action was relatively unimportant except in the initial separation of the province from its seaport (as already suggested, probably a net retarding influence), the provision of legal and administrative procedures for the orderly distribution of Crown lands, and certain changes in tariff policy which may have assisted the growth of agricultural exports.

---

[8] George P. de T. Glazebrook, *A History of Transportation in Canada* (Toronto: Ryerson Press, 1938), Chapter 5; Easterbrook and Aitken, *op. cit.*, Chapter 14.

Whereas an expansionist pattern in this first sense may properly be contrasted with an "intrinsic" pattern of development, expansionism in the second sense, namely, the strenuous and continued efforts to improve the St. Lawrence route as a corridor for freight originating outside Canada, calls for some other contrast. This was the expansionism of a commercial economy, whose potentialities for development were conceived as lying not so much in production as in trade. For close parallels one must look to the Dutch economy in the seventeenth century or the economy of New England in the eighteenth. Certainly in central Canada in this period few conceived of the future of the economy as lying in either manufacturing or a continued expansion of agricultural settlement. The key to the development of central Canada was thought to lie in trade or, in other words, in attracting down the St. Lawrence corridor the exports and imports of the American midwest. This was the final goal of Montreal's commercial ambitions.

This conception of the role of central Canada as an artery of commerce persisted throughout the first half of the nineteenth century. Its influence was slow in dying, although by the late 1860's it was being challenged by the newer conception of expansion into the western prairies. The goal was never achieved—Montreal never captured more than a small fraction of the American midwestern trade— but its attainment was never so far distant as to kill all hope that, with a little more effort or ingenuity, it might be. A few cents cut from the costs of the through route, a canal here, a branch railroad there, a train ferry at Detroit, a railroad bridge at Montreal, and the prize might yet go to Montreal. Such at least was the vision; the Welland Canal, opened in 1829, the St. Lawrence Canals, completed in 1848, the Grand Trunk Railway, with a line from Sarnia to Portland in 1859, and its competitor, the Great Western, linking Windsor, Toronto, and Hamilton in 1856, were attempts to translate the vision into reality.

The Western Prairies and the Pacific Coast

Developments on the western prairies and the Pacific Coast in the period before Confederation can be summarized briefly. Until the discovery of gold in British Columbia in 1856, the dominant economic activity throughout this area was the fur trade.[9] The expansionist phase

9 Easterbrook and Aitken, *op. cit.*, Chapters 10, 15; Harold A. Innis, *The Fur Trade in Canada* (New Haven: Yale University Press, 1930), Chapter 4, and his

of the fur trade had ended in 1821, when the long struggle between Montreal and Hudson Bay was concluded by the absorption of the North West Company by the Hudson's Bay Company. By this date the area of exploitation had been extended from its original limits around the Great Lakes across the prairies, into the Mackenzie River basin, across the Cordilleras, and onto the Pacific slope. Throughout this area the trade was controlled by a single organization—the Hudson's Bay Company, operating under an exclusive charter received from the Crown in 1670.

The policy followed by the Company after 1821 was one of planned conservation. The destructive struggle with the North West Company had resulted in ruthless exploitation of fur resources, unsound trading practices, and uneconomic duplication of trading posts. Under the energetic direction of George Simpson, governor of the Company in North America, these wastes were largely eliminated by 1826. The organization of the trade was brought under tight centralized control and a policy of conserving fur resources in areas that had been over-trapped during the period of competition was instituted. Such a policy was possible only under conditions of monopoly.

In certain areas, however, the Company was still exposed to competition, and conservation policies could not be applied. The first of these was on the Red River, near the present-day city of Winnipeg, where a small agricultural colony had been established by Lord Selkirk in 1812, partly in an attempt to relieve distress in the highlands of Scotland, partly as a tactical move designed to interfere with the North West Company's pemmican supplies. In general the attitude of the Hudson's Bay Company toward agricultural settlement was hostile, because the trade in fur could not survive in any area where settlers managed to gain a foothold. The colony on the Red River, which had been established under the auspices of the Company, was a partial exception; it served as a labor pool for the supply brigades and as a convenient location for retired or superfluous personnel. But even there the Company did all it could to hold agricultural expansion within bounds, to keep the colony economically and politically dependent on the Company, and above all to prevent the development of economic ties with the United States. This last objective led to continual friction, for American traders from Minneapolis, St. Paul, and Pembina regarded the colony as an important source of furs and a market for

---

Introduction in R. H. Fleming, ed. *Minutes of Council, Northern Department of Rupert Land, 1821–31* (Toronto: Champlain Society, 1940).

manufactures, and the possibility of American annexation of the colony, with the consent of a majority of its inhabitants, was never far distant. By 1865 it was clear that the Hudson's Bay Company could not restrain American expansionism much longer in this area and that the colony could not indefinitely be denied a measure of self-government.

On the Pacific Coast, as on the Red River, the Company met the spearheads of American expansionism, adopted a policy of containment, and finally was compelled to make a strategic withdrawal. The movement of American settlers into the Oregon Territory was the dynamic factor in this instance. Immediately after 1821 the Company had begun intensive exploitation of the fur resources of the Columbia and Snake River area. The commercial prospects of this region were not at first considered encouraging. But the Columbia area was one of the last remaining untapped fur preserves, and furthermore the Company's operations there would make possible a "defense in depth" against American expansion. By the Convention of 1818, it will be remembered, Great Britain and the United States had agreed to joint occupancy of the Oregon Territory, but there was never very much doubt that the latter would in the end annex most if not all of the territory so occupied (although the exact boundary remained in dispute). The Company's policy therefore was to exhaust the fur resources of the area as quickly as possible and at the same time to restrain, by all peaceful means, the spread of American settlement. In Governor Simpson's words, the Columbia-Snake River area was "a rich preserve of beaver . . . which for political reasons we should endeavour to destroy as fast as possible." [10]

Throughout the period of joint occupancy, up to 1846, the Hudson's Bay Company functioned explicitly as the agent of the British government on the Pacific Coast, maintaining close contact with the Foreign Office in London and executing (and to some degree forming) official British policy. The final withdrawal to the 49th parallel was far from unexpected, and full preparations had been made. The entire policy of containment and planned withdrawal must be considered a success, for certainly a fur-trading organization never could have been expected to hold the line against the stream of American immigrants pouring in over the Oregon Trail. Almost completely unexpected, however, and a far greater shock to the Company's position, was the discovery of gold on the Frazer River in 1856–57. Against agricultural settlement the Company had fought a successful delaying action; a gold rush was

[10] Frederick Merk, ed. *Fur Trade and Empire: George Simpson's Journal, 1824–1825* (Cambridge: Harvard University Press, 1931), p. 46.

something against which a fur-trading organization could not hope to stand. Nevertheless, the Company was then the sole representative of the British Crown in the area and had to accept responsibility for the maintenance of law and order. To be sure, a colony had been formed on Vancouver Island in 1849, but its Governor and the local Governor of the Company were the same man, and its employees formed the majority of the population.

The influx of gold miners, many of them from California, completely transformed the situation and ended the rule of the Company. Sir James Douglas formally severed all connection with the Company upon accepting the governorship of the new colony of British Columbia in 1858, and in the same year the Company's exclusive trading rights on the mainland were revoked. By 1859 the population of British Columbia had risen to 17,000, excluding Indians. The problems that remained included finding some relatively secure economic base for the colony (especially after the decline of gold production in 1865), preventing its annexation by the United States, and connecting the colony economically and politically with the other British colonies in North America—the province of Canada on the St. Lawrence, the isolated colony on the Red River, and the Maritime Provinces. Confederation in 1870, with its promise of a transcontinental railroad within ten years, was expected to solve these problems.

It requires little imagination to regard the Hudson's Bay Company as playing the role of "the state" throughout western Canada from 1821 to 1870. The pattern of development encouraged by the Company in this period was the very antithesis of expansionist. In most of the Company's territory in western Canada the keynote of policy was conservation, and the over-all goal was to preserve the area as a source of furs for the markets of Europe. Such a policy could not be followed in the Red River colony, the Oregon Territory, or British Columbia after the discovery of gold, and the Company was compelled to cede part of its control to other agencies. Forces of expansion, emanating principally from the United States, could not be contained by any defensive measures available to a fur-trading organization. Only by union with the other British colonies could the necessary resources be mobilized to hold the lines of defense against American expansionism and create a national transcontinental economy.

CONFEDERATION AND THE "NATIONAL POLICY"

During the 1840's Canadians had seen the economic structure of the British Empire dismembered piece by piece, as the Corn Laws and the

Navigation Acts were repealed and the differential timber duties reduced to a nominal level. Cast off, as they felt, by the mother country,
they had flirted briefly in the late 1840's with the idea of annexation
to the United States. Later the idea of reciprocal free trade in natural
products seemed to offer an acceptable substitute for annexation; and
in 1854, with the signing of the Reciprocity Treaty, central Canada and
the Maritimes seemed content to accept the status of an economic
satellite of the United States. With the victory of the protectionist
North in the Civil War and the abrogation of Reciprocity in 1866,
this prospect also disappeared. Unable to secure preferential tariffs
from either Great Britain or the United States, Canadians finally and
hesitatingly turned to the possibility of transcontinental federation.
Political deadlock between the French and English factions in the legislature of central Canada provided one urgent stimulus to action. The
possibility of agricultural expansion into the western prairies, already
threatened by American encroachment, served as another.

The passing of the British North America Act in 1867, uniting under
a federal legislature the provinces of Canada, Nova Scotia, and New
Brunswick, paved the way for a federation of all the scattered colonies.
This was accomplished by the purchase of Rupert's Land from the
Hudson's Bay Company in 1868 and the admission of Manitoba,
British Columbia, and Prince Edward Island as provinces in 1869–70.
The political details of the confederation arrangements are familiar
and need not be repeated here. The economic policies which were to
strengthen the political skeleton are of prime importance for our purpose, however, for in these measures the role assigned to the state in
the development of a transcontinental economic system becomes clearly
evident. These measures are known to Canadian historians as the
"National Policy," a term applied in a narrow sense to the system of
protective tariffs adopted in 1878, and in a broad sense to the general
strategy of defensive expansionism adopted by the new federal government after 1867.[11] In these measures we see for the first time a fading
of the older conception of the St. Lawrence as an artery of trade for the
midwest, and a dawning of the newer conception of transcontinental
expansion.

At the heart of the National Policy was the determination to
strengthen Canada's east-west axis by the construction of a trans-

[11] Vernon C. Fowke, "The National Policy—Old and New," *Canadian Journal of
Economics and Political Science*, 18:271–286 (August 1952), and "National Policy
and Western Development in North America," *Journal of Economic History*, 16:
461–481 (December 1956).

continental railroad. This would offset the increasing north-south pull of American markets and at the same time make possible agricultural expansion into the western prairies beyond the intervening barrier of the pre-Cambrian Shield. Central Canada—now the provinces of Ontario and Quebec—would become the manufacturing and financial center of the new dominion, and by the transcontinental railroad manufactured goods could be sent west to the prairie market and agricultural produce east to the St. Lawrence provinces and Europe. To this grand design all other aspects of the National Policy were to contribute. The protective tariff would check the importation of American manufactures and funnel freight of Canadian origin along the east-west artery. The retention by the federal government of the natural resources of the western provinces, to be administered "for the purposes of the dominion," made possible centralized direction of immigration and settlement policy and the use of land grants to facilitate railroad construction.[12]

Agricultural expansion in the west was basic to the whole design. Wheat was the new staple to which the transcontinental economy was geared. The first essential was construction of the transcontinental railroad. British Columbia had been assured in 1870 that such a road would be begun within two years of admission of that province to the dominion and completed within ten, but it soon became evident that this promise could not be carried out. The principal railroad then operating in Canada—the Grand Trunk—was willing to extend its system to the west only on condition that it could build south of the Great Lakes, through the traffic-producing territory of Michigan, Illinois, Wisconsin, and Minnesota, rather than across the barren lands north of Lake Superior. This was unacceptable to the federal government: Canada's transcontinental axis had to pass entirely through Canadian territory—it was unthinkable that the United States should be permitted to control any part of it. This stipulation excluded the Grand Trunk from participation in the transcontinental project for the time being. The federal government also received an offer to build the railroad from a group of capitalists ostensibly headed by Sir Hugh Allen, a prominent Canadian steamship operator, but actually representing the Northern Pacific group in the United States under the leadership of Jay Cooke. This offer also was refused on the ground that the rail-

[12] Arthur S. Morton and Chester Martin, *History of Prairie Settlement and "Dominion Lands" Policy* (Toronto: Macmillan Company, 1938); Herbert Heaton, "Other Wests than Ours," *Journal of Economic History*, Vol. 6, Suppl. (1946), pp. 50–62.

road had to be under Canadian control. For a time no further offer was received. The federal government undertook preliminary surveys of the prairie and Rocky Mountain areas and began building a line south from Winnipeg to the United States boundary to connect with the St. Paul and Pacific. It began to appear as if the nationalistic insistence of the federal government on Canadian control and an all-Canadian route had indefinitely postponed construction of the transcontinental line.

The assistance offered by the federal government to any company contracting to construct the Pacific railroad had originally been generous and became increasingly so. During the first period of Canadian railroad construction, in the 1850's and 1860's, government aid had typically taken the form of guarantees of bonded debt, and the provincial governments had been in financial difficulties as a result. Remembering this experience, the federal House of Commons, in approving the resolution for a transcontinental railroad, stipulated that government assistance should consist of land grants and cash subsidies. In line with this policy the government in 1872 offered a grant of not more than 50 million acres and $30,000,000 in cash. This was later amended to $10,000 in cash and 20,000 acres per mile of track, and again amended in 1878 to a total grant of 100 million acres—according to estimates made at that time, about two thirds of the total area suitable for agriculture and pasture in the prairie region.

It was not regarded as feasible or desirable that the government construct the railroad itself. This had already been tried on the Intercolonial Railway between Montreal and the Maritimes with dubious results, and this experience, combined with the slender and inexperienced administrative resources available to the federal government, may have made contracting with a private syndicate appear more attractive. Opinion differed, however, between the Liberal and the Conservative parties: the latter insisted on construction by private enterprise, while the former toyed with the idea of step-by-step government construction across the prairies westward from Lake Superior, with the line never advancing far beyond the area of settlement. Some measures were actually taken to put this latter conception into effect. It never caught the public imagination in the way the more ambitious project did; on the other hand, the possibility of relying on shipping on the Great Lakes for the connection between the prairies and central Canada was attractive from the cost viewpoint. It would have avoided the necessity of laying rails through the barren area of the pre-Cambrian

Shield north of Lake Superior—the reason for the reluctance of private enterprise to accept the government's offer.

Not until 1880 did a group of private entrepreneurs come forward who both met the government's requirements as to national affiliation and possessed the resources and talent required for the task. Paradoxically, these men had made their reputation in railroading by their successful reorganization of a twice-bankrupt American road, the St. Paul and Pacific. Two of them, however, Norman W. Kittson and James J. Hill, were of Canadian origin, and their principal associate, Donald A. Smith, was a chief commissioner of the Hudson's Bay Company. The other members of the original Canadian Pacific Railway syndicate, George Stephen and Richard B. Angus, were president and general manager respectively of the Bank of Montreal. None of them was associated at this time with any major American Pacific railroad (although Hill later withdrew and devoted himself to expansion of the Great Northern system). These affiliations and the increasing evidence that it would be long before another offer would be made, if this were rejected, satisfied the government's insistence on Canadian control. The contract with the government was signed in October 1880. The C.P.R. was to receive $25,000,000 in cash and 25 million acres of land; all sections of the railroad already completed by the government were to be handed over to the Company without charge, and sections already under contract were to be completed at government expense; the construction of competing railroads between the C.P.R. line and the American boundary was to be prohibited for 20 years; and other concessions of minor importance were added.[13]

With this assistance and later emergency financial help from the government, highly competent management and construction techniques already perfected in the United States, the through line of the C.P.R. from the Pacific Coast to central Canada was completed in 1885. Before World War I its facilities were supplemented by two additional transcontinental lines, the Canadian Northern and the Grand Trunk Pacific, both constructed with federal and provincial government assistance; the whole formed a transport network considerably in excess of the country's needs at the time. Thus did the problem of excess capacity, which had plagued central Canada after the completion of

[13] Easterbrook and Aitken, *op. cit.,* Chapter 18; Glazebrook, *op. cit.,* Chapters 6–11; Harold A. Innis, *A History of the Canadian Pacific Railway* (Toronto: McClelland and Stewart, 1923), Chapters 1–3; James B. Hedges, *The Federal Railway Land Subsidy Policy of Canada* (Cambridge: Harvard University Press, 1934).

the canals in 1848, reappear in the first half-century of the new dominion.[14] Defense against American economic expansion necessitated
transcontinental expansion in Canada; but its costs, borne originally
by the government but finally by consumers in high freight rates and
a high tariff, made the maintenance of national economic unity extremely difficult.

Meanwhile in 1878 the second foundation stone of the National
Policy, the protective tariff, had been firmly laid. Here the power of
the state was applied directly to forging national economic unity and
erecting bastions against American expansion. The question is not
why Canada turned to protection, but why protectionism came so late.
Lingering hopes for a renewal of reciprocity are part of the explanation; the strenuous opposition of the Maritime Provinces, another part;
and the weakness of domestic industries, a third. Yet as early as 1858
A. T. Galt, Minister of Finance, had stated the function that the protective tariff was to perform as a means of stimulating traffic along
east-west transport routes and encouraging the development of manufacturing in central Canada. Not until two decades later, however, was
Galt's policy of "incidental protection" converted into an admittedly
protective tariff, and then only under the pressure of the major depression of 1876–79. By this date hopes for reciprocity had dwindled;
railroad construction, by lowering transport costs, had increased the
vulnerability of Canadian manufacturers to foreign competition; and
a more rapid rate of industrialization was coming to be recognized as
essential if the over-all conception of a transcontinental national economy was to be realized. In addition, the emergent spirit of Canadian
nationalism, already noticed in its effect on the planning of the Pacific
railroad, fostered a conviction that the nation must reduce its dependence on outside conditions by developing its own sources of manufactured goods.

Between the protective tariff and railroad construction in the west
there was a close connection. When the tariff kept out foreign goods
and encouraged manufacturing within Canada, prospects of freight on
the east-west transport artery and an adequate level of earnings by the
railroads were improved. When goods entered over the tariff barrier,
customs revenue could be applied to meet railroad deficits and support
the debt incurred by the state for western expansion. This was the
philosophy first stated by Galt in 1858. It underlay the whole National

[14] Harold A. Innis, "Unused Capacity as a Factor in Canadian Economic History"
and "The Political Implications of Unused Capacity," in *Political Economy in the
Modern State* (Toronto: Ryerson Press, 1946), pp. 201–228.

Policy program from 1878 onward and was not seriously modified until the onset of depression in the 1930's.

Both in tariff legislation and railroad construction the state after confederation assumed an active role in promoting Canadian development. The responsibility for creating a national economy and the conditions in which it could survive lay with the state. Extending far beyond the basic constitutional framework of government, internal security, and justice, this responsibility embraced also the construction, in partnership with private enterprise, of the east-west transport system; the erection of tariff barriers behind which an industrial complex could develop; and the promotion of immigration and a flow of investment capital from Europe. The over-all objective of the policy was to make possible the maintenance of Canadian political sovereignty over the territory north of the American boundary: that is to say, to prevent absorption by the United States and to build a nation state that could guide its own economic destiny, and assert its independence from both the mother country and the United States, within limits no more restrictive than those necessarily applicable to an economy dependent on staple exports for its overseas earnings. Sustaining the policy was an emerging sense of national identity and purpose, analogous to the sense of manifest destiny which had colored the expansion of the United States.

Whether the initiative in stating and implementing this policy is to be ascribed to private enterprise or to the state is a question on which opinions will differ. The assertion that the state in the form of the federal government was merely acting as the agent or instrument of private economic interests—the same interests that had worked to achieve confederation, the sale of the Hudson's Bay Company's lands, and the chartering of a Pacific railroad—could probably be supported. But if the distinction between "the state" and "private enterprise" is to be retained (as applied to Canada, the distinction often seems artificial), the weight of the evidence seems to indicate a contrary view. The secular decisions at this stage of Canadian development were made by governmental bodies; the basic developmental policies to be pursued were stated by government officials; and the implementation of these policies involved the exercise of initiative by governments.

THE TWENTIETH CENTURY

I propose to use three aspects of Canadian development in the twentieth century to exemplify the ways in which the state has continued to influence the rate and direction of economic change: the fostering of the pulp and paper industry in central Canada; the construction of the St. Lawrence Seaway; and the control of the oil and natural gas industries.

Pulp and Paper Industry

The primary instrument of state assistance to the pulp and paper industry has been the tariff. Exploitation of Canada's forest resources for the manufacture of paper and allied products dates from the introduction of the first methods of manufacturing paper from wood pulp in the 1860's. Today the manufacture of pulp and paper is Canada's leading industry, whether the criterion be value of output, capital invested, or wages paid. The spectacular growth of the industry has been due partly to Canada's rich resources of timber and hydroelectric power; partly to a mass demand for cheap newsprint in the United States; and partly to a consistent government policy of discouraging the export of raw pulpwood and encouraging its manufacture into newsprint and pulp within Canada.

Government policy concerning the industry has centered in a systematic attempt to induce pulp and paper mills to migrate toward the source of the raw material.[15] Basic to the success of this policy has been the secularly bouyant demand for newsprint in the United States and the progressive exhaustion of its pulpwood supplies. By 1900 it was clear that American newsprint consumers could no longer rely exclusively on domestic supplies unless they were prepared to pay considerably higher prices. The cheapest and most convenient source of imports was Canada, where costs of production were generally somewhat lower and the danger of exhaustion of supplies was more remote. Canadian provincial governments controlled by far the largest proportion of the country's forest resources and recognized at an early date that they were in an unusually strong position to reinforce the pull of cheap raw materials by imposing duties on the export of the unmanufactured product. The implementation of this policy clearly involved the risk of retaliatory action by the United States, not to mention the hostility of politically influential newspaper chains, but

[15] John A. Guthrie, *The Newsprint Paper Industry: An Economic Analysis* (Cambridge: Harvard University Press, 1941). See also "The Pulp and Paper Industry in Canada," *Canada Year Book, 1952–53* (Ottawa, 1953), pp. 467–475.

was nevertheless pushed through with surprising consistency. British Columbia led the way in 1891 by prohibiting the export of timber cut on Crown lands; Ontario followed with a similar prohibition in 1902; and Quebec in 1900 imposed in effect an export duty on pulpwood by reducing the fees on timber cut on Crown lands by about one third on condition that the wood was manufactured within the province. Within the next 13 years the remaining provinces adopted similar legislation.

The ability of the United States to retaliate by imposing higher import duties on Canadian pulpwood was limited by the reluctance of newspaper publishers to pay the cost in higher newsprint prices. A compromise passed by the American Congress in 1909 reduced the tariff on the lowest grade of paper to three sixteenths of one cent, on condition that the exporting country removed all restrictions on pulpwood exports. When the Canadian provincial governments refused to reverse their policy, a retaliatory duty of $2.00 per ton was imposed on Canadian paper. The burden of this tariff, however, was borne principally by American newspapers, whose demand for Canadian newsprint was highly inelastic. Pressure for the removal of the retaliatory duty resulted in a provision for free admission of Canadian newsprint in the proposed reciprocity agreements of 1911, which, however, were rejected by Canada after having been accepted by the Congress. In 1913 American newsprint consumers finally won a conclusive victory in the Underwood Act which provided for the free admission of newsprint paper valued at not more than 2.5 cents a pound, together with mechanical and chemical pulp. Subsequent increases in the price of Canadian newsprint have been met by raising the 2.5-cent limit, so that since 1913 Canadian pulp and newsprint have entered the American market free of duty.

The history of the Canadian newsprint industry is important principally as the only instance wherein Canadian producers and governments have been able to exploit a quasi monopoly in the marketing of a staple product. The embargoes and restrictions on the export of the raw material admittedly would not have been effective without the underlying locational pull of cheap pulpwood and hydroelectric power. Nevertheless, the determination of the provincial governments to exploit fully the strong bargaining position given them by control of pulpwood supplies undoubtedly hastened the migration of newsprint production to Canada.

St. Lawrence Seaway

We have noted the construction of a system of canals between Lake Erie and tidewater at Montreal as the dominant theme of economic development in central Canada from 1815 to 1849; the inspiration of this series of transportation improvements by a vision of central Canada as an artery of commerce between the American midwest and Europe; and the slow transition from this phase of development to that of transcontinental economic expansion.

The recent construction of the St. Lawrence Seaway constitutes an emphatic restatement of the older theme. The conception of a transport system that would permit ocean-going vessels to go to the heart of the continent by way of the St. Lawrence was never abandoned; rather, it was cast into the shadow by the newer and more practicable proposals for a transcontinental railroad. Now, with the opening of new resources of iron ore in Quebec and Labrador and the pressure of new conceptions of continental defense strategy, the original idea has been translated into action. The agreement to build the Seaway signed by the Canadian and United States governments in 1954 was, in essence, the realization of an idea that has influenced Canadian development for more than 150 years.[16]

Since 1841, when the private interests that had constructed the first Welland Canal were bought out by the Canadian government, the completion, maintenance, and enlargement of the St. Lawrence – Great Lakes canal system has been regarded as a responsibility of the state. By the early years of the twentieth century, successive governments had brought into existence a chain of canals between Montreal and Lake Ontario giving a minimum depth of 14 feet throughout, and deepened the ship channel below Montreal to 35 feet. Between Lake Ontario and Lake Erie the Welland Canal, which had been deepened between 1873 and 1887 to 14 feet, was already proving inadequate for the traffic; and construction of the Welland Ship Canal, to provide a channel 25 feet deep, was begun in 1913. Between Lake Huron and Lake Superior, at Sault Ste Marie, an American canal had been built in 1853–55; and a similar canal on the Canadian side was begun in 1887 and completed in 1895.

Despite these successive enlargements and extensions, it was still impossible for the large steamships that operated on the Great Lakes to

---

[16] Easterbrook and Aitken, *op. cit.*, Chapter 21; "The St. Lawrence Seaway," *Canada Year Book, 1955*, pp. 885–888; U. S. Senate, 83rd Congress, 2nd Session, Document No. 165, *The St. Lawrence Seaway Manual* (1955); Royal Institute of International Affairs, *Springs of Canadian Power* (London, 1953).

pass down the St. Lawrence to Montreal, and for the ocean-going vessels that touched at Montreal to proceed to the Lakes. The bottleneck of the 14-foot St. Lawrence canals meant that water-borne traffic had to be transshipped twice between the Atlantic and Lake Erie—at Montreal and at Kingston. By enlarging and deepening these canals, Canada could have overcome this bottleneck without help from the United States. Its participation was highly desirable, however: better use could be made of the natural channel of the St. Lawrence (the international boundary over much of the distance above Montreal), and the heavy financial burden involved could be borne more easily by two federal governments than by one.

Early attempts to find some formula for joint construction proved abortive. Commissions of inquiry appointed by both federal governments in 1895 produced no positive results. In 1921 the International Joint Commission, which was established in 1909 to arbitrate questions involving the boundary waters of Canada and the United States, recommended joint construction, but no decision to implement the recommendation followed. Later inquiries and recommendations produced the St. Lawrence Deep Waterway Treaty of 1932, which was rejected by the U. S. Senate in 1934, when opposition came principally from the eastern seaboard states and American railroad interests. The Great Lakes – St. Lawrence Agreement of 1941 also failed to secure congressional approval. Faced with the prospect of indefinite further delay, the Canadian Parliament in 1951 created the St. Lawrence Seaway Authority, a Crown corporation authorized to construct a deep waterway between Montreal and Lake Erie either wholly within Canada or in conjunction with the United States if Congress finally agreed to participate.

Meanwhile the economic significance of the project had been completely transformed. Originally regarded almost exclusively as a transport improvement, it was increasingly considered as a power resource. Industry in central Canada has developed on an energy base made up partly of bituminous coal imported from the United States and partly of hydroelectricity generated within Canada. In 1945 Canada had a total installed hydroelectric turbine capacity of just over 10.25 million horsepower, of which 5.9 million was in Quebec, and 2.7 million in Ontario. Of the total energy consumed in Ontario and Quebec in 1943, water power contributed 37.8 percent, and coal 52.6 percent.[17]

[17] *Report of the Royal Commission on Coal,* W. F. Carr, chairman (Ottawa, 1947); John H. Dales, "Fuel, Power, and Industrial Development in Central Canada," *American Economic Review,* 43:181–198 (May 1953).

The rate of industrial development in these two provinces since 1900 has hinged on the rate of hydroelectric power development. The principal power sites have been at Niagara Falls and on the St. Lawrence and the rivers of its drainage system.

Recognition of the importance of the St. Lawrence Seaway project as a potential source of cheap hydroelectric power dates from the late 1920's, when it was partly responsible for a marked growth of interest in the project in the United States. Several large American corporations were keenly interested in the hydroelectric aspects and threw their influence on the side of American participation, in alliance with the Lake cities, such as Cleveland, Detroit, and Chicago, which had always been attracted by the transportation aspects. Not until after World War II, however, did hydroelectric power become the critical factor. In Ontario, where primary load requirements had increased by 88 percent from 1945 to 1954, an acute shortage of electric power was imminent. In New York State and Quebec it seemed certain that existing generating facilities would be inadequate within a few years. In these circumstances the development of the last remaining water power resource of any significance in the area—the St. Lawrence River—became imperative. The total power available from the St. Lawrence between Lake Ontario and Montreal is estimated at 5.4 million horsepower; of this, only some 1.4 million had been developed at that time.

Joint participation in the development of hydroelectric power proved easier to secure than in the navigation improvements. In 1951 the Canadian government announced its intention of proceeding independently with the Seaway development. Negotiations on the electric power aspects continued, however, and in 1952 parallel petitions for approval of joint development of the hydroelectric facilities were submitted to the International Joint Commission by the two federal governments. Permission was readily obtained and plans were approved, with Canada still accepting exclusive responsibility for the construction and operation of the deep waterway.

In the meantime another major development had taken place: the opening of the iron ore deposits in the Quebec-Labrador region.[18] The existence of large iron ore deposits in this region was known to

18 Royal Institute of International Affairs, *op. cit.;* Dominion Bureau of Statistics, *Chronological Record of Canadian Mining Events from 1604 to 1947 and Historical Tables of Mineral Production in Canada* (Ottawa, 1948); "Canada's Mineral Resources," *Canada Year Book, 1954,* pp. 482–506; "The Iron-Ore Resources of the Quebec-Labrador Region," *Canada Year Book, 1950,* pp. 505–512.

Canadian geologists as early as 1893, but the impossibility of extracting the ore and delivering it to Canadian and American smelters, with the existing transportation facilities, at prices competitive with Mesabi and Newfoundland shipments prevented commercial development. Commercial surveying did not begin until 1938. Between 1942 and 1944 extensive surveys revealed very large deposits of low-phosphorus iron ore, and by 1944 reserves of more than 300 million tons of high-grade ore had been proved. The first shipments of ore from this development were made in July 1954. Production was geared initially to a rate of 10 million tons a year. Meanwhile plans were pushed for a similar development of iron ore deposits in Ungava, north of the original discoveries.

The capital for the initial exploration of the Quebec-Labrador deposits came from Canadian mining interests. The Iron Ore Company of Canada, however, the concern now working the deposits, represents a union of Canadian and American capital; five leading American steel corporations are large shareholders. Development of the Steep Rock deposits in Ontario has been similarly financed and organized. In both cases American interest stems largely from the approaching exhaustion of the higher-grade deposits in the Mesabi range. It has been estimated that by 1960 Canada will be one of the world's largest exporters of iron ore. Despite the rapid growth of the Canadian steel industry, it seems clear that most of Canada's iron ore exports will go to the United States.

The relevance of these developments for the St. Lawrence Seaway project is obvious. If iron ore from the Quebec-Labrador deposits was to be transported to the iron and steel producing centers south of Lake Erie, radical improvements in the existing canal facilities were indispensable. The increased cost of reliance on either the existing 14-foot canals or rail transportation would have destroyed the economic feasibility of the scheme.

Opinions can reasonably differ as to whether the United States would have agreed to participate in construction of the Seaway in the absence of these developments in Quebec-Labrador. It seems, however, that the prospect of obtaining competitively priced high-grade iron ore from Canada was a major influence producing American participation after almost three-quarters of a century. Estimates by the U. S. Department of Commerce, made shortly before construction of the Seaway began, put the total annual traffic between the Gulf of St. Lawrence and Lake Erie at not less than 57 million tons. Of this total, it was estimated that iron ore from Ungava and Quebec-Labrador would contribute 30 million tons. Economic and strategic considerations combined to emphasize the importance of a transportation improvement that would open this massive new resource to the industrial centers of the American heartland. In the absence of these considerations the bills for American participation in the Seaway that were finally approved by Congress in May 1954 might well have had a much rougher passage.

The construction of the Seaway represents, as has been said, the realization of one of the most persistent aspirations of Canadian development. The role of the state has included not only the obvious responsibility for construction and finance but also that of exerting diplomatic and political pressure on the government of an interested, friendly, but disappointingly uncooperative power—the United States. This is of course a developmental function that no other organization could have performed. It may be emphasized, however, that the Seaway illustrates Canada's changing satellitic role vis-a-vis the United States and Great Britain. The Seaway was originally thought of as a means of enabling Canada to capture and control part of the transit trade between Great Britain and the American midwest: the idea reflected Canada's role as an economic satellite of the former. In its final form, however, the Seaway is largely facilitating the export of Canadian raw materials to the United States. The St. Lawrence River, throughout most of Canada's history a symbol of a dominant orientation toward Europe, now serves to strengthen Canada's economic ties to the United States.

Oil and Natural Gas Industries

Until the years immediately after World War II, Canada's production of crude oil and natural gas was insignificant. Oil fields in the southwestern peninsula of Ontario, between Lake Huron and Lake Erie, were first exploited in 1858 and reached a peak production of 795,030 barrels in 1890. Thereafter they were important only for local supplies of natural gas. The Turner Valley oil field in Alberta was discovered in 1914 and by 1930 was producing one million barrels a year. Canada remained, however, a large net importer of crude oil.

During World War II the speed of exploration for new Canadian resources of crude oil increased markedly, partly as a result of tax concessions by the federal government, and new discoveries were made in areas distant from the Turner Valley field. In 1946 the Conrad and

Taber oil fields near Lethbridge, Alberta, came into production, and were followed within a few months by the Lloydminster field lying across the Alberta and Saskatchewan boundary. These finds, important in themselves, dwindled into relative insignificance with the opening of the Leduc field near Edmonton in 1947, which was of first-class importance. A period of intensive surveying followed, with American oil companies playing a leading role, and within a few years several major oil deposits were discovered. Most of the early discoveries lay within Alberta, but by the end of 1953 the area of active exploration included Saskatchewan and Manitoba, the northeast corner of British Columbia, and the Northwest Territories south and west of Great Slave Lake. By 1954 proven recoverable reserves had reached a total of 2.5 billion barrels. Total crude oil production rose from about 8.5 million barrels in 1945 to 29 million in 1950 and almost 61 million in 1952.

These discoveries represent completely new development potentials for the Canadian economy, and their full significance will not be apparent for some time.[19] They have posed certain problems of national policy, which have centered around the construction of pipe lines for the export of natural gas to the United States. There is a certain understandable suspicion in Canada concerning the extent to which its resources have come to be owned and controlled by American corporations. It is recognized, on the one hand, that American capital is important in stimulating and supporting Canadian development, particularly since this capital tends to flow into the more venturesome and speculative projects.[20] On the other hand, Canadians, who have only recently attained full independence and self-determination in the political sense, are reluctant to see their natural resources—the full richness of which is just coming to be appreciated—exploited in the interests of industries of another country. This sentiment is particularly marked in the case of the spectacular new developments of resources such as prairie oil and gas.

In comparison with the Texas and California fields, for example, the original oil and natural gas discoveries in the western prairies suffered

---

[19] Easterbrook and Aitken, *op. cit.*, Chapter 21; "Canadian Crude Petroleum Situation," *Canada Year Book, 1954*, pp. 540–544; The Royal Bank of Canada, "Oil and Gas Bulletins"; Royal Institute of International Affairs, *op. cit.*

[20] Easterbrook and Aitken, *op. cit.*, Chapter 23; A. E. Safarian and E. B. Carty, "Foreign Financing of Canadian Investment in the Post-war Period," in American Statistical Association, *Proceedings of the Business and Economic Statistics Section* . . . , *September 10–13, 1954*, pp. 72–79.

from one major handicap: their distance from water transportation. The markets that Alberta oil and gas could reasonably expect to serve were in central Canada and on the Pacific Coast. To reach these markets the construction of pipe lines was indispensable. In the case of oil pipe lines no government restriction of any importance was encountered. In 1949 the Interprovincial Pipeline Company, a subsidiary of Imperial Oil, began construction of a line from Edmonton to Superior, Wisconsin. This was completed late in 1950, and construction was begun on an extension south of Lake Superior, across the Mackinac Straits to Sarnia, Ontario. During 1952 an additional line was constructed to carry refined products from Sarnia to Toronto. In 1952 construction also began on the Transmountain Pipeline from Edmonton to British Columbia, and plans were made for its continuation to new refineries to be constructed in the state of Washington. No Canadian government interposed any obstacle to the construction of these pipe lines, despite the fact that part of the eastern line ran through the United States and the western was planned to terminate at refineries in that country.

A very different policy was adopted concerning natural gas pipe lines. At an early date the government of Alberta announced that exports of natural gas from the province would not be permitted until reserves had been proved adequate to provide a 30-year supply for the province and to meet the prior needs of the Dominion. The first of these two conditions was satisfied in 1951, and in 1951–52 government approval was given for two pipe lines to carry natural gas to the United States: one to serve the Anaconda Copper Company's plant at Butte, Montana, the other to serve industrial consumers in Portland and Seattle. With these two exceptions, the export of natural gas to the United States was prohibited. A statement by the Canadian federal government in March 1953 made clear the policy: no permits would be granted for the export of natural gas until the government was convinced that there could be no economic use, present or future, for that gas in Canada.

Literally interpreted, this statement implied an indefinite embargo on natural gas exports. By what rational process could a government ever convince itself that there could be no present or future use for a major energy resource within Canada? In practice, however, the government's policy has been interpreted to mean that sanction will not be given for the export of natural gas to the United States until a pipe line has been constructed entirely through Canadian territory to convey natural gas from the prairie provinces to Ontario and Quebec.

The apparent discrepancy between the Canadian federal government's policy concerning oil and uranium, completely free export of which has been permitted, and that concerning natural gas and hydroelectric power, export of which has been permitted only under very unusual conditions, has occasioned considerable critical comment. The rationale of the policy is that hydroelectric power and natural gas are considered sources of industrial energy, whereas oil and uranium are not. Access to cheap Canadian industrial power will be restricted to plants within the political boundaries of Canada; it is hoped that this inducement, combined with the protective tariff, will encourage manufacturing within Canada and counteract the tendency for Canadian resources to be exported in their natural condition to industries in the United States.

The analogy with the policies successfully pursued in the case of the newsprint industry is obvious, as is the analogy with the federal government's insistence in the 1860's and 1870's on the construction of a transcontinental railroad entirely within Canadian territory. In all three cases the state has acted to offset the pull of markets in the United States. The state has interpreted its function as the preservation of national economic unity along an east-west axis as a defense against the divisive north-south pull of the United States.

Conclusion

In broad outline the story of Canadian economic development until the early years of the twentieth century is a simple one. The rate and direction of development have been determined by the economic characteristics of a number of staple products: fish, fur, timber, wheat, and minerals. Each of these staples has posed its own particular problems of organization and marketing, and each has cast Canada in the role of an economic satellite and marginal supplier of other more advanced areas, chiefly Great Britain and the United States. Fish, fur, wheat, and square timber kept Canada within the economic orbit of the former; lumber, metallic minerals, and more recently crude oil drew Canada closer to the latter. Great Britain and the United States have also been the principal sources of capital imports and of the immigrant labor supply.

The role of the state in Canadian development has been that of facilitating the production and export of these staple products. This has involved two major functions: planning and to some extent financing the improvement of the internal transport system; and maintaining pressure on other governments to secure more favorable terms for the marketing of Canadian exports. In relation to economic development, the escape from colonial status and the achievement of political independence in Canada have meant primarily the creation of a political apparatus competent to perform these functions effectively.

The course of economic development in Canada can be called expansionist, but with two qualifications. First, expansionist tendencies have not infrequently been frustrated, partly by changes in demand conditions in foreign markets, partly by the temporary inability or unwillingness of the state to underwrite the capital investments required for further growth. Second, expansionism in Canada has been largely induced rather than autonomous. It has been contingent on state action both in the political integration of widely separated regional economies and in the provision of indispensable transport facilities. Throughout Canadian development expansionism has been defensive in character. It has been part of a general strategy of containing the expansionism of the stronger and more aggressive economy of the United States and preserving a distinct political sovereignty over the territory north of the present international boundary. Each phase of expansion in Canada has been a tactical move designed to forestall, counteract, or restrain the northward extension of American economic and political influence. Primary responsibility for maintaining and strengthening this policy of defensive expansionism has fallen on the state.

4 THE STATE AND ECONOMIC DEVELOPMENT: RUSSIA, 1890–1939

George Barr Carson, Jr.

As an example of a state in which economic development can be characterized as expansionist, dominant, and induced, it might be hard to find a more logical choice than Russia. Although there was some division of opinion in Russia during the 1890's as to whether a great amount of foreign aid was required, or should be permitted, most of the historical development of the country was certainly weighted toward a consistent pattern. The notably authoritarian political organization reinforced the influence of historical tendencies.

HISTORICAL BACKGROUND

Three important conditions combined from the sixteenth to the twentieth century to explain many of the problems of Russian development. These were (1) the feeble economic development of the Russian empire, (2) the heavy demands made upon the population by the state, and (3) the prevalence of a concept of the state as general proprietor as well as ruler.

The feeble economic development of the Russian empire was noticeable in 1890 in both a relative and an absolute sense. Any comparison of Russian agriculture with that of other leading European states was to its disadvantage in level of cultivating technique; productivity per unit of land, labor, or capital; and stability of income for the majority of cultivators. In industry Russian achievement lagged, except in the rate of building railroads, and Russian domestic and foreign commerce was at a fairly low level. In an absolute sense Russia was in sight of bankruptcy in the 1880's, if not on the verge of it. The proportion of military and naval expense in the Russian ordinary budget was heavy, but this was not the only burdensome item. The currency inflation and the rise in the public debt as a consequence of the Crimean War and the Turkish war of 1877–78 imposed further suffering on the country; debt service absorbed 25 percent of the annual expenditures in the imperial budget. The state had assumed additional heavy responsibilities in the emancipation of the serfs in the 1860's and in promoting the transition from a natural to a capitalistic economy. In the last analysis the burden of these expenses had to fall on the peasantry, not because they were sufficiently prosperous to carry the load but because their overwhelming preponderance in the population made theirs the only branch of production extensive enough to meet the requirements. Redemption payments for the lands transferred to the emancipated peasantry and increased taxes were the consequence. Yet in the end these measures failed; in the 1890's the stabilization of the paper ruble at two thirds of its face value was engineered by Finance Minister Witte's introduction of a gold standard, and a decade later redemption dues were abolished because the peasants were almost hopelessly in arrears.

For the Russian autocracy national defense was the overriding consideration. In part because of the geographical configuration of the empire and perhaps in part because of the experience with foreign invasion in the nineteenth century, an extremely large military establishment was required. The heavy demands that this imposed on the population restricted its capacity to contribute to economic development. Because of heavy collections from the population, the state was the unavoidable arbiter as to how resources were to be employed; the state held the most significant portion of disposable resources. In an autocratic political organization it was possible for defense considerations to remain dominant and for the nature or necessity of economic development to be decided by the small group that participated in government, without effective influence by other groups. Indeed it required the impact of the unsuccessful Crimean War to impel the dominant group to necessary social and economic change. Even then only the demonstrated insufficiency of the prevailing level of economic development to sustain national defense prompted action.

As late as the reign of Peter the Great, the concept of the state as the general proprietor still prevailed. Only after Peter's death in 1725 did the landed class of serfowners acquire full private property rights in land, and the state continued to be the preponderant landholder until the Bolshevik nationalization of land in 1917–18. The new industries opened by Peter the Great were frequently state owned, although operated by private parties and for private profit; the state continued to be a significant owner of manufacturing and mining properties until the emancipation of the serfs. When railroad construction was undertaken on a large scale, the state played a prominent role not only in subsidizing construction but in actual operation. Although an important part of the mileage was built by private enterprise—guaranteed against loss by the state—the purchase of railroads in the 1890's and later led to a high degree of state ownership in an enterprise that by 1914 employed nearly half the nonagricultural workers in the empire. State proprietorship was by no means limited to the imperial government but was evident also in the zemstvos and municipalities, whose budgets reflected the operation of productive enterprise. In view of the extensive nationalization of productive property during the Soviet regime, the relatively short interlude when state proprietorship gave way to widespread private holding of productive property was an exception to the general tradition in Russia of the state as proprietor as well as ruler.

From the emancipation of the serfs to the end of the 1880's the policy of the Russian government was not particularly directed toward major changes in the traditional development of the economy. The 1860's, when many reforms in Russian life were under consideration, were on the whole characterized by the conviction that Russia was and should remain a primarily agricultural country. Owing to the extensive cultivation of grain, Russia could advantageously exchange agricultural products for all kinds of manufactured goods from abroad, and it was therefore unnecessary to expand native mining and manufacturing industries. This policy explains not only the rather feeble growth of these industries during the period but also the failure to offer effective inducement or protection against foreign competition. One consequence was the small buying power of an overwhelmingly agrarian society. In 1890 it was estimated that the demand for manufactured articles was at the rate of only 17 rubles per capita.[1]

The rational basis for this policy disappeared with changes in the world grain market after 1870 and the competition of large-scale grain production in the Americas. The price of grain was reduced by one third or more, which meant that maintaining a rate of export sufficient to pay for imported manufactured articles was possible only at an increasing loss to the Russian agrarian population. Since these effects were traceable to an officially accepted view of the nature of economic development, it was incumbent on the state to make changes

[1] *The Industries of Russia: Manufactures and Trade,* Vol. I, translation ed. by John M. Crawford for the World's Columbian Exposition (St. Petersburg, 1893), p. xiii.

in policy that would affect the course of this development. There was probably also some compulsion toward state initiative and leadership after 1890 because of a series of cataclysmic losses that required social effort to replace—private resources available in Russia could not have met the need in a reasonable time. Among these disasters were the serious famine of 1891–92; famine again in 1902; the riots of the Russo-Japanese War period, which caused losses of about 2 billion rubles; and the cost of that War.

The most notable feature of the way in which the state exacted from its people the heavy requirements for its budgets was the relatively low proportion of direct taxes and the increasingly high proportion of indirect taxes. The regressive character of this taxation is indicated by the following estimates: In 1890 the average per capita annual income was about 35 rubles.[2] The average per capita share in the imperial tax load was between 7.5 and 8 rubles per year.[3] The largest single revenue item in the state budget was the excise tax on alcoholic beverages; 2 rubles 37 kopecks, or nearly 30 percent of the average per capita tax bill, came from that source.[4] The greater part of this burden was borne by the low-income agrarian population, for as a consumption tax this was widely distributed regardless of income. The industrial worker, whose average annual wage was about 187 rubles,[5] was somewhat better off than the agrarian, but the greater affluence of the industrial workers could not have made any vast difference in the distribution of the excise tax because of their small numbers.

The structure of local taxation was slightly different, and the total revenue involved was far less significant. The total revenue of the

---

[2] Peter I. Lyashchenko, *A History of the National Economy of Russia to the 1917 Revolution* (New York: Macmillan Company, 1949), pp. 697–698, gives estimates of national income for 1900–1913. For 1890 I have estimated on the basis of the ratio of state budget income to estimated national income, using budget figures from P. A. Khromov, *Ekonomicheskoe razvitie Rossii v XIX-XX vekakh, 1800–1917* (Moscow, 1950), Table 25b, p. 501; Table 25g, p. 508. The ratio declined from 26 to 20 percent during the period. I have estimated on the basis of 26 percent for 1890 since there is no evidence that the state budget took a smaller proportion before 1900 and may have taken more. The precise figure is not needed to indicate the relative burden of certain imposts on the population. See Khromov, p. 275.

[3] S. S. Kh., *Finansy Rossii v sviazi s ekonomicheskim polozheniem eia naseleniia* (2nd ed.; St. Petersburg, 1908), p. 97.

[4] See Khromov, Table 25b, pp. 498–499; and *Finansy Rossii*, Table 21.

[5] *The Industries of Russia*, Vol. I, p. 514.

zemstvos in 1890 was 47 million rubles, and that of municipalities approximately 54 million rubles.[6] The zemstvos' primary sources of revenue were taxes on immovable property, income from their own capital and property, and increasingly after 1899 grants-in-aid from the imperial government. A minor fraction (about 4 percent) of the zemstvos' income came from taxes on trade and industry and from various duties. The major part (57 percent) of municipal revenue, on the other hand, came from town property and municipal enterprises, the next from grants-in-aid (26 percent), a poor third (about 11 percent) from taxes on land, and the small remainder from licenses, fees, and other duties.

Table 1 shows the resources available to the state in 1890 and indicates the degree of dependence upon indirect and consumption taxes.

TABLE 1. IMPERIAL REVENUES BY SOURCE, 1890

In thousands of rubles

Ordinary		
Duties	54,844	
Commercial licenses	34,339	
Excise tax, spirits	268,381	
Other excise (tobacco, sugar, kerosene)	64,685	
Customs	141,939	
Forests	16,734	
State railroads and share in profits of private railroad companies	88,065	
Redemption operations	88,232	
Other income	182,726	
Capital receipts	3,741	
		943,686
Extraordinary		
Loans	72,149	
Receipts from return of expenses for railroads and balance of railroad capital	16,470	
Receipts from special capital and other sources	6,708	
War indemnity military compensation	8,360	
		103,687
Total ordinary and extraordinary		1,047,373

Source: Based on Khromov, *op. cit.*, pp. 498–499, 501.

6 Margaret S. Miller, *The Economic Development of Russia, 1905–14* (London: P. S. King & Son, 1926), pp. 169–170.

In order to influence the economic development of the country, the government might divert collections for specific developmental measures or modify the tax structure to encourage selected economic activities. The extent to which the government resorted to both these courses can be traced in the expenditures during the following decades and in the effect of alterations in tax bases. Another influential factor was the degree to which the state refrained from interference (in 1905–14, and 1921–26, for example) or withdrew from an area where it had exercised restraint (labor policy and labor organization), or by its currency and fiscal policy permitted private development where it did not publicly intervene. Russian currency stabilization or other monetary policy, however, has been a secondary influence and determined by the requirements of other policy decisions.

From 1890 to 1913

Since a major part of the Russian national income was derived from agriculture, ready and mobile capital was not plentiful. Private resources were limited, and private holders were unwilling or unable to advance major investment funds. At the same time Russian consumers were dependent on the importation of manufactured goods because of the poor development of domestic industry. Agricultural consumers and landowners dependent on the export of grain favored free trade or low customs duties, to avert increasing prices of imported manufactured goods. As long as this policy continued (protective measures were introduced by the tariff of 1877), Witte's statement of Russia's economic position was essentially incontrovertible: "The economic relations of Russia with western Europe are fully comparable to the relations of colonial countries with their metropolises." [7] In the political organization of tsarist Russia, hostility of the landlord class to protection was a powerful influence.

Dependence on Foreign Trade

Russian dependence on foreign trade was the result of several factors. First, an important part of the national debt (estimated at as much as 75 percent [8]) was held abroad, and the service on it had largely

[7] Theodore H. Von Laue, "A Secret Memorandum of Sergei Witte on the Industrialization of Russia," *Journal of Modern History*, 26:66 (March 1954).

[8] See Miller, *op. cit.*, p. 121.

to be met in gold. Gold did not circulate in Russia and the paper ruble suffered from a heavy discount abroad. To avoid a ruinous drain on the treasury, a policy of collecting customs duties in gold at the frontier had been adopted; this in itself substantially increased the amount of duties without changing the rates. Second, the government met budget deficits through foreign borrowing. Capital for railroad development had also been raised abroad. It was essential for the government, therefore, not only that foreign trade be maintained, but that a favorable balance be achieved. Between 1882 and 1913 Russia had such a favorable trade balance in every year except 1899.[9]

Russian exports throughout this period were chiefly agricultural and consisted primarily of grain. In 1890 grain accounted for 49 percent of the value of all exports; next in value were flax and "forest products," each of which accounted for about 8 percent. Until 1911 grain continued to account annually for 46–52 percent of the value of all exports, except in the years following crop failures (34 percent in 1892, 41.5 percent in 1899, etc.) [10] It is an important indicator of government policy that the level of grain exports remained high, despite famine conditions among the peasantry in years following partial or total crop failure over extended regions. The landlords, whose estates were the source of most of the exportable surplus in these years, did not profit more; rather the peasants suffered more. For example, government expenditures to combat famine and cholera in 1891 (when the harvest was more than 380 million bushels short of that in 1890) and 1892 reached about 150 million rubles, but grain to the value of 165 million rubles (paper) was exported in 1892 and the favorable balance maintained.

An even more striking demonstration of the extent to which the Russian government used agriculture to support the level of foreign exchange is provided by the level of grain consumption per capita. Russia was not an importer of grain during this period; the per capita share of the harvest in 1883 *after* deduction of exports for that year was approximately 18 poods. In 1897 it was 14, in 1906 it was 13, and in 1912, 14 again. In 1912 the value of grain exports fell to 36.3 percent of the total value of exports, the lowest since the crop failure of 1892.[11] In relation to the basic role of cereals in the Russian peasant

[9] Khromov, *op. cit.*, pp. 469–471.
[10] *Ibid.*, pp. 474–475.
[11] Calculations based on *Finansy Rossii*, Table 21; Khromov, *op. cit.*, pp. 452–455, 474–475; Miller, *op. cit.*, pp. 48–49.

diet, the substantial export trade was at the price of a decline of more than 20 percent in per capita domestic consumption.

Between 1895 and 1912 the grain harvest had increased from 2,681 millions of poods to 3,778 millions. With the exception of the bumper harvest of 1913 (4,240 millions of poods), the 1912 harvest and the 3,848 millions of poods collected in 1909 represented a high volume of production. While the grain harvest increased by 40 percent, however, the population of the empire increased by about 35 percent. Interestingly enough, the total numbers of cattle, poultry, and hogs changed very little between 1897 and 1914, and Russian food supplies were not supplemented by heavy imports of livestock products.[12] The increase in grain production was largely the result of increasing numbers of cultivators rather than of significant advances in technique. The state's contribution to the increase came primarily from its land policy after 1890, and from its efforts to emancipate the more productive peasant element from the drag of communal tenure in the mir after 1906.

Land Policy

The government held lands of enormous extent in Siberia and in the southeastern areas recently added to the empire—for the most part unsettled. Before 1892 the government generally had no extensive colonization program. There was a serious problem of population pressure on the land in the long-settled provinces of central European Russia, partly because of its primitive agricultural technique, partly because of the small size of allotments for cultivation following the Emancipation. Colonization was thought of only in terms of relieving the agrarian problem of central European Russia. With the building of railroads into the eastern territories, however, the colonization of the land along the routes and the development of production in the new lands became more important, especially since the annual natural increase of the population in the central provinces was equal to the losses through migration.

The bad harvests of the early 1890's, particularly in the Volga region, stimulated a spontaneous peasant colonization movement. Insofar as the government had a policy for Siberian emigration, it was inclined to be restrictive, but the officials at the border failed to enforce the ban on settlers rigorously. The number of new colonists increased

---

[12] Khromov, *op. cit.*, pp. 466–467, 478–479.

from 48,776 in 1890 to 87,432 in 1891 and 92,146 in 1892.[13] It declined in the next two years, but government policy was altered to regularize the process rather than to check it. In 1892 the Committee on the Trans-Siberian Railway was established; among its functions, in addition to planning the railroad, was the preparation of lands for colonists. Construction began in 1894 and greatly shortened the duration and the difficulty of the emigrants' journey. In 1895, 120,000 colonists were admitted, and in 1896 more than 202,000. In 1897 the number was cut to about 86,000 by a specific government prohibition—the number of colonists was outrunning the ability of government agencies to survey and prepare allotments for them. But there were 205,645 in 1898, 223,981 in 1899, and 219,263 in 1900. The numbers declined thereafter, reaching a low point during the war with Japan, when the Trans-Siberian Railway was fully occupied with movement of troops and supplies. Furthermore, the revolutionary threats of 1902 and the years immediately following apparently led many peasants in European Russia to hope that they might receive more land at home, thus causing a temporary suspension of the pressure to move to the virgin lands in the east. The dashing of these hopes after 1906 was followed by a resurgence of colonization, which reached a peak of over 664,000 in 1908.

The movement of surplus population from the central provinces was subsidized by the state, at first indirectly and then directly. In 1894 the Trans-Siberian set fairly low rates for the transportation of colonists and their baggage. The government set up a procedure for selecting the point of immigration by requiring prospective colonists to send an advance agent for inspection. One agent might select locations for several parties, of course, but his expenses were a part of the cost of colonization. Ultimately the state provided a series of subsidies: for the trip, for building a preliminary shelter for the first winter, and for public works (roads, irrigation, or amelioration), as well as subsidies in kind for seed or stock. By 1903 the amounts were running to 400 rubles per household in the Amur region, between 250 and 400 rubles in the Transbaikal region, and 250 rubles in other parts of Asia. The trip costs were usually nonreimbursable. Even so, the subsidies con-

---

[13] Vladimir Sineokow, *La colonisation russe en asie* (Paris, 1929), pp. 91ff. Donald W. Treadgold, *The Great Siberian Migration: Government and Peasant in Resettlement from Emancipation to the First World War* (Princeton: Princeton University Press, 1957) was published after this paper was written, and contains a thorough discussion of land and colonization policy.

stituted a heavy burden on the rural economy. After the revolutionary movement of 1905 most or all of the subsidies were nonreimbursable and amounted to public assistance, which often had an enervating effect rather than stimulating repayment and consequent gain in production.

The so-called Stolypin land settlement program after 1906 was directed not so much at increasing the amount of land under peasant cultivation as at favoring the more productive peasants in the redistribution of land. The basic assumption was that by freeing peasants from the collective responsibility feature of the mir and by consolidating holdings, the efficiency of some peasant farming would be improved, while the less efficient producer would be driven off the land altogether. The wasteful and time-consuming strip system would be eliminated, and individual enterprise would be free to introduce new techniques or mechanization without the brake of the commune and its least-common-denominator level of operation. Since the program was in effect scarcely a decade, and was carried through gradually and on a permissive rather than a forced basis, the results were limited. It is estimated that the 13 or 14 million peasant holdings could be classified roughly in the following categories at the outbreak of war in 1914: 5 million in unchanged repartitional tenure; 1.3 million covered by the arbitrary dissolution law of 1910 but not actually in operation; 1.7 million partially individualized under the same law; 4.3 million with fully established hereditary title but still in strip; and 1.3 million partly or fully consolidated.[14]

To facilitate the changes in peasant holdings envisaged by the Stolypin program, the operations of the Peasant Bank were changed. During the decade 1895–1905 the Bank sold a total of some 504 estates amounting to an area of 961,000 dessiatines, which had been bought chiefly from landlord owners. Its capital was increased and its activities expanded after 1905. In 1906 many landowners unloaded property, and the Bank handled more acreage than in the entire preceding decade—700 estates of 1,144,000 dessiatines. In 1907, however, the Bank handled 1,191,000 parcels or a total of 1,520,000 dessiatines; during 1906–15 it sold 3,257,000 estates or a total of 4,326,000 dessiatines.[15] It is evident that in the latter period the transactions primarily involved subsistence allotments, and reflect the redistribution under the

[14] Geroid T. Robinson, *Rural Russia under the Old Regime* (New York: Longmans, Green and Company, 1932), pp. 226–227.

[15] Lyashchenko, *op. cit.*, p. 749.

Stolypin program by which the richer peasants were buying out the poorer in the dissolving communes. If 1,258,000 dessiatines transferred by the state are included, the Bank disposed of about 6,400,000 dessiatines between 1895 and 1915. Since the peasants held over 116,000,000 dessiatines of land, the Bank's activities affected only a small percentage of peasants and of peasant lands: approximately 10 percent of households acquired full private title to consolidated allotments. There was undoubtedly some net gain, since surveys conducted by the government indicated that, whereas many peasants sold out and became wage earners, one third to one half of those selling did so in order to settle in new areas on better and more independent terms, as in Siberia.[16]

None of these measures was directed at the root of the agricultural difficulties in Russia; in view of the political power of the landlord class, probably no thorough attack on the land problem was feasible. In general, the colonization program, the Stolypin measures, and the activities of the Peasant Bank merely made more land available for cultivation by the peasants without modifying their cultivating technique. The total amounts of land held by landlord and peasant classes respectively were not extensively changed, and since the bulk of the landlords' land was cultivated by peasants the state program was simply shoring up the old society.

Granted that the state did not directly contribute to the agricultural sector, on which most of the national income depended, did government policy contribute indirectly through facilitating mechanization or internal improvements in communication and transport? The state's policy of maintaining a favorable balance of trade was criticized on the ground that the protective tariff tied the peasantry to primitive methods of production by keeping the cost of agricultural machinery high. In general, the cost of manufactured goods was high as a consequence of the tariff policy, and this raised the cost of living, impoverishing the peasant to the point where he could not maintain livestock, which further reduced his production and deprived him of necessary manure for his plot.

Tariff Policy

The state's tariff policy was plainly guided by the interest in protection rather than revenue. Witte argued vigorously for the policy

[16] *Ibid.*, p. 750,

and claimed that the sacrifices it required were justified by tangible results.[17] After the Crimean War Russia had moved toward free trade until 1876, under the influence of the thesis that Russia should remain agricultural and import manufactured goods. Imports rose but revenue did not rise correspondingly, and the period after 1877 was marked by a steady increase in protective rates, intended to foster native industry. The tariff was levied on finished goods to protect native manufacturing, since the latter employed imported materials. During the 1880's a satisfactory rate of growth in native manufacturing became evident, but there was not a corresponding growth in extractive industry and production of raw materials. Until late in the nineteenth century most iron production in Russia was still based on charcoal fuel processes because the working ore fields were near forests. The fields of southern Russia, where coal and iron ore were found in close proximity, were not opened until 1869 (and by Englishmen), under the stimulus of contracts for rails at high prices. The charcoal process, whose heavy labor demands were supported by the system of serfdom, was not abandoned until after the Emancipation and the growth of railroads. Ural iron enjoyed the advantage of cheap river transport—during the navigation season—until rail lines were able, by about 1890, to bring the more modern and efficient southern works into competition.

The protective purpose of the tariff is evident in the discriminative rates under the schedules of 1891. For example, to encourage the production of native sulphur and the manufacture of sulphuric acid for the chemical industry, a duty on raw sulphur was imposed. But since the major deposits in the empire were in the Caspian regions and the cost of transport to any but the southern provinces was excessive, the tariff was 5 kopecks per pood on imports through the Black Sea frontier, and only 2 kopecks per pood on the other frontiers. This was supposed to protect the region of the natural internal market without unduly burdening the chemical industry in other regions.[18] Another type of schedule is illustrated by the rates on wool. Before the 1880's the duty on raw wool, combed wool, and wool tissues had been the same, and the import of combed wool had increased. In order that spinning mills should not be dependent on foreign half-finished goods, and to encourage native wool production, the schedule was changed. The 1891 schedule placed a duty of 2 rubles per pood on raw wool,

[17] Von Laue, *op. cit.*, p. 67.
[18] *The Industries of Russia,* Vol. I, p. 436.

5.5 rubles per pood on combed wool, and 9 rubles per pood on wool tissues.[19] The industrial policy behind the 1891 tariff, therefore, was to foster Russian industry at all stages—production of raw materials, half-finished materials, and manufactured goods—and thus to add new sources of wages and increase the buying capacity of the country.

Although tariff policy after 1891 protected a native industry which was woefully inadequate for providing cheap manufactured goods for home consumption, and was criticized for keeping prices high, Witte saw it as a creative measure if used in conjunction with foreign capital. Behind the tariff barrier foreign capital could be used to develop industry more quickly than would have been possible with Russian resources alone. Any obstructions to the flow of foreign capital would merely delay the maturing of a powerful industrial establishment and prolong the burden imposed on the populace by high prices for manufactured goods.[20]

Use of Foreign Capital

The assumption in most writing about Russian economic development before 1914, both by Witte and others who believed in the industrialization of the economy, was that Russia could not develop industry in a reasonable time without extensive foreign assistance in capital, technique, and equipment. Those who made this assumption failed to envisage the degree of coercion that post-World War I governments were able and willing to exercise on their peoples. Nevertheless, whether foreign capital could play the role expected of it in the development of the Russian economy remains a legitimate question.

Witte estimated in 1899 that the accumulation of recorded savings in Russia ran at the rate of 200 million rubles per year, of which 130 million went into land operations and was therefore not available for private investment in railroad or industrial development.[21] In the decade since 1887 imported foreign capital had amounted to 376 million rubles, and the more recent years accounted for substantial parts of the total. In 1896, 92 million rubles of foreign capital was imported; in 1897, 77 million rubles. Most of these funds went for the establishment of foreign corporations in Russia, and a small part for investment in Russian joint stock companies. The foreign capital for in-

[19] *Ibid.*, p. 438.
[20] Von Laue, *op. cit.*, p. 73.
[21] *Ibid.*, p. 68.

vestment in Russian industry at that time was larger than the domestic capital for investment in the same part of the economy. To these figures should probably be added the amounts of imported capital goods, i.e., goods long protected by the tariff but still required by producers rather than consumers in Russia—98 million rubles of imported capital goods in 1896, and 82 million in 1897.

The contribution made by foreign capital to Russian development appears significant in these terms, but it appears less significant when Russian government operations are taken into account. For construction and improvement of railroads the government spent 132,358,000 rubles in 1896 and 130,671,000 rubles in 1897.[22] The alcohol monopoly and railways were the two main government enterprises; subsidies to private railroads, the sums for purchase of private railroads to add to the state operation, and funds for investment in distilling facilities also would be properly included in the public investment in the economy. The fact was that private capital, whether domestic or foreign, was not sufficient for adequate industrialization of the Russian economy. Even with government participation the rate of growth was moderate; between 1900 and 1913 the increase in national income (figures are available for European Russia only) amounted to 79.4 percent.[23]

Negative Aspects of Government Policy

The issue of coercion is relevant in assessing this rate of growth since the role of government in economic development includes negative as well as positive features. The government refrained from taking steps to force the redistribution of wealth, whether by income tax or other means, or to compel a major shift of wealth from agriculture to industry. Social and political organization may constitute a real barrier to economic development; the primary requirement always for increased wealth is a type of society conditioned to produce it. Russian society was not adapted to the pattern of European industrial society at the beginning of the twentieth century, and it cannot be said that the government's general policy was conducive to the creation of such a society. Between 1903 and 1913 the budgetary category of educational and productive expenditures did increase by 146 percent, which exceeded even the increase in national defense expenditure (77 per-

22 Khromov, op. cit., p. 522.
23 Lyashchenko, op. cit., p. 698.

cent). But in absolute amounts nearly as much was spent in 1913 in the former category for the department of agriculture and for land settlement (135,800,000 rubles) as for the ministry of education (143,-000,000 rubles); and the educational and productive expenditures remained only 15.5 percent of the total government expenditures.[24] The general and technical education on a mass scale required to diffuse the skills necessary for modern industrial society was simply not available in prewar Russia.

Even in newly added frontier lands, as in Turkestan where the government took an active interest because of the importance of a domestic supply of cotton for the textile industry, production increased in spite of the handicaps of local social organization rather than because of changes imposed by the government. In 1890, 71 percent of cotton worked in Russian mills was foreign, and not until after 1907 was Russian cotton 50 percent or more of all cotton worked; 80 percent of domestic cotton came from Turkestan.[25] The government contributed to this development by (1) securing the introduction of more productive American types in place of native cotton plants; (2) constructing railways to enable Turkestan cotton to be marketed in European Russia (the Transcaspian Railroad to Tashkent in 1898, and the Tashkent-Orenburg Railroad in 1906, the latter removing the necessity of transshipment by the Caspian Sea); and (3) imposing a tariff that provided protection for domestic growers. The rate of 4.15 rubles per pood, on the basis of 1909 prices, indicates that about 75 percent of the revenue went to equalize costs, which were high for Turkestan cotton because of more primitive technology, the requirements of irrigation, and long overland transport, and about 25 percent remained as a bonus to growers.

Government policy did little, however, to alter the weaknesses that afflicted cotton production in Turkestan because of its local social organization and forms of land tenure. Cultivation was by individual peasant labor on very small holdings. The infinitesimal size of plots precluded crop rotation and made the peasants dependent on cash crops, while the pattern of landholding made machinery impractical and prohibitively expensive. Dependent on a cash crop, the peasant required credit to operate in a money instead of a natural economy, and

[24] Khromov, op. cit., pp. 527–529; and A. M. Michelson and others, Russian Public Finance during the War (New Haven: Yale University Press, 1928), pp. 64–65.

[25] Khromov, op. cit., pp. 460–461; John Whitman, "Turkestan Cotton in Imperial Russia," American Slavic and East European Review, 15:198 (April 1956).

fell easily into the hands of the large purchasing establishments that bought the crop in Turkestan for processing in Russia.[26] Without a system of government credit for the peasants, to keep credit charges down to the level available to the cotton marketing firms or speculators, and without any industrial development to offer Turkestan peasants alternative employment, the state did nothing to change a pattern of social organization that affected economic growth negatively as much as state-built railways affected it positively. The acme of this exploitation of a colonial area of the tsarist empire came after the outbreak of war in 1914, when a state Committee of Cotton Supply, whose members were manufacturers and traders, set a procurement price in mid-1915 below production costs. In 1916 a low price was again set after planting. In 1917 the peasant response was to cut planting by 200,000 dessiatines (from the 1915 high of 524,000 dessiatines).[27]

In the long run, economic development must come from native saving. If domestic capital in large quantities cannot be secured, any development program has failed to produce one of the essential features of an advanced industrial economy. Although studies of Russian industrial growth show an impressive rate of about 7–8 percent per year in the 1890's, and 6 percent per year from 1907 to 1913, this development came at the expense of the level of living and the rate of growth in agriculture, lagged in absolute terms far behind that of other large industrial countries, and was heavily concentrated on military power rather than welfare. By 1913, the last "normal" year of the tsarist regime, the level of consumption of industrial products was still extremely low. Per capita income had increased since the beginning of the century, but agriculture continued to be the chief source. Per capita consumption of metal, sugar, and other goods was a fraction of what it was in such countries as the United States, Great Britain, or Germany, and the normal per capita reserve of goods was very low.[28]

Thus the fruits of economic development were not particularly sweet as a result of the policies followed by the state over nearly 25 years. In 1913 half of the ordinary revenue of the state came from the liquor monopoly and operation of the railroads (see Table 2). The national debt had grown—almost in step with the rising national income—

26 Whitman, op. cit., pp. 197–200.

27 Ibid., p. 203.

28 S. O. Zagorsky, State Control of Industry in Russia during the War (New Haven: Yale University Press, 1928), p. 18.

TABLE 2. IMPERIAL REVENUES BY SOURCE, 1913

In thousands of rubles

Ordinary	
Direct taxes (largest item, state tax on industry: 150,118)	272,517
Excise taxes (largest item, customs: 352,917)	708,101
Duties, licenses, fees	231,230
State monopolies (largest item, spirits: 899,299)	1,024,883
State property and enterprises (largest item, railroads: 813,604)	1,043,740
Alienation of state properties	2,858
Redemption payments	1,194
Compensation for expenses from state treasury (payments by railway companies, etc.)	116,677
Other income	16,160
Total ordinary	3,417,360
Total extraordinary	13,845

Source: Based on Khromov, *op. cit.*, pp. 506–507, 510–511, 513.

from 6,392 million rubles in 1901 to 9,055 million rubles in 1909. By 1913 it had been reduced to 8,824 million rubles, and Russia stood second among the nations of the world in absolute amount of national debt.[29] In amount of payments per year on service of the debt, however, Russia was first; in 1913 this ran to 424,378,000 rubles. The amount of Russian debt held abroad slightly exceeded the amount held at home.

EFFECTS OF WAR AND REVOLUTION

An economy such as that of Russia in 1914 was peculiarly vulnerable to the disruption of war. Since half the national debt was already held abroad, one third of the capital of all joint stock companies was foreign, certain industries were dependent on imports, and half the budget revenue was derived from the operation of state railroads and a liquor monopoly, the Russian economy had to undergo drastic change when foreign ties were broken by the outbreak of the war. Even so, Russia secured 7,788 million rubles in foreign credits during the war years, out of a total of some 25 billion rubles of war debt accumulated up to 1917.[30]

It is, however, in a sense irrelevant to point out the vulnerability of the state's program of economic development to war conditions, for we are mainly concerned with whether the general pattern of domi-

[29] Khromov, *op. cit.*, p. 375.
[30] Michelson and others, *op. cit.*, pp. 320–322.

nant, autonomous, expansionist development was continued or modified under the conditions of the war years, and whether the government took steps to remedy the weaknesses of its prewar policy.

At the outset of the war the sale of alcoholic drinks was prohibited, and the lucrative state monopoly on distilling was abandoned. This entailed an immediate loss of revenue which had to be made up by increases in excise taxes and taxes on commerce and industry. The state railway operation continued to show a paper profit, but a large part of railroad business was the movement of troops and supplies, which was charged to other government accounts. In short, the main methods of raising revenue were not changed; continued reliance on the same indirect taxes provided sufficient revenue by 1917 to balance the ordinary budget because of somewhat increased rates and increasing collections. With the wartime growth and inflation, consumer demand increased and a substantial part of income went for luxury as well as consumption items. The result was a budget for the revolutionary year 1917 that estimated receipts approximating those of 1913.[31] Extraordinary expenditures and the balance for the ordinary budget were met by loans.

The only new tax of major importance was the income tax, and this was not passed until 1916 and did not become operative until 1917.[32] There was no revenue from it, therefore, until after the overthrow of the tsarist regime. The significance of socialist parties in the provisional government, especially after May 1917, led to the adoption of enormously increased rates for the new tax. It is somewhat paradoxical that when the traditional Russian reliance on indirect taxes was justified to some extent by the pattern of spending of wartime incomes, the political changes made necessary a "soak the rich" tax which seemed unlikely to effect a major increase in revenue. The optimistic estimate of 200 million rubles from the income tax, with its almost confiscatory rates on joint stock companies and high incomes of individuals, was a fairly small percentage of the 3.5 billion ruble revenue of the ordinary budget, although more than sufficient to balance the anticipated deficit.

From 1890 until the middle of 1917 the major decisions on the direction of the economy and the channeling of investment had been made in the last analysis by public authority. Government policy on the

[31] *Ibid.,* pp. 189–190.

[32] There was considerable discussion in print, during the 1890's and after the revolution of 1905, about the possibilities of an income tax.

protective tariff, on the maintenance of the favorable trade balance (which broke down only with the outbreak of the war), on land and colonization, on railroad building and defense, was the determining factor. The government was the largest customer for an important part of heavy industry, whose growth it fostered above consumer industry by encouragement of foreign capital investment and by restriction of labor. But except in certain fields, such as railroads, distilling, and some forest and mineral exploitation, the operation of the economy was private, not public. The character of the political organization of Russia may have meant that the decisions were arbitrary and favored certain classes of the population, but progress in improving the comparatively feeble economic development is nonetheless traceable to state initiative. That the state's policy of economic development did not satisfy the demands of a majority of the population would be irrelevant if it were not for the fact that the dissatisfaction led to political change and an alteration in the pattern of development. It is not clear whether without state pressure the rate of saving in the primitive Russian economy would have been greater, or the rate of foreign investment higher; but a higher rate of voluntary saving was not likely in a society where the level of living was so low that the average income was inadequate even for necessities.

The full passage of economic decision-making from private to public hands followed the second, or Bolshevik, revolution of 1917. The new regime proved in the end to be not less but more arbitrary than the tsarist; and state decisions on economic development prevailed just as in tsarist times, without regard to an educated and independently expressed public opinion concerning what was in the public interest. But the new Soviet regime did introduce the logical extreme of the policy the state had followed before: the Soviet regime eventually controlled economic development in the interest of defense and industrialization not merely indirectly by protective policy and purchases, but directly by public ownership and operation of all forms of productive property except land. In the case of land, the policy of indirection remained; but the willingness of the Soviet regime to coerce its populace up to the limits of security for the regime and its superior ingenuity in applying coercion led to a far more rapid rate of development than the program of the tsarist regime.

It is not clear that the Soviet regime could have limited consumer sovereignty and freedom of choice as it did without the circumstances of war and civil war to 1920 and a carefully nurtured fear of war

thereafter. Once again the combination of feeble economic development, heavy demands of the state on the people, and the conception
of the state as proprietor worked toward the adoption of public rather
than private control. The destructiveness of World War I and the
civil war in Russia is well known, and the extremely low level of both
agricultural and industrial production in 1920–21 is an incontrovertible fact, regardless of argument over the responsibility of the
Soviet regime's policies in bringing about the decline. Nevertheless,
the needs of defending the country against foreign invasion played
into the hands of the Bolshevik leaders in their effort to overcome the
low level of productivity, to make heavy exactions on the populace for
defense purposes, and to establish state proprietorship for all forms
of productive property in Russia.

At the outset of the revolution the Soviet regime proceeded toward
a nationalization, on paper, of productive property. The operation of
nationalized property in the beginning depended on local control.
From 1918 to 1939 there was a progressive centralization of public
control and operation of the economy. In this process the only major
departure of the Soviet regime from the pattern followed by the
tsarist regime was the strengthening of the "dominant" nature of the
development, and the effort to dispense with foreign capital.

To begin with, the Soviet regime cancelled all state debts, including
guaranties of loans made by other institutions, and in 1919 all loans
and debts of zemstvo and municipal units from the tsarist period.
The cancellation of the state debt, especially the foreign debt, immediately removed one of the largest requirements of former state budgets
—service on the national debt. At the same time, to be sure, the step
closed off all foreign sources of capital for some time. Second, the
Bolsheviks inaugurated a program of paper money inflation, which
practically destroyed the utility of those prewar taxes whose collection
was attempted. Until 1921 the Soviet regime, properly speaking, had
no budget that could be compared with tsarist budgets.

The most important source of state revenue during the civil war
period, consequently, was the collection of agricultural produce. This
was supposed to be in exchange for manufactured goods, but of these
the state soon had almost none because of the decline in production.
Financing of defense and production needs during the civil war was
by confiscation of all peasant produce over the minimum requirements
of peasant consumption. As already pointed out, the tsarist policy had
reduced per capita grain consumption from the 19 poods per capita

considered desirable in the 1880's to about 14 poods per capita before the war. In 1920–21 consumption dropped to an average of about 11 poods per capita.[33] It was only when this level had been reached, with attendant famine in many districts because of the state's coercive collection to supply urban districts regardless of peasant requirements, and widespread passive resistance by the peasants, that the Soviet regime returned to more normal budgeting and a money accounting.

The New Economic Policy

The New Economic Policy (NEP) involved a temporary return to securing government revenue through money taxation on economic activity. Since agricultural activity was the most readily susceptible to restoration—the principal requirement was that the state promise to leave the cultivator a reasonable portion of his harvest—the major concession was the abandonment of requisitioning and the levy of a tax in kind, announced in advance of sowing. The surplus could be traded, which would also introduce an economic activity subject to tax, since trade had virtually disappeared under the civil war conditions. Indispensable for the resumption of economic activity was state initiative. In stabilizing the currency the state undertook to limit the free printing of paper rubles by which cash needs had been met, and introduced more rigid control of expenditure to reduce the deficit. Achievement of a favorable balance of trade also was required for successful stabilization of the currency.

While the NEP measures involved a partial return to private as against public decision-making on economic development, the extent of the transfer should not be exaggerated. It was true that the peasant could decide whether and how much to plant. Even in the period of most extreme requisitioning, he had held the power of deciding whether to plant; under the NEP, how much to plant was actually determined by the state when it stipulated the amount of tax in kind. The national income in 1921 was little more than one third that in 1913, and an overwhelming proportion of it was derived from agriculture; industry contributed only half its prewar proportion.[34] But the rapid restoration of a sizable budget, combined with the direct control retained in

[33] Gregory Y. Sokolnikov and others, *Soviet Policy in Public Finance, 1917–1928* (Stanford: Stanford University Press, 1931), p. 87.

[34] Serge N. Prokopovicz, *Histoire économique de l'URSS* (Paris: Au Portulan, 1952), pp. 582–583.

industry and the indirect control in agriculture, left basic decisions in public hands.

It is significant that under the NEP the Soviet regime relied substantially on the same sources of income used by the tsarist regime. The excise tax produced the most revenue of any item in the state budget.[35] This is unavoidable so long as the holding of property is not widely diffused, and the average income is low. The categories that produced the chief income were the same as before the war: taxes on alcoholic beverages, sugar, tobacco, salt, and petroleum products. The role played by customs duties in state revenue was slightly altered by the state monopoly of foreign trade. The cheapness of foreign manufactured goods compared with Russian was offset by the government's retention of import duties and regulation of importing concerns through centralized control of licenses and exchange. Foodstuffs no longer constituted the major part of exports. Commercial agriculture was largely peasant agriculture after the revolution, and as long as the peasant controlled the distribution of his surplus he preferred to eat better rather than to market more exportable grain. Imports in general remained the same—manufactured and semifinished goods.

Direct taxes constituted the lesser part of the budget revenue. The most important of these was the agricultural tax, which as a money tax after 1924 was in fact an income-property tax on peasants. It was based on a complicated assessment of the income-producing value of peasant property. The income tax proper was collected from urban residents and business enterprises. Since gross production in private hands dropped from about 25 percent of all production in 1923–24 to 18 percent in 1926–27, the income tax was not a particularly large item. Socialized state enterprises made substantial contributions in the form of deduction from profits, and through the craft tax, a graduated licensing and equalization tax.[36]

Not until 1926 did the state budgets exceed those of 1913. This achievement, however, had considerable meaning for the development of the economy. In view of the nationalization of 80 percent of the industrial economy, the paucity of state financing of agriculture, and the reduced expense of servicing the national debt,[37] an important

---

[35] Franklyn D. Holzman, *Soviet Taxation: The Fiscal and Monetary Problems of a Planned Economy* (Cambridge: Harvard University Press, 1955), p. 114.

[36] *Ibid.*, pp. 112–113.

[37] The NEP saw a return to state loans and some national debt; loans were very short-term and remained small in amount until 1927 (*ibid.*, p. 203).

part of the budget went into investment in productive enterprise. After the 1923 decree on trusts, state enterprises were forced to operate on a money accounting basis, but they were established with capital from socialized sources, and a high percentage of investment in industry was state investment during the NEP. Investment in agriculture and in trade continued to be largely private, and therefore independent of direct control by the state. By 1926–27, when the national income was estimated to have reached the prewar level, the government decided to resume the effort to control all productive property rather than the limited part represented by industry. Without large-scale foreign investment, the further expansion of the Soviet economy required heavy exactions from the populace, and particularly from the agricultural sector, to provide capital. The participation of the state in the economy consequently underwent a phase of intensification.

INTENSIFICATION OF STATE ECONOMIC ACTIVITY

The level of state participation in economic development had fluctuated considerably after 1890. On the one hand, the government had encouraged or financed the establishment of new enterprises (including colonization and new agricultural enterprise) and then left them to operate on their own. On the other hand, it had operated directly enterprises such as railroads, distilling, and communications. The latter tendency had been enhanced during the war by the inevitable expansion of control over procurement and distribution of vital materials, such as fuel.

The Bolsheviks, in theory, preferred complete direct operation of the economy by the state. In practice they discovered this was not feasible, for lack of the necessary administrative apparatus. Experimental attempts to develop the necessary apparatus meant continual fluctuation in the level of state operation. During the civil war complete control failed because the administrative machinery inherited from the previous regime was inadequate and there was not time to develop a new one. The resulting economic collapse meant that the primary problem of the NEP was the resumption of economic processes. Political considerations had to be secondary until about 1926, when recovery to approximately prewar levels was achieved—"normalcy" or its equivalent by Russian experience.

Once the economic processes had been resumed, the primacy of political considerations could be reinstituted. The NEP concession had restored some respect for individual rights as against the total claims of the state; but the concession was one of expediency, not one of principle. It became evident, once the level of "normalcy" was restored, that further development of production required either continued lifting of restraints on individual and private entrepreneurial initiative, or intensification of state pressure.

Russian experience since the late nineteenth century promised very dubious returns from adoption of the first alternative. In a predominantly peasant economy capital accumulation might be expected to be slow, and industrial development would again become heavily dependent on foreign capital and imports. The lessons of the World War and the intervention period, for the Bolshevik leadership, were many: in comparison with the other leading industrial states Russia, despite the progress made since 1890, still suffered from relatively feeble economic development; wartime interruptions seriously affected an industrial development tied to foreign sources of supply; in view of the open hostility of the other major governments to the Soviet regime as such, heavy reliance on foreign assistance was either unrealistic or likely to be possible only on terms insuring Russian economic dependence. Left to themselves, the peasants showed considerable unwillingness to make sacrifices for capital accumulation; when manufactured goods were not available—and they were short relative to demand in the NEP period—the peasant did not surrender his produce. Obviously he would produce if consumer goods were available; this would foster the development of consumer industry, but not of heavy and defense industry, which the leaders of the Soviet regime believed to be essential to free them from dependence on the hostile West.

The conflict of interest between the agricultural producer and the security of the Soviet regime could be resolved by conceding more individual rights at the cost of rapid industrial development, or by sacrificing individual rights to the necessity to industrialize at a forced pace. The decision to attempt the latter led to the abandonment of the NEP and the inauguration of extensive economic and administrative reforms after 1928. Capitalism, as developing in trade and in parts of industry during the NEP, might become strong enough to be a political danger if private control of productive property was retained and expanded. The inauguration of the five-year plans signalized the resumption of the Soviet regime's basic offensive against the private ownership of productive property and in behalf of its monopoly by the state. With state proprietorship, industry could be expanded and the numerical weight of the propertyless industrial wage-earner in the population could be increased, without the political menace of expanding private industry. The political danger of peasant proprietorship, even if it were retained, would be diminished as expansion progressed and an increasing proportion of the population shifted from agriculture to industry. The problem in this decision was primarily how to extract surplus produce and labor from agriculture, without repeating the disastrous experience of the peasant strike which had destroyed the requisitioning policy used by the state to finance its program during the civil war.

Collectivization

Although the Soviet regime does not exploit agriculture to pay for foreign capital to the extent the tsarist regime did, the Soviet policy does exploit agriculture to pay for heavy and rapid industrialization, with essentially similar consequences for the peasant. The basis for the first five-year plan was the capital and reserves accumulated, in important degree by agriculture, during the relatively relaxed years of the 1920's. To capitalize on the peasant achievement of agricultural recovery in the 1920's, and to harness peasant productivity for the support of rapid industrialization, the Soviet regime devised the now famous collective farm (kolkhoz). Some experimentation with its form occurred in the early period, but since the 1934 model statute for agricultural artels the general principles have been fixed. The kolkhoz is a producers' cooperative, which has the status of a private corporation in Soviet law, with perpetual-use right in the land, although the ultimate title to land is still vested in the state. Kolkhozes were formed by pooling the land allotments, equipment, and stock of the original members, who then shared in the proceeds from operation of the cooperative. As an added inducement certain categories of peasants, the so-called "rich" peasants, were excluded from the program and their holdings expropriated for the kolkhoz. In the initial program, mechanization of agriculture was intended to accompany collectivization, in order to maintain and even increase the level of productivity reached by the peasants in the 1920's, and to do so with fewer hands. The agricultural labor thus relieved would, of course, be recruited into industry.

If the regime had moved slowly, collectivization might have been accepted without large-scale revolt. Many features of the collective farm in the artel form had been familiar to peasant experience in Russia for generations. Cooperative ownership and restrictions on cultivation were a heritage of the old Russian agrarian commune, the mir. Mechanization, furthermore, added distinct advantages to collective cultivation. But the regime could not move slowly; it depended on agriculture for the capital to pay for industrial equipment—in exports of raw materials exactly as in tsarist days—and for food for an increased number of industrial workers. It also depended on the peasantry to supply recruits, immediately and in quantity, for the new industrial labor force. In effect this, too, was confiscation, because the productive work of the peasant in agriculture was lost when he went into industry, and only after he had gone into industry could he make the machines to replace him in agriculture. The peasants remaining in agriculture were the victims, with an increased load on fewer shoulders. The peasant, faced with loss of his individual plot of land and not supplied with the promised machines in sufficient quantity to secure immediate benefits from mechanization of agriculture, resisted again. Under duress he went into the collective—but as empty-handed as possible. A major casualty (besides human life) was livestock, which the peasant slaughtered rather than contribute to the collective farm.

Concessions to peasant opposition in the early 1930's brought two new features into the artel structure which are essential characteristics of the kolkhoz today. One was the recognition of the members' right to an individual household plot for private cultivation. The Soviet regime has tampered with the size of allotments and from time to time has indirectly restricted exploitation of private cultivation, but it has never touched the right. The household plot is recognized as an essential contribution to peasant subsistence, and its yield is the basis for the personal income tax paid by artel members. The second feature was the workday unit, a complex system of accounting by which the artel determines the individual member's share in the proceeds of joint cultivation. There has been experimentation with this system also; the most notable trend has been toward a highly differentiated level of income, in contrast to the strongly egalitarian character of the prerevolutionary agrarian commune.

The importance of the kolkhoz for the peasant and capital accumulation lay in the relationship of the kolkhoz to the state as owner and operator of most nonagricultural segments of the national economy. During the five-year plan era, just as in the civil war period, the Soviet regime as proprietor tried under the collectivization program to determine how the land should be utilized, what constituted surplus, and how this should be disposed.

The peasant worked for two accounts, his own and that of the state. When he worked on his household allotment his entire time was charged to his own account. When he worked for the kolkhoz his time was divided between his and the state's account in a proportion varying widely among kolkhozes. The peasant sometimes tried to support himself solely on his allotment; to prevent this, legislation requiring minimal standards of kolkhoz work was promulgated. Kolkhoz production went to the state in three principal forms: corporate taxes paid by the kolkhoz; forced, quota sales to the state, at less than market prices, for stock-piling and reserves; and payments for services by the state-operated Machine Tractor Stations (MTS), which owned the bulk of heavy agricultural equipment. Flexibility in the application of these exactions determined whether the pressure on the peasantry was heavy or light. But the pressure was always great enough to insure that the kolkhoz could not meet its obligations without resorting to the advantages of mechanized cultivation and modern crop rotation. Since the means of mechanization were not under the control of the kolkhoz but were retained by the state, the kolkhoz, a private corporation in theory, could not become independent in fact. The annual contract between the kolkhoz and MTS, which provided agronomic and technical advice as well as equipment, became a device for determining planting and crop rotation and, through contract payments, for the extraction of surplus. Thus the major share of kolkhoz production became available to the state for capital purposes. The balance was distributed in cash or in kind to the kolkhoz members and supplemented personal income from the household allotment.

Control by the Ruble

The administrative advantage of the kolkhoz to the Soviet regime is that it can deal with one large unit rather than many individual producers. In industrial organization the system is only superficially different. By retaining control of the operation of heavy industry during the NEP, the state developed a system for administering productive industrial property that could expand with the economy. The Supreme Council of National Economy (VSNKh) administered industry through a descending hierarchy of Chief Administrative Commissions (Glavk), trusts, and individual enterprises. The second decree on trusts in 1927 made enterprises independent, but ended their competition in the public market; they were to operate to fulfill the plan, which replaced competition as an efficiency factor. Each enterprise was chartered as a public corporation with a fixed capital and functioned on a *khozraschet* basis, i.e., a system of economic accounting that showed the effect of management in profit or loss terms.

In the 1930's the Supreme Council of National Economy was superseded by a series of industrial commissariats, each responsible for some major branch of the economy and organized internally on essentially the same basis as the Supreme Council. The principle of *edinonachalie* introduced the concept of a single responsible head of management for each enterprise. Assigning property and capital to a state corporation made possible control of property through accounting methods. Financial statements went to the Commissariat for Finance. The procedure was a device to save bureaucratic personnel for supervision; checkups provide incentive because of management's opportunity to show results in the statements—to call attention to ability as well as incompetence. Investigation is for the purpose of determining whether the planning agency or management is at fault or deserves credit for achievement. In order to keep the *khozraschet* system in operation, a form of tariff for domestic purchasers is maintained. The pegged ruble gives Russian purchasers a profit-and-loss statement advantage over Russian suppliers; if a plant buys in the cheaper foreign market, the management must allocate from its budget a cost amount equal to the difference between the pegged rate and the cost in the Russian market.

After 1928 the state in effect determined allocation, expansion, and limitation of foreign participation, but as a consequence of *edinonachalie* and *khozraschet* removed itself to second-level participation. The state bureaucracy and the budget financing of the economy are a compromise between supervision and regulation of private industry, and direct budget operation of state-owned industry. The financial mechanism for accomplishing economic development is the traditional Russian reliance on indirect taxes borne by consumers.

The total budget revenues show an enormous change between 1928 and 1938, as the state's program of industrial expansion developed (Table 3). The 8.3 billion rubles for 1928–29 is only about double the prerevolutionary level (current rubles in each case); but the 156 billion rubles for 1939 bears no resemblance to any revenue figure before 1928 and reflects the extent to which the state, exercising its monopoly ownership of productive property, was able to expand its budget resources. The pressure on the populace by which this was accomplished is indicated by the decline in total consumption by households from 71.5 percent of gross national product in 1928 to 66.3 percent in 1937. Correspondingly, defense plus gross investment increased from 25.7 percent in 1928 to 30.6 percent in 1937; but the increasing burden of defense is shown by the percentage of gross investment alone—23.2 percent in 1928 and 22.9 percent in 1937.[38]

TABLE 3. SOVIET BUDGETARY REVENUES

Year	Realized receipts (billion rubles)
1928–29	8.3
1929–30	13.0
1931	23.8
1932	31.0
1933	40.2
1934	53.7
1935	67.4
1936	83.8
1937	96.6
1938	127.5
1939	156.0

Source: Franklyn D. Holzman, *Soviet Taxation* (Cambridge: Harvard University Press, 1955), Table 9, p. 57. By permission.

The relative role of direct and indirect taxes is shown in Table 4. Grains, alcohol—the old standby for excise revenue—and sugar produced more than half of the total receipts from the turnover tax.

In industrialization and expansion of the national economy, according to Soviet writers, capital construction played a leading role: "The question of construction has always been for us not only an economic question but also a political one." [39] The rationale of the allocation of investment lies in political considerations of defense, and the development of the heavy industry on which it is based. In a real sense consumer sovereignty ceased to exist in the Soviet Union after 1928; the planning decisions of state authorities determined the varieties and quantities of consumer goods that would be permitted. But even

[38] See Abram Bergson, *Soviet National Income and Product in 1937* (New York: Columbia University Press, 1953); and Oleg Hoeffding, *Soviet National Income and Product in 1928* (New York: Columbia University Press, 1954).

[39] V. M. Molotov, *O stroitelstve i zadachakh stroitelei* (Moscow, 1935), p. 27.

in an authoritarian political structure the extent to which political considerations can be made independently of existing economic conditions is questionable.

TABLE 4. DISTRIBUTION OF ESTIMATED SOVIET TAX RECEIPTS, BY TYPE OF TAX
In billions of rubles

Year	Turnover	Craft and excise	Profits	Other indirect	Direct	Gov't. bonds *	Social ins.	Total
1928–29	–	2.9	3.3	0.8	1.1	0.1	1.2	9.4
1929–30	–	4.6	5.4	1.3	1.1	0.7	1.4	14.5
1931	11.7		6.0	1.1	1.6	1.6	2.2	24.2
1932	19.6		6.6	1.1	2.4	2.4	3.6	35.7
1933	27.0		7.3	1.3	3.5	3.2	4.3	46.6
1934	37.6		6.4	1.5	3.8	3.4	5.7	58.4
1935	52.2		7.8	2.1	3.2	3.8	7.0	76.1
1936	65.8		14.2	2.7	3.8	3.5	8.9	98.9
1937	75.9		16.9	3.3	4.0	4.3	6.6	111.0
1938	80.4		15.7	3.8	5.1	6.1	7.2	118.3
1939	96.9		26.3	4.6	7.0	6.7	7.6	149.1

Source: Franklyn D. Holzman, *Soviet Taxation* (Cambridge: Harvard University Press, 1955), Table 52, p. 252. By permission.
* Holzman argues that the nature of government bonds and the terms of payment —or better, nonpayment—are such that they must be treated as a form of tax.

The consolidated state budget in the Union of Soviet Socialist Republics, under which investment allocation can be centrally controlled even in local budgets, depends heavily on the turnover tax. The budget sets the percentage of collection that may be retained in the individual republics, and this percentage is very much higher in the Kazakh Republic (51.3 percent) than in the Russian Republic (3.5 percent).[40] Officially, the explanation of the varying rates is the interest of the regime in promoting the industrialization of formerly undeveloped regions of the USSR. This is compatible with the party propaganda on the brotherly assistance given to each other by the several nationalities of the union, and with a policy of building up basic industry far from the western frontiers and the historic path of invasion. In fact, the percentage increases in gross output of large-scale industry for certain regions from 1913 to 1937 are impressive. The output for 1937 exceeded that for 1913 by 157 times in the Tadzhik Republic, and by 116 times in the Kirgiz.[41] The actual figures are

[40] *Current Digest of the Soviet Press,* 8 (1):3 (February 15, 1956).

[41] S. S. Balzak, V. F. Vasyutin, and Ya. G. Feigin, eds., American edition ed. by Chauncy D. Harris, *Economic Geography of the USSR* (New York: Macmillan Company, 1949), p. 206.

another matter—in the Tadzhik Republic 1913 production was valued at 1 million rubles, and 1937 production at 157 million rubles, but the latter is not a particularly impressive figure in comparison with those for other industrial areas.

If the percentages of total output in the several regions are compared for 1913 and 1937 (Table 5), it is evident that the great expansion in industrial output was in accordance with an established pattern of distribution. This is not to deny the spectacular expansion of the economy in certain areas, but simply to point out that the great growth in absolute production and the speed of its achievement were not obtained under the Soviet regime by starting in new and undeveloped regions. The decline in the Ukraine's percentage of the nation's industrial output—i.e., in a frontier region in the direct path of invasion—is offset by increased percentages in the Ural and Eastern Siberian regions of the Russian Republic, but this can hardly be called a major relocation. If the distribution is substantially altered now, World War II should be held responsible, not the original planning.

TABLE 5. PERCENTAGE OF GROSS INDUSTRIAL OUTPUT, BY REGIONS, 1913 AND 1937

	1913	1937
Regions of Russian Socialist Federated Soviet Republic	70.7	73.6
European North	1.8	1.8
Northwest and Central	50.5	49.5
Volga	6.2	5.4
North Caucasus and Crimea	4.2	5.2
Urals and Western Siberia	6.1	8.5
Eastern Siberia and Far East	1.9	3.2
Soviet Socialist Republics		
Ukrainian	20.3	17.7
Belorussian	1.1	1.9
Azerbaidzhan	3.6	2.5
Georgian	.5	1.0
Armenian	.15	.2
Turkmen	.32	.28
Uzbek	2.6	1.6
Tadzhik	.09	.17
Kazakh	.54	.9
Kirgiz	.1	.15
Total, USSR	100.	100.

Source: Based on Balzak, Vasyutin, and Feigin, *op. cit.*, Table 17, p. 206. The table gives output in million rubles for large-scale industry, by regions.

In one respect the Soviet regime differed markedly from its predecessor. A systematic effort was made to reduce or eliminate illiteracy, and thus bring the whole population to a level of education which would facilitate economic advance. Furthermore, the state in effect put a bounty on population increase by the financial assistance offered to families with numerous children, and by tax rates discriminatory against bachelors and childless couples. The state also undertook a program of social security for employees of state enterprises, designed to encourage the growth of the industrial labor force at the expense of the agricultural.

Conclusion

In conclusion it may be noted that the Russian experience with expansionist, dominant, induced economic development offers some evidence that the state cannot promote such a program without forcing social change. A vast increase in the extent of the state apparatus accompanied the growth of the economy under the Soviet regime. If one reviews the political activity of the regime that accomplished the increase in industrial production—gross output of large-scale industry in 1937 was more than eight times that in 1913—it is difficult to escape the conclusion that growth of the state apparatus was always a direct prelude to an increase in state intervention in the economy. The effect in agriculture is perhaps the most marked. The postrevolutionary peasantry was not a good market for agricultural machinery. To mechanize Russian agriculture the state forced the creation of the kolkhoz. The original administrative structure of the kolkhoz was relatively simple, but rapidly became more complex. The collective farm is administratively as top-heavy as industry, as it must be if agriculture is to achieve the degree of central planning that is characteristic of industry. The Soviet regime has acted on the logical principle that the peasant is an anachronism and has tried to convert him and his work to factory-type enterprise, with piecework rates and division of labor.

The repressive and regulatory character of the Soviet regime has been dictated (or excused) by the necessity to overcome a once feeble economic development and to control the allocation of resources in what is still an economy of scarcity rather than of abundance for the consumer. From both a theoretical and a practical standpoint an economy of abundance would mean the end of the regime as now constituted, i.e., a rigidly authoritarian machine to maintain a perpetual mobilization against enemies at home and abroad. The justification of the collectivist approach in Russia has been that only that approach could make the insufficient means of production accessible to all.

Whether future development in Russia will continue to follow this pattern is a question that only the foolhardy would attempt to answer. One suggestion, nevertheless, may be hazarded. It is true that with sufficient social cooperation each individual need not own a lawn mower, or washing machine, or automobile. But the entire philosophy of industrial mass production is precisely to make possible a universal individual ownership of all articles of consumption. Therefore, once the mobilization of productive forces has been maintained for a sufficient length of time (without major wars to reduce physical accumulation) for mass production to reach the point where every individual can own his own lawn mower, washing machine, automobile, etc., the pattern of expansionist, dominant, induced development may presumably be modified in one or another particular. Since abundant production would destroy the basic economic necessity for the police state and its mobilization of resources to overcome feeble economic development, the heavy demands made on the populace by the state might in time be relaxed, even if the state continued as traditionally to be the general proprietor of productive property.

5 OPPORTUNITIES, GOVERNMENTS,

AND ECONOMIC DEVELOPMENT

IN MANCHURIA, 1860–1940

Edwin P. Reubens *

The record of Manchuria is a revealing case history of the various roles of the state in promoting or hindering economic development. The history of Manchuria exhibits, in fact, several different "states," operating not only in succession but sometimes also in parallel. Each of these "states" engaged in a distinct *gestalt* of functions: substantially differentiated from the others, diversely related to economic life in negative or permissive or positive ways, and strongly marked with reference to the conditions of the society and the scope of private activity.

Manchuria's growth during the past century may certainly be described as extensive or expansionist development, although the region was not "new and empty" in the same sense as America or Australia before the coming of the white pioneers. And the region's political and economic status during most of that period was distinctly nondominant, being subordinate to foreign powers as well as dependent on foreigners for markets, capital, technology, and immigrant labor. The essential character of the developmental process in Manchuria, however, is not so readily described as either autonomous or induced, and indeed experience casts some doubt on the validity of that twofold classification of the role of the state. For these reasons it seems advisable to state explicitly the model of economic development and the concept of the state that are used in this paper.

The model that is implied by the autonomous vs. induced classification is applicable to "decisions" that "lead to" growth and for which the responsibility is ideally assigned either to government or private parties. It seems more useful here to employ not a "decisions" model of discrete acts, but a process model based on emerging "opportunities."

* The author is indebted to Henry Aubrey, Alexander Eckstein, and Fred Greene for helpful comments on the first draft of this paper.

148

This process model involves five elements: potentialities, means, agents, obstacles, and aims. The potentialities are conceived as existing circumstances of natural resources, population, quality of labor force, markets, terms of exchange, technological knowledge, and the like. The means are operable facilities for exploiting the potentialities in the interest of production, and consist of both directly productive instruments and "overhead" facilities and arrangements. The agents are the natural and artificial persons, including interest groups and government agencies, who carry on economic activity and form state policy in accordance with their powers and commitments. The obstacles include certain lacks (the absence of the corresponding potentialities, means, and agents), certain costs (which may exceed what people will tolerate), and above all the whole socioeconomic structure of the society (which presents a kind of inertia). The aims embody the values and standards of the society in general as well as the special interests of various agents.

In the actual process of economic development, according to this model, the dormant opportunity is activated when various agents, pursuing their own aims, recognize certain potentialities, find or create the means to exploit them, and remove or overcome intervening obstacles. The opportunities are not merely *found;* they arise from the social process, but they arise *creatively,* as innovations which lead to discovery of new materials and rearrangement of old ones. The agents and events of development are therefore only aspects of the entire social process: the process carries along all the elements and is continuously redirected by their interactions.[1]

---

[1] The process model differs not only from the decisions model but also from the usual stimulus-response model; for the process model does not postulate a stimulus that is independent of, and external to, the responding subject. Rather, it emphasizes the ways in which the influences to action, or opportunities, are within the evolving situation. Likewise, the process model does not assume that channels of response are already established, but emphasizes the existence of opportunities to create new means and to remove obstacles. In general terms, the model seeks to unify, in terms of the concept of process, the elements that are left discrete and static in both the decisions model and the stimulus-response model.

The intrinsic character of the development process is a sustained but limited disequilibrium: usually a situation of demand exceeding the current supply of goods and services (both finished items and productive factors), so as to encourage agents to take steps to raise the supply; but in some respects disequilibrium involves an excess of supply over current demand, notably in certain social overhead items, whose supply is not very elastic and therefore must in advance show sufficient idle capacity to reassure the entrepreneur. These disequilibria are subject to a "range

With reference to the role of the state in economic development, the process model seeks to avoid any simple opposition between autonomous development (amounting virtually to laissez faire) and induced development. In the process model there is no distinct "original cause." The state appears as various kinds of agent, dealing with other agents positively or permissively or negatively, in regard to means, obstacles, and aims, as they all bear on potentialities. Thus the state is treated as one agent among many: an institution distinguished from other institutions by certain representative functions on behalf of the whole population, as well as by a limited monopoly of compulsive power; and yet a social conveyance which, like other institutions, expresses certain dominant needs and aims and changes its behavior in accordance with their changes. This paper attempts to show for Manchuria not only the actual roles performed by the state at various times, but also the interrelations of the state with the other agents and the other elements in the process model.

The history of Manchuria up to World War II may be conveniently divided into three principal stages: Stage I, up to about 1860, characterized by a native nomadic civilization gradually overlaid by Chinese influences; Stage II, 1860–1931, marked at first by slow but later by accelerating economic growth, traceable largely to foreign penetrations of the "sphere of influence" type; and Stage III, 1931–41, the "Manchukuo" era of Japanese occupation and rapid industrialization. The experience during each stage may be summarized in the following propositions:

I. During the premodern era in Manchuria, the complicated apparatus of the state was Imperial Chinese at the topmost level and tribal at the bottom level, with an intermediate hierarchy semifeudal in character. At most levels the attitudes of this "state" toward economic development were markedly negative; consequently there were few real economic opportunities, despite the existence of great physical potentialities in the nearly empty lands. Actual development was very limited and very slow.

---

of tolerance" such that if the excess of demand becomes very great, the developmental movement will end in some kind of inflation; whereas if the excess becomes very small, the movement will dwindle away into stability. As long as the disequilibrium persists within the range of tolerance, the process of development will continue. The interaction among the five elements outlined, including public policy, determines whether a limited disequilibrium will persist or will pass the limits into either explosion or collapse.

II. During 1860–1931 the functions of the state were divided among the Chinese, the Russians, and the Japanese, with a lesser share for the British. The attitude of the Chinese authorities toward economic development gradually shifted from negative to permissive, and in very limited respects became positive. Meanwhile, the Russian and Japanese authorities shouldered aside the Chinese government's obstructionism, established permissive conditions in their "zones" of authority, undertook positive but limited action by directly constructing and operating certain facilities (mostly transportation and other forms of social overhead capital), and generally created attractive opportunities for private enterprise. The chief agency in this was the South Manchuria Railway Company, a semi-official Japanese organization. Private action, notably by Japanese businessmen and by Chinese land-companies and immigrant peasants, was vigorous and accounted for the bulk of Manchuria's advance in productive capacity and actual production.

III. During the 1930's the Manchurian state was "Manchukuo," which meant a local Chinese facade with real power in the hands of Japanese, i.e., immediately in the hands of the Kwantung Army, which was loosely responsible to the Tokyo government. With regard to economic development, this decade falls into two periods:

a. The years 1931–37, when the puppet government took very positive developmental action, including direct undertakings in heavy industrial fields, restriction of private enterprise in those fields, and strong influences over many other sectors of the economy;

b. The period following 1937 and running into the war years, when the puppet government intensified its positive action through a Central Plan and directed many lines of production and certain other phases of the economy, but at the same time revised its policy on private enterprise by limiting its own undertakings and offering attractive opportunities to a new group of Japanese capitalists, with whom the authorities set up an uneasy and unstable partnership.

These efforts to accelerate the industrialization of Manchuria brought substantial increases in productive capacity and actual production. But after 1937 Japan's ability to support this development was progressively impaired by political and military actions outside Manchuria, and finally collapsed in 1945. Consequently the full significance of the Manchukuo era in economic terms—as distinguished from political and moral judgments—becomes a matter of speculation dependent on a theory of economic development.

MANCHURIA BEFORE 1860

The first stage of Manchuria's history is significant here chiefly as background for the modern evolution, with its contrasting patterns. The region known to Westerners as Manchuria was called by the Chinese the "Three Eastern Provinces." It lies at the northeastern corner of China Proper and is delimited on the west by Mongolia, on the north and east by Siberia, and on the southeast by Korea. It has access to the ocean via the Yellow Sea. The total area of the three provinces is over 380,000 square miles, nearly equal to that of the states of Washington, Oregon, Idaho, and Montana combined; and if the province of Jehol (taken from Inner Mongolia by the Japanese in 1933 and annexed to their puppet state of Manchukuo) is added, the total area becomes 446,000 square miles (equal to the four states plus half of Wyoming). Manchuria lies in approximately the same latitudes as those states, but its climate is more severe: winters are long and bitterly cold (although not very snowy), whereas summers are short and hot, with moderate rainfall fortunately concentrated during the growing season.

The chief agricultural tract is the rich central Manchurian Plain, drained by the extensive Liao and Sungari river systems. Surrounding this vast plain are uplands suitable for pasture, and mountains which contain the chief timber resources remaining in all China. The mineral resources of Manchuria have proved to be substantial, notably in coal, iron ore, and oil shale; but only a very small fraction of these were known and worked before the foreign penetrations, and some of the richest ore deposits were discovered only shortly before World War II. The demographic penetration of this whole region was mainly by northward migration, chiefly from China Proper. The actual rate of migration was so slow that the total population of Manchuria was estimated to be no more than 14 million in 1900, and only 20 million as late as 1916; in the latter year the over-all density per square mile was only 53 persons, broken down among the three provinces of Liaoning in the south, Kirin in the center, and Heilungchiang in the north, as 133, 63, and 12 persons per square mile, respectively.[2]

For centuries Manchuria had been primarily a land of nomadic tribes whose life followed the familiar and repetitive pattern of herd-

---

[2] These figures are estimates by the South Manchuria Railway Company and like many other Manchurian statistics, especially for the earlier years, are not entirely reliable; different sources give diverse estimates. By way of broad comparison, indi-

ing, hunting, and warfare. Those activities, in differing degree among the Manchus and the Mongols, fixed the ranking of social values and left agriculture, manufacturing, and trading near the bottom of the scale. The complicated social organization was tribal at the lowest levels, quasi-feudal (the "banner" system) in the middle ranks, and topped by military governors appointed by the Manchu emperor in Peking. The structure was static, although the turnover of individual leaders was considerable.

A significant feature of this era was the alternating hostility and tolerance of these native nomadic peoples toward the immigration of the neighboring Chinese, who looked longingly northward from the overcrowded North China valleys. Manchuria was not a land lying passive before the Chinese foreigners. It was not the kind of country that Europeans found in America, Australia, southern Africa, and other regions where the aboriginal population was not only sparse but at a cultural level vastly different from that of the newcomers. On the contrary, the Manchus and Mongols were warlike peoples whose well-organized hordes over the centuries had repeatedly conquered and ruled all or part of China Proper; and who in turn were intermittently conquered by Chinese armies and subjected to pervasive influences from Chinese culture. Consequently, the Chinese peasant migrating to thinly settled Manchuria during the nineteenth century was entering a population containing both friendly Chinese and tolerant or hostile Manchus and Mongols, and an articulated social order not altogether different from his own; in particular, he was seeking a place within a land-tenure system that had already established some kind of property rights over all the available land. The Chinese immigrant was, in early American terminology, not so much a pioneer as a settler—a colonist who acquired his land on long-term contract from a local lord, land company, or other private owner, and settled on the outer edge of an existing community.

When the Manchus conquered the imperial throne of China in 1644, they sought to isolate their land of origin and to preserve the

---

cating that Manchuria has been one of the most sparsely settled regions of the Far East, the densities of population in other countries around 1920 were:

Japan, almost 400 per square mile;

Korea, about 200 over-all (but only 45 in its northern provinces);

China, about 100 over-all (but over 600 in the Yellow River Valley alone).

The over-all population density of the United States in 1920 was only 35.5 per square mile, ranging from 566 in Rhode Island to .7 in Nevada.

fierce and warlike quality of its people. The Manchu emperors therefore forbade the immigration of the Chinese, who represented the tamer civilization of sedentary agriculture. The administration of this prohibition was intermittently relaxed, however, and was specifically liberalized in the 1880's (although full-scale immigration was not actually sanctioned until after the turn of the century). By 1900 the stream of immigrants had gradually brought the numbers of Chinese to some 80 percent of the total population of Manchuria. The interests and activities of the Chinese were in marked contrast to those of the indigenous tribes, and provided the early development of the area. The Chinese engaged mainly in agriculture of a substantially commercialized type, raising cereals and soy beans for local consumption and for shipment to other regions, chiefly South China. They developed an elaborate commercial organization and practices, as well as extensive transportation using the natural waterways of the country.[3]

Thus the premodern situation comprised the political dominance and economic conservatism of the Manchus, together with the expanding role of Chinese enterprise, using traditional Chinese technology but largely oriented to distant markets. The society of Manchuria was therefore already in flux when Western influences began to penetrate that region in the second half of the nineteenth century. In some ways this situation paralleled that of Japan at about the same time, when the increasing commercialization of the economy under the tottering political regime of the Tokugawa prepared the way for major transformations once the foreigners provided the catalyst. But transformation in Manchuria was neither so rapid nor so far-reaching, for reasons now to be indicated.

Manchuria under the "Spheres of Influence"

The period 1860–1931 was marked by the interaction of the slow Chinese expansion and the more ambitious and more potent activities of the British, Russians, and Japanese. The first important breach in

---

[3] These main features of Manchuria's early economic history are summarized from *Economic History of Manchuria*, prepared by T. Hoshino for the Bank of Chosen (Seoul, 1920), Introduction and Chapter 1; Owen Lattimore, *Manchuria: Cradle of Conflict* (New York: Macmillan Company, 1932), Chapters 1–3; F. C. Jones, *Manchuria Since 1931* (London: Royal Institute of International Affairs, 1949), pp. 5–6, 9, 169; South Manchuria Railway, *Report on Progress in Manchuria, 1907–1928* (Dairen, 1929), Chapters 1–2; George B. Cressey, *Asia's Lands and Peoples* (New York: McGraw-Hill Book Company, 1944), Chapters 1, 3, 6.

Manchuria's isolation from the Western world came in the 1860's, when the British opened the port of Newchwang (Yingkow) to foreign trade as a result of the Treaty of Tientsin (1858), which followed the so-called Arrow War with China. This port, located near the mouth of the great Liao River which drains South Manchuria and East Mongolia, furnished new markets for the produce of the interior, especially soy beans and their products. These markets in turn stimulated expansion of production, the spread of trade and trading influences, the construction of cities along the trade routes, and the inflow of both Chinese and foreigners. The British who came to Newchwang were mostly traders, operating on their own private account; British officials there were chiefly diplomatic and consular.

After an initial spurt of growth, Newchwang's progress was slow during the 1870's and early 1880's, but the relaxation of the immigration barriers provided a stimulus in the later 1880's. Progress accelerated again when the end of the Sino-Japanese War brought a great expansion of Manchuria's trade with Japan.[4] The history of this port illustrates the advance of private action once political action opened opportunities that hitherto had been closed.

The Japanese had only minor interests in Manchuria prior to the Sino-Japanese War, but became very active there following that conflict. This was not the result of territorial seizures (Japan was forced by the European powers to give up the territorial cessions she had exacted from China in 1895), but rather of the knowledge of Manchuria's potentialities that was acquired by the Japanese military who overran the country during the war and by the businessmen who followed the troops. The new interest was concentrated not so much on minerals as on soy beans and bean cake. The beans were found to be cheaper, delivered in Japan, than the same varieties grown in Japan, and were particularly desirable for replacing fish manure, the supply of which had become inadequate for Japan's agricultural needs. As trade developed, Japan quickly came to take one third of the growing total of Manchurian exports through Newchwang. At the same time, Manchurian agriculture "began to be conducted on a much larger scale and to push its way further into the interior, and the farmers, unable to utilize the land they had taken up to the full, came to depend largely upon hired labour, causing . . . a large amount of labour to be yearly imported from the northern provinces of China. . . . Thus

[4] From the detailed account by Hoshino, *op. cit.,* pp. 18–23.

dawned a new period for Manchuria, not only in trade but also in agriculture." [5] In that country, endowed with unused resources and newly provided with mobility, the excess of demand over supply—foreign demand over current Manchurian supply—generated a large expansion of production.

The first direct and positive undertaking by a foreign government in the development of Manchuria was Russian. At first the Russian influence was indirect, via the Siberian settlements established after 1860 by the Russian authorities, at considerable expense to the State Treasury, along the northern and eastern frontiers of Manchuria. These settlements were intended for military security as well as for emigration from European Russia and for exploitation of the agricultural and mineral resources of the area. The settlements were supported by village and urban construction and by steamship and other means of transportation, all subsidized by the Russian government. But "the Russian immigrants, who were neither good farmers nor good traders, had to depend largely upon their southern neighbors across the [Amur] river, the Chinese, for their daily necessaries, which fact alone was sufficient to draw large crowds of profit-hunting Chinamen to the frontier districts." [6] Chinese towns and villages soon sprang up in these regions of northern Manchuria.

The greatest Russian impact came after 1896, when Russia obtained from China, still staggering from the Sino-Japanese War, the right to construct a railway across the heart of Manchuria and to administer a "zone" flanking the railway line on both sides. The Russo-Chinese agreements of 1896, which included a mutual assistance pact against Japanese aggression, also provided that the railway would be turned over to the Chinese government without payment at the end of 80 years. This line was to connect the Transbaikal section of Russia's Trans-Siberian Railway (whose construction had begun some years earlier) with the Ussuri section leading to the terminus at Vladivostok. The new route, running from the northwest corner of Manchuria to the southeast corner, was supplemented by a branch line running, at a right angle to the main line, from Harbin in central Manchuria southwestward to Port Arthur at Manchuria's southern tip on the Yellow Sea; these two lines thus lay diagonally across Manchuria in the form of a great T. Construction of this system, named the Chinese

[5] *Ibid.*, p. 30.
[6] *Ibid.*, p. 32.

Eastern Railway, was pushed rapidly, so that both the main line (925 miles long) and the branch line (617 miles) were open to traffic by 1903. The financing of the construction and equipment was handled by the Russo-Chinese Bank, an ingenious "private" institution which, under the control of the Russian Ministry of Finance, served to obtain French private capital for the Asiatic projects of the Russian government.[7]

The economic impact of these new railroad lines was tremendous. Millions of rubles were paid to coolies for construction work and to Chinese farmers and merchants for all sorts of supplies and services.[8] As the Chinese migrated to the new opportunities, boom towns grew to substantial proportions. At Harbin the Russians built a great new city, something like early San Francisco, where life was hectic and violent and fortunes were made overnight. All along the main railway, and especially around Harbin, idle lands were put into cultivation and crop production soared. Many Chinese merchants seized the trading opportunity and accumulated large fortunes. Altogether, this frontier-land, where immigration and trade had been making quiet gradual progress, suddenly was plunged into a fever of new projects and opportunities. Railway construction did for northern Manchuria what the discovery of gold had done for the American West. On the other hand, the effects of the branch line through southern Manchuria were much less powerful, since the southern regions were already considerably developed, fairly well-populated, and provided with other means of transportation.

The next act of the Manchurian drama saw a head-on collision between the Russians and Japanese. The Russians had begun to develop Port Arthur as a naval base for their Pacific fleet and to construct a modern commercial port at the neighboring city of Dairen (which they called Dalny). In 1900, on the occasion of the Boxer uprising, Russian troops set up a virtual occupation of all Manchuria. By this time the Japanese were eagerly exploring Manchurian opportunities for trade, colonies, and personal advancement.[9] Fearing for their

---

[7] Paul H. Clyde, *The Far East* (New York: Prentice-Hall, 1948), pp. 261–264; Jones, *op. cit.*, p. 101.

[8] The construction costs of this railway amounted to 375 million rubles, according to the *Japan-Manchoukuo Year Book, 1934* (Tokyo, 1934), p. 580; additional construction at terminal cities, ports, and other points brought the total outlay eventually to 588 million rubles.

[9] Hoshino, *op. cit.*, pp. 60–62.

commercial and territorial interests in both Manchuria and Korea, the Japanese attacked the Russians in 1904, and to everyone's astonishment were quickly victorious. The subsequent peace treaty provided for the expulsion of Russia from southern Manchuria, by transferring to Japan the "leased territory" of Kwantung in the Liaotung Peninsula, together with most of the branch line and accompanying railway zone and mines of the Chinese Eastern Railway, i.e., the portion running from Ch'angch'un (Hsinking) to Port Arthur.

Russia retained the main line of her railway together with the now abbreviated branch from Harbin to Ch'angch'un. She continued to dominate Harbin and other northern cities, and to exploit the mining, lumbering, and agricultural resources in her railway zone; but her southward expansion in Manchuria had been halted.[10] In fact, the Chinese Eastern Railway was never extended nor much improved, and the Russians even began a parallel railroad (the Amur Railway) within Siberian territory and raised trade barriers against Manchurian industrial products in the interest of Siberian industrial development.[11] Finally, in the mid-1930's, Russia sold her remaining holdings in the Chinese Eastern Railway to the Japanese puppet state of Manchukuo. It was not until World War II that Russia resumed her drive into Manchuria.

South Manchuria Railway Company

The Japanese, in contrast, advanced in Manchuria by leaps and bounds after 1905. The chief agency of this advance was the South Manchuria Railway Company, whose remarkable character and performance deserve a detailed account. This Company was organized in 1906 under the Japanese title of Minami Manshu Tetsudo Kabushiki Kaisha (meaning Southern Manchuria Railway Joint Stock Company), commonly abbreviated to *Mantetsu* in the Japanese and to SMR in the English literature. While the organization was in legal form a private joint-stock company, in operation it served as an arm of the Japanese

---

[10] Russia's sphere of influence in North Manchuria was confirmed but limited by successive treaties with the Chinese and the Japanese governments. It survived the Allied Intervention of 1918 and the Russo-Chinese hostilities of 1929, but was outflanked and rendered almost valueless by the Japanese establishment of Manchukuo in the 1930's. See Clyde, *op. cit.*, pp. 334, 345–348, 412–423, 555–557, 665.

[11] Hoshino, *op. cit.*, pp. 72–76. The total of Russian investments in Manchuria grew but moderately, according to Charles F. Remer, *Foreign Investment in China* (New York: Macmillan Company, 1933), Chapter 18, covering 1904–30.

government and was subject to the general supervision of the governor of the Kwantung Leased Territory; it was in fact the first of several huge "semiofficial" companies and banks organized under government auspices to pursue Japan's economic and political interests in Asia. The Japanese government appointed the president, vice-president, and directors, and held one half of all the shares. Initially the Company's authorized capital was 200 million yen, of which the government's half was contributed in the form of the railways, mining properties, and associated Manchurian assets obtained from Russia by the Treaty of Portsmouth. The other half was designated for private ownership, but up to 1920 only 80 million of the 100 million yen had been called. These shares were offered to the general public, including Chinese, but were subscribed chiefly by the Zaibatsu.[12] The Japanese government guaranteed the payment of interest on debentures and the repayment of principal, and for the first 15 years a dividend of at least 6 percent on paid-up capital. The government retained a number of supervisory and restrictive powers over the Company.[13]

The government's intentions regarding the SMR were made explicit in an "Order" issued August 1, 1906. The Company was instructed to operate the lines acquired from Russia; reconstruct and modernize those lines (especially by changing them from Russian wide-gauge to standard gauge, and by double-tracking the most important stretches); provide for connections between land and water transportation at the ports; provide facilities for lodging and meals of passengers and warehouses for goods; engage in "accessory" lines of business "for the convenience and the profit of the railway," specifically mining, water transportation, electrical enterprises, brokerage, warehousing, real estate management, and "in addition, any business for which Government permission has been given"; and "make the necessary arrangements for engineering works, education, sanitation, etc." within the Railway Zone, and to collect fees to defray the expenses for these services.[14] It is evident that the Company was given a positive man-

12 Jones, op. cit., p. 103. The Zaibatsu were the great business houses, at once financial, industrial, and commercial, which dominated the Japanese variety of capitalism. They were organized around a family nucleus and were controlled along familial lines, but operated as vast diversified holding companies.

13 Details from the "Articles of Incorporation of the South Manchuria Railway Company," in its Report on Progress in Manchuria, 1907–1928, pp. 207–214.

14 Summarized from "Order Regarding South Manchuria Railway Company," reproduced in ibid., pp. 204–205.

date, yet its scope was not to extend much beyond what now is called "social and economic overhead capital." The prescribed activities referred to transportation, other functions closely associated with it, and general social services. The chief item outside this range was mining, and even this was primarily for coal for locomotives. Conspicuous by their absence from the prescribed activities were agriculture, ordinary trade and banking, manufacturing, personal services, and other forms of production which were intended, on the whole, for private enterprise.

Up to the events of the 1930's the SMR was faithful to this conception of its mandate. Table 1 shows the aggregate amount of fixed

TABLE 1. FIXED INVESTMENT * OF SOUTH MANCHURIA RAILWAY TO MARCH 31, 1928

Category	Value in thousands of yen	Percentage of adjusted total
Railways	239,518	35.9
Workshops	8,760	1.3
Steamships	4,045	0.6
Harbors	59,789	8.9
Coal mines	102,731	15.3
Ironworks	20,748	3.2
Public works †	164,679	24.5
Other	44,572	6.7
Actual total	644,842	
Plus divested properties: ‡		
Electrical plants	15,238	2.6
Gas works	5,434	.7
Hotels	2,370	.3
Divested total	23,042	
Adjusted total	667,884	100.0

Source: South Manchuria Railway, *Report on Progress in Manchuria, 1907–1928*, pp. 72, 92.

* Book values, after allowance (probably inadequate) for depreciation. The value of the initial properties of SMR in March 1908 was 101 million yen.

† Comprising urban facilities, housing, medical and educational facilities, and institutions for research, agricultural extension services, and resource conservation.

‡ These are the values, as of March 1923, of SMR properties transferred to newly established independent companies between 1925 and 1928; actual values may have been closer to 30 million yen. Other properties in steamships and dockyards, of relatively small value, had been divested in 1918 and 1923.

investment by the Company up to March 31, 1928. The figures represent the 100-million yen appraised value of the initial properties acquired in 1906, plus the annual investment outlays in yen values of each year, apparently after allowance for depreciation and for divestment of certain properties. From 1908 to 1928, the stated total of fixed capital was multiplied more than sixfold.[15]

Transportation facilities—the first four categories in the table—accounted for nearly half of the total investment. The Company did not materially increase the total mileage of its railroad lines after 1907, but concentrated on improving the existing lines and double-tracking the main portions. In addition, it built for Chinese ownership various lines which served as "feeders" to its own network.[16] Other notable transport installations were the large railroad repair shops, the tripling of rolling stock, the Yalu River bridge connecting the SMR lines with the Korean railway network, and the development of Dairen into one of the chief ports and commercial centers of the Far East.

Equally notable is the allocation of one fourth of the total investment to "public works," in which are included all kinds of urban facilities —from housing, schools, and hospitals to water supply and sewage systems—as well as model farms and experimental stations, technical research laboratories, economic research institutions, and other facilities for social services. In the frontier conditions of Manchuria, these constructions were vital to various kinds of direct production, as well as important in improving the quality of products, the efficiency of operation, and the confidence of entrepreneurs. These constructions, together with the transportation facilities, were indispensable for con-

[15] This measurement is made in current yen, without price deflation. No suitable price index is available for Manchuria during this period. However, a rough guide is provided by the indices of unit values of manufactured exports (both finished and semifinished) from Japan, which was the principal source of capital equipment for Manchuria. According to these indices, equipment installed during 1908–16 was obtained at prices roughly 15 percent below those prevailing when the initial properties were appraised in 1906; and equipment installed during 1917–28 was priced on the average about 70 percent above the 1906 price levels (based on *Oriental Economist*, "The Foreign Trade of Japan," Tokyo, 1935, p. 699). These indices throw no light on the movements within Manchuria of local prices and wages entering into capital installations.

[16] "Of the 1,500 miles of Chinese railways [in Manchuria in 1928], over 695 miles were built with Japanese capital," in the form of loans to the Chinese government, and an additional 466 miles were built partly with British capital. See *Report on Progress in Manchuria, 1907–1928*, pp. 48–49.

verting Manchuria's natural resources into economic resources, and more broadly for transforming Manchuria's potentialities into positive opportunities.

The rate of progress in utilizing these facilities is measured in part by the almost continual rise of the SMR's output/capital ratio (Table 2) in the face of repeated additions to the capital stock. As the economy expanded, freight traffic swelled from 1.5 million tons in 1907–08 to 18.4 million tons in 1927–28, the chief items by tonnage being coal and soy beans. Traffic was already sufficiently large in 1907–08, after the railway had been in operation for only four years under the Russians, to show an operating profit that was the main contribution to the whole Company's net profit in that first year. In subsequent years the twelvefold multiplication of traffic meant greatly improved utilization of capacity, since the total track mileage was not increased (although it was double-tracked) and the rolling stock was enlarged not much more than threefold. The freight rate schedules were framed with a view to earning a profit, but not shortsightedly: exorbitant rates which would have stifled the growth of traffic were avoided and, as the Company stated, "special reductions in rates . . . [were] made from time to time to encourage local development and assist in relief work." [17]

TABLE 2. SOUTH MANCHURIA RAILWAY RATIOS OF ANNUAL RECEIPTS
TO EXISTING FIXED CAPITAL

Year	Over-all ratio *	Railways alone †
1908	1:8	1:3.5
1913	1:6	1:5
1918	1:4	1:3
1923	1:3	1:2.2
1928	1:2.8	1:2.1

* Calculated from data in *Report on Progress in Manchuria, 1907–1928*, p. 72.
† Calculated from *ibid.*, p. 81. Capital values have been adjusted to include the 25 million yen of original property excluded from "railway investment" in the cited source.

A similar record is found in the development of coal mining, which exploited a rich resource and was intended to supply the needs of the Railway itself as well as other consumers in Manchuria, Japan, and elsewhere in Asia. Coal mining was profitable and continuously expanded. Output rose from 233,000 tons in 1907–08 to nearly 7 million

[17] *Ibid.*, p. 78. Such rate reductions were particularly important in promoting the immigration of Chinese.

tons in 1927–28. The Company's coal profits were not merely book-keeping profits, produced by transfers at high prices in the accounts; the SMR itself took less than one fifth of the total value of coal sold in 1927–28, and the remainder was sold at market prices, both domestic and export.[18]

Some of the Company's other undertakings showed very different performance. The ironworks at Anshan are the most notable example of accounting losses, which have usually been taken to indicate "uneconomic" allocation of resources. The fact is that these works used low-grade ores, were constructed at inflated capital costs during 1917–20, and were operated far below capacity. Naturally the works showed substantial annual losses from 1919 to 1928. Yet "Japan was pressed by the necessity of this product to meet her ever-developing industry," as the Company explained.[19] Research on the technology of the plant and its by-products was consequently intensified, production was stepped up, capitalization was reduced by more than half the original investment, and the charges for coal and the salaries of executives were reduced. By the end of the 1920's annual output was above 200,000 tons of pig iron, after having been only about 75,000 tons a year during 1920–26. The chronic losses were first cut down in 1927–28, and then converted into operating profits in the next two years—only to revert to losses in 1930–31 under the impact of the world-wide recession.[20]

In raising funds for all these activities, the Company managers at first sought to avoid diluting the initial stock ownership and concentration, and even preferred not to call up all the stock subscriptions. They turned instead to the issue of debentures in the London capital market; four issues, aggregating 14 million pounds (but yielding about 2 percent less as a result of discounts and underwriters' commissions), were floated during 1907–11, at stated interest rates of 5 and 4.5 percent. Beginning in 1917, the Company floated all subsequent debentures in Japan at somewhat higher interest rates (except for one issue of 14 million pounds in London in 1923). The total of outstanding debentures was 278 million yen on March 31, 1928. In addition, the

---

[18] The highly competitive export market absorbed almost half of the total coal sales, and more than half of the exports went outside Japan, Korea, and Formosa (*ibid.*, p. 87).

[19] *Ibid.*, p. 89.

[20] South Manchuria Railway, *Third Report on Progress in Manchuria to 1932*, pp. 121–122.

capitalization of the Company was enlarged after World War I from the original authorized 200 million yen to an authorized 440 million yen. The Japanese government acquired half the increment, or 120 million yen worth of shares, by taking over 14 million pounds of debentures previously floated in London. The public's half of the stock increment, like the original stock issue, was not fully called, so that in March 1928 only 138 million yen of the total public allotment (220 million yen) had been paid up.

A major source of capital funds was the reinvestment of profits. And during this period profits from the successful undertakings (especially the railways and coal mines), the losing undertakings (mainly the ironworks and the hotels), and the nonprofit undertakings (chiefly social services), taken together, were decidedly substantial. The Company showed an annual surplus, of current revenues over current expenditures,[21] running between 15 and 21 percent of total revenues. Dividends were paid to the individual stockholders from the first fiscal year in amounts gradually rising from 6 to 10 percent of par value of the stock; and a dividend was paid to the government on its shares from 1909 on, amounting to 4.3 percent a year during the 1920's. From 1907 to 1928 the Company built up a legal reserve of 17.5 million yen and a special reserve of 127.4 million yen; the total of 145 million yen is sizable compared with the paid-up capital of 358 million yen in 1928 and the debentures of 278 million outstanding on that date. In the single year 1927–28, the net profit of 36.3 million yen was allocated as follows: dividends, 61 percent; bonuses and retirement fund, 7 percent; legal and special reserves, 30 percent; unallocated balance, 2 percent carried forward. This emphasis on reinvestment appears to have been fairly steady over two decades.[22]

Other Economic Expansion

The economic growth of Manchuria during this period was not confined to the direct undertakings of the SMR, although most other

[21] Depreciation allowances, at an apparent annual rate of about 2 percent of the book value of company property, were probably inadequate, but accorded with the practice of the times. In addition, fixed capital charges were held down by the seizure rather than purchase of the original properties from Russia, and their transfer by the Japanese government to the SMR in exchange for stock rather than bonds.

[22] Of the small initial profits of 2 million yen in 1908, about 40 percent were plowed back. These data on profits are from *Report on Progress in Manchuria, 1907–1928*, pp. 72–73.

activities showed their influence. Private enterprise, both Japanese and Chinese, expanded gradually but quite steadily, and in total magnitude exceeded the direct undertakings of the SMR.[23] Agricultural and commercial expansion took place throughout Manchuria; industrial growth was more concentrated in the SMR and the Chinese Eastern Railway (Russian) zones.

The most massive advance of private enterprise was in agriculture. As population rose through both immigration and natural increase, settlers pushed northward. Between 1919 and 1930 the area of cultivated land more than doubled, according to some estimates. At the same time productivity increased greatly, perhaps doubling the yield per acre for such crops as soy beans, wheat, and rice. Output of all cereals and soy beans together is reported to have tripled from 1914 to 1927. The spread of soy bean cultivation was of outstanding significance not only for its contribution to physical output but also for its role in transforming the economy: being a cash crop intended for export, in contrast to the cereals raised for subsistence, soy cultivation

[23] The following data (SMR *Third Report . . . to 1932*, p. 48) show the magnitude of the Japanese investment in Manchuria as of March 1931:

	Million yen
SMR	
Direct undertakings	742.07
Loans and advances to affiliates, Chinese railways, private industry, etc.	320.74
Japanese government guaranteed loans to Chinese government	98.73
Japanese corporations	
Direct undertakings	439.00
Loans to Chinese government and individuals	20.28
Japanese individuals	94.99
Total	1,715.81

The total, which was equivalent to 850 million U. S. dollars at the exchange rate then current, excluded government property in Manchuria owned by the Kwantung government and the Japanese Army, private property of Japanese residents in Manchuria, and the annual grant made since 1906 by the Japanese government to the Kwantung government; these excluded items were estimated at 460 million yen.

No estimate is available for total capital investment in Manchuria from all sources, but all foreign investment there as of 1931 was estimated by Remer (*op. cit.*, p. 73) at 880 million U. S. dollars. This estimate implies a much smaller absolute amount for the Japanese investment than is given in the SMR *Third Report*, for Remer (p. 606) assigns a value of 261.8 million dollars to the Russian investments in Manchuria (other countries had negligible amounts there); nevertheless, the Japanese share remains decidedly predominant.

advanced the commercialization of agriculture and the broad spread of the market nexus. Other primary activities, chiefly lumbering and fishing, had also been carried on in small volume, with primitive methods and mainly for subsistence, until the Japanese influence was felt. After 1905 these activities were substantially modernized and expanded.[24]

The exploitation of minerals and the development of transportation did not attract much private enterprise. Both these fields were left almost entirely to the SMR.

In contrast, the fabricating industries were mainly in private hands. Table 3 indicates the growth of "factories" by five-year intervals from 1909 to 1929, in the area "within Japanese jurisdiction in Manchuria," including the Kwantung Leased Territory, the Railway Zone, and Consular Districts. A different tabulation, compiled for the depression year 1931 and presumably including more small-scale enterprises, showed 2,025 manufacturing plants in South Manchuria, with 73,336 regular workers and a total output valued at 224 million yen. The greater part of these enterprises was engaged in primary processing: soy-bean oil milling accounted for one third of the total output, and food products represented another fifth; cotton spinning, metal products, and machinery and tools together accounted for only one third of the total; the remainder comprised chemicals, glass, paper, ceramics, and other fields.[25] In North Manchuria, according to figures for the late 1920's, there were about 600 manufacturing establishments (including 147 soy-bean oil mills, 62 liquor distilleries, and 52 flour mills), located chiefly in the cities of Harbin and Mukden.[26]

The influence of Japanese economic activities on the Chinese may be traced in both working skills and entrepreneurship. A considerable number of Chinese acquired technical skills in Japanese-run training

[24] This description of trends in primary activities is derived from the *Report on Progress in Manchuria, 1907–1928*, pp. 114–115, and *Third Report . . . to 1932*, pp. 140–141 and 151–154; Hoshino, *op. cit.*, p. 136; and Chu Hsiao, "Manchuria: A Statistical Survey," in Institute of Pacific Relations, *Problems of the Pacific* (1929), pp. 383–389. The data, especially for the earlier years, are not entirely reliable and exhibit several inconsistencies.

[25] Calculated from data in *Japan-Manchoukuo Year Book, 1934*, pp. 599–600. The metal products and machinery and tools, comprising less than one fourth of the total manufacturing output, were produced mainly in plants of the SMR and its affiliates (*ibid.*, pp. 610–614).

[26] SMR *Third Report . . . to 1932*, p. 157.

schools and through employment in Japanese firms. The SMR in 1908 employed 6,135 Japanese workers and 4,129 Chinese, and 20 years later, 11,865 and 13,677 respectively; these numbers exclude the coolie day laborers who were nearly all Chinese.[27] In factory employment the ratio of Chinese to Japanese workers was over 7 to 1 in 1929, the result of a rising trend in the numbers of Chinese during the 1920's while the Japanese total remained about stationary.[28]

TABLE 3. MANUFACTURING IN SOUTH MANCHURIA

Year	No. of factories	Capital investment	Value of products
		In thousands of yen	
1909	152	16,132	6,139
1914	244	24,537	20,799
1919	450	123,572	242,883
1924	658	192,937	139,901
1929	789	302,080	126,915

Source: South Manchuria Railway, *Third Report . . . to 1932*, p. 157. These figures represent only the larger enterprises, those employing more than 5 workers, but not exclusively those owned by Japanese. Capital investment and value of product are given in current yen (not deflated for price changes) and therefore are somewhat misleading as to real trends, especially for 1919, which was marked by severe price inflation. (In Japan, according to the Bank of Japan's wholesale price index with 1909=100, the price level stood at 119 in 1909, 126 in 1914, 312 in 1919, 273 in 1924, and 220 in 1929.)

Even more important for the future, numbers of Chinese found opportunities for independent enterprise of modern types in medium-scale industries. Chinese entrepreneurs followed the lead of foreigners in establishing themselves in such fields as flour milling, soy-bean oil extraction, beet-sugar refining, tobacco products, and cotton textiles.[29] A few Chinese became officials in the SMR's "district councils" for local administration in the Railway Zone; some became executives of the Company and of other Japanese enterprises, where they functioned largely as go-betweens in Japanese-Chinese relations; some were directors of joint Sino-Japanese companies in extractive industries, public

[27] *Report on Progress in Manchuria, 1907–1928*, p. 69.

[28] *Third Report . . . to 1932*, p. 158. Wages for Chinese workers were far below those for their Japanese counterparts, but at the same time Chinese in Japanese-owned factories were paid at higher rates than their counterparts in Chinese-owned factories.

[29] *Report on Progress in Manchuria, 1907–1928*, pp. 131–137.

utilities, commerce, etc.; and some served in cooperative Japanese-Russian-Chinese undertakings in public health and other social services.[30]

To summarize the trends during the second period of Manchuria's development, it is possible roughly to distinguish private from governmental actions and to distinguish native from foreign agents. The Japanese government, operating mainly through the SMR, was the principal leader; Japanese private agents closely followed its lead; Chinese private parties followed more slowly, although occasionally accelerating (as in the surge of immigration during 1927–29); the Chinese government was the least active of these four groups (its chief positive actions related to immigration and railroad feeder lines).

Efficiency of Allocation of Resources

A question should be raised regarding efficiency in the allocation of resources under the SMR regime: Did the Japanese administration waste resources—of Manchuria or of Japan itself—either by forcing certain investments into Manchuria or by retarding the rate of development? The Lytton Commission, which surveyed the Manchurian situation for the League of Nations in 1931–32, suggested that the Company had sought to prevent and to stifle Chinese railway competition; that it had financed and constructed for Chinese ownership only such lines as would feed the SMR's system, although "it is doubtful if their construction, in certain cases, was justified on purely economic grounds"; and in general that the Company had failed to develop an adequate transportation network.[31] This somewhat qualified charge was reiterated in more extreme form by F. C. Jones.[32]

There are, of course, well-known difficulties in attempting to make a judgment as to the economic or uneconomic allocation of resources in any actual case at a particular time. These difficulties are vastly compounded in attempting to make such a judgment over a long period and in relation to major structural changes; the attempt may involve a loss of historical perspective and some embarrassing rebuttals in the subsequent event. In the process of economic development, high direct

---

[30] *Ibid.*, pp. 8–9, 92–93.

[31] League of Nations, *Report of the Commission of Enquiry (Lytton)*, Publ. Series C.663. M.320. 1932. VII (Geneva, 1932), pp. 42–49, and Annexes, pp. 41–42.

[32] Jones, *op. cit.*, pp. 104–105. For similar charges of extreme waste of resources, referring chiefly to the Manchukuo period, see pp. 185–186, infra.

costs at the outset may in the longer run be offset by the internal and external economies of increasing scale and progressing efficiency. More specifically, the rail lines that had been constructed in the 1920's, only shortly before the Lytton Commission made its survey, needed several years of increasing traffic to prove their worth—just as the original lines built by the Russians showed small direct return until freight traffic began to grow enormously, as local production expanded in response to the new transport facilities.[33]

To return to the larger aspect of resource allocation, it would seem that development under the SMR regime followed fairly closely the apparent pattern of comparative advantage. Manchuria's most evident potentialities lay in the field of agriculture, and this showed the most massive expansion. Similar advantages characterized the exploration and exploitation of Manchuria's coal and mineral resources, except that private capital played a small role, while in the chemical industry, designed to utilize the available Manchurian materials, there was greater participation by private Japanese industrialists. Even the iron-works, the most frequently cited case of "wasted resources," were founded on the local deposits of coal and iron ore, and progressed from losses in the short run to a competitively efficient performance in the long run. A great deal of investment was poured into urban construction, power plants, and other public utilities and services; many of these are not susceptible to any simple measure of "efficiency," let alone "profitability," but the outlays in these fields do not seem far out of proportion to those in other activities with which they were associated. In the directly productive industries, where private management prevailed, profits in Manchuria appear often to have exceeded those earned in North China or in Japan. This performance may have been aided by the SMR's provision of social overhead capital; but for all that, the SMR itself showed a substantial net profit, not the losses to be expected from a primarily subsidizing operation! The conclusion seems inescapable—when Manchuria's development is viewed in proper historical perspective, and apart from very important political and moral considerations—that there was efficient use of available resources under the SMR regime.

These considerations lead to an examination of the underlying factors that gave such crucial importance to social overhead capital,

[33] Jones himself indicates (pp. 109, 114–115) the great growth of traffic on the non-SMR lines during the 1930's.

and that prevented both the Chinese government and private Chinese entrepreneurs from performing the whole developmental function. Such an examination must begin by comparing the trends since 1860, with those during earlier decades and earlier centuries.

Underlying Factors and Economic Changes

If Manchuria had been left to her own devices during this period, there can be little doubt that economic life would have continued in the traditional patterns of North Chinese agriculture and handicrafts alongside the still more primitive economics of nomadic life. Since technology, capital, and other means were stagnant, and the economic agents were unchanged, while structural obstacles persisted and social values continued to be hostile to material transformation, undoubtedly there would have been only a very slow growth of output, as population increase (from both natural increase and a trickle of immigration) gradually drew frontier resources into use. Unfortunately, this proposition cannot be demonstrated, so as to satisfy the "method of difference," by eliminating the roles of the state and the foreigners from the course of history. It is certainly significant, however, that even after the creation of the foreign zones in Manchuria there was little development in transportation, mining, or manufacturing outside those zones. And this pattern was not notably altered even after the republican government came to power in China in 1911. The reasons why the Chinese ignored the developmental opportunities appear to lie deep in the traditional social system.

The behavior of the Chinese immigrants in Manchuria is probably most revealing. They came into Manchuria reluctantly, pushed by overcrowding in the old areas as well as pulled by offers of new land. According to one interpretation, the Chinese immigrant was fearful of losing contact with his old home and Chinese culture, and he continually looked backward. In the new location he tended to prefer the already settled areas, to stay close to his fellows, and to cling to familiar methods, whether in agriculture, industry, or social organization. He did not undertake to conquer the wilderness; he sought rather to compromise with it. The return migration to China Proper was heavy, representing not only the movements of seasonal farm labor but also the return of settlers, merchants, and small industrialists—some driven back by failure, others riding high on success. Success in Manchuria was for many Chinese only peripheral to success in China—a step toward status in the traditional structure, not a means of transforming it.[34]

This picture of the Chinese approach to Manchuria's development, if correct, has important implications. It suggests, first, that without Western intervention and without participation by the Chinese government, the economic development of Manchuria would have been slow and intermittent. Second, even that government could not remain aloof while Russian and Japanese colonizers attempted to move into Manchuria. If the Chinese government was to keep out these invaders, it had to attract Chinese settlers into the frontier regions by offers of tempting land grants and grubstakes. But these offers were almost bound to fail because of the reluctance of the migrants, and the chief result was the passing of large tracts into the hands of a few individuals (or firms) who settled down to wait patiently for the tide of migration to move up to them. Third, when at last major appropriate actions were taken to improve opportunities, the response of migrants was enormous and cumulative; from this point of view, the flood of migrants during the 1920's was not only a flight from famine and disorder in North China but also a response to the Japanese "intervention," especially by railway building. The Chinese government officials, however, were not interested in doing what the foreigners did in developing, commercializing, and rationalizing economic activities; rather, they were willing to adopt Western methods only insofar as necessary. They saw a fundamental opposition between Western methods and Chinese ideals of civilization, and sought to subordinate the former to the latter. This was an intractable problem, perhaps impossible of solution; and in any case the rest of the world would not wait.

This interpretation of the Chinese as developers has been formulated mainly in terms of social values. Much the same conclusions are reached by considering the socioeconomic structure and the obstructions it posed. Here we must take account of such factors as the family

---

[34] For details of these attitudes and practices, see Lattimore, *op. cit.*, especially Chapters 3, 4, 9; and C. Walter Young, "Chinese Colonization and the Development of Manchuria," in Institute of Pacific Relations, *Problems of the Pacific* (1929), especially pp. 435–437, 441–444. Filmer S. C. Northrop in *The Meeting of East and West* (New York: Macmillan Company, 1946), especially Chapters 8–9, contrasts the "aesthetic component," or emphasis on immediate experience, in Eastern attitudes, with the "theoretic component" which he finds dominating Western attitudes and calling forth endless pursuit of verification and validation.

and its restrictive control over innovation and the innovator (the issue of "conformity vs. deviance"); inheritance by division of property rather than by primogeniture; the reliance on personal status rather than impersonal contract in business transactions; the formulation of criteria of achievement in cultural and particularist terms, rather than in material and universalist terms; the importance of the ancestral village and the prestige of the local landed gentry; the origin of most government officials in the conservative landed gentry, and the consequent close ties between these two functional groups.[35]

An outstanding feature of this pattern was the failure of the merchants and the money lenders to undertake modernization of the economy. These classes were outside the traditional class hierarchy, and were also rich and powerful. They were therefore the potential entrepreneurs of a modernizing China; but instead they tended to use their wealth for the purchase of land, which was their means of entering the gentry class and paving the way for their sons' entry into the official bureaucracy. These and other features of the Chinese social structure reveal the lack of suitable agents to undertake economic development, and the concentration of power in groups that were indifferent or actually hostile to social and economic change.

It was left to outsiders to recognize the potentialities and to treat them as opportunities. The British, Russians, and Japanese provided the technologies and the capital for social overhead as well as direct production; they introduced aggressive agencies and individuals; they adapted or circumvented the local forms of organization; and they brought a powerful drive for material progress. In this situation the response of the Chinese was sluggish, both within the foreign zones and outside them: as already noted, a few Chinese rose to positions of power and creativity in the new superstructure and many more filtered in at the bottom, but most of the Chinese in Manchuria ignored the qualitatively new opportunities and made their progress only along traditional lines. Thus even when foreigners provided a new economic

[35] The role of the family in retarding China's evolution has been particularly stressed by Marion J. Levy, Jr. See his *Some Problems of Modernization in China* (New York: Institute of Pacific Relations, 1949); also Shi Kuo-Heng and Marion J. Levy, Jr., *The Rise of the Modern Chinese Business Class* (New York: Institute of Pacific Relations, 1949). Some of Levy's points were anticipated in two remarkable monographs by H. D. Fong, "Industrial Capital in China" and "Industrial Organization in China," *Nankai Social and Economic Quarterly*, April 1936, and January 1937.

environment, the vital resistance—so to speak—of the Chinese way of life prevented any broad or deep involvement in the Western ways.[36]

The development of Manchuria, however, could not be accomplished by private foreign agents alone. Active though they might be, relatively well endowed with capital and experience and eager for the reputed riches of the region, they could not overcome without governmental aid the material obstacles of distance, terrain, and climate combined with the social obstacles of a conservative population and a hostile bureaucracy. The prerequisite was social overhead capital in very large amounts. In many countries the provision of such capital is left largely to the state because the investment is necessarily so massive, and the returns so distant, so uncertain, and often so difficult for private investors to appropriate.[37] But in Manchuria the ordinary material dimensions of the problem were greatly enlarged by the social obstacles and risks. Only a foreign government could take the measures essential for opening the opportunities. In other words, the long-run net social-marginal product was expected to be large, and the long-run net private revenue would also be large; but the short-run social-marginal product was small, and the private net revenue would for a while often be less than zero; consequently, only a state which was not concerned with maximizing net revenue in the short run could undertake this kind of development. Thus without foreign governmental auspices, the private foreign ventures in Manchuria would not have amounted to much. When the political aims of the Russians and the Japanese were added to those economic necessities,

[36] The most striking Oriental contrast to this record is the modern evolution of Japan Proper: an aggressive and rapid modernization by means of remarkable adaptations of Western methods to Japanese conditions. See Marion J. Levy, Jr., "Contrasting Factors in the Modernization of China and Japan," and Edwin P. Reubens, "Foreign Capital and Domestic Development in Japan," in Simon Kuznets, Wilbert E. Moore, and Joseph J. Spengler, eds., *Economic Growth: Brazil, India, Japan* (Durham: Duke University Press, 1955), pp. 511–536; 180–181, 198–200, 210–211. See also William W. Lockwood, *The Economic Development of Japan* (Princeton: Princeton University Press, 1954), especially Chapters 4, 5, 9, 10. It is also noteworthy that the "overseas Chinese," who encountered in Southeast Asia a different ethnic group and a separated and distinct society, considerably Westernized in the port cities, have shown much assimilation to Western economic ways.

[37] In many essentially capitalist systems there may be other motives for state preemption of public utilities, etc.: e.g., to prevent or eliminate monopoly, to manipulate the rest of the economy, to ensure military requisites. Motives of this kind, which were prominent in the British nationalizations under the postwar Labor government, appear in the Manchukuo period of Manchuria's evolution.

the predominance of various states in Manchuria's development became inevitable.

THE MANCHUKUO ERA OF THE 1930's

By 1931 Manchuria had reached a fairly advanced stage of quasi-colonial development. The main occupation of her population, now over 34 million persons, was still agriculture, which was carried on with a small-scale and simple type of technology but was substantially commercialized and oriented to foreign markets. Agriculture and the traditional handicrafts (sometimes a full-time occupation but often a supplementary activity in the peasant home) supplied the bulk of popular consumption. Factory production in Manchuria and imports of manufactured goods were increasing but still constituted a small proportion of total consumption. The few large-scale enterprises in manufacturing and mineral extraction were almost all in foreign hands. The native economy was capable of showing considerable surpluses above minimum subsistence, but these surpluses tended to flow into additional consumption, luxurious construction, expenditures by warlords, and remittances to China, rather than into productive investment. The economy was expanding gradually in volume of output, capital facilities, geographic scope, and population (by both immigration and natural increase). The drive, however, was exogenous and the local inertia was massive; consequently the rate of growth was moderate, and the character of growth was a gradual diffusion rather than a revolutionizing upheaval.

It is conceivable that this type and rate of growth might have continued in Manchuria if the Japanese Kwantung Army had not intervened in 1931. Commercial agencies, following the lead of semigovernmental agencies, would have continued the gradual development of the country. At least, no important event had occurred within Manchuria to obstruct that evolution. But drastic changes had taken place in the surrounding conditions. The economic crash of 1929 and the prolonged world-wide slump that followed brought a sharp drop in the demand and price of Manchuria's principal export, soy beans. For Japan, the world-wide slump meant increased difficulties in exporting its manufactured goods, and intensified trade rivalries with the British and other nations. These adverse events, however, would probably not have sufficed to call forth aggressive action in Manchuria if it were not for more profound stresses and strains.

The Kwantung Army officers who came to dominate Manchuria at that time had attitudes and motives quite different from the civilian bureaucrats, small businessmen, and Zaibatsu agents who formerly had administered that territory. The whole complex of these attitudes and motives extended beyond Manchuria to the structure and tensions in the society of Japan itself. The control of Japanese society had been the object of struggle for several decades among the Zaibatsu, the Army, and the Court aristocracy. Other larger groups of the population were more or less loosely attached to one or another of these protagonists. Thus, the peasantry and small landowners tended to support the Army, which drew both its enlisted men and officers chiefly from the overcrowded countryside. Small business and professional men tended to align themselves with the Zaibatsu, who in the economic arena were perhaps more collaborators than rivals of small businesses.[38]

Over the course of Japan's modernization, these groups had adjusted their interacting roles in a complex and thoroughly Japanese mingling of collaboration and opposition. During the 1920's, however, the Zaibatsu drew well ahead of their rivals, largely as a result of the material prosperity of the country, but partly as a result of the Allied victory in World War I over Germany (the model admired and copied by the Japanese militarists), and postwar setbacks to the Japanese Army's militarist and expansionist ambitions in China and Siberia (especially the failure of the Allied Intervention in 1918–20) and in international military parity (the Washington Conference of 1922).[39] While the Army officers were glowering over this damage to their pride, prestige, and influence, the depression of the 1930's hit Japan with severe though brief impact. The status of the Zaibatsu and their policies of peaceful economic penetration abroad were shaken; and the military seized the opportunity to promote a surge of popular feeling for vigorous, and if necessary ruthless, direct action of the kind that Army officers could lead. The Army's scheme to occupy all of Manchuria was thus a lever to force the Zaibatsu into acquiescence or to topple them from power altogether and was in fact considerably successful for a time, although it later had to be qualified, as will be indicated below.

[38] Cf. T. Uyeda, *The Small Industries of Japan* (Oxford: Institute of Pacific Relations, 1938); and Edwin P. Reubens, "Small-Scale Industry in Japan," *Quarterly Journal of Economics*, 61:577–604 (August 1947).

[39] Cf. Edwin O. Reischauer, *Japan Past and Present* (New York: Alfred A. Knopf, 1947), Chapters 10, 11.

In this struggle with the Zaibatsu, the Army aimed at certain larger objectives. Its ideologists, who for years had studied the German military system, were influenced by the rise of Hitler and worked out for Japan a version of the national-socialist doctrine. While the home country was admittedly perhaps not yet ready for such a system, Manchuria appealed to the younger officers as a splendid proving-ground for the "new ideas," and possibly as a means of beating the Zaibatsu at their own economic game. In addition, the Army could mobilize considerable public support for the ideas that the economic stresses of the 1930's must be met by autarky within a Greater East Asia Co-Prosperity Sphere; that war with Russia and perhaps other powers was inevitable, so that strong industrial foundations for military force must be laid down; and that such foundations required not only the natural resources of both Manchuria and Korea but also their industrialization so as to provide semifinished goods and perhaps end products in widely dispersed regions of the Empire.

At this juncture in history, the government of China under the Kuomintang was showing signs at long last of putting its house in order politically and of undertaking a positive economic program of reform and construction. From the Japanese viewpoint, this meant a danger that Manchuria might soon be drawn out of their hands. Indeed, the Chinese seemed to have already signaled their intentions in the bitter railroad competition after 1924—in both rate wars and construction of parallel lines—which the Japanese viewed as an effort to stifle the SMR and crowd out other Japanese enterprises.[40]

All these influences and motives conspired to spell for Manchuria a Japanese military intervention in the early 1930's, followed by a state-socialist regime of forced industrialization. The Army made it clear from the outset that the newly occupied territory would be developed in accordance with a central plan, in place of the limited and gradualist approaches used by the SMR and the ordinary commercial methods used by private entrepreneurs.

The First Five Years of Manchukuo

An "Economic Construction Programme" was announced by the new Manchukuo government in March 1933. According to the preamble of the Programme, four basic principles would prevail in Manchukuo: "the interests of the people as a whole will be made the keynote and efforts will be made to prevent any exclusive class of people

[40] Cf. Jones, *op. cit.*, pp. 105–106.

from monopolizing the benefits"; "national control will be exerted on important economic activities"; "the principle of the open door and equal opportunity will be observed"; and "emphasis will be placed on securing cooperation between the two nations" (Manchukuo and Japan).[41] These principles did not immediately produce a fully articulated plan, and the Manchukuo authorities actually never undertook comprehensive detailed allocation of resources in the Soviet style. The years from 1932 to 1937 were devoted chiefly to strengthening the substructure of the new regime, reorganizing the existing economy, and fashioning appropriate new institutions, while the specific orientations of the new structure were first being surveyed and then determined.

During this period the rule of the new Manchukuo regime was made effective over most of the territory and its population. The transportation and communication system was improved and vastly extended; railway mileage in 1940 was double the 1931 total.[42] Existing installations in mineral extraction and heavy processing were reorganized and enlarged, production was pushed close to capacity, and new facilities were built to take advantage of the most promising opportunities. Urbanization proceeded rapidly, the most conspicuous feat being the construction of the modern city of Hsinking as the capital of Manchukuo at the site of the old Chinese town of Ch'angch'un. The economic frontier was pushed out by vigorous exploration and surveying of resources, resulting in the discovery of large rich deposits of iron ore in the Tungpientao region, and other mineral reserves. Research on low-grade resources, both mineral and agricultural, was intensified and yielded more or less practicable processes for working the low-grade iron ores, extracting oil from shale, sifting alluvial gold deposits, utilizing alumina shale instead of bauxite for aluminum, growing upland cotton and rice, improving livestock breeds, etc.[43] Agriculture was something of a stepchild amid all this activity, being left mostly to the effects of demand and supply;

[41] SMR *Report on Progress in Manchuria to 1936,* p. 98.

[42] *Manchoukuo Year Book, 1942* (Hsinking, 1942), pp. 585–588. The figures for both dates include the mileage of the Chinese Eastern Railway, which the Manchukuo government bought in 1935 from the Russians; the latter thus extricated themselves from an untenable strategic and economic position, whereas the Manchukuo regime was enabled to unify the railway system.

[43] According to H. Foster Bain, the Japanese innovations in the roasting and sintering of low-grade iron ores put the Manchurian iron and steel industry in a strong competitive position among other steel centers. The oil and aluminum processes, however, continued to be high in cost. See "Manchuria, a Key Area," *Foreign Affairs,* 25:116 (October 1946).

but crop research was supported, and there were the rudiments of an agricultural extension service, new facilities for rural credit, railway rate concessions, and the formation of special agencies to promote the cultivation of desired crops (cotton, rice, sugar beets, cordage fibers, castor beans, etc.). On the other hand, the inflow of farmers was curtailed by obstacles put in the way of the immigration of Chinese, in a rather unsuccessful effort to promote colonization by Japanese.[44]

The Manchukuo regime also proceeded to reform the basic financial institutions. The currency and banking systems were brought from their previous disorder (outside the SMR Zone) into an orthodox "sound" condition. Specialized financial institutions (Central Bank of Manchu, Industrial Bank of Manchu, Rural Credit Association, etc.) were instituted to serve particular developmental needs. The fiscal system was also revised, chiefly by reforming and centralizing the administration and by enlarging the scope of state monopolies (salt, matches, alcohol, opium), and extending the land tax, the business tax, and various excises (wine, tobacco, etc.). Export and import duties were amended, partly to stabilize revenue but more particularly to encourage trade in certain commodities and discourage trade in others.[45]

The Manchukuo government's ordinary revenues rose by about 80 percent during its first five years and its current expenditures rose correspondingly. But the amounts in these categories were small, and the government's investments in industry and other capital formation were financed not from ordinary revenues but from bonds issued in Japan, loans from the Bank of Japan, and loans from the Central Bank of Manchu. The total of the government's internal borrowings was relatively modest up to 1937, for Japanese investors were providing most of the finance for industrial development, and most military costs were borne by the government of Japan.

The most complex problem of structure and values during 1932–36 concerned the respective roles of private and state action. The Kwantung Army leaders were apparently not clear in their own minds as to desirable policy in the relatively unfamiliar arena of economic affairs, for they failed to specify in the 1933 Programme the "important economic activities" in which the state was to predominate. Certain areas were evidently destined for state domination, especially transportation,

[44] These activities in utilizing resources are summarized from SMR *Report on Progress in Manchuria to 1939*, pp. 58–63.

[45] *Ibid.*, pp. 82–94; and Jones, *op. cit.*, Chapter 7.

mineral extraction, metallurgy, and heavy chemicals. Certain other areas were almost as evidently destined to be more or less free of state intervention, notably agriculture, commerce and services, handicrafts, and some of the modern establishments for producing consumer goods. Between these two sets of areas was terra incognita, and until 1937 no sharp line was drawn through it. The need for such a line was to some extent postponed by the choice of an instrument to execute the government's industrial policies. This was to be the SMR, with its old and new subsidiary companies, in all of which private parties could take a very subordinate share. As a semiofficial agency with deep roots in the Manchurian situation and substantial independence of the Japanese Zaibatsu, the SMR seemed admirably adapted to the Army's scheme for excluding the Zaibatsu and eclipsing their achievements. In addition to assigning many new industrial undertakings directly to the SMR, and authorizing the Company to more than double its capital stock (again reserving half for the Japanese government) and its funded debt, the government also authorized the creation of "semispecial" companies. The latter were largely private concerns operating "important economic activities," and were assisted and closely supervised by the SMR, by the government, or (unfortunately for the particular concern) sometimes by both. The Manchukuo government also established a number of "special" corporations, largely financed by the Treasury and wholly controlled by the authorities.

During 1932–36 this vaguely mixed system of governmental primacy and residual private action worked reasonably well toward the ends in view. Difficulties began to appear when the authorities raised their program targets in 1936, for the enlarged goals involved new technologic needs which could not be met with the existing institutions. It seemed time for a major reorganization with more comprehensive planning, and new possibilities for state-private collaboration were presented.

The Second Period of Manchukuo, 1937–41

Early in 1937 the Manchukuo government issued its "Second-Period Construction Program" for the five years 1937–41. This program was designed "to meet the need of strengthening the Japan-Manchukuo economic bloc and to enable Manchukuo to develop resources necessary for her national defense and for the eventual establishment of self-sufficiency of goods for consumption within the country as well as to supplement the resources of Japan." [46] The program was framed in terms of (a) production targets for various economic sectors; (b) investment expenditures, public and private, for the several sectors; and (c) certain institutional changes and innovations. A five-year industrial plan specified targets and expenditures for various branches of mineral extraction and processing, for wood pulp, and for electric power, and provided in more general terms for the expansion of manufacturing, especially automotive products, aircraft, and munitions. For the agricultural sector specific target outputs were set, and expenditures for research and extension services, irrigation, crop loans and grubstakes, subsidies, etc. were intended to help farmers achieve the targets. Not only was total output to be increased and productivity raised, but production was to be diversified—partly to free the farmers from excessive dependence on the one-crop culture of soy beans, as Japanese propaganda declared, but partly to make Manchukuo self-sufficient in foodstuffs (especially wheat and rice) and to provide crops needed in Japan's "quasi wartime" economy (especially cotton, kenafe, flax, and beet sugar). Rural credit was to be improved and large-scale Japanese immigration was to be promoted. In transportation and communication, only moderate expansion of railways was projected, but extensive construction of highways was programmed.[47]

The "Construction Program" was far-reaching but not fully comprehensive. It emphasized heavy industry, agriculture, and transportation, and virtually ignored light industry and services. Furthermore, it did not make detailed allocations in the Soviet way, but relied on setting targets, fixing government outlays, and influencing private action by propaganda, regulation, and institutional adaptation. The pattern of these influences over the private sector deserves further specification.

Manchuria's economy after 1937 was of the mixed type. Not so comprehensively nationalized and planned as the Soviet system, the economy of Manchukuo moved further toward government ownership and direct controls than either Germany under the Nazis or Japan under the quasi wartime economy of the late 1930's. In comparison with the postwar British economy under the Labor government—which nationalized chiefly coal, steel, and the public utilities, and restricted its control to certain strategic operations—the Manchukuo

[46] SMR *Report . . . to 1939,* p. 58.
[47] *Ibid.,* pp. 58–64.

economy was subject to much more extensive and intensive intervention by the state. The state dominated certain industrial fields and left others to private action. The Law Controlling Important Industries, issued in May 1937, reduced the ambiguity of the 1933 Programme by listing 21 industries subject to close state control of operations and investment.[48] These included virtually all the heavy industries and the greater part of the other large-scale industries, for most of which specific output and investment goals had been set up. In agriculture, the goals were implemented not by specific controls but by a combination of inducements and penalties (such as reduction in supplies of rationed consumer goods), together with state monopsonistic agencies which manipulated crop prices. Finally, the small-scale industries, handicrafts, and services were free of both specific control and specialized regulation. All economic activities, however, were affected by broad governmental regulations, which included control of the total supply of labor (especially by control of immigration) and allocation of part of that supply, priorities for the granting of bank credit, fiscal concessions, and regulation of exports and imports.

From the institutional point of view, the state implemented its most urgent programs by establishing special companies (largely government-owned) or semispecial companies (partly financed and closely regulated by the government) in the industries deemed vital: mining and metallurgy, chemicals, electric power, automobiles, aircraft, transportation, colonization, and banking. It is noteworthy that in other countries many such companies are owned or closely regulated by the state, because of their "public utility" or "national security" character. Formally, private enterprises had a place even in the area of vital industry, and they prevailed throughout the rest of the economy. At the end of 1938 there were in Manchuria 41 of the special and semispecial companies with a paid-up capital of 1.15 billion yuan, of which about one third was held by the Manchukuo government; but there were altogether nearly 4,000 companies and partnerships with an aggregate paid-up capital of 2.48 billion yuan.[49]

Of all the structural shifts, the most outstanding was the curtailment of the South Manchuria Railway Company in favor of a new instrumentality. By 1937, the SMR had become "over-extended and over-

48 *Ibid.*, p. 183.

49 *Ibid.*, pp. 76–77; and Elizabeth B. Schumpeter, ed. *The Industrialization of Japan and Manchukuo, 1930–1940* (New York: Macmillan Company, 1940), p. 400.

burdened, and it suffered from both managerial and financial difficulties." [50] It had become a gigantic holding company for a great diversity of "subsidiary" firms, some of which were in an unprofitable stage of growth while a few had very dubious prospects. In addition, the SMR was becoming more and more involved in the financing and supervision of the semispecial companies. In fact, it had been pushed into central planning functions for which it was unsuited, since it was still essentially a private, profit-seeking corporation. Its business-minded and rather conservative management was suspected of being "not always in sympathy with the aims and methods of the Manchurian administration." [51] Furthermore, the Company was not a very good channel for obtaining new capital from Japanese investors, since its 8 percent dividend rate (on the privately held shares) was not very attractive in comparison with booming opportunities in Japan in this period.

These deficiencies of the SMR as a tool of the Manchukuo regime became apparent in 1936–37 as its leaders prepared to move from the stage of strengthening the structural foundations of their system to that of concrete and rapid expansion. To carry out the five-year industrial plan vast increases in capital investment and in technical services would evidently be required. The most readily available sources of both were the Zaibatsu and other business groups in Japan. As it happened, there had recently developed certain new Zaibatsu groups (especially the Nippon Sangyo Kaisha, commonly called Nissan) who were relatively free of the traits that the Army opposed in the older Zaibatsu (Mitsui, Mitsubishi, Yasuda, Sumitomo). The new Zaibatsu were chiefly engaged in the same heavy industries that the Manchukuo regime wished to promote, and their company shares were fairly widely held, rather than closely concentrated in families as in the older Zaibatsu. The Army could collaborate with these "new men" without losing face.

In this situation a huge new agency, the Manchuria Heavy Industry Company (Mangyo), was created as an equal partnership of the Nissan interests and the Manchukuo government. This company took over most of the industrial enterprises controlled by the state, including many subsidiaries of the SMR, leaving to the latter its transportation enterprises and some associated activities. The government, which

[50] Jones, *op. cit.,* p. 146.
[51] Schumpeter, *op. cit.,* p. 377.

supervised the new company and appointed its president and vice-presidents, guaranteed a minimum dividend of 6 percent.[52] The new company was inaugurated with much fanfare and optimism in December 1937, and quickly expanded its investments in most branches of heavy industry. It soon ran into managerial difficulties, however. Although it had nominal control of the subsidiary operating companies, its real control was undermined by the Manchukuo officials, who had their own independent lines of contact with those companies. The Nissan people who headed Mangyo were "business men interested in efficient and profitable management and they had frequent feuds with Army theorists and bureaucratic State planners."[53] In 1941 Mangyo was reorganized more tightly, but before the results could be seen the outbreak of war in the Pacific changed the whole situation.

To implement the vast plans of the "Construction Program," it was estimated that 2.5 billion yuan would be required (the Manchukuan yuan was maintained at parity with the yen, which was valued at about 28.8 U. S. cents in 1937). One fifth of this amount was to be raised in Manchukuo and the remainder in Japan. It was calculated that these sums, on an annual basis, would not be more than about 15 percent above the rate of actual investment in Manchuria during 1935. The government announced a policy of "sound finance," to cover the largest possible amount of the expenditures with tax revenues, and to this end revised the land tax, the customs, and the state monopolies. For investment purposes, however, the government also decided to float substantial loans as well as enlarge the supply of credit available to business firms. In 1938 the original goals were greatly stepped up, and the programmed expenditures were doubled, reaching the comparatively huge figure of 5 billion yuan (1.42 billion U. S. dollars at the 1938 exchange rate) for the five-year period. (In September 1938 they were raised still further, to 6 billion.) Of the 5 billion total, 1.7 billion was to be raised in Manchukuo, the amount to be sought in Japan remained at 2 billion as in 1937, and the remainder was to be raised abroad.

Long-term foreign capital from non-Japanese sources actually was not forthcoming, although some 80 percent of the estimated requirement of 850 million yuan for 1938 was secured during that year. About two thirds of this amount came from Japan, in the form of investments

[52] SMR *Report . . . to 1939*, pp. 70–72, and "Administration Act," pp. 193–202.
[53] Jones, *op. cit.*, p. 150.

by private and semiofficial companies and by individual investors. During 1939 such Japanese investments provided over 1 billion yen and made possible a Manchurian import surplus of nearly equal magnitude; 26 percent was obtained by stock calls and bond issues of the SMR, 66 percent was obtained by other Manchurian corporations, and only 8 percent was procured by bond flotations of the Manchukuo government. The government's intended contribution to real capital formation during these years was large but cannot be specified, since it was absorbed in the "Special Accounts Budget," which showed estimated expenditures of just over 1 billion yuan in 1938 and 1.29 billion in 1939 (these amounts were over 3 times as large as the totals in the "General Accounts Budget" which chiefly covered ordinary administration rather than capital outlay). The government raised the capital for at least part of this program, primarily from domestic, nontax sources; internal borrowing in 1939 was scheduled for nearly 400 million yuan, an increase in currency issue for another 230 million, and additional sums were to be provided by advances from the Central Bank of Manchu. Over the four years 1936–40 the currency in circulation nearly quadrupled.

In consequence of such inflationary financing, prices began to rise rapidly in 1937. The government applied price and wage controls and rationed scarce consumer goods. These controls were not very effective, although the wage limitations were as usual more effective than the price restraints. Thus the inflation probably had the effect of holding down real consumption. For a time workers actually may have been stimulated by the money illusion to make greater efforts, but eventually real sacrifices and unrest set in. The inflation, as Mrs. Schumpeter suggests, also appears to have encouraged Japanese and Chinese entrepreneurs to invest in the semiofficial companies and to undertake the many ventures left to them amid the more massive projects of the government. In addition, as Cheng indicates, the relatively greater rise of Manchurian prices than of Japanese prices stimulated Japanese exports to Manchuria and discouraged the latter's exports. The balance of Manchuria's trade had swung from a long-standing surplus to a deficit after 1932, and this deficit tended to grow at an accelerating tempo. From 1929 to 1935 this trend represented chiefly the sharp world-wide slump in agricultural exports and the increasing importation of capital goods into Manchuria. After 1935 the recovery of soy bean prices more than compensated for the low export quantities (compared with predepression levels), but imports of capital goods, operating supplies, and consumer goods for new immigrants rose greatly. Meanwhile exports were restricted by the growing use of domestic products in Manchuria's own development and by delays in completing the new facilities for increasing production.[54]

The achievements of the Manchukuo regime are difficult merely to measure, let alone evaluate. An interval of only a few years had been available for constructive projects, when Japan's plunge into World War II turned most of her economic efforts from capital construction to current production and dislocated the flow of many supplies. Even before Pearl Harbor, Japan's ability to support the development of Manchuria was increasingly impaired by warfare in China, enlargement of Japan's armed forces, expansion of her economic war-base, and after 1939 the Allied blockade cutting off German supplies and technology. Consequently, Japan was unable to deliver all the capital goods, operating supplies, technicians, and other requisites for her ambitious Manchurian projects. Our information on what actually occurred is defective because many important statistical series were suppressed during this period. The available data and qualitative reports suggest that Manchurian productive capacity and actual production greatly increased after 1937, particularly in minerals and mineral products and also in the manufacture of heavy machinery and electrical equipment; meanwhile the expansion in cotton textiles and in railway lines—which had been growing rapidly since 1932—was slowed. Agriculture was the chief laggard. Output, which had never fully recovered from the slump of the early 1930's, suffered subsequently from a labor shortage as the industrialization program drew men off the land, and was further impaired by the low purchasing prices fixed by the government's exclusive marketing boards, which were set up in the late 1930's for several important crops.[55]

When it comes to evaluating the Manchukuo era, the uncertainties are still larger and the dangers of misinterpretation are more serious. Several analysts have taken the view that the Japanese committed themselves to an enormous waste of capital and resources by attempt-

[54] The financial details in the foregoing three paragraphs are from SMR *Report . . . to 1939*, pp. 64–69, 147–150; Schumpeter, *op. cit.,* pp. 397–399; *Oriental Economist,* March 1940, p. 152; Jones, *op. cit.,* pp. 136–138, 196–205, 217–218; and Yu-Kwei Cheng, *Foreign Trade and Industrial Development of China* (Washington, D. C.: University Press, 1956), pp. 203–207.

[55] Based on data in Jones, *op. cit.,* pp. 112, 153–164; Schumpeter, *op. cit.,* Table 103, p. 388; SMR *Report . . . to 1936,* p. 164, and *Report . . . to 1939,* p. 156; Cheng, *op. cit.,* pp. 187–194.

ing to industrialize Manchuria beyond its comparative advantages, in the pursuit of primarily political, military, and monopolistic aims. The data presented in evidence of such waste are rarely analytic, and consist chiefly of historical records showing small returns on the investment, strong inflationary pressures, and difficulties with the balance of international payments.[56] The principal difficulty with this view is the short historical perspective. If all intensive efforts had to be justified by immediate returns, there would be little constructive work done in the world—whether in individual investments, national development, or even scholarly research. The choice of the proper period for study, the proper definition of "costs" and "returns," and the proper recognition of both "stability" and "progress" are intricate and debatable matters; and they are not well resolved by adopting the most mechanical and importunate standards. A broad outlook is particularly important in dealing with large undertakings that alter the parameters of a whole society. For these undertakings eventually alter the profit showings, the comparative advantages, and the levels at which stabilization becomes possible and desirable, both for individual firms and for the whole economy.

To be sure, some of the Manchukuan projects represented strategic rather than economic aims and depended on special Japanese markets and support. And it is easy to point to certain high-cost efforts, such as the extraction of oil from shale and from coal (although even here there remained possibilities for technological advance, including the application of methods already developed abroad). But the main body of projects in Manchuria represented an industrialization effort that, like comparable earlier movements in Japan itself or the early industrial revolution in the West, could only justify itself in an ultimately transformed and more productive economy, which would find its appropriate place in the world economy.

Thus, the economic worth of the Japanese undertakings in Manchuria during the 1930's must be judged in the light of the developmental potentialities and obstacles, the trends of developmental efforts during the period, and the probable economic outcome if the Japanese leadership had not embarked on aggressive and destructive

---

[56] See, for example, John R. Stewart, *Manchuria Since 1931* (New York: Institute of Pacific Relations, 1936), especially pp. 8–9, 46; and Lockwood, *op. cit.*, p. 538. Lockwood allows for the possibility of "myopia" in this judgment. The most extreme treatment is by Irving I. Kramer, *Japan in Manchuria* (Tokyo: Foreign Affairs Association of Japan, 1954).

adventures first in China Proper and then in World War II. In other words, the indictment of Japanese militarism rests on such strong *moral* grounds that it does not require dubious and misleading arguments as to the *economic* aspect.

CONCLUSION

The significant role of the state in Manchuria's economic development may be formulated by recapitulating the record in terms of the process model of "opportunities."

Manchuria before the coming of the foreigners was marked by: rich economic potentialities; scanty and inefficient means of production; agents who operated on a small scale and along conservative lines; massive obstacles in the political bureaucracy, the system of land tenure, and other features of the social structure; and the traditional culture and social aims, which deprecated economic affairs and stressed continuity and compromise rather than change and transformation. This situation could not present large opportunities for development until the conditions were altered by some kind of force.

The foreign governments, especially the Japanese, supplied this force. They explored the potentialities; introduced advanced technologies and capital, carried on research, enforced peace and order, and set up needed facilities; took important leads, which were followed slowly by the Chinese authorities, and more rapidly by private agents who entered into the many complex operations of production and marketing that appeared unsuited to official agencies; broke through or circumvented many social practices and structural obstacles; and insisted on developmental aims. Thus the foreign governments introduced in Manchuria the essential disequilibria which opened the opportunities for cumulative development.

Up to the 1930's, governmental activities were concerned chiefly with the framework of the Manchurian economy. During the 1930's, when the puppet state undertook a more positive role and greater participation in direct production, the economy was not nationalized and tightly centralized after the Soviet pattern, but held to the fascist model of mixed enterprise with governmental domination of "important" sectors.

Alternative agents who might have performed the same developmental functions as the foreign governments were neither plentiful nor powerful. It is doubtful that private foreign entrepreneurs, without their governments' pioneering and aid, could have done the same job. It is virtually certain that potential Chinese entrepreneurs under the pre-existing conditions would have accomplished very little, at least in the period before 1930. On the other hand, the economic yardstick is not the only criterion; against the economic achievements of the Japanese in Manchuria must be set their political and military aggression, and the cultural and personal costs of drastic social change.

Conditions in Manchuria were relatively favorable for economic development, as compared with many retarded countries today. There are, nevertheless, some general implications for criteria of developmental action. It should be clear that the process of development in Manchuria was not "steady" or "gradual"; it did not maintain continuous "balance"; and it did not maximize current income, let alone current "welfare." On the contrary, the development of Manchuria exhibited wide leads and lags in the interrelations of demand, capacity, and output; it showed sharp discontinuities in production functions and in structural change; it gave varying emphasis to the several economic sectors; in the short run and in the medium run it incurred substantial waste and sacrifice. In sum, the development of Manchuria —like many other real processes of social behavior—does not agree very closely with many of the prevalent rationalist criteria for maximizing current results. This is not to say that such criteria are not useful for indicating base lines and the degree of departure from them, for describing the logical limits of possibility under specified conditions, or for improving actual performance. The danger is that such criteria will be used mechanically to tie the hands of the state or other economic agents and prevent them from taking constructive action which would also be disequilibrating. A sustained but carefully limited disequilibrium is not a mere unfortunate accompaniment of development; it is of the essence of "opportunities," and the process of cumulative development.

6 ECONOMIC GROWTH IN GERMANY

Norman J. G. Pounds

"The German Empire has been built," wrote Keynes, "more truly on coal and iron than on blood and iron." [1] The German Empire was well endowed with coal, iron ore, and certain other raw materials, but it was not because she possessed these assets that she developed a powerful manufacturing industry. In fact, Germany was well on the road to industrialization before the richness of her natural endowment was discovered. And if these resources had proved to be much smaller and less valuable than they were, Germany's industrial objective would probably have remained unaltered, although her course might have been changed in detail.

Germany's advantages were not limited to fuel and minerals. A tradition of careful craftsmanship and qualities of industry and devotion to duty in her people combined with a degree of state assistance, not always enlightened but generally opportune, to build up in the nineteenth century the most impressive modern industry in Europe.

The expansion of the German economy has been characterized as intrinsic, dominant, and autonomous.[2] There can be little doubt that it was intrinsic in the sense that it did not, in Toynbee's phrase, experience the "stimulus of new lands." It was autochthonous: it grew up within the territorial limits allotted to the German Confederation in 1815. Both the United Kingdom and, to a limited extent, France were expansionist in the sense that new sources of materials and new markets were revealed as the course of empire in effect expanded the territorial limits of the state. But the German colonial empire came late and only after the colonial plums had all been picked by Germany's neighbors and rivals.

It must not be assumed, however, that the expansive aspect was entirely lacking. No less than three phases in German industrial growth can be described as expansionist within the meaning employed in this volume.

[1] John M. Keynes, *The Economic Consequences of the Peace* (New York: Harcourt, Brace and Howe, 1920), p. 81.

[2] Hoselitz, "Patterns of Economic Growth," *Canadian Journal of Economics and Political Science,* 21:427.

Germany was left at the end of the Napoleonic Wars as a congeries of some 50 states, each enjoying a quasi sovereignty within a loose and ineffective Confederation. No more than half a dozen had, or were ever to have, any considerable industrial importance. They remained, apart from the mining carried on in some of them, predominantly rural and agricultural. During the nineteenth century, all these territorial units were incorporated into a single politico-economic whole, first through the operations of the Zollverein, then by the formation of the North German Confederation, and finally by incorporation into the German Empire. The industrial development in the nuclei of German industry that were already established profited greatly from the expanding economic opportunities that resulted from the incorporation of other units into their commercial sphere.

The German economy was expansionist, also, in the acquisition of new and contiguous territory—Alsace and Lorraine. Economic motives were probably not foremost in the minds of the German rulers in 1871, when they dictated the terms of the Treaty of Frankfurt. But the iron ore of Lorraine and, to a much smaller extent, its coal soon came to support an iron industry that was of immense significance to the German economy as a whole.

Lastly, Germany succeeded during the later years of the nineteenth century in establishing a kind of economic empire over the lands of the Austro-Hungarian monarchy. Germany not only dominated the foreign trade of this area but also established within it manufacturing units that were subsidiaries of German firms. In Russia, too, where the high tariff wall with which the Tsars surrounded their empire prevented the influx of more than a small proportion of the imports that could have been taken, German industrialists established works either on their own initiative, as in the iron industry of Dąbrowa, or at the invitation of the local authorities, as in the case of the cotton mills at Łódź.

Although in these three respects German economic development in the nineteenth century may be defined as expansionist, the economy remained essentially intrinsic. Germany in 1815 was a well-settled country, in process of shaping its own techniques and skills and using these to develop its own resources.

The description of the German economy in the nineteenth century as dominant or independent—in the sense that its growth was based only on the domestic accumulation of capital and locally developed skills and techniques—is also true in the main, but certain qualifications may fairly be made. Non-German capital was not significant in German industrial enterprises established in the nineteenth century. Belgian capital was invested in some of the earlier concerns in the Ruhr, and there was a little French capital in some West German coal mines. Until the end of the century foreign capital was of negligible importance in industrial undertakings in Central and West Germany. On the other hand, Germany relied heavily on skills and techniques evolved in other countries, particularly in spinning and weaving and in iron smelting, iron refining, and steel making. It is probable that Upper Silesia owed its early lead in the iron-smelting and refining industries to its acceptance of British technology. British technicians were brought to Upper Silesia before 1800, on the initiative of the Prussian state, to impart their knowledge to local craftsmen. That English craftsmen achieved so much in Silesia and so little in France, where they were brought a few years earlier, suggests that resources and skill alone are an inadequate basis for an industry.

Greater exception may perhaps be taken to the generalization that German industrial development was autonomous, as defined on page 2 supra. The German state never consciously and deliberately adopted a laissez-faire policy, such as was practiced in England. During much of the period under discussion, the governmental authorities made decisions that vitally affected the growth of industry, and many of these decisions were intended to encourage industrial expansion in specific directions.

The active role of the state was more clearly demonstrated in the Prussian province of Silesia than elsewhere.[3] The modern iron industry of Upper Silesia was created by the Prussian state, which itself operated both coal mines and ironworks. It also controlled most of the lead mining and smelting; the only branch of heavy industry in this region in which the state did not participate was zinc working. In the Ruhr area the Prussian state for a time operated a coal-mining company. The coal mines of the Saar were taken over by the Prince of Hesse-Nassau in the eighteenth century, and during much of the nineteenth century were run as fiscal mines. Elsewhere in Germany there were

<hr/>

[3] O. Simmersbach, "Die Begrundung der oberschlesischen Eisenindustrie unter Preussens Königen," *Stahl und Eisen*, 31:213–217 (1911); K. Wutke, "Aus der Vergangenheit des Schlesischen Berg und Hüttenlebens," *Der Bergbau im Ostens des Königreichs Preussen*, Vol. 5 (Breslau, 1913); N. J. G. Pounds, *The Upper Silesian Industrial Region*, Indiana University Publications, Slavic and East European Series, Vol. 11 (1958).

state-operated works, most of which catered in one way or another to military needs, but served other ends as well.

In addition to direct participation in industrial enterprises, the Prussian state exercised close supervision over works that were in private hands.[4] It was particularly concerned in the technical conduct of industries of military significance and, until the *Direktionsprinzip* was abolished in 1864, arrogated to itself the right to nominate the technical directors of certain types of works. The Prussian state also manifested concern for the economic welfare of its industries by protecting them as much as it thought necessary from foreign competition. The report of the *Eisen-Enquette-Commission* of 1878 is a monument to the solicitude of the German government in this respect and, furthermore, was produced at a time when other European countries were adopting a policy of laissez faire.

Although private initiative was not unimportant, it was overshadowed in certain areas, notably Silesia, at least in the earlier phases by the operations of the state. Whether in the long run these operations were beneficial or served as a drag on private initiative remains to be seen.

ECONOMIC DEVELOPMENT OF UPPER SILESIA

The case of Upper Silesia is admittedly an extreme one. The province of Silesia, which was annexed to the Prussian crown by Frederick the Great in 1741, was a forested, sparsely populated area. Much of it was divided into large estates and held by a numerically restricted aristocracy. The inextensive agricultural land was tilled by primitive methods by a peasantry which was in part landless and bound to the soil of its masters. Here one would not look for liquid capital awaiting investment opportunities nor for a pool of labor suited to the needs of factory industry.[5]

Yet it was in the forests of Upper Silesia that technical advances

---

[4] A. Serlo, "Beitrag zur Geschichte des schlesischen Bergbaues in den letzten Hundert Jahren," *Festschrift zur Feier des hundert-jährigen Bestehens des Königlichen Oberbergamtes zu Breslau* (Breslau, 1869); *Handbuch des Oberschlesischen Industriebezirks,* Festschrift zum XII Allgemeinen Deutschen Bergmannstage in Breslau (Kattowitz, 1913); A. Steinbeck, *Geschichte des schlesischen Bergbaues* (Breslau, 1857); Ezechiel Zivier, *Geschichte des Bergregals in Schlesien* (Kattowitz, 1898); Oberbergrath Gedike, "Geschichte der schlesischen Bergbau-Privilegium," *Zeitschrift für Bergrecht,* Vols. 13–15 (1872–74).

[5] Fritz Redlich, *History of American Business Leaders,* Vol. 1 (Ann Arbor: Edwards Brothers, 1940), pp. 36–38.

were made, in both the working of iron and the extraction of minerals, that were of the greatest significance for the development of industry in Germany as a whole. A primitive mode of ironworking had long been used. Ore, extracted in small nodules from the shallow swamps, was smelted with charcoal on a hearth. The resulting poor-quality iron was used to fabricate the simple tools of an agricultural society. An iron industry of this primitive kind was carried on in most parts of Europe, and during the nineteenth century disappeared from almost all of them.

In 1753 the Prussian government established the *Malapane Hütte,* a small but, for the times, modern blast-furnace works and foundry. Its purpose was to cast ordnance, and the location in Upper Silesia was chosen rather than one more favorably endowed with mineral resources because of the proximity to the probable future battlefields along the boundary of Austria.[6]

The initiative of the Prussian state was manifested in other ways. The most precious industrial asset of the area at this time seemed to be the deposits of lead ore (galena) in the Triassic limestone beds. Lead was a regalian mineral; the Prussian King had, if he chose, an exclusive right to mine lead. This right probably derived from the military importance of lead as the material from which shot was customarily made. Coal was known to exist in Upper Silesia, but until the middle of the eighteenth century was not mined because there was no conceivable use for it.

The conjuncture of coal, iron ore, and certain nonferrous metals was not uncommon, but to synthesize them into a manufacturing industry called for initiative and foresight, technical skill, and capital. All these the Prussian government supplied. One of the more positive characteristics of Frederick the Great was his capacity for choosing subordinates. His choice of F. A. von Heinitz to head the mining and manufacturing division of the Prussian government was a wise one. As his chief lieutenant in Silesia, von Heinitz chose Graf von Reden. To these two men is due the implementation of the government's plans.[7]

---

[6] Hermann Fechner, "Geschichte des Schlesischen Berg- und Hüttenwesens in der Zeit Friedrich's des Grossen, Friedrich Wilhelm's II und Friedrich Wilhelm's III, 1741 bis 1806," *Zeitschrift für das Berg-, Hütten- und Salinenwesen im preussischen Staate,* Vols. 48–50 (1900–1902).

[7] F. A. von Heinitz, "Mémoire sur les produits du règne minéral de la Monarchie Prussienne," in Honoré Gabriel Riquetti, comte de Mirabeau, *De la Monarchie Prussienne,* Vol. 2 (London, 1788), pp. 213–303.

The motives that inspired the Prussian government were military in character. The newly acquired territories might have to be defended. Roads were bad, and hauling military supplies to the Austrian border was excessively difficult. So, not for the last time in industrial history, industrial development sprang from the need to establish an armory close to an expected scene of conflict. Thus the initiative of the Prussian government owed little to the exceptional natural resources of this area. If there was a single resource that recommended Upper Silesia as a site for an iron industry, it was the vast expanse of virgin forest which could provide charcoal in plenty.

In 1779 von Reden was appointed to the office of *Oberbergamt* for Silesia, and at once applied himself to improving the technology and extending the scope of the Upper Silesian industry. Some mystery surrounds the visit of von Reden to England to learn about the new technical processes that had been perfected there, as it does a similar visit by vom Stein. But von Reden was able to persuade William Wilkinson, brother of one of the most distinguished and successful ironmasters, to accompany him to Silesia.[8] Experiments at the *Malapane Hütte* in smelting with coke followed; the results were not satisfactory but at least showed promise. Another furnace was built, presumably according to Wilkinson's specification, and operated with greater success.

Malapane lay almost 40 miles from the nearest known outcrop of coal. The next step, also instigated by von Reden, was the erection of a blast furnace on the coal field. Gleiwitz was chosen for the new operations, and the first blast furnace to operate on the Upper Silesian coal field was successfully brought in by a Scottish iron founder, John Baildon.

It is impossible to record the steps by which the Prussian government went on to establish the *Königshütte,* long one of the largest and most efficient iron-smelting works in Europe. The puddling process of making soft or weld iron from high-carbon pig iron had been patented in England in 1781. Not long afterwards it was successfully used at the Royal Prussian works in Upper Silesia.

The initiative of the state was not confined to the establishment of ironworks. By law the state possessed the sole right of mining certain minerals, a store of which was supposedly of national importance. These included bullion, of course, and also lead. The *Friedrichsgrube* was developed under von Reden's direction into a major source of

---

[8] W. O. Henderson, *Britain and Industrial Europe, 1750–1870* (Liverpool: University Press, 1954).

lead for the Prussian state. Here was established the first steam engine, of English design, for pumping water; and a state-owned coal mine was opened to supply fuel for the lead smelter and subsequently for the ironworks.

Private enterprise on any considerable scale came later, and was of little importance until 30–40 years after the establishment of the fiscal works. The privately owned works owed much to the example of the state-owned enterprises. The latter were very efficient for their time and aroused the envy of ironmasters elsewhere. A writer in 1842 described the industrial complex of Upper Silesia, with pardonable exaggeration, as "the equal of England and foremost on the continent of Europe." [9] If indeed it had attained this position, it was because of the initiative and example of the state.

Until the law was changed in 1864, certain categories of private industry, including the mining and metallurgical, were obliged to accept technical directors nominated by the state. The purpose of this *Direktionsprinzip* was to assure a high level of technical efficiency in a range of industry deemed to be of strategic importance. Undoubtedly, the directors trained and assigned by the Prussian state were able and efficient, and the high technical level of Upper Silesian industry in the first half of the nineteenth century, in contrast with that in other parts of Germany, was probably due largely to this means of disseminating technical knowledge.

Two questions may fairly be raised: Did the *Direktionsprinzip* inhibit the formation of companies and thus restrict economic growth; and was it continued too long? The first question is difficult to answer because in Silesia the number of entrepreneurs was smaller and their available capital less than in other parts of Germany. Nevertheless, if we compare the rash of little ironworks in Central and West Germany with their relative paucity in Silesia, it is possible to argue that the system did restrain the small-scale entrepreneur. It can also be argued that it made him more efficient. In the technical journals which began to proliferate in the 1830's and 1840's, a mass of evidence indicates that the conduct of many ironworks in various parts of Germany was characterized by crass ignorance of technical processes and by gross inefficiency. The absence of serious complaint about the conduct of the privately owned works in Upper Silesia suggests, though it does not prove, that they were better operated. If so, it may have been due in part to the example of the neighboring state-owned works. Iron-

[9] *Berg- und Hüttenmännische Zeitung,* 1:58 (1842).

works, some of considerable size, established by the great landowners of Upper Silesia, in particular by Hohenlohe, Renard, and the two branches of the Henckel von Donnersmarck family, were highly efficient by the standards of the first half of the nineteenth century.[10] In their operation the influence of the state-owned works is easily traced, even to the sharing of the services of John Baildon, who was brought over from Great Britain by the Prussian government.[11]

As to whether the *Direktionsprinzip* was maintained too long, it is perhaps easier to give a direct answer. By the middle of the century several small merchant groups were interested in establishing iron-works, and technical knowledge was more accessible. There is evidence that several technical periodicals were widely read. The state and its officials no longer had a monopoly of technical knowledge, and it is possible that the technical directors had become somewhat conservative and old-fashioned in their methods. Apparently it was better to leave technical advance to private initiative and the profit incentive.

From the middle of the century economic growth in Upper Silesia lost something of its *élan* or, at least, lagged in relation to that in other parts of Germany. During these years the entrepreneur was very active in the Rhineland and to a lesser extent in Central Germany, and Upper Silesia was soon exceeded by other regions in the total volume of production. Coal production, which reflects the volume of industrial activity, grew much faster in the Ruhr than in Silesia; and when given the opportunity, investment capital chose the Rhineland rather than Silesia. The abandonment of the *Direktionsprinzip* was followed in Upper Silesia by the formation of many companies, and by investment by banks in metallurgical undertakings. One is forced to conclude that the state's control over industry had deterred large-scale investment of private capital in Upper Silesia before the 1870's.

CONTRASTING DEVELOPMENTS

The attempts to stimulate industrial growth in Saxony and Thuringia in the first half of the nineteenth century afford an interesting contrast with those in Silesia. We know now that the raw materials

[10] L. Wachler, "Die Lage des Eisenhüttenbetriebes in Oberschlesien," *Zeitschrift für das Berg-, Hütten- und Salinenwesen,* 2:130–158 (1855).

[11] W. Paley Baildon, *Baildon and the Baildons,* Vol. II (London: St. Catherine Press [1912–26]), pp. 491–494.

of the former area are insufficient to support a large industry, but this fact was not apparent a hundred years ago. Indeed, the variety of craft industries, the relatively dense population, and its purchasing power—so much higher than that of Silesia—might have been thought to hold excellent promise for industrial growth. Yet attempts to develop industry there were generally unsuccessful. In spite of the presence of raw materials that were adequate for industry at that stage of its development, and of market possibilities, a smelting and ironworking industry failed to take root. A writer in 1850 laid this failure to "the conservatism of the older men, an unwillingness to progress with the times, and, in many instances, a lack of carefully trained and skilled workmen." [12] A works near Zwickau, in Saxony, where materials of adequate quality appeared to have been used, failed. The same journal commented on the lack of technical skill at the furnace and attributed the failure to this lack.[13] The technical literature of this period indicates many instances of such failures to develop industries—most of them attributable to technological ignorance and incapacity.

It seems possible to divide the nineteenth century into two periods, during the earlier of which industrial growth was in some measure induced. Such were the conditions, technical and economic, that perhaps any carefully conceived and executed plan of industrial development could become successful, provided it received the wholehearted support of the state. Location and resources were of much less importance than initiative. In the economic and social conditions in Germany a century and a half ago, only the state could induce technicians from other countries to bring their skills and apply them to the German resources. The establishment of the textile industry at Łódź is an analogous example of successful governmental promotion of industry.

During the second period industrial growth had more of an autonomous quality. It was characterized by greater mobility of skilled personnel and easier access to technical knowledge. There was a greater number and a wider circulation of technical journals. The level of scientific education was higher; and a very important factor in its spread, a vocabulary with which to describe scientific and technical processes, had developed and gained wide acceptance. The net effect was to raise the level of technical knowledge and achievement. Some

---

[12] *Berg- und Hüttenmännische Zeitung*, 9:257–258 (1850).
[13] *Ibid.*, 8:83–84 (1849).

industries and areas remained technically backward, of course, but these became fewer year by year.

Competition in this second period forced firms to adopt the newer technologies in order to remain in operation. But another influence began to assert itself, as the expanding network of transport facilities created something of a common market. The excellence and abundance, or other characteristics, of local deposits of ore and fuel had mattered little when competition between iron-producing regions was inhibited by difficulty of transport or by tariff barriers. The local market of each producing unit was highly protected. But the gradual creation of a common market had a selective influence on producing areas: there was a process of concentration of production in a few specially favored areas. Of these, the best endowed and most conveniently located was the Ruhr area of the lower Rhineland. This industrial region experienced neither the invigoration of Prussia's drive and efficiency in the early stages, nor the stultifying effect of state control when this had lost its freshness and originality. By about the middle of the century the Ruhr drew into first place as a producer of iron goods, and during the present century has gradually increased its lead. Other producing areas, which had shown promise in the 1840's, declined in both relative and absolute importance and by the end of the century had ceased to count. During the second period, then, market considerations in Germany at large and to some extent outside Germany were the chief influence on location and growth. It is difficult to define the limits of the two periods in which industrial growth was respectively induced and autonomous, but the effective completion of the *Zollverein* about 1860 may serve as an arbitrary point of separation.

In summary, we may say that the early phases of development of the German iron industries were heavily dependent on the initiative and support of the state. Given such support, intelligently applied, an industry could hardly be other than successful. The role of capital was minimized because the volume of investment in an early ironworks was relatively small. On the other hand, the availability of technical skill was, after an intelligent *dirigisme,* the most important single factor in the growth of an industry. During the so-called period of autonomous growth, the role of the state in Germany changed from one of active participation in the running of industry to one of more remote control. The government never ceased to manipulate duties in the interests of industry and, as is witnessed by the report of 1878, went to great pains to ascertain what exactly were the needs of industry. It is of some interest to compare the *induced* industrial growth in Germany with the failure of the government of France in the years preceding the Revolution to achieve a similar development. The details of the French experiment are familiar: the mission of Gabriel Jars to England to inquire into the new industrial processes; the publication of his voluminous report; the prolonged stay of William Wilkinson in France for the acknowledged purpose of instructing the French in new methods of furnace management; the experiments at Hayange, Alès, and Le Creusot.[14] Step by step, there is a remarkable similarity between this sequence of events in France and that in Silesia only a few years later. Yet the French enterprise was an ignominious failure, and the Silesian perhaps the outstanding example of state-promoted industrialization before the twentieth century.

The contrast is not easy to explain. There is no reason to suppose that the materials employed in the French enterprises were inferior in quality or inadequate in quantity. The government of France was no less anxious than the Prussian to establish a gun-forging industry. Yet the record of events in France is characterized by chicane and intrigue. Vested interests of individuals stood in the way of the enterprise. In the end, the Le Creusot works were diverted to the production of gewgaws for the royal court.

In contrast with the industrial development in Prussia, that in eighteenth-century France was grossly mismanaged by a corrupt and inefficient government. Achievements analogous to those in Upper Silesia were attained at Le Creusot, Alès, and St. Étienne some 40 to 50 years later, but by the enterprise of private individuals.

In 1744 the French government reformed the mining law, in a way likely to encourage efficient mining. In Artois, one area where the new law was enforced, it led to the opening of the "hidden" northern coal field by Desandrouin.[15] Elsewhere, the government was generally not strong enough to enforce its own legislation.

[14] C. Ballot, "La révolution technique et les débuts dans la métallurgie française," *Revue d'Histoire des Doctrines économiques*, 5:29–62 (1912); N. J. G. Pounds and W. N. Parker, *Coal and Steel in Western Europe* (Bloomington: Indiana University Press, 1957), pp. 68–74.

[15] Édouard Grar, *Histoire de la Recherche, de la Découverte et de l'Exploitation de la Houille dans le Hainaut français, dans la Flandre française et dans l'Artois* (Valenciennes, 1847–50); Pounds and Parker, *op. cit.*, pp. 91–94.

The clear-sightedness, ruthlessness, and efficiency of the Prussian government, more than any other single factor, explain the early advances in the metal industry of Germany. The ineptitude and failure of the comparable efforts of the French at this time only point up the importance of this factor in German economic growth.

7 NATIONAL STATES AND NATIONAL DEVELOPMENT: FRENCH AND GERMAN ORE MINING IN THE LATE NINETEENTH CENTURY

William N. Parker *

Over the past 200 years the principal Western countries have all experienced periods of rapid economic expansion. During this time they have been joined—at times more closely than at others—in a single network of trade and communication. The vivid picture drawn by Keynes in 1919 remains in our minds today because it represents an ideal with which the reality of the Western countries has never quite lost touch.[1] Capital, goods, skill, and technological knowledge did indeed move relatively readily among these countries before World War I.

Must not the common progress of this whole area be attributed to those elements whose international movement made them the common property of all? If so, differences in levels of activity and rates of growth in different portions of this area must be traceable to differing resources (relative to the prevailing industrial technology), and in lesser part to cost differentials arising from imperfect mobility of labor. From this viewpoint, the appropriate unit of study appears to be the whole international, intercommunicating region. Its long-run dynamics derive mainly from technological change and population growth, considered as independent variables to which economic life responds. The national economy as such then fades into nothingness; the state as an economic actor withers away. Where it has insisted

* The material for this paper was gathered in connection with another project, which was carried out with the assistance of a grant-in-aid from the Social Science Research Council in 1954–55. I also wish to acknowledge the support of Resources for the Future, Inc., which has permitted this extension of my earlier work.

[1] John M. Keynes, *The Economic Consequences of the Peace* (New York: Harcourt, Brace and Howe, 1920), Chapter 2. See also I. Svennilson, *Growth and Stagnation in the European Economy* (Geneva: United Nations Economic Commission for Europe, 1954), pp. 16–18.

on action, this appears as an embarrassment, misdirecting the stream of international investment and distorting the international price-cost system.

The view generally taken of the state's role in Western economic history does not contradict this impression. When tariffs, specific monetary and fiscal arrangements, and other examples of state interference are examined for a period predominantly laissez-faire, the impression is often confirmed. The national state is a political creature, and the fumbling fingers of many states in an international economy have generally warped the price system somewhat in directions suitable to the short-run designs of national politicians. Tax systems, tariffs, exchange controls, migration restrictions, all operating within arbitrarily defined regions, find slender and infrequent excuse as instruments for the economic development of an international area.

This is not to say that elements distinctive to national regions may not have had an important bearing on their rates of growth. Even in technology, perhaps the most communicable and international element in production, regional peculiarities impose themselves.[2] Though essentially governed by intellectual rather than economic developments, technological change is responsive to local needs and opportunities. The region where a technology originates hence often has a considerable advantage in its application. At least, every region needs a vigorous native engineering tradition to adapt foreign technology to its own uses. This holds true particularly in agriculture, mining, and smelting, which deal with natural materials in all their endless variations. A region's industrial career depends then in part on ability to train its own engineers. If this is important in technology, it is indispensable in entrepreneurship—a skill especially rooted in a particular social and geographical setting. Economic unit or not, the Western world has been splintered by language and cultural differences, and these have permitted differing responses to economic opportunity. The growth characteristic of Western nations in recent times may indeed have had a common set of causes in each. But these cannot

---

[2] For further treatment of this subject, see Norman J. G. Pounds and William N. Parker, *Coal and Steel in Western Europe* (Bloomington: Indiana University Press, 1957), Chapter 9, and the references cited therein. The adaptation of coking technology to the qualities and prices of local coals and the market for coke oven products is a particularly intriguing subject which still awaits treatment. For material on adaptation of blast furnace construction and practice, see Fred Clements, *Blast Furnace Practice*, 3 vols. (London: E. Benn, 1929–33).

lie exclusively in those elements of production that move freely in the international network of trade and communication. A set of immobile elements, reproduced within each national region, may account for similarities as well as for some differences in the records of Western nations. It is not essential that these separate elements be identical from one national society to another, but each society's set of elements must function together to give an effective response to economic opportunity.

In the Western world a special feature of the state is that its political organization has been roughly coterminous with the social organization imposed by the national culture. An example may suggest the general effect of this fact on the growth of the national economies. From a comparison of the operation of several social elements in production as they were combined historically within each of two national societies, the role of the national state in shaping these elements and in adjusting them to one another may become apparent.

RESPONSES OF TWO SOCIETIES TO SIMILAR ECONOMIC OPPORTUNITY

For such a comparison, a situation of similar economic opportunity in two societies must be found, and their responses to the opportunity must be measured. A similar response to similar opportunity would suggest similar effectiveness in the organization and motivation of economic life in the two societies. Comparison of the aggregate rates of growth of, for example, France and Germany would be the task of a full-scale economic history; but with a narrower focus on individual industries the two societies may be compared. Here, however, the movement of the economy outside an industry—movements of demand and factor cost rates—must be taken as given, combined with technology and the real costs of resources to provide the limits of economic opportunity for the particular industry. The record of such an industry is measurable largely in terms of its output, and of changes in inputs.[3]

Full comparison of the ore mining and smelting industries in French and German Lorraine in the period 1871–1914 would require much more detailed research than has yet been done, but there is here an unusually favorable opportunity for analysis. Differences in natural

[3] The long-run correspondence of price to production cost is also an important measure. Historical data, however, are rarely good enough to give more than an approximate output trend. Input measures are notoriously difficult, and measures of the profit rate are nearly impossible.

conditions on the two sides of the famous 1871 boundary [4] could be compensated to a large degree by use of different types of mining equipment and different mixtures of ores in smelting. Demand for ore, and even for pig iron, was to some extent international, and the two regions had somewhat similar home markets.[5] Relative to the movement of demand, it is not unlikely that factor cost rates moved somewhat similarly for each region.

If the opportunity for development of a profitable mining and smelting industry did appear and grow in a similar manner in French and German Lorraine, then a great interest attaches to the similarity in their records of output. From 1871 to 1914 output movements of iron ore and pig iron were very close for the two regions.[6] With respect to pig iron after 1900, the movements and the absolute amounts were almost identical. A similar opportunity and a similar result would suggest an equal effectiveness of response. One who knew nothing of the organization of the two industries might suppose that he was faced with the handiwork of two national planners, equally enterprising and farsighted, and equally constrained by considerations of cost and price. But the facts are very different. Several of the complex elements producing the response differed sharply in the two regions.

Differences in Mining Laws

The most striking differences were in their mining laws.[7] The mining law governing the exploration of French Lorraine was the Napoleonic

[4] See Richard Hartshorne, "The Franco-German Boundary of 1871," *World Politics*, 2:209–250 (January 1950); and for a brief but intriguing account of French exploration after 1871, Lucien Cayeux, *Les Minerais de Fer Oolithique de France,* Fasc. II (Paris: Imprimerie Nationale, 1909–22), pp. 70–71.

[5] The French ore and iron moved naturally west and northwest into France and Belgium, the German into the Saar and the Ruhr. In the rather smaller French market the French products had no serious competitors, whereas the German ore and iron met growing competition from imports of Swedish ore into the Ruhr. See Pounds and Parker, *op. cit.,* Chapter 10, for an analysis of the interregional balance between these areas.

[6] For data on iron ore production, see J. Raty & Cie., Societé des Hauts Fourneaux de Saulnes, *Les Mines de Fer Françaises* (Nancy, 1954), pp. 104–105; on German pig iron, *Vierteljahreshefte zur Statistik;* and on French pig iron, *Statistique de l'Industrie Minérale.*

[7] The French law, as amended, is summarized in C. Dumanet, *Traité d'Exploitation des Mines,* 2nd ed. by A. Dufrane-Dumanet, Vol. 3 (Brussels, 1898), pp. 427–438; pp. 440–444 contain a summary of the Prussian law. See also Gerhardt Boldt, *Staat*

law of 1810, amended in minor particulars in 1838, 1852, and 1880. Without relinquishing the state's prior claims to mineral deposits, it set up the machinery by which these rights might be conceded to private individuals. A license to explore was required even of the owner of the surface rights, whose consent was required before such a license could be given to anyone. Application for a license was made at the local prefecture and then followed a rather long route to and in Paris for approval. Licenses were usually limited to a term of 1–2 years, and in themselves gave no title to any minerals discovered. The explorer was required to make a payment to the owner of the surface rights, whose special permission was required for drilling near and under buildings on the property. If minerals were discovered and a concession to exploit them was given to someone other than the finder, or was reserved to the state, an indemnity was paid to the finder. The exploitation of mineral deposits was a privilege conceded under a special grant from the state. Each concession was a separate arrangement, the terms of which were contained in the *cahier des charges,* but certain standard provisions were made in all such arrangements. These included the rents to be paid to the owner of the surface rights and the boundaries of the concession. In addition, the law of 1810 provided for a flat tax per hectare and a percentage tax on net revenues (not to exceed 5 percent) to be paid to the state. The operation of a mine, once begun, was subjected to close control from the *administration des mines,* which might even require it to raise its rate of output and could forbid it to shut down. Concessions and shares of stock in mining companies were of course salable, but one concession could not be combined with another, broken up, nor abandoned without permission of the state.

In sharp contrast to this restrictive policy was the system of *Bergbaufreiheit,* which was set up under the famous Prussian law of 1865 and applied with minor changes to Alsace-Lorraine in 1874. Under this law the state was required to grant a license to explore for minerals, even over the protest of the owner of the surface rights, to any applicant unless damage to the public interest was clearly involved. The sole right to exploit any minerals found was vested by the law in the finder, who might fix a field of any size and shape up to 200 hectares

---

und Bergbau (Munich: Beck, 1950), pp. 1–11. For the text of the Prussian law as applied in Alsace-Lorraine, see Robert Courau, *Législation des Mines en Alsace et Lorraine, 1871–1918* (Paris: H. Dunod & E. Pinat, 1918).

and up to 2,000 meters from the point of initial discovery.[8] Except for deciding what constituted a bona fide discovery the state had very little discretion; it could not decide that minerals were not exploitable nor reserve any right in them to itself. Fields might be sold, abandoned, divided, or joined. As against the surface owner, the mine owner possessed large rights. The surface owner could not object to duly authorized digging on his property, nor was he entitled to any share in the minerals found or to any other rents. The mine owner even had the right to appropriate certain materials on the property for his own use and might erect buildings on the surface, although in that case the surface owner might force him to buy the land for the purpose. The principal protection given to the surface owner was his power to prohibit digging under his buildings or within a radius of 62.8 meters of them.

Roles of the Bureaucracy

These two mining laws imply a different role for the bureaucracy in the two countries.[9] In the operation of mines the law of 1865 gave

[8] These limits applied only to Alsace-Lorraine. For Prussia, they were 219 hectares and 4,185 meters, respectively.

[9] No comment in this section should be construed as an attempt to compare French and German entrepreneurs—either bureaucratic or private. Alexander Gerschenkron has repeatedly called for such a comparison, both in discussion of the suggestive work of John E. Sawyer and David S. Landes on the French entrepreneur and in a Comment on Bert F. Hoselitz, "Entrepreneurship and Capital Formation in France and Britain since 1700," in Universities – National Bureau Committee for Economic Research, *Capital Formation and Economic Growth,* Special Conference Series No. 6 (Princeton: Princeton University Press, 1955); see especially pp. 297–311, 373–378, 385–393.

The attempt here is simply to compare certain elements in the institutional structure within which the mining industry operated in the two countries. Until the measures of growth for the two economies—both aggregate and by sectors—are closely reviewed, it is dangerous to proceed far into explanatory elements. Comparison of the recent studies by François Perroux and associates with the estimates by Paul Jostock indicates a growth in the deflated income per capita in France not markedly inferior to that in Germany between 1870 and 1914. This represents a sharp revision of the relative movements shown by Colin Clark, and some reconciliation of the estimates seems called for. The recent studies are contained in International Association for Research in Income and Wealth, *Income and Wealth, Series III,* Milton Gilbert, ed. (Cambridge, England: Bowes & Bowes, 1953), and *Series V,* Simon Kuznets, ed. (London: Bowes & Bowes, 1955); Clark's data are in his *The Conditions of Economic Progress* (2nd ed.; London: Macmillan & Co., 1951), pp. 80, 101.

the Prussian bureaucracy various supervisory powers, and it appears to have exercised them mainly to reduce the risks of long-term investment. Here again we must argue from examples. In the introduction of electricity into coal mines at the end of the century, the work of safety inspectors of the *Oberbergamtsbezirke* was significant.[10] No general code for electrical installations in mines was adopted until 1903, except a code governing all electrical equipment, issued by the *Verein deutscher Ingenieure*. Instead, each separate installation was made under the supervision of a government inspector. In this case the risk of an important innovation was reduced and transferred in part from the mine operator to the government. Since the German electricity industry was aggressive and the mine inspectors were not averse to exercising their authority, electrification in the German mines proceeded rapidly. In France, where the dangers of explosion were admittedly greater, the innovation was not similarly encouraged, and greater boldness on the part of a mine operator was needed to introduce it. Even in minute regulatory functions the German state appears rather more protective than restrictive of industrial operations. Cooperative enterprises among producers were common in exploration, research, and worker training; the trade association, the *Verein,* and the cooperative flourished—with considerable legal encouragement.[11] In France, where these forms of self-help were less common, the function of the bureaucracy as protector and adviser of producers may well have been fulfilled slightly differently. In the mining industry, at least, exploration appears to have been carried on not infrequently by state geologists and engineers, alone or in association with private companies. Whereas in Germany a private activity was protected and regulated by government officials, in France a state activity was farmed out to private producers. One must be careful not to generalize the tendency evident in mining; toward manufacturing both governments may have pursued an equally liberal policy.

[10] H. Denis, *Étude sur la transmission et l'utilisation de la Force dans les Mines* (Paris, 1909), pp. 50–54.

[11] In Germany, for example, the *Bergbauhülfskassen* were organized originally by the state, financed by a levy on mine owners, and in 1883 turned over to the owners, to be run by them, although membership appears to have remained compulsory. The concept of the privately run organization in which membership was compulsory was applied after 1913 to the coal cartels. These *Bergbauhülfskassen* undertook numerous common projects, such as supporting training schools for miners, and contributing in the Ruhr to the construction of the Rhein-Emshäfen Canal. See Adolf Arndt, *Bergbau und Bergbaupolitik* (Leipzig: C. L. Hirschfeld, 1894), pp. 197–200.

Training of Mining Engineers

To understand how the different mining laws and their administration produced apparently equivalent results in Lorraine, it would be necessary to consider the character and motivations of the prospectors and mine operators in the two national regions. A number of these men in both countries were mining engineers, and all the major mining and metallurgical firms had such engineers in their employ. Some light is shed on this difficult subject by comparison of the French and German methods of training mining engineers during this period.[12] Both countries had state mining schools that dated back to the turn of the century or earlier. In Prussia the *Bergakademie* at Clausthal had been established by Frederick the Great; the *École des Mines* in Paris was founded in the Revolutionary period. There were other *Bergakademien* in Berlin and Freiburg, and a second *École des Mines* in St. Étienne. Instruction in mining engineering was also given at the *Technische Hochschule* in Aachen.

The French and German schools differed sharply in most respects, and in ways quite upsetting to naive preconceptions of French and German "national character." Admission to the French schools was extremely difficult, depending on a competitive examination possible for most students only after two years at the *École Polytechnique* or equivalent special preparation. Five to six years of scientific training, mostly in mathematics, was the rule for the French applicant to the *École des Mines;* indeed, it was estimated that he had ten times as much mathematics as his German counterpart. In Germany, the tech-

---

[12] This comparison is based largely on a revealing public discussion in the *Révue de Metallurgie,* 1906 and 1907. At this time French technical education was coming under heavy criticism. The *Révue* controversy was set off by the report of an inspection trip to Germany by A. Pelleton, deputy director of the *École des Mines,* under official orders from the Minister of Public Works. Pelleton appears to have visited most of the ten *Technische Hochschulen* as well as the three *Bergakademie,* and to have been greatly impressed. His report elicited comment—largely critical of his comparisons—from the directors of several French technical schools, the president of the *Aciéries de Longwy,* a former president of the *Association des Anciens Élèves de l'École des Mines.* The spokesman of a student group at the *École* contributed to the discussion some complaints about courses, relations with professors, and work loads. This controversy is interesting for the critical views expressed concerning both the French and German systems. Discussions of the German system appear elsewhere, e.g., E. C. Meyer, "Industrial Education in Germany," in U. S. Department of Commerce and Labor, *Special Consular Reports,* Vol. 33 (Washington, 1905).

nical schools were open to all graduates of a *Gymnasium, Realgymnasium,* or *Oberrealschule*. The result was that the successful French applicants began their special training to be mining engineers at about age 25, and were ready to take a job with the government or private industry at 28; the German student was at work well before he was 25.

Instruction and the relations of students to professors were also strikingly different. The German training was specialized almost from the start. Four alternative courses led to degrees in mine operation, topology, ferrous metallurgy, and nonferrous metallurgy in the Berlin *Bergakademie*. The *Technische Hochschulen* were equally specialized. In the first two years some general science and mathematics were required, but practical subjects predominated and some actual experience in a mine or factory was included in the program. In contrast with this specialized and practical approach, the *École des Mines* offered virtually no choice of courses, but included a long array of courses worthy of a general engineering school. To some extent it was such a school, for it trained metallurgical and industrial engineers as well as mining engineers. All were required to take essentially the same curriculum and only one kind of diploma was given. The course was encyclopedic and largely theoretical; job training as such was left until the graduates were on the job.

With the rather wide choice of courses in the German schools there was also freedom in other respects. Professors were dependent, not simply for their self-respect but also for part of their income, on the numbers of students in their classes. An established professor might double his income through his students' fees, a percentage of which he retained. At the beginning of his career a *privatdozent* received from the school nothing but a lecture room and depended for his whole livelihood on fees for his courses. Students in the *Technische Hochschulen* might move freely from professor to professor and from school to school, and some movement between these and the *Bergakademien* was also possible. The French student, on the other hand, continued to be treated as a schoolboy until graduation. Discipline was strict, relations with the faculty were even more formal than in Germany, and as choice among courses was narrow, choice among professors was inconceivable.

The French training, in short, was general, theoretical, highly mathematical, intensive, and compulsory; the German was specialized, practical, rather less intensive, and permitted rather wide choice. The

French student, carefully selected and several years older, was kept under discipline in a highly academic atmosphere. The German student was free to roam, and was generally required to get some job experience before receiving his degree.

One would be foolish indeed to attribute an absolute superiority to either system of instruction. The engineers they produced almost certainly represented two rather different kinds of men. The German may have moved easily from school into a specialized job, where little direct supervision was needed to hold him to a workmanlike performance. His faults must have been those of one who specializes early, a certain lack of imagination, and an inability to move readily from one task to another. An industrial and bureaucratic organization that protected him, kept him in a secure niche in the system, and permitted him patiently to exploit a limited range of opportunity could best use the trained mind that he brought to industry. The French engineer, on the other hand, was released from 6–10 years of academic training, as from a military school. He almost certainly needed an apprenticeship before he was ready for responsible work in a plant or mine.[13] On the other hand, his mind would be more sharply and more widely trained than the German's, and over a whole career this might prove to be a considerable advantage. Men with the French engineering training, however, on entering the mining industry, might well need some guidance from trained engineers, especially since many of the best students went from the *École des Mines* into the government service. The more highly specialized abilities of the engineers of the government's *Corps des Mines* were available in service anywhere in France, rather than in the employ of an individual firm.

Other Elements in the French and German Economies

It is not possible, on the basis of such evidence, to reconstruct adequately the social and legal setting in which the exploitation of the Lorraine ore deposits took place in France and Germany. Reflected in the relation between the legal and the educational systems, however, certain elements in the French and German economies in this period became evident. France was clearly drawing on an intangible social capital in a tradition of education and administration whose elements

---

[13] Those who supported the French system claimed, probably with some justice, that the supposedly practical training of the Germans did not in the least obviate a similar need of apprenticeship.

were to some extent adjusted to one another. With the virtual termination of population growth, the phase of increasing productivity through increasing specialization of labor was largely over. The "problem" (to speak as an economist rather than a historian) for the French economy was to exploit native resources and adapt new technology to domestic use, without the advantage that growing scale and specialization would promise.[14] The "solution" to the problem lay in maintaining the hand of government, representing the maximum scale in the economy, somewhat stronger in France than in Britain or Germany, while retaining an educational system designed to prepare engineers for a varied experience. The advantage of these two elements in the system undoubtedly was felt in the settlement of the colonial empire. It cannot be imagined that it produced an industrial upsurge in France comparable to that in Germany. Perhaps a major weakness—derivable from intellectual traditions rather than economic circumstances—was that technological change in France, stemming from general science and mathematics, produced inventions of general application, which contributed less to France than to the rest of the world. It would be surprising, for example, if the failure of the automobile to gain favor in France as quickly as in the United States was a failure in French entrepreneurship.

The situation of the German economy was quite different. National administration and national technical education were in the process of formation, but local organization and the system of apprenticeship had deep roots. A nice balance could be struck between centralization and decentralization in the school system, and between freedom and control in government policy toward business. The economy at the same time could look to a growing population to permit important increases in productivity through specialization. At least in the heavy industries, adaptation of British and French technique was of first importance. Such adaptation required engineers with specialized training and ability to make numerous minor innovations.

The adaptation of the French and German structures of industrial organization to the different situations of the two economies is a

---

[14] The advantage of scale in a single intercommunicating society exists for native technology and technological education; but it exists also in the ability of native firms to specialize, particularly in such products as machinery. The weakness of the French electrical and chemical industries noted by John H. Clapham, *The Economic Development of France and Germany, 1815–1914* (Cambridge, England: Cambridge University Press, 1948), pp. 256–257, might well be examined in this light.

matter for separate examination. Any superiority in German performance in this period, however, must be examined against differing opportunities offered by resources (particularly coal), population growth,
and the international movement of demand and of technology. In the
exploitation of Lorraine ore, where the opportunity was unusually
wide, the French and German systems appear to have operated with
equal success. The German system of law and education may have
been unusually well-suited to the peculiar situation of other German
industries. Only after such elements have been taken into account can
a direct comparison of French and German entrepreneurs be made.
Such a comparison would be enormously delicate and difficult, and it
is not yet clear how the available materials could be made to yield
meaningful results.

Such broad study may show that the role of the secular state in the
West has been to form rational, economic men through public education, while shaping a legal and administrative system suitable for
putting the specially trained products of that education to their maximum economic use. Only in such a way can the persistence of high rates
of growth in so many Western countries in the nineteenth century be
reconciled with the minor, but numerous, differences in state policy,
social organization, and "national character." The alternative to such
an explanation is to assume that, even taken one by one, such differences are really of no importance at all. Although attractive to an
economist, such an alternative is excessively harsh and insensitive to
the wonderful variety of which human nature is capable. National
economies may rather be delicately compared to national cuisines. The
countless examples of both these forms of social activity share three
important characteristics. They satisfy hunger, they use predominantly
local materials, and they are generally considered tolerable (sometimes
even exciting) by those who have been brought up in them.

8 THE GROWTH OF THE SWISS NATIONAL ECONOMY

Alfred Bürgin

A specifically Swiss economic history dates only from the period during which the Swiss economic area separated itself from upper Germany to embark upon a development of its own.[1] The sixteenth century was crucial, although some structural characteristics of the later Middle Ages were important for the ensuing age. Certain conditions, which resulted from the political structure and geographical environment, speeded up subsequent economic development.

FOUNDATIONS OF THE NATIONAL ECONOMY

The area that today is Switzerland lay on the intersection of vital medieval communication routes.[2] The lively trade of Italy with the textile-producing area of the Netherlands, of the Baltic and German ports, and of Frankfurt, the outstanding city of fairs, largely traversed the Swiss Alpine passes and the Rhine River Valley. East-west commerce moved from the Danube area via upper Germany through Switzerland to the Rhone area (there were fairs at Geneva and Lyons), southern France, and the Iberian Peninsula. As a result of this extremely favorable intersection of routes, hostelry, transportation, and activities of middlemen came into being. Opportunities for foreign sales of Swiss products were created; and it is important that this commerce was concentrated in the hands of Swiss merchants. Because of the particular political structure, a stratum of monopolistic middlemen did not emerge.

In handicrafts, only the textile industry achieved some importance. Eastern Switzerland controlled a considerable part of the upper-German linen trade. St. Gall with its environs was a significant center of linen weaving in the later half of the fourteenth century.[3] The linen was

---

[1] See Traugott Geering, *Grundzüge einer schweizerischen Wirtschaftsgeschichte* (Berne, 1912).

[2] H. Ammann, "Die wirtschaftliche Bedeutung der Schweiz im Mittelalter," in *Aloys Schulte zum 70.Geburtstag* (Düsseldorf, 1927), pp. 112 ff.

[3] Hermann Wartmann, *Industrie und Handel des Kt. St. Gallen auf Ende 1866* (St. Gall, 1865).

sold in Venice, Milan, Genoa, southern France, and Spain; from the Frankfurt fairs it reached northern and eastern Europe. In Fribourg the woolen cloth industry developed in the fourteenth century; the products were sold at the Zurzach and Geneva fairs.[4] The long established *Grautucherei* of Zurich and Basel also exported its products in the thirteenth and fourteenth centuries, but continued to have little significance. In Basel *schurlitz* weaving (cotton) flourished to a certain degree as an export industry in the first half of the fifteenth century.[5] The silk industry, not known in upper Germany, began to take root in Zurich in the thirteenth century,[6] played quite a large role there in the fourteenth century, and vanished completely in the middle of the fifteenth.

Two aspects of the medieval Swiss economy should be kept in mind. First, a considerable accumulation of capital was possible even at that time, mainly from commercial and handicraft sources. Rich merchants and craftsmen are known to have lived in the cities as early as 1400. They rose out of the common townspeople, acquiring wealth in a relatively short time through profits from trade and handicrafts.[7] Around the middle of the sixteenth century Swiss merchants contributed significantly to French crown loans.[8] The capital that had accumulated in the fifteenth and sixteenth centuries could be preserved even to modern times because of the continuity of events, and despite the partial displacement of the European trade network that resulted from the New World discoveries and the decline of silk and woolen cloth manufacturing. Thus, medieval conditions favored a widely dispersed accumulation of property. Equally predetermined were the manner and direction of investments: as a result of geographical position, investments in Swiss shipping enterprises were out of the

[4] H. Ammann, *Freiburg und Bern und die Genfermessen* (Langensalza, 1921).

[5] Traugott Geering, *Handel und Industrie der Stadt Basel* (Basel: F. Schneider, 1886), pp. 259 ff.

[6] Adolf Bürkli, *Geschichte der zürcherischen Seidenindustrie* (Zurich, 1884).

[7] See H. Nabholz, "Zur Geschichte der Vermögensverhältnisse in einigen Schweizer Städten in der 1. Hälfte des 15. Jh.," in *Festgabe Paul Schweizer* (Zurich, 1922), pp. 93 ff. Sombart's theory of capital accumulation in a craft economy does not apply to Swiss conditions because the insignificance of the nobility meant that there were only limited possibilities for "derived" capital accumulation *(Der moderne Kapitalismus,* Vol. 1 [2nd ed.; Munich, 1916], pp. 608 ff.).

[8] See E. Wild, *Die eidgenössischen Handelsprivilegien in Frankreich, 1444–1635* (St. Gall, 1915), pp. 30 ff.; Richard Ehrenberg, *Das Zeitalter der Fugger,* Vol. 2 (Jena: G. Fischer, 1922), pp. 81 ff., 99.

question and so were the acquisition and development of colonial possessions. For natural and political reasons Swiss agriculture was unsuited for large estates, and there were only limited possibilities for investing capital by acquiring large tracts of agricultural land. Natural resources did not exist in appreciable quantities. There was, however, great potential for investment in industry. One of the aims of this paper is to demonstrate the forces and conditions that enabled this potential to develop.

Second, the linen manufacturer in eastern Switzerland was able to adopt capitalist modes of production. Because of the political structure of this area its development was not hampered by regional economic policies. In contrast, when economic decline set in, the upper German cities became ossified in the guild system and were swallowed up by the absolutist territories, losing their cultural strength and ability to organize governments.[9] But St. Gall, with its industrial development, was able to take part in the modern economy. The economic development of Germany, despite its similar origins, was funneled into a course sharply different from that of Switzerland. In the sixteenth century, when the former commercial and craft prosperity of Germany began to wane, and the Thirty Years War exterminated economic life throughout Germany, Switzerland laid the groundwork for her industrial and capitalist future. It was then that she blossomed as an early center of industry into which flowed the assets of preceding centuries, namely, a relative wealth of capital and a qualified labor force, which had been trained in the self-governing cities of traders and craftsmen. Under new conditions, these assets were thoroughly developed.

FORMATIVE FACTORS IN SWISS ENTREPRENEURSHIP

We shall pass over the problem of relations between capitalism and Protestantism,[10] but the more conspicuous aspects of the immigration of religious refugees must be mentioned. Not only Switzerland but the whole of non-Catholic Europe profited considerably and permanently

[9] See Eberhard Gothein, *Wirtschaftsgeschichte des Schwarzwaldes* (Strassburg: K. J. Trübner, 1892); Willy Andreas, *Deutschland vor der Reformation* (Stuttgart: Deutsch Verlags-anstalt, 1948); F. Rörig, *Die europäische Stadt im Mittelalter* (Göttingen, 1955).

[10] Suffice it to mention the work that started scientific discussion of the relation of capitalism and Protestantism: Max Weber, "Die protestantische Ethik und der Geist des Kapitalismus," *Gesammelte Aufsätze zur Religionssoziologie* (Tübingen, 1947).

from the refugees, who brought an advanced business culture and more highly developed processes of production and trade with them. In Switzerland the refugees found political conditions that enabled them to live in large numbers as free citizens alongside the guild members, and to inject new life into the urban crafts which had a tendency to stagnate organizationally and to discourage new forms of production and technique. Switzerland profited from the very first wave of emigration of religious refugees in the second half of the sixteenth century, whereas the German cities attempted to deny them admission until towards the end of the seventeenth century. There, too, modern manufacturing enterprises were founded by their initiative, but the results of the immigration were different. While in Switzerland it gave new or increased impetus to the cities, preserved them from the straightjacket of guilds, and contributed to their political and cultural leadership, in Germany a century later the immigration brought about a strengthening of princely and absolutist power because of the political weakness of the cities.

Switzerland directly or indirectly owes the greater part of her modern industry to the initiative of the refugees.[11] In consequence of their influx, the urban middle class consisted more or less exclusively of refugees, and many city officials were recruited from them.

Industrial development in the Protestant sections of Switzerland was far more intensive than in the Catholic. This situation was noticed even by contemporary observers, and its significance needs no further elaboration. It seems worthy of reflection, however, that cities and areas in which trade and handicrafts flourished before the Reformation were receptive to its ideas and became its centers.

Another factor must be recognized if we are to understand the Swiss managerial class: as a result of a democratic political structure, which enabled the competing individual to acquire political power, the demands of Protestant attitudes for work were coupled from the start with the will to influence affairs of state and society. In Germany the economically active bourgeoisie was deprived of participation in political life, becoming immobilized in an apolitical outlook. By contrast, in Switzerland, particularly in the nineteenth century, all large entrepreneurs were engaged simultaneously in politics and in economic

---

[11] W. Bodmer, *Der Einfluss der Refugiantenwanderung von 1550–1700 auf die Schweizerische Wirtschaft* (Zurich, 1946); Johann C. Moerikofer, *Geschichte der evangelischen Flüchtlinge in der Schweiz* (Leipzig, 1876).

activity, thus spreading and realizing liberal ideas and doing pioneer work for the modern liberal state.

THE POLITICAL FRAMEWORK

The growth of the Swiss economy cannot be grasped in isolation from foreign relations since the economy received its most decisive impulses from the outside. As a small neutral, Switzerland knew how to profit economically and politically from the economic goals and competitive policies of other states as well as from the wars of the great powers. Its democratic and federalist structures left the individual to make use of available opportunities as best he could. These structures explain in part both the important role played by the Swiss merchants in European trade, and how Swiss industry by making use of their trade relations could grow to such proportions.

Lack of a Central Authority

Until 1848 the Swiss Confederation was an association or union of states, without a central authority. Because of this federalist structure,[12] mercantilism, the economic policy best suited to absolutism, could not gain a foothold as an over-all economic concept. Furthermore, there was no universal economic policy for all Switzerland at that time. Various cantons had concluded temporary economic agreements, and had also made a few joint attempts to defend their commercial interests in foreign lands. Only the cantons, therefore, as political units, were in a position to pursue a mercantilist policy. Swiss mercantilism is of interest here merely in connection with state intervention to foster an active trade balance through encouragement, on the spot, of industry and trade. The measures taken to this end were very limited in scope and differed from canton to canton. No significant industrial or trade relations were established in consequence of direct governmental action.

The beginnings of a mercantilist economic policy were most clearly visible in the cantons ruled by aristocracies, especially in the Republic of Berne. Nor was this accidental. Berne enlarged its territorial possessions during the fifteenth and sixteenth centuries by campaigns of conquest. In many ways this led to a change from a city economy to an expanded territorial one. The city was the administrative center for extended territories; it was not a corporative city in the true sense. The

---

[12] W. Bodmer, "Tendenzen der Wirtschaftspolitik der eidgen, Orte im Zeitalter des Merkantilismus," *Schweiz, Zeitschrift für Geschichte,* 1(4):562 ff. (1951).

interest of the burghers lay in politics and military service. No specifically bourgeois traits could thereby mature in the ruling strata, so the city lost its role as a center for the arts and handicrafts.[13] The territorial and economic policies of the government were intended to further the introduction of new handicrafts in the whole state rather than merely in Berne, and also to check the unemployment resulting from increases in population.

The government's efforts to import new industries, however, had little success. The largest textile industries of the eighteenth century, linen production, cotton spinning and weaving, calico printing, and clockmaking originated without administrative assistance. Only the relatively unimportant hosiery and silk industries—also brought in by the refugees—received official assistance.

Similarly, the Chamber of Commerce in Lucerne, copied from that in Berne, tried to start new trades via the granting of privileges. The home industry production of floss silk, financed by the state, soon went bankrupt. Subsequently, however, some citizens decided to continue this industry privately; in other words, the state had stimulated private initiative. In Solothurn, toward the middle of the eighteenth century, members of the Council sometimes borrowed money from the treasury for their own new industrial enterprises. In Geneva the Council granted privileges to certain refugees in the sixteenth century for the introduction of new handicrafts. Calvin himself emphatically recommended the furtherance of industries to the Council. Nonetheless, in Neuchâtel, clockmaking, calico printing, and lacemaking originated without any direct assistance by the state.

In the guild-dominated cantons, mercantilist principles from the beginning had but little influence on economic policy. There, naturally, corporative interests dominated. The Councils insisted on applying principles of urban economy and strove to control the rural home industry in order to concentrate trade within the cities.

In Zurich, only the sixteenth century saw interference on the part of the Council in favor of new textile industries. Even in the eighteenth century, the Council of Basel repeatedly attempted to further wool and cotton spinning, as well as hosiery, in the country. These were temporary measures for combating unemployment. In the eighteenth century

[13] Compare the statement in *Helvetische Monatsschrift*, 6:85 (1806): "Several foreigners and some nationals have for some time accused the government and burghers of Berne to the effect that 'they despise and suppress trade or fail to support it sufficiently,' comparing them unfavorably with Zurich, Basel and St. Gall."

the newly founded cotton industry of St. Gall eluded the control of the city guilds and was able to develop in complete independence.

In the rural cantons industry enjoyed complete mobility since no guild-ruled cities tried to control and localize the handicrafts through measures favoring the urban economy. Free of regulation were the cotton industry and cotton printing in Glarus and Appenzell and the floss silk manufacture in central Switzerland. Except for the cattle trade and transactions for immediate consumption, export and transit trade in most cantons was left entirely to the merchants.

This general survey shows that in Switzerland there was no significant promotion of industry, in the mercantilist sense, through conscious government action. Consequently, the genesis and spread of Swiss industries cannot be ascribed to planned government assistance. In the seventeenth and eighteenth centuries, paradoxical as it may seem, a positive balance of payment in some cantons resulted precisely from the absence of mercantilist economic policies. The lack of government economic policies greatly aided the activities of the Swiss merchants and entrepreneurs since they were always able to appear in foreign markets as private individuals, not as exponents of an unwelcome foreign power.

Neutrality

Another factor aiding the free mobility of Swiss merchants was the political neutrality of the Swiss federation. Neutrality made feasible the full preservation of the individual's freedom to form his own attitude toward powers at war. Neutrality began as a by-product of the defeat suffered by the Confederate Army at Marignano through Francis I, and was confirmed by the Permanent Peace with France in 1516 and the *Soldbündnis* (alliance including use of mercenary troops) with the French Crown, concluded in 1521. The defeat put an end to the joint conquests of the cantons. Henceforth the warlike and battle-hardened contingents—much in demand by all sovereigns—from Switzerland's valleys and towns became the mercenaries of foreign wars. The reason for this change, fraught with consequences, must not be sought in an accidental defeat following brilliant victories or in military weakness. Rather, it was the inevitable outcome of the essential quality of Swiss political life which is not monarchical but is organized communally, flowing from the common will, not from personal, dynastic interests.

The primary concerns of a political cooperative community *(Genossenschaft)* are autonomy, self-administration, and the preservation of liberty, not domination and increased power. The Swiss confederate pacts were entered into for the sake of protecting the individual spheres of the confederates, not in order to rule over foreign areas. Hence, after the victory over Austria (1474) and over Burgundy (1476) and after secession from the Empire (1499), there was no longer a common goal in the foreign policies of the cantons. Even before the Marignano disaster, the unity of the federal army had disintegrated, and the western expansion of Berne at the beginning of the sixteenth century was not assisted but opposed by the other cantons.[14]

Trade Privileges in France

The peace treaty of 1516 with France opened undreamt of possibilities for the Swiss industries. It has been referred to as the *Magna Carta* of the later industrialized Switzerland.[15] In that treaty the contracting parties were mutually guaranteed free trade for all time. At that time France did not levy protective tariffs. Following the strengthening of the centralized power of the French Crown, however, mercantilist economic practices became noticeable. In 1550, when France adopted protective tariffs, the Swiss merchants invoked the treaty clauses. Since Switzerland had a distinctive type of military alliance with France and since France urgently needed Swiss mercenaries, the merchants time and again obtained valuable trading privileges which gave them an advantage over German and Italian traders. From 1550 on, Swiss exports to France were largely dependent on repeatedly renewed privileges. The French kings failed to revoke them only because of the agreement concerning mercenary troops.[16] Until the Revolution France remained the main market for Swiss products, becoming the principal stimulant of Swiss industry.

The commercial opportunities resulting from the wars among the surrounding great powers could be exploited because of these three basic circumstances: the absence of mercantilist economic policies,

[14] See Werner Naef, *Die Schweiz in Europa* (Berne: Herbert Lang et Cie., 1938), pp. 26, 37.

[15] H. Honegger, *Die Entstehung des schweizerischen Industriestaates aus dem Wirtschaftsliberalismus des Spätmittelalters* (Zurich, 1945), p. 16.

[16] E. Wild, *op. cit.;* R. Feller, "Bündnisse und Söldnerdienst 1515–1798" in *Schweizer Kriegsgeschichte,* No. 6 (Berne, 1916), pp. 10 ff. L. Weisz, *Die Zürcherische Exportindustrie ihre Enstehung und Entwicklung* (Zurich, 1937).

political neutrality, and the possession of trade privileges in France. Nonetheless, in contradistinction to England and the Netherlands, Switzerland, being a nonmaritime nation, did not profit from distant wars. Consequently, the wars fought at sea (the Wars of Liberation of the Netherlands, the Nordic Wars, those of Frederick II, and the American Revolution) do not come within the purview of our study; our concern is primarily with the Thirty Years War, the wars of Louis XIV, the War of the Spanish Succession, and the French Revolutionary Wars.

Developments during the Wars

The neutrality of the Swiss during the Thirty Years War enabled them to oust France from the German market. New markets were found almost without effort in northern and eastern Germany, at the Frankfurt fairs, in Austria and Bavaria. During the wars of coalition against Louis XIV, German-French trade was interrupted by blockade measures, which enabled the Swiss to acquire largely and permanently the role of middlemen between France and Germany.[17] Merchants from St. Gall exported not only Swiss merchandise but also linen from southern Germany and Silesia to France. Swiss merchants bought iron, copper, and other metals for armaments for the French from German, Austrian, and Hungarian mines. The huge demand for French cavalry horses was met, apart from large Swiss contingents, through imports from Germany. The Swiss traders also took care of French exports to countries at war with France.[18]

[17] The blockade measures also resulted in the introduction of new branches of production. One example among many is found in the "Family Tradition" of the Hoffmanns of Basel: "When the Franco-German war broke out in 1688 and the import of French wares into the Empire was forbidden, my father had the idea to manufacture silk ribbon *à la française* which sold so well in peace-time Germany. We know now (1721) that this, too, was successful and has brought still more divine blessing and food to town and country."—Traugott Geering, *Handel und Industrie der Stadt Basel*, p. 636.

[18] In a memorandum in 1697 the Swiss merchants of Lyon pointed out the usefulness of their commerce to the French authorities: "Our relations with foreign countries whither we export many French commodities in the face of danger and, often, losses, since during wars they are not allowed there, were highly advantageous to the King and to his subjects; . . . although the high price for silk and wool as well as the fluctuations of currency rates held up the sales of French goods, we exported more thereof than all Frenchmen together."—*Der schweizerische Grosshandel in Geschichte und Gegenwart* (Basel, 1944), p. 64.

Financial transactions acquired great importance. From their own resources and their uninterrupted connections with the anti-French areas, Swiss firms came to the rescue of Louis XIV's exhausted gold reserves. With the help of their international connections they took charge of money orders from France to French agents and armies operating in enemy territory. Merchants from Geneva and St. Gall helped finance the French wars through loans. These close financial relations with the French Crown led to a situation wherein, at the end of the eighteenth century, six Swiss were at the helm of French banking with Necker from Geneva handing the bill to the French monarchy as the representative of French capital and in the name of the French bourgeoisie. When Napoleon founded the Bank of France in 1800 he appointed one director from Neuchâtel; the shareholders appointed the second from Zurich.[19]

The key to the personal careers of Swiss merchants and to the confidence they enjoyed at foreign courts was their independence from national ties and ambitions. This enabled them to take advantage of every attractive opportunity, and they adjusted to new circumstances with amazing flexibility. Their characteristic traits were sobriety and matter-of-factness, developed in a bourgeois democratic environment, and a clever, calculating weighing of chances of success, which is the forte of the self-reliant. Their realism and purposefulness compensated for lack of power. Their love of freedom made them circumvent the trade restrictions of foreign potentates without qualms since they regarded these restrictions as arbitrariness, not law. When accused, Swiss merchants cited the laws of the seventeenth and eighteenth centuries, according to which the wars of the sovereigns must not disturb the peaceful activities of the subjects.

INDUSTRIAL DEVELOPMENT

Commercial expansion may be due to such factors as interstate and transit commerce and trade with domestically produced goods. The continuity of trade through the centuries is guaranteed only when its vital sources continue to flow despite the displacement of trade routes and markets and changes in consumer preferences. Interstate and

---

[19] See *ibid.*, pp. 63 ff.; H. Lüthy, "La République de Calvin et l'essor de la Banque Protestante en France de la Révocation de l'Edit de Nantes à la Révolution," in *Schweizer Beiträge zur Allgemeinen Geschichte*, Vol. 11 (Berne, 1953), pp. 73 ff.; *Die Tätigkeit der Schweizer Kaufleute und Gewerbetreibenden in Frankreich unter Ludwig XIV und der Regentschaft* (Aarau, 1943).

transit commerce are by their very nature dependent on foreign centers of production, which can be lost in the wake of many kinds of events. The strength of Swiss trade lay in the existence of home industries based on the putting-out system—Switzerland's predominant method of production before the industrial revolution.

Under early capitalism with this predominant system of home industry, production required, above all, capital for buying the raw materials to be processed. In Switzerland, capital accumulation occurred in good part as a result of commercial profits, the influx of refugee capital, profits from financial transactions, and earnings from foreign military service.[20] Because of the rudimentary state of production the chances for capital accumulation were relatively small in the industrial sector. With the available technology and degree of development, increased accumulation was possible not through intensifying the production process but only by increasing the number of working hands, perfecting the organization of labor, or introducing new types of income.

These were the only outlets for capital within the orbit of the arts and crafts. And conditions for expansion were optimal in Switzerland because of its peculiar social structure. The extraordinary density and expansion of industrial home work were consequences of these conditions. Home work was common to all of Europe before the Industrial Revolution. What was typically Swiss, however, aside from the greater distribution of home industries, was the predominance of rural industrial activity compared with urban—in other words, a separation between city-based trade and rural production.

Conditions Underlying the Development of Home Industries

A Free Peasantry. Rural home work presupposes to a certain extent the availability of a free peasantry. In the Alpine cantons the peasants had rid themselves of serfdom as early as the Middle Ages. In the other cantons the Reformation removed most of the master-serf relations that still remained. However, this liberation did not remove the feudal corvées, etc.; these survived, in somewhat different shapes, even under the new conditions. That is to say, the cities and individuals became the recipients of deliveries from the peasants.

These shifts had two essential consequences. First, in the urban cantons [21] the free peasant emerged as a political subject of the city

[20] Cf. Julius Landmann, *Der schweizerische Kapitalexport* (Berne, 1916).

[21] The formation, within the Confederacy, of the Swiss city states (i.e., dependent territories dominated by a politically and economically privileged township com-

without enjoying the privileges accompanying urban citizenship. Hence he drifted into the occupational orbit of an urban, businessminded citizenry. Whenever the city became a center for export industries in addition to local handicraft products, the political dependence of its rural subjects was compounded by economic dependence, as the rural home industry was tied to the trade monopoly of the city. Second, deliveries by the peasants were no longer used for the upkeep of a nobility engaged merely in consumption, but were channeled into productive processes of various kinds.

While the impulse for engaging in home work often came from the city, residents in the open country in turn tended to favor this development. Home work, besides military service in foreign lands, provided often-needed and always welcome additions to the income of peasants who faced overpopulation, poor soils, and long winters.

Capital Accumulation. The capital accumulated by the bourgeoisie through trade and crafts called for investment. This was best provided by home industry, which at the given technological level required only simple manual equipment that could be installed anywhere. Local concentration was therefore not necessary. Because of the combination with agriculture, wages could, at a pinch, be kept below the subsistence level.

Usually, only the women were engaged in spinning and weaving, while the men worked on the land all day during the summer. The family knew how to employ its own specific strength as a productive unit. Orders could be varied according to the demand, and temporary unemployment was absorbed by agriculture. The spread of home industry to the remotest villages and valleys was conducive to wide training of skilled workers and to the growth of a relatively progressive population.

The organization of home work varied throughout the country, in keeping with the variegated political structure. The industrial process

---

munity), like Zurich and Basel, did not lead to the emergence of princely, territorial states as in Italy and Germany. The annexation of new areas to the city cantons was rarely by violence; instead, it was achieved by purchase or as a result of forfeiture. By means of a plebiscite an area was given the right—temporarily at least—to participate in internal and foreign affairs. This rule by a citizenry engaged in trade and handicrafts was of paramount significance, as we shall see, since capital accumulation, which increased as the result of political dependence, was used for productive economic activity. This was, thus, a "bourgeois monopoly." On the part of the ruling stratum there was no tendency toward introduction of a feudal order.

initiated by home industry was thus not the same everywhere, as two examples from the cotton industry will show.

Political Influences on Organization of the Cotton Industry. The cotton industry and related activities were Switzerland's most important prior to the French Revolution. The beginning of the cotton industry can be traced to the fourteenth century. Yet, only toward the end of the seventeenth century did it take a powerful upward swing after refugees introduced fine spinning and muslin weaving. Cotton was imported from Egypt, Asia Minor, and the Americas via the ports of Venice, Marseilles, and Genoa.

In the canton of Zurich the cotton industry was not subject to any restrictions in the fifteenth and sixteenth centuries. It grew up primarily in the rural districts where small-scale entrepreneurs (putters-out) established themselves gradually. They bought the raw materials at the fairs, had home workers spin and weave them, and then sold the finished cloth themselves. Later, the rural entrepreneur had to compete with his counterpart in the city. Since the rural population depended politically on the city, the city burghers managed to seize the exclusive trade monopoly (except in the town of Winterthur) during the second half of the seventeenth century. From 1662 on, the rural entrepreneurs were under obligation to transport all cloth to the city for sale to an urban trader; after 1693 this rule applied to all threads. At the same time the city obtained the monopoly for buying up raw cotton, the rural home workers were no longer allowed to work for a foreign entrepreneur, and the founding of commercial associations between a city dweller and a rural entrepreneur was forbidden. The city's commercial monopoly led to concentration of capital and the rationalization of the process of buying and selling cotton and cotton goods. Capital concentration, combined with cheap and dependent labor, enhanced the accumulation of capital. Parallel with this process was a more rationalized organization of home work, which was tantamount to increased labor productivity. The large urban commercial firms bought cotton wholesale in the ports of arrival and shipped it to Switzerland. From Zurich they sold it to rural entrepreneurs on credit or in exchange for threads and cloth.

In the village the entrepreneurs maintained stores for cotton, thread, and cloth. Every week the spinners and weavers brought their goods to the stores, were paid by them, and received new raw materials. The city merchants who originally were putters-out as well, and thus had direct relations with the home workers, later specialized in organizing the labor process and in buying and selling.[22] From this a well-contrived network of commercial industrial relations had developed by the close of the eighteenth century.

Developments were different in the rest of eastern Switzerland, where the cotton industry emerged as late as the eighteenth century. In 1714 cotton spinning was begun in Glarus, and between 1730 and 1750 in St. Gall, Appenzell-Ausserrhoden, and the Toggenburg; in the later half of the seventeenth century it was established in the Rhine valley and in Appenzell-Innerrhoden. Weaving was begun in St. Gall in 1721, in Appenzell in 1747, in the Toggenburg in 1760, and in Glarus and Thurgovy in 1770. Developments took a different course in these cantons due to the absence of a territory-holding city and, consequently, of a subject population dependent on a city bourgeoisie. Numerous, scattered centers of commercial activity developed, with many kinds of labor organization and dependence.

Here, economic spontaneity emanated not only from local merchants who operated on a larger scale but also from men who spun and wove themselves and whose work had expanded to where they could put out some to others. This situation, even before the French Revolution induced the rural population in the urban and aristocratically ruled cantons to achieve political equality, led to increasing numbers of autonomous small entrepreneurs whose strength and indestructibility were rooted in the peasantry, whose independence was embedded in the democratic and regional political structure. Because of the absence of urban trade monopolies, however, there was no excessive capital accumulation in relatively few hands. It is not accidental that, in contrast, textile manufacturing and, in its wake, machine building developed fastest in Zurich Canton where capital was amply available.

Clockmaking. Free home work also dominated the clockmaking industry until the period of large-scale manufacture. In this case raw materials were of less importance, and tendencies toward centralization and monopoly through control of sources of raw material and use of the lever of political dependence need not be considered. From the start the emphasis was on qualified, intensive labor by politically and economically free home workers.

In this industry, too, the disintegration of the medieval socioeconomic order created conditions favorable to the new modes of production. In

---

[22] Cf. William E. Rappard, *La Révolution industrielle et les origines de la protection légale du travail en Suisse* (Berne: Staempli et Cie., 1914).

a unique way, clockmaking in the stage of incipient mass production indicates the degree of capitalist progress, since chronometry became a universal and decisive factor. Although the first clocks were made outside Switzerland, it emerged as the world center of clockmaking. The reasons are not far to seek. It was in Switzerland that feudal ties were first dissolved and that bourgeois capitalist society evolved in an uninterrupted process. A contributing factor undoubtedly was the country's scarcity of raw materials and the resulting concentration upon processing and industrial art *(Kunstgewerbe)*. This explains why heavy industries could not come into being, but in no way elucidates why specialized industrial activities developed at all.

In the canton of Neuchâtel the clock industry began as a native enterprise without any assistance from the refugees. The chief demand for clocks and watches came from France. To a certain extent Neuchâtel's location on the French border caused the industry to take root where it did. Furthermore, precision metallurgy was carried on in the mountain valleys as early as the sixteenth century. Yet the "birth" of the watch industry was somewhat accidental: In 1679 a locksmith apprentice, D. J. Richard, was able to repair a watch that a local citizen had brought from England, and thereupon proceeded to make one himself. His shop became the birthplace of watchmaking in Neuchâtel, where in the early eighteenth century many peasants engaged in watchmaking during the winter months, in complete independence and without any guild or administrative supervision. They were not motivated by the interests of urban craftsmen but merely by the knowledge that free, landholding peasants could engage in profitable trades.[23] It must be kept in mind, however, that the employers were a city bourgeoisie that had become wealthy by trade and crafts; hence the growth of the

[23] In 1836 the English House of Commons sent a member, Dr. John Bowring, to Switzerland to analyze industrial and trade conditions there. His enthusiastic report supplied Sir Robert Peel with arguments for free trade. Bowring obtained the following information on the Neuchâtel clockmaking industry from a manufacturer, Houriet of Locle: "Strangers are surprised to see the surface of these mountains covered with a multitude of scattered habitations, even in the most retired and inaccessible situations, and each of them surrounded with a small enclosure for a few heads of cattle. This circumstance, however, has had a very great influence upon the extension, and it may be said upon the creation, of our industry and commerce, for all these petty proprietors are occupied with their families, during the long winters which reign in our climate, about one or other of the respective branches of watchmaking, and for this reason they live more economically and more independently than if they were concentrated within towns or villages. They have also more

industry can be understood only in relation to the over-all bourgeois development.

Subsequently, watch manufacturing evolved in accordance with its own laws. Certain processes of production, especially the more minute and complicated ones, were concentrated gradually in the larger villages, whereas the simpler processes were carried out on the farms. The home workers began to abstain from agricultural pursuits. Before the French Revolution, a large segment of the population—men, women, and children—worked in their homes or in small shops. With greater division of labor a stratum of merchants was gradually recruited from former watchmakers. Some of these became large-scale exporters, who took up manufacturing by employing workers in homes or small shops, paid them in cash, and sold the watches and clocks that had been made to order or accumulated in storage. Technological progress and division of labor led later to modern industrial production. By mobilizing its own resources, the clockmaking industry in Neuchâtel created the conditions for modern capitalist industry: capital accumulation through concentration of capital in relatively few hands; then as now a predominance of small enterprises; qualified work by the home industry, competing for orders; determination to deliver high-quality goods; and, at a later stage, the establishment of trade schools providing a high level of occupational training.

In Geneva, clockmaking and many other crafts were introduced in the sixteenth century by French and Italian refugees. In the late seventeenth century the city had 100 masters with 300 apprentices, and in the late eighteenth century about 1,000 masters and several thousand apprentices. There were several causes of this amazing growth. The beginning was decisive. When Calvin arrived in Geneva, he found an environment that other revolutionaries had to create for themselves, namely, absence of the traditional secular and ecclesiastical powers, the legacy of the Middle Ages. The nobility and the bishop had left the city as an aftermath of the battles against Savoy. Guilds had been unable to ensconce themselves in the city, since it was the temporary center of the Savoyan nobility and host to fairs. Thus, the precon-

---

resources in the event of adversity; and, lastly, their manner of living, half agricultural and half manufacturing, is more salubrious, and exposes them less to the temptations of luxury and expenses. The morality of the population is, likewise, better preserved than it could possibly be amidst a great accumulation of working classes."—John Bowring, *Report on the Commerce and Manufactures of Switzerland* (London, 1836), p. 35.

ditions for modern forms of organization were present. It was considered a religious duty in Geneva more than anywhere else to grant haven to religious refugees; and this policy was not opposed by any guild. Thus, thousands of Italian and French refugees, highly trained for specific occupations, were able to settle and carry on their trades. The economic dynamism generated by this situation was enormous.

During the eighteenth century an extremely diversified division of labor developed in the clock industry, and *de facto* leadership slipped into the hands of the merchants. Here, too, the typical process of concentration set in at the city level, and without direct interference from the government.

THE NINETEENTH-CENTURY PATTERN OF DEVELOPMENT

We have noted that before the French Revolution production was organized differently in the industries of every canton as a consequence of their varied political development. Yet certain common characteristics stand out, and these determined the configuration of Swiss industry in the nineteenth century.

Individualism

The separation of trade and handicrafts—with commerce located mainly in the cities and work in the open country—led to antagonism, which was overcome by the revolution of 1798 and the Regeneration of 1830–31. The leaders of radical movements came primarily from the rural districts. It must be kept in mind that classical Swiss democracy had been corporative; traditional Swiss liberty had not meant the autonomy of equal individuals vis-a-vis the state, but had meant, exclusively, the collective autonomy of a valley or town community. The new factor that led to the Swiss federation of 1848 was the concept of individual liberty that was carried into Switzerland by French revolutionary propaganda, i.e., the idea of the naturally equal human being as the basis of the political community. It is fundamental for the understanding of modern Swiss democracy that the individual, equipped with new rights and heightened self-confidence, was received into the protection of a continuing community and consequently had to conform. Swiss individualism was not under compulsion to assert itself, as a radical antithesis to feudal institutions, by revolutionary destruction of all that had been. The founding of the federal state, guaranteeing the modern freedom of the individual, did not amount to the liquidation of the old communal cooperative *(genossenschaftlich)* state, but to its modernization.

Importance of Exports

An almost disproportionally large section of the Swiss economy was devoted to export industries. The Swiss economy, furthermore, was (and is) interwoven to an extraordinary extent with the world economy. The preservation of markets for export and of the sources of raw materials, in view of their scarcity, came to be regarded as the foremost task of Swiss economic policy. Questions relating to foreign trade relations were much in the foreground during the nineteenth century. The general demand for free trade and an open economic order repeatedly derived its decisive arguments from the country's economic situation.

In order to remain competitive in the foreign markets, Swiss industrialists insisted on a high degree of occupational training. The foundation of the Federal School of Technology was, as it were, symbolic of the new state. They also demanded cheap foodstuffs—which had to be increasingly imported because of the preponderance of industrial activity—cheap raw materials, and inexpensive labor. All these could be provided only by free trade. While these demands were made on the basis of prevailing conditions, freedom of buying and selling had been taken for granted for centuries. To this situation was added, in the nineteenth century, the universal political liberty of the individual. The reasoning was that political liberty was prerequisite for economic liberty. This freedom-loving ideology determined economic policy and was maintained even when new markets had to be sought primarily overseas, because of the protective tariffs of the surrounding countries; this search for new markets was often accompanied by ruthless unemployment. The dangers from foreign protectionism were met by the Swiss economy by ever increasing specialization and more intensive occupational training, not through protective measures. In 1830 a speaker at the annual opening ceremony of the Zurich Technical Institute stated: "Only fast progress in all fields of scientific and technical education can enable us to compete permanently with other manufacturing and trading countries. . . . We must strive for a farther spread of our goods in foreign parts. That we can do only by learning foreign languages and if we are in the forefront technologically and produce cheaply." [24] This was the period of rapid progress in general and scientific education.

[24] *Der schweizerische Grosshandel in Geschichte und Gegenwart,* pp. 94–95.

Factors in Swiss Adaptability to External Conditions

What made it possible for Swiss industry to adapt itself to the ever changing sales picture in the outside world? Swiss adaptability stemmed originally from an elastic labor market and a capacity for sudden change which were the result of the domestic system of manufacture; furthermore, the wealth of available capital always enabled the producers to seize promising chances.

Only private persons participated in industrial activity, and up to the emergence of the federal state there was hardly any nation-wide state organization. Besides, the federal structure of 1848 had been advocated mainly by men who expected more and better industrial output from better internal communications. Consequently, there was from the beginning neither ideological nor factual ground for state planning or direction of industry. To the extent that the individual was outside the guild order, he was completely on his own so far as his economic existence within the democratic and regional environment was concerned. This situation encouraged strength and the will to be independent, self-preservation, and the spirit of enterprise. These qualities found expression in the patient pursuit of aims and in virtuosity in adapting to the needs and wants of others.

Another factor was Switzerland's lack of basic raw materials. No industry based on the country's natural resources could originate, and there was a vital national interest in the maintenance of the industries that had developed.

Finally, the limited internal market did not make possible large-scale business except in communications and electricity, which later were transferred to state or semistate management. In place of big business, and as a reaction to the protective tariff policies of other countries, a special type of large-scale business came into being with small and medium enterprises spread over the world and directed from Switzerland by Swiss engineers and businessmen. This development provided another stimulus to free trade.

ECONOMIC DEVELOPMENT AND SOCIAL POLICY

The industrial revolution was followed inevitably by political changes.[25] Factory mass production required the concentration of sufficient numbers of workers in industrial centers and hence free mobility

[25] Cf. Rappard, *op. cit.;* Bernard de Cerenville, *Le Système continental et la Suisse 1803–1813* (Lausanne: G. Briedel et Cie., 1906); H. Nabholz, "Die Entstehung des

of the population. Greater movements of commodities and raw materials required better communications, unified currency and postal systems, freedom from tolls, and a common business law. No single canton could answer these demands. Prior to the nineteenth century every canton producing for export had found its own sales market. Given the economic structure of Europe as it then existed, each canton could look after its economic security alone. There was no need to tighten the loose federal structure that kept the cantons together. The driving force behind the unification of the national realm was the leaders of modern business. The new bourgeois, liberal, and capitalist world crystallized itself by means of the federal constitution of 1848. Its spirit permeated state and society, giving free rein to the economic sphere. The new constitution was greeted with approval by most cantons and the vast majority of the people. The genesis of the constitution or of the patterns of political behavior that it expresses was not merely a reflection of nineteenth-century mentality but of a process that covered six centuries and in which three main currents were apparent: the communes striving in the late Middle Ages for continued autonomy and self-rule; the ideas of the Reformation during the Renaissance— e.g., Zwingli's concept of the unity of the confederacy in relation to the federal constitution; and Rousseau's doctrine of popular sovereignty in conjunction with influences emanating from the American constitution, the French Revolution, and German Idealism.

Special Conditions of the Industrial Revolution in Switzerland

The special conditions under which the industrial revolution took place in Switzerland and the process itself, which thereafter contributed to the direction taken by economic policies, must be considered, as must certain characteristic traits of the federal states' economic policy.

Manufacturing in the rural regions, along with the relative freedom and autonomy of the rural populations, brought about a relatively high level of occupational training. This became especially effective after the revolution when town and country had become politically and economically equal. Numberless small entrepreneurs and rural manufacturers suddenly enjoyed total independence. They made use of

Bundesstaates, wirtschaftsgeschichtlich betrachtet," in *Ausgewählte Aufsätze zur Wirtschaftsgeschichte* (Zurich, 1954), pp. 195 ff.; *Der schweizerische Grosshandel in Geschichte und Gegenwart, loc. cit.*

their experience and skill to establish commercial relations of their own, for the rich rural manufacturers, in spite of their ability to buy and sell raw materials and finished goods themselves, were among the most outspoken opponents of the urban monopoly of trade.

The introduction of machine-equipped factories gave rise to a second "wave" of modern manufacturers. This new business world was at first recruited from all strata of the population: peasants who had sold their farms, master artisans, innkeepers, workers, carpetbaggers, merchants. Machines were set up in shacks, cellars, backyards, improvised sheds. Savings, modest as well as substantial, were used for buying machinery. Mechanized spinning and weaving mills sprang up like mushrooms where once domestic handicrafts had flourished. Nonetheless, the fact that the cities had always left manufacturing to the rural areas while keeping the trade had definite economic results, for only through the politically enforced commercial monopoly was it feasible to accumulate the capital required for large-scale spinning and weaving plants. In other words, for a monopoly to arise while capitalism was still little developed, the political dependence of the producers was prerequisite. Increasing mechanization, however, changed the political dependence into its economic counterpart. This meant that the individual who was unable to possess means of production was dependent on the owner of such means. What had changed was the mode of acquisition of surplus value. A glance at an early nineteenth-century map of Swiss industrial expansion shows that mechanized spinning and weaving mills were far more frequent in areas under the sway of urban monopolies.[26]

The process of the industrial revolution was strongly influenced by events in the world at large. Spinning machines had been built in eighteenth-century England, and the first mass product of English industry, cheap machine-made thread, flooded the continent. Even at that time France was largely excluding English goods, but the Swiss cotton entrepreneurs bought the English thread all the more eagerly. The spinners who had worked by hand and had become unemployed now took up weaving by hand. As a result of its flexibility and of the free import of English threads, the Swiss cotton industry enjoyed its last boom prior to the French Revolution.

[26] There were about 60 mechanized spinning firms in the canton of Zurich in 1814, 74 in 1817, and 126 in 1827, whereas the cantons of St. Gall and Appenzell together contained only 24 spinning firms in 1820. As a result of competition the number of spinning firms decreased after 1827, while the number of workers rose (see Rappard, *op. cit.*, p. 53).

The exclusion of English competition from European markets, following Napoleon's Continental System, enabled Switzerland to adopt mechanical spinning quickly, thus initiating modern industry. The first permanently successful large-scale spinning plant was established in the canton of Zurich in 1802. In the city of Zurich the spinning firm of Escher, Wyss & Co. developed a machine plant that became known throughout the world. The cotton industry thus gave birth to the machine-producing industry, and mechanized spinning plants multiplied. As early as 1810 they could provide 25 percent of the thread needed by the cotton industry. In 1812 Escher, Wyss & Co. planned and equipped the big spinning factory of J. J. Rieter in Winterthur, which soon opened its own machine-building plant and was exporting spinning machines by 1832. The cessation of the Continental System could no longer hurt Swiss industry. By the 1870's Swiss thread production held second place in the world.

The transition to mechanical weaving brought bitter hardships to the population engaged in weaving by hand. For them there was now no escape into another craft and no governmental economic policy to lend a helping hand. Only emigration remained. In 1845 alone, nearly one sixtieth of the population of the canton of Glarus emigrated to America.

The rapid expansion of the cotton industry was due to the machine-producing industry, which was by now wholly independent, and turned Switzerland—a country barren of coal and iron—into a leading center of machine construction.

Federal Economic Policy

To understand Swiss economic policy from 1848 on, one must bear in mind that the Constitution of 1848 was instrumental in bringing about an over-all identity of interests between the state and its individual citizens. The relative harmony of interests in the population—whose economic interests and capacities almost suffered from hypertrophy—led to a conception of the state that provided security for the pursuit of economic interests. Under Swiss economic conditions this could only mean guarantees of freedom of trade and industry.

The demand for freedom of trade and industry amounted to confirmation of the existing state of affairs or of an existing trend, except where it concerned the local guilds or improvements in domestic communications. Christopher Bernoulli opposed the still existing, though rather insignificant, guild system in his theory of free trade; he did not oppose state monopolies or protective tariffs, which did not exist. This stand, which was influenced by the English classical economists, looks somewhat modest in contrast with the demands for free trade advanced by foreign liberal theoreticians.

In other countries the bourgeoisie strove for political and economic emancipation. Consequently, the bourgeoisie's ideas of economic liberalization had bellicose ideological traits, forcing the economists to work out universal theoretical systems of economics. It is not surprising, therefore, that Switzerland did not produce classical economists known to the outside world, despite her wide recognition as an outstanding example of manifestations of classical economics. In their writings Swiss economists dealt with the solution of concrete problems arising out of current and constantly changing situations.[27] Their attitude was in keeping with their realism; they were interested in contemporary events and were shaped by a bourgeois environment that was concerned with goals and hence averse to thinking in terms of systems and theories.

Historically speaking, freedom of trade and industry as codified by the constitution is not to be confused with the slogan of laissez faire, laissez passer, but rather represents positive law as fashioned by actual life. Yet this freedom was also a program, aside from being a confirmation of a state of affairs.

Constitutionally, the state was in no position to interfere directly in the economic process. The levying of tariffs was stated to be the sole concern of the federal government. Economic discussion was stimulated, however, by the arguments as to how to levy tariffs, since their revenue constituted the backbone of the federal budget (income and property taxes went to the cantons). The first tariff of 1850 was purely fiscal with very low rates that in no way restricted trade. Vital raw materials and foodstuffs came under minimum rates, manufactured products and luxury wares under maximum rates. It was characteristic of this system that raw materials and foodstuffs were not exempted at the expense of manufactured goods. That would have led to a situation where some industries enjoyed more protection than others, which would have been considered inadmissible from the view of legal equality alone. Preferen-

---

[27] See, for instance, the writings of Th. Hoffmann-Merian, J. J. Speiser, W. Schmidlin, H. Bovet-Bolens, Numa Droz, George Baumberger. They are poor in theoretical results, and in the main defend free trade and condemn protectionist policies.

tial taxation benefiting some producers or occupational groups at the expense of society would have been incompatible with the constitutional thesis of the equality of all citizens before the law.

This principle thenceforth determined the decisions on tariff policy. Along with the fact that the Swiss economy is highly dependent on the fluctuations of the world economy, this basic attitude stands in the way of a comprehensive, modern policy of full employment and adjustment to the business cycle *(Konjunkturpolitik)*. The economy is supposed to be the concern of private persons. This attitude, moulded through the centuries by typically Swiss conditions, is now hardly questioned.

Nevertheless, the high living standard of the Swiss people does not permit the conclusion that the so-called "free economy" alone is responsible for their prosperity. In this essay we have stressed historical factors of growth because the developments under examination were made possible by specific and unique historical conditions which will also contribute to the shaping of the future.

9 ETATISM IN TURKEY, 1933–50

Robert W. Kerwin

Modern Turkey represents an excellent case for study of the role of the state in economic growth. Immediately after World War I a new, nationalistic Turkish state was born. One of the first acts of its leaders was to embark on an intensive program of economic development.

The state traditionally has played a leading part in the economic growth of Turkey. As far back as the early nineteenth century the Ottoman government had established military factories and encouraged private artisans and industrial entrepreneurs by introducing tax exemptions, government gifts of land, and preferential state buying. After World War I a somewhat similar policy was followed, especially through the Law for Encouragement of Industry, passed in 1927. A protective tariff and semiofficial financing of industrial enterprise, through the organization of a commercial bank investing in industry, were also introduced in the 1920's. Faced with the economic crisis of the 1930's, however, the nationalistic Turkish government in 1933 adopted a clearcut economic policy of state intervention in industrialization; this was called etatism[1] and remained official policy until 1950.

Within the terms of reference of the present discussion, the development of etatist Turkey may be classified as intrinsic, dominant, and induced. The country was fairly well-settled by the end of World War I. Natural resources were relatively plentiful. Strong nationalism led the Turks to rely on their own resources in economic growth. Foreign financial assistance was largely limited to an industrial equipment loan from the Soviet Union, and foreign capital was expropriated or placed under severe restrictions. The policy of etatism was in itself an effort to induce economic growth.

OBJECTIVES AND ORIGINS OF THE POLICY OF ETATISM

The Turkish economic development efforts launched in 1933 were aimed at attaining national self-sufficiency. Aspirations for prestige,

[1] The Turkish word for this economic policy is "devletçilik," which is the equivalent of the French *étatisme*. In translation the writer has chosen to anglicize the widely known French word rather than to use the direct English equivalent of "statism," in order to differentiate clearly between the specific Turkish economic policy and statism in a broader sense.

237

so often associated with nationalism, may have been involved, but apart from these the Turks considered economic independence a matter of national defense. Their recent experiences in military defense of their country against European powers, as well as the semicolonial nature of the Ottoman Empire with its system of capitulations which gave foreigners a privileged position in Turkey, led the Turkish Nationalists to seek industrialization as a means of achieving a strong, better balanced, and independent economy. Foreign capital investment and foreign goods were considered threats to national independence. Furthermore, economic development efforts during 1923–33, when private enterprise had been given encouragement and material assistance by the state, showed clearly that accumulation of capital within Turkey left much to be desired. Entrepreneurs were relatively nonexistent, and there was a shortage of trained technical personnel. An objective of etatism, therefore, was the actual participation by the state in industrial and mining pursuits to fill the gap left by private enterprise. A hybrid economy resulted. While the Turkish government became by far the largest single investor in industry, private entrepreneurs continued to receive state encouragement and aid in the etatist period.

Apart from the nationalistic reaction to foreign domination of the economy in Ottoman Turkey, the world economic crisis of 1929–30 was itself one of the strongest influences in the adoption of the policy of etatism. The value of the Turkish lira and the trade and payments situation were of serious concern in Turkey just when encouragement of industry was being undertaken, and when countries of the West were enjoying their greatest prosperity. By the commercial agreement that was part of the Lausanne settlement, the Turks were bound from 1923 to 1928 to apply the specific tariff schedule of 1916, as adjusted to allow for wartime depreciation of the lira, to all imports from the countries signatory to the Lausanne Convention. This made protection of native industry very difficult, and resulted in an influx of foreign goods into Turkey as advantage was taken of the favorable customs rates, especially in the year or two preceding the termination of the temporary tariff limitation. The trade situation was aggravated further by continued drought, which seriously impeded Turkey's developmental efforts. Turkey did not have a favorable balance of trade during these years, and the value of the Turkish lira fell rapidly. Moreover, as a producer of raw materials and agricultural products, Turkey felt the world economic crisis in its earliest stages.

The effect of the depression years on Turkish thinking is well illustrated by an editorial in the journal *Kadro,* which in 1932–34 was very influential in promoting etatism and in essence played the role of spokesman for nationalistic reasoning on economic policy:

... in our opinion Turkey is not a part of the world crisis but stands outside it. ... It is, of course, not possible to overlook the effects on Turkey of the world-wide structural depression. It is especially impossible not to see the reactions upon our peasant population of the drastic fall in prices of such raw materials as cotton, wool and goat's hair. But this is true largely because of our passive attitude toward the world's industrial centralization. It is plain that when Turkey can make use of her own raw materials, she will, with respect to these three products, stand outside of any world-wide economic depression ... Turkey and countries like Turkey stand really outside the crisis as far as the meaning of their National Independence activities is concerned.[2]

The Turks were also becoming increasingly aware of the anticapitalist trend in Fascist Italy and Nazi Germany. State planning as practiced in Germany particularly interested Turkish intellectuals. At the same time they were watching communist experiments in the same field in Russia. There is no doubt that both the German and Russian systems influenced Turkish etatism, and both countries gave some technical and material aid to the Turkish industrialization program, but the influence of these foreign economic systems should not be exaggerated.

Even though the Turks admired both Nazi and Soviet ideas of planning and control of national economies, they attempted from the beginning to distinguish between the Fascist-Nazi or communist systems and a strictly Turkish nationalist policy. This can be illustrated by comparisons made in *Kadro:*

Fascism is a movement to save semi-capitalist Italy from capitalism's class conflict, from the internal anarchy which that conflict brings forth, and from the demagogy and bureaucratic administrative paraphernalia—democracy and parliamentarianism—which are a reflection of that anarchy.

... The Turkish nation, on the other hand, because it has begun its revolution with a national structure not divided into social classes, will reject and take measures to make impossible such dividing into classes. This is the reason for assigning to the government the principal means of production, and the acceptance of the progressive and planned *étatism.*

Fascism, even in the post-war period when colonialism was disappearing, has, because of democratic necessities, been compelled to make colonialism one

---

[2] *Kadro,* No. 6 (June 1932), pp. 46–47. All references to this source are from the English translation by John Kingsley Birge.

of its main points. . . . Kemalism [the Turkish Nationalist Movement] is a revolt against colonialism. . . . It rejects opposition and conflict of interest both internally and externally, that is, from the point of view of both social classes and nations.

Fascism, since it is a movement peculiar to semi-capitalist structure, is not suitable to structures that are either wholly capitalist or not yet capitalist at all. . . . Kemalism will constitute the ideas and source of ideology for those countries which have not yet brought to realization their National Independence Activities.[3]

The social structure of Turkey and the background of the nationalist leaders also played an important part in the adoption of the policy of etatism. As early as the sixteenth century, Ottoman society was divided into clear-cut occupational groups: those earning their livelihood by the sword, those employing the pen, cultivators of the land, and merchant traders. The last group was considered the lowest class. In later centuries of Ottoman rule this division of occupations took place along national and religious lines. The Christian and Jewish minorities formed the commercial and entrepreneurial class; the Turks were largely soldiers, government officials, or peasants.

When Turkey emerged from World War I there were few Turkish nationals to fill the shoes of the departed Armenians or the Greeks who were exchanged as part of the aftermath of the Lausanne settlement. Moreover, Turkey's leaders were mainly military men to whom a system of government planning and direct participation in economic development was bound to appeal. Kemal Atatürk, the architect of modern Turkey, as a military man was relatively inexperienced in the business and economic fields, but he furnished much of the new spirit. To a handful of intellectuals and relatively inexperienced administrators fell the lot of translating aspirations into action. The mechanism of the state was the only known means of attaining Turkey's aims in the economic field. State intervention in economic activity was not only traditional but inevitable.

METHODS OF ETATISM

The policy of etatism was initially confined to state participation in specific fields of economic activity. On January 9, 1934, the Minister of Economy announced the inauguration of a five-year plan for the development of three categories of industries: (1) industries for which

[3] *Ibid.*, No. 8 (August 1932), pp. 38–39.

the raw materials were produced in Turkey but in which domestic production was not sufficient to meet the needs of the country; (2) industries that could process local raw materials for export in a finished or partly finished state; and (3) those that could produce goods consumed in the country in considerable quantity even though the raw materials had to be imported. The specific fields in which development was scheduled included certain chemical industries, ceramics, iron and steel, paper and cellulose, sulphur and copper mining, cotton and woolen textiles, hemp, and the sponge industry.

In 1936 a second five-year plan, which was in the nature of an extension of the first plan, was prepared. In 1938 several changes were made in this second plan and its duration was reduced to four years. World War II, however, interfered greatly with the execution of the plan, and in the latter part of the etatist period such plans began to lose meaning.

The principal mechanisms for the implementation of the Turkish etatist plans were the Sümerbank and Etibank, which may be classified as state industrial and mining holding companies, even though they have carried out minor commercial banking functions as well. It should again be noted that in creating the state holding-company banks the Turkish government did not intend to curtail private enterprise. On the contrary, the laws establishing the Sümerbank and Etibank provided for their giving assistance to private industrial and mining development. In practice, however, such assistance did not work out. It should also be noted that the tax concessions and other benefits of the 1927 Law for Encouragement of Private Industry remained in force until 1942.

THE STATE HOLDING-COMPANY BANKS

Their Organization

A clear-cut pattern of organization for Turkish state economic activity was discernible by 1938. In that year the Law for State Economic Enterprises (No. 3460), a general law on organization, administration, and control of the holding-company banks, was passed. This provided for certain operational autonomy but reserved final policy control for the Turkish Parliament.

A General Economic Commission, composed of various government ministers and chairmen of economic committees in the Grand National Assembly, as well as the directors of the state banks and other organizations covered by the Law for State Economic Enterprises, reviewed annually all operations and programs of enterprises in which the government owned 50 percent or more of the stock. Only the State Revenue Monopolies and transportation and communications agencies were excluded from this law. A Central Auditing and Control Board was set up in the Prime Minister's office to report annually to the General Economic Commission on the management and operations of the state enterprises.

Sümerbank and Etibank have also had their own boards of directors, appointed by the government. Under these boards a general management has supervised operations of the state-owned factories and mines.

Considerable effort was directed toward attaining a businesslike organization of the state economic enterprises. Special personnel regulations were provided, and annual bonuses were paid to employees if earnings reached a satisfactory level.

The relative autonomy of the state economic enterprises, compared with other government departments, can best be seen in the financial field. The state holding companies have not been subject to standard government adjudication procedure in purchases of raw materials, capital equipment, and supplies. The budgets of the special economic enterprises have only indirectly been subject to approval by the Grand National Assembly through review by the General Economic Commission. Thus they have been allowed to operate with a business-type budget, which allocates expenditures in accordance with earnings.

The financial provisions applied to the Sümerbank and Etibank are most significant because they have permitted state economic enterprises to determine their own investment programs. Allowed to retain their net earnings for additional investment, the holding-company banks have been able largely to finance their own expansion.

Financial Resources

The funds for establishing and operating industrial plants and mines under the Sümerbank and Etibank during 1933–50 came from four sources: allocations in the national budget; earnings of the Sümerbank and Etibank enterprises themselves; borrowing from the Central Bank of Turkey; temporary deposits of the state Treasury. All these financial resources represent involuntary savings on the part of the Turkish people.

The state Treasury turned over existing military factories to the

Sümerbank on its inception in 1933; and from time to time mines that were expropriated from private owners by the government were given to Etibank as part of its capital assets. The total of government contributions to the capital of the holding-company banks in the form of installations or monetary grants from the national budget reached 118.8 million Turkish lira by the end of 1949.[4]

From their earnings Sümerbank and Etibank added a total of 55.8 million Turkish lira to their capital. The profits of Etibank were somewhat misleading, however, since the price of coal was subsidized by the government. In addition to recorded profits, the two institutions amassed a total of 181.1 million Turkish lira in reserves and 140.1 million in depreciation funds. Thus, through self-financing, they added the significant sum of 380.4 million Turkish lira to their financial resources.[5] It should be noted that no earnings of the state holding-company banks reverted to the general government accounts up to 1950.

As the activities of Sümerbank and Etibank expanded, further need of funds developed, and eventually inflationary financing by borrowing from the Central Bank was permitted. After 1938 various state organizations were accorded the right, with the approval of the Council of Ministers of the government, to issue bonds for rediscounting at the Central Bank. These bonds were guaranteed by the Treasury and were valid for nine months, renewable any number of times. They became in effect a permanent floating debt of the state enterprises at the Central Bank, bearing a nominal interest rate of 4 percent of which three fourths was paid by the Central Bank to the Treasury and finally reverted to the enterprise issuing the bonds. Thus the effective rate of interest on these Central Bank rediscounts was 1 percent. Up to the end of 1949 Sümerbank and Etibank borrowed a total of 165.7 million Turkish lira from the Central Bank on this basis. In addition Sümerbank had rediscounted some 11.0 million Turkish lira from its portfolio of other commercial paper at the Central Bank.

The importance of the banking functions of these organizations can also be seen from the fact that Sümerbank had a total of 10.2 million Turkish lira in deposits on December 31, 1949, and Etibank 22.2 million. However, 19.8 million of the latter were for the account of the

[4] The official exchange rate in 1949 was TL. 2.80 to $1.00. Prior to 1946 the official rate was TL. 1.40 to $1.00.

[5] All financial figures for the Sümerbank and Etibank are based on balance sheets and other data furnished to the writer by these organizations.

Treasury. These had been temporarily placed in Etibank, pending appropriation of the government coal subsidy for 1948.

Development of Industries and Mines

By the end of 1949 Sümerbank had established 7 cotton textile factories with 146,988 spindles and 3,370 looms; 5 woolen plants of 29,629 spindles and 449 looms; a rayon mill of 204 spindles; a hemp skutching plant of 4,000 tons annual capacity; a paper mill producing 20,000 tons of paper products annually; a leather and shoe factory turning out some 2.5 million pairs of shoes a year; 2 cement plants with an annual capacity of 115,000 tons; 2 brick and tile yards producing about 3 million bricks and 4 million roofing tiles annually; a firebrick factory with a capacity of 2,000 tons of silica brick per year; and an iron and steel mill with an annual capacity of 300,000 tons of coke, 150,000 tons of pig iron, and 110,000 tons of finished steel products. Sümerbank also participated in the operation of cotton gins, retail stores, insurance companies, and other banks and commercial enterprises.

By 1949 Etibank was operating bituminous coal mines producing about 4 million tons of unwashed coal per year, subbituminous mines producing nearly 1 million tons, chrome mines turning out about 200,000 tons of ore, iron mines producing 210,000 tons, copper mines with an annual output of about 11,000 tons, and sulphur mines producing 3,000 tons per year. In addition Etibank had minor stock holdings in an insurance company and a commercial bank.

EXPANSION OF ETATISM

While Sümerbank and Etibank accounted for most of the major industrial developments under etatism, the government also became involved in several other economic enterprises as etatism ran its course. The ever increasing activities of the state significantly influenced the attitudes of the Turkish people toward the etatist policy.

One interesting form of state participation in economic enterprises in Turkey has been investment through mixed ownership. As early as 1924, with the establishment of the Is Bank—a semiofficial commercial institution, which was owned largely by political leaders and subject to government policy control, but which relied on private savings deposits as a major source of capital—investments that to some extent combined private and state resources were made in several fields. The largest of these investments was in the Sugar Trust, which was jointly owned by the Is Bank, the Sümerbank, and the State Agricultural Bank. Some 135,000 tons of sugar were produced by four plants in Turkey in 1949. The Is Bank also invested in coal mining, textile mills, insurance companies, banks, and other industrial mining and commercial enterprises. By 1950, however, the Is Bank had liquidated most of these investments. A large part of its industrial holdings were transferred to Sümerbank, and all of its mines were sold to Etibank. As the Is Bank developed into Turkey's largest commercial bank, it retained only its interests in sugar factories, a glass and bottle factory, a silk and woolen weaving mill, and minor commercial undertakings.

In the agricultural field, also, the state entered into economic enterprises. Many of these undertakings were financed through the State Agricultural Bank, originally created by the government in 1889 for the purpose of making crop and land improvement loans to farmers. This bank operated a cotton ginning and baling plant and a vegetable oil and soap factory. It also helped to finance state farms, which included both model farms and large-scale combine farms, wine distilleries, a tea plant, and a dairy products enterprise; an agricultural equipment distribution agency, which sold machinery, seeds, and fertilizers; the state Soil Products Office, a crop price support and purchasing organization somewhat akin to the U. S. Commodity Credit Corporation, and Agricultural Sales Cooperatives for the processing and marketing of Turkish agricultural products. The cooperatives caused particular controversy as to the role of the state in economic enterprise. Nominally made up of private producers of such items as figs, hazelnuts, and cotton, these organizations were under strict government control. In fact, membership in cooperatives was virtually obligatory, and they became bureaucratic organizations operated by officials appointed by the government.

In 1937 all forest resources in Turkey were placed under government control, and a State Forestry Exploitation was set up. In various parts of the country peasants who had depended largely on lumbering for their livelihood had to switch to agricultural pursuits. This often resulted in economic hardship and other problems as well as severe criticism of the government.

The Turkish Ministry of National Defense continued to operate a number of military factories during the etatist period. The state also was heavily involved in the transportation and communications field. The State Railways and State Airlines were a government monopoly. The government operated a shipping company which competed with private shipowners; and several regulatory laws gave the state a virtual monopoly of large-scale coastal shipping. Postal and telecommunications services were provided by a government agency. The building of roads and electric power plants was also the province of the state.

In 1925 the Turkish government expropriated tobacco, salt, explosives, and alcoholic products revenue monopolies that had been accorded to foreign concessionaires under the Ottoman Public Debt Administration toward the end of the nineteenth century. By 1932 these monopolies were combined under a single government agency. By 1950 the State Monopolies employed some 30,000 persons in 6 tobacco and cigarette factories; 8 alcohol distilleries, wineries, and beverage plants, and 2 breweries; numerous salt installations; a match factory, a box factory, miscellaneous lumberyards, shops, and foundries; a tobacco research institute and farm; and many depots, warehouses, and distribution offices throughout the country.

The state also entered the petroleum field. A government office, the Minerals Research Institute, operated a small oil field in eastern Turkey. The Turkish government intervened in the distribution of petroleum products during World War II. Originally set up as a regulatory agency for rationing imports of oil, the government-owned Petrol Office became a commercial company, selling petroleum in competition with foreign distributors. With a privileged position in regard to government buying and access to foreign exchange, the Petrol Office expanded until it equalled or surpassed the distribution facilities of any of the major foreign oil companies in Turkey. This government activity became the subject of bitter criticism on the part of foreign businessmen.

PUBLIC CRITICISM OF ETATISM, 1948–50

As already pointed out, the Turkish economy after 1933 was a hybrid, comprising both state and private enterprise. Private Turkish entrepreneurship developed considerably in the commercial field, and private investors were found in industries where the state was absent, where private enterprise had existed prior to the advent of etatism, and in a few cases where demand was so great that both state and private investments were attracted. The principal fields of private industrial investment were cotton, woolen, and silk textiles; leather tanning; rubber processing; cement, bricks, and tiles; food processing; vegetable oils and soap; foundries and machine shops; furniture, plywood, and veneer manufacturing; and chemicals and pharmaceuticals.

An important development in the etatist period was the emergence of a private industrial and commercial class. On the other hand, in the state enterprises a number of engineers and economic specialists were trained. It is significant that these new classes in Turkish society began to form a core of opposition to the etatist policy after World War II. The private enterprise group criticized the state for neglect of private businessmen and investors in favor of government enterprise, while many of the economists and technical men in state enterprises criticized the etatist hierarchy as being inefficient and bureaucratic.

The institution of multiparty politics in Turkey, beginning in 1946, set the stage for clear-cut public opposition to etatism. Previously a single party as inheritor of the Atatürk reform movement had reigned in Turkey. After World War II there was free criticism and competition between political parties, and a new opposition emerged in the Democrat Party.

The first opportunity for extensive expression of criticism of etatism was found in the National Economic Congress held in Istanbul in November 1948. This meeting was called by the Istanbul Merchants Association and included representatives of such groups as the Chambers of Commerce of principal cities, the regional Industrialists Associations, the Association of Economists (largely university professors) and the Turkish Economic Society (an Ankara organization composed principally of government officials). The congress discussed three major questions: etatism, foreign trade, and taxation. Committees were appointed to report on each of these. Preliminary papers prepared for the congress by leading economists and the final reports of the committees were published and fairly widely circulated in intellectual and business circles. Views on etatism expressed by individuals at the congress varied from criticism of the policy for not being enough like British socialism, to condemnation of etatism for maladministration and expansionism.

The congress' final report on etatism indicated that the opinions of the delegates were largely concerned with the state's failure to give proper recognition to private enterprise and with criticism of the expansionist and monopolistic nature of state enterprise in Turkey. The right of the government to promulgate social welfare regulations and to engage in such enterprises as transportation, large power installations, forestry, technical education, credit institutions, and even industrial undertakings in backward regions of the country where private capital could not be attracted, was clearly recognized. A distinction was made between enterprises that have a public service character and those that do not. Foreign capital was welcomed, and scientific study of the national economy was recommended.

The congress occasioned many comments in newspapers and elsewhere on economic policy. Advocates of etatism defended the policy as a historic necessity and cited its role in economic and social development along with the failure of private capital to do what was needed. Private merchants and industrialists, on the other hand, recognized the historical justifications of etatism but stressed the inefficiency of state enterprise and the adverse influence of its expansionism on the development of private enterprise. It is significant that, in contrast to the situation before the adoption of etatism, extremist views on national self-sufficiency, fear of capitalist monopoly, and distrust of foreign intervention in Turkish internal affairs were not publicly expressed. These views had dimmed in importance as the Turkish Republic became a strong political entity.

As early as 1948 American observers also began to criticize Turkish etatism. In view of the developing relations between the two countries, this had an important influence. It began to be generally thought that Turkey's internal regime should be more palatable to the United States in order to assure better understanding and to justify economic assistance. The writings of Max Thornberg were important in this connection. His conviction that the curtailment of etatism and the favoring of free enterprise in developmental efforts were prerequisites of American aid [6] had an impact on a wide and influential audience.

Major results of American aid under the Marshall Plan were a new emphasis on agriculture and recognition of the importance of roads in developing the Turkish economy. Some aid had been given to agriculture after 1933, particularly through crop and equipment loans to farmers, but the concentration on state investment in industry meant that agriculture generally had been neglected. The Turkish Nationalists had been convinced that industrialization made a state modern, and they failed to realize that agricultural development was essential for industrial growth in Turkey. Agriculture is particularly important in relation to the necessity of developing consumer purchasing power. In 1948 Turkey's participation in the Marshall Plan was predicated on estimates of the country's potentialities as a "bread basket" for Europe. Large numbers of tractors and other agricultural machines were

[6] See Max Weston Thornberg, Graham Spry, and George Soule, *Turkey: An Economic Appraisal* (New York: Twentieth Century Fund, 1949).

brought to Turkey with American aid. Extension work under the Turkish Ministry of Agriculture was stepped up considerably with American technical assistance. Most significant was a new cooperative Turkish-American highway program, which resulted in better roads, development of Turkish ability to build and maintain highways,[7] and access to areas that had been isolated both economically and culturally. Markets began to develop for both agricultural crops and consumers' goods. The Anatolian interior began to experience an economic boom.

The extensive public criticism of etatism finally led to its re-evaluation by the political parties in power after 1948. The People's Republican Party toward the end of its quarter century in power exhibited a growing tendency to cater to Turkish and foreign private enterprise, even though the etatist policy continued in force. Foreign trade was less restricted than prior to World War II; accumulated foreign exchange reserves were rapidly spent for industrial investment, a large part of which was financed by private entrepreneurs. The government began to talk of limiting its sphere of economic activity. To attract capital from abroad a law was passed late in 1947, which allowed the Ministry of Finance to guarantee repatriation of earnings and principal of foreign investments in Turkey. In discussions between the Turkish government, the International Bank, and local bankers and industrialists, the establishment of an Industrial Development Bank to make medium- and long-term loans to new or expanding private industrial firms was considered. On April 27, 1950, 17 days before the national elections, the People's Republican Party in its platform defined etatism as 100 percent state intervention only in large-scale mining, electric power, heavy industry, defense industries, and transportation and communications. Other fields, with the exception of sugar refining and meat packing, were to be left open for private investment, including foreign capital. Furthermore, an attempt was made to convince the voters that competition between state and private enterprise in certain fields benefits national economic development.

The election manifesto of the Democrat Party, on the other hand, emphasized the lack of stability and security for private enterprise under etatist policy, and pointed out that a healthy climate for private enterprise was necessary to entice much-needed foreign capital to Turkey.

The surprising electoral victory of the Democrat Party in 1950 meant that the public had rejected etatism as an economic policy at least for

[7] See Robert W. Kerwin, "The Turkish Roads Program," *Middle East Journal,* 4:196–208 (April 1950).

the time being. It is most important, however, that the reactions to etatism as a national policy were largely negative in character. Criticism was generally limited to the grievances of private entrepreneurs and of well-meaning state officials enmeshed in the bureaucracy of the etatist hierarchy. Even the intellectuals in Turkey failed to espouse the free-enterprise system as a means of development, except in terms of hopes that foreign capital would come to the aid of Turkey. Private enterprise was not well defined in the minds of the critics of etatism, and the role of the state in economic growth was not often conceived as more than a matter of degree. Furthermore, although the criticism of etatism led in part to a search for a new approach, most of the opposition to the policy came from those who felt that the government had not intervened sufficiently in their own behalf.

For the purpose of the present discussion, it should be noted that the gradual postwar change in the economic policy of Turkey meant that its economic development became less intrinsic in nature as previously uncultivated land was brought into cultivation and the interior of the country was opened by the road-building program. The economy could also be considered less dominant in character after 1948 because of the extent of American aid, and somewhat more autonomous because of the trend toward greater reliance on private investment toward the end of the etatist period. Nevertheless, continuation of a large-scale investment program in state industry, in expanded government assistance to agriculture, and in transportation, communications, and power meant that economic growth in Turkey was still essentially of the induced type.

RESULTS OF ETATISM

Taking as a convenient frame of reference the factors cited by Hartshorne in Chapter 11 (pages 297 ff. infra), we can summarize some of the problems and accomplishments of Turkish etatism.

Transport facilities: The development of a railway system serving major points all over the country, coastwise shipping jointly owned by state and private enterprise, a government operated airline reaching many parts of the interior, and some new roads were among the gains from the policy of etatism. Much of this development probably would not have occurred without state intervention. On the other hand, the neglect of roads as an integral part of the development of transport facilities in the earlier years meant that economic growth was forced from the top as compared with the more spontaneous growth that was kindled in many areas of the country after 1948, when emphasis was placed on highway development.

Capital goods: The physical plant created under etatism became a showpiece of modern Turkey. The new factory chimneys have been called "Atatürk's minarets." There is no doubt that much of the industrial equipment that was acquired in Turkey from 1933 to 1950 was a direct result of state investment. On the other hand, the major part of these capital goods had to be imported, and because of this situation foreign exchange pressures have been continuously experienced in Turkey. Government concentration on industrial investment meant a preference for capital goods in setting foreign exchange priorities. Private industrial investment and consumers' goods had to take second place in regard to spending of foreign exchange earnings up to 1946.

Mechanical energy: Most of the factories established by state enterprise in Turkey had their own power plants and used coal mined by the Etibank at Zonguldak. This made necessary the maintenance of standby power capacity at most of the isolated plants. Private industrial undertakings were more often centered in the large cities and profited from municipal power sources, which also used coal as fuel. The only large power plant developed prior to 1950 was a 60,000 kw. thermal plant at the coal mines in Zonguldak. One major result of etatist development, however, was that the Turks became "power conscious." A scientific study bureau to survey power needs and potential, particularly hydroelectric possibilities, was organized in the latter part of the period. The bureau's studies were used as a basis for applications for foreign aid in the energy field.

Raw materials: State intervention in the industrialization of Turkey proved to be a partial boon to the development of raw materials. Cotton growing became a major agricultural pursuit, to feed the textile factories built by state and private investors. Substantial development of coal mining for general energy uses took place. Such minerals as iron, manganese, coal, and sulphur were extracted for use in the state iron and steel industry. State enterprise may be criticized, however, for failing to develop certain industries in accordance with the availability of raw materials produced in Turkey. Paper mills were set up without any source of wood pulp. Woolen mills used only imported wool tops since Turkish wool is coarse and suitable only for homespun and carpets. While these enterprises produced goods that were in demand in Turkey, their contribution to over-all economic development was less than that of enterprises using Turkish raw materials.

Entrepreneurship: It is on the human side that the problems of Turkish economic growth are most evident. The basic justification for the entrance of the state into industrial production was the absence of private entrepreneurship. This remained a weak aspect of Turkish economic development to the end of the etatist period. A commercial class developed, largely from selling imported capital goods to the state for its enterprises, but industrial entrepreneurs remained relatively few. Fear of state competition only partly explains the hesitancy of private investors to risk capital in industry. Merchants were beginning to consider industry as a field for investment toward the end of the period. Other classes of Turkish society did not have the capital for such investment. On the other hand, the claims of the few private entrepreneurs that state enterprise stifled private activity undoubtedly had considerable validity.

Finance capital: Another major justification for the policy of etatism was the shortage of capital in Turkey. Even with the marshaling of capital by the state, however, the accumulation of capital was insufficient to meet demands. The resort of the government to inflationary financing of state enterprise after 1938 proves this point even though it must be admitted that the state industries and commercial enterprises were often inefficient and wasteful. There was also a certain amount of misdirection of investment under etatism. Capital accumulation, moreover, is still the greatest problem in Turkey's economic development. It is significant that, as a result of trying etatism, the Turks reverted to hopes of inducing foreign capital investment in Turkey despite the experiences of Ottoman times and the strong nationalism that had motivated economic policy under the Republic.

With regard to finance capital, another important point is that the bill for the etatist economic growth fell largely on the peasants who bought the textiles and other products of state enterprise. A definite policy of charging high prices for textiles to amass earnings for investments in other fields was followed by state industry. Private enterprise in the textile field let the state enterprises set the price and profited greatly. Partly for this reason private entrepreneurs did enter the textile field, despite the potential state competition. Moreover, the capital for government investments in Turkey came from involuntary savings. It might be said that, because of the way it was financed, state enterprise bit the hand it was trying to feed.

Labor: During the etatist period a limited class of skilled workers gradually emerged. This was no mean feat. Labor turnover in state factories was a constant problem. The location of factories in rural areas—a definite policy measure aimed at raising their level of development—meant that labor had to be enticed from the farms to the factories. Seasonal fluctuations in labor supply were frequent because workers were accustomed to returning to the land for the harvest and planting seasons.

The social welfare measures introduced by state enterprise in Turkey have been cited as one of the real accomplishments of etatism. Factory workers in both state and private enterprise did profit from the furnishing of housing, hot meals, work clothing, recreational facilities, and many social security benefits, such as health care, unemployment, old-age, accident, and maternity insurance, and protection of employment rights. On the other hand, the paternalism of the social welfare measures under etatism may also be criticized for impeding the development of labor unions as well as individual aspirations on the part of the worker.

Consumer markets: The greatest weakness of the etatist policy was that in many cases state enterprises in Turkey indulged in production for production's sake. Factories were often built for the sake of national self-sufficiency or for prestige. Technicians were trained and then became obsessed with the problems of attaining production, often overlooking cost and the necessity of guiding production in terms of consumer demand. The bureaucratic government organizations in the economic field were very weak in marketing. High price policies on the goods that were in greatest demand limited the market even further. There was a definite imbalance between what was produced and what was in demand. When costs were considered in production, the tendency was to expand the plant in order to lower costs rather than to make better use of existing resources.

In summary, reference may be made to some of the points raised by Hoselitz (Chapter 12 infra). Creation and accumulation of capital remained Turkey's major problem. Etatism resulted in new forms of productive organization, but these were limited to industry and not necessarily the most important in relation to consumer demand.

It is most significant that the people of Turkey as a whole benefited relatively little from the policy of etatism. According to official data, per capita income, figured at constant prices (1948 factor cost prices), rose only from 423.3 Turkish lira in 1938 to 442.9 in 1948.[8] This in-

---

[8] Based on national income data in Republic of Turkey, Prime Ministry Central Statistics Office, *Istatistik Bulteni,* No. 18 (August 1955), and population data from Central Statistics Office Publication No. 350, *Umumi Nüfus Sayim, 22 Ekim 1950.*

crease of 10.6 Turkish lira equalled only $3.79 at the official rate of exchange.

In conclusion, we may say that etatism as an economic development policy was hampered by the narrow outlook that motivated it. The concern of the Nationalists with the introduction of industry for the sake of national prestige as well as self-sufficiency was a limiting factor. It was coupled with idealistic hopes for regional development and social welfare aims that benefited only a small group in the population. Because etatism was not all-inclusive and permitted mixed development of state and private enterprise, a major effect was the development of attitudes critical of the policy itself. The Turks of their own accord turned from etatism to some extent, but still recognized the need for a strong role for the state in the economic growth of the country. Argument revolved about limiting state participation to definite fields. Etatism made the Turkish people more conscious of their fundamental economic problems and stimulated a desire to progress, which was not so much based on narrow nationalism as on true aspirations to raise standards of living for the whole population.

Major problems of capital formation, development of entrepreneurs, and attainment of productivity as distinguished from production remained in Turkey as the etatist policy came to an end with the elections of 1950. Moreover, a fundamental conflict between centralization, or the extent of induced development, and decentralization, or the need for more autonomy in economic growth, since 1950 has given the Turks the real problem of defining a new government policy for attaining economic growth. Recognition that the state must play a role in the economic development of Turkey remains a part of the Turkish mentality.

10 THE ROLE OF THE STATE

IN ECONOMIC GROWTH

IN EASTERN EUROPE SINCE 1860

Nicolas Spulber *

This study is focused on the characteristics, methods, and range of state activity in the various stages of economic development of Eastern Europe as a whole. The area studied is comprised of Czechoslovakia, Poland, Hungary, Rumania, Yugoslavia, and Bulgaria, countries which are today centrally planned economies. The individual countries are discussed with the sole object of determining or illustrating trends for the whole area. Three periods are considered: the formative years up to 1914; the interwar period, 1920–38; the era of centralized planning, from 1947 to the present day.

Study of these three periods poses numerous difficulties in the construction of uniform tabulations and of long-term series. The main difficulties are due to wide territorial and population displacements, and to the absence of any uniformity in the scanty data available. Given the complexity of the subject, this study can attempt only to delineate the broad lines of development during the three periods.

DEVELOPMENT BEFORE 1914

General Characteristics

A century ago the present East European area was divided among Austria-Hungary, Russia, Germany, and the Ottoman Empire. In the period of maturation and expansion of the West European capitalistic system, the second half of the nineteenth century, only the Czech lands (Bohemia, Moravia, and Silesia), Slovenia, and some of Russian Poland underwent significant industrialization. In the rest of this part of Europe certain centers, such as Warsaw, Budapest, and Zagreb, ex-

* This paper has benefited from the comments of various participants in the Conference on the State and Economic Growth. I am particularly indebted to Alexander Erlich, who kindly made his comments available in writing and thus helped me to clarify various important points in the final draft. I wish also to express my thanks to Franz Gehrels for helpful criticism of the earlier draft.

perienced a slow, limited, and very unequal process of development; outside these centers the most primitive economic conditions continued to exist. Except in the developed areas, an overwhelming segment of the population was engaged in agriculture. The domestic demand for manufactured goods was satisfied mostly by handicrafts, very small local industries, and limited imports. The exports of the area consisted of agricultural produce, foodstuffs, and raw materials.

The Czech lands, because of their location, resources, and favorable political factors, became the industrial basis of the Austro-Hungarian Empire. Thanks to the broader market of the Empire, encompassing some 35 million people in 1870, Bohemia, Moravia, and Silesia had already succeeded in developing a highly articulated industrial structure, consisting mainly of food processing and light industries, construction materials, and mining. By 1870, along with the continuous concentration and increased mechanization in food processing and light industries, the establishment of heavy industries had started. At that time the Czech lands were producing over 6 million tons of bituminous coal and nearly 4 million tons of lignite, but were dependent on imported iron. In the ensuing years the steel foundries and metalworking industries were built up—the Vitkovice Works and the Skoda Complex (at Plzen) and others at Kladno and Teplice. By 1913 the output of bituminous coal had increased to 40 million tons and that of lignite to 23 million tons, while the steel output was over 1.2 million tons, more than one half of the total for the dual monarchy.

The railroad network developed concomitantly with the growth of industry. The first line was built in 1845, but the greatest expansions occurred around 1867 and again after 1880. By 1914 there were over 6,700 kilometers of track in Bohemia alone and a total of 9,500 in the Czech lands, or 41 percent of the total in Austrian territory.

Wide shifts in the occupational structure of the population and in trade illustrate the broad changes undergone by the Czech economy during the period. In 1890 nearly 41 percent of the population of Bohemia were engaged in agriculture. By 1910 this proportion had decreased to 32 percent, while that dependent on industry and handicrafts had risen to 41 percent.[1] In their turn the exports of the region showed the shift toward a highly diversified industrial output.

[1] Karl Franzl, "Neuzeitliche Entwicklung der böhmischen Industrie und des böhmischen Handels," in Z. V. Tobolka, ed. *Das Böhmische Volk* (Prague: Prager aktriendruckerie, 1916). See also *Manuel Statistique de la Republique Tchecoslovaque* (Prague, 1928), p. 300.

While this process was occurring in the Czech lands, three divergent developments were taking place in Poland, according to the divergent interests of the three partition powers (Germany, Russia, and Austria).

Except in Silesia, German Poland developed on the basis of extensive agricultural production. The only manufacturing facilities were for food processing and often only the first stages of processing (for instance, sugar works for raw sugar only, to be refined in Germany). In Upper Silesia there were important developments in the coal and iron industries. By 1870 the output of coal was close to 6 million tons. By 1913 it was over 34 million tons. The output of iron was quite irregular and apparently was sacrificed to the cartelized German interests; up to 1914 it increased by rather narrow increments. By that time, however, the crude steel output of the region had reached over 1.1 million tons. Even so, while Bohemia and Moravia were the main industrial bases of Austria, the easternmost provinces of Germany were considered of only secondary importance to her, and their growth was far less rapid than that of the rest of Germany. Thus, in 1871 Upper Silesia supplied 15 percent of the cast iron produced in Germany; in 1913 the Silesian share was only 5 percent.[2]

Russian Poland (called Congress Poland or the Polish Kingdom) struggled against the persistent efforts of Russia to suppress the development of Polish agriculture. Some favorable factors, however, such as the Russian demand for manufactured goods, encouraged industrial expansion in various centers: metalworking industries in Warsaw, textiles in Łódź, and iron and steel foundries in the coal basin of Dąbrowa. In 1877 Congress Poland counted some 8,000 plants of all sizes, with some 90,000 workers. By 1910 the number of plants had increased to nearly 11,000 and provided jobs for over 400,000 workers. By that time most of the plants were concentrated in textiles (one third of the total), food processing (one fifth), and metalworking industries, which had started to expand greatly after 1860. Notwithstanding these developments Congress Poland remained strongly dependent on agriculture, and by 1914 an estimated 60 percent of the population were still engaged in that sector.

Austrian Poland (Galicia) developed from very primitive conditions. Although it represented a large segment of the Austro-Hungarian territory and 25 percent of its population, by 1900 only 10 percent of the

---

[2] See Witold Kula, *Historia Gospodarcza Polski, 1864–1913* [Economic History of Poland, 1864–1918] (Warsaw, 1947), pp. 93 ff. It is difficult to determine to what extent this disparity in growth was due to differences in natural advantages.

population of Austrian Poland were engaged in industry and handi-crafts and only 5 percent in mechanized manufacturing. The most significant developments were in the production of raw materials, such as oil.

In the three parts of Poland the railroad system developed according to the immediate interests of the partition powers, and was evidently oriented toward Berlin, Moscow, and Vienna. The best-developed net-work was in the West. In Poland as a whole, the total length of track increased from 2,400 kilometers in 1880 to nearly 10,000 in 1901, after which it increased slowly to 12,400 in 1913. By that time there were in the area some 6 kilometers of track per 1,000 inhabitants, as against 11–12 kilometers per 1,000 inhabitants in the West.

In Hungary a decisive turn toward industrialization was taken only after 1879. For a number of years, development outside agriculture was represented by a modest growth of the milling industry and of the railroads, while Budapest became a processing center for the raw materials brought from the areas outside the Magyar settlement (Slovakia, Transylvania, and Croatia). After 1879 there was substantial growth in Budapest of textile industries, machinery construction, and the chemical industry. The importance of these developments may be gauged by the increase in the percentage of the total population of Hungary engaged in industry, from 4 percent in 1867 to 16 percent in 1910.[3]

The countries dependent on the Hungarian Crown developed very unevenly. In Slovakia the pressure of surplus agricultural population was heavy and continuous, and emigration reached high levels in the 1880's. After the start of her industrial development, however, Hun-gary tried "to find Bohemia in Slovakia." In 1900 a significant number of plants in Slovakia employed over 20 workers each, and many small enterprises were meeting the needs of the domestic market and some Hungarian needs. Notable expansion or improvement had occurred in the production of iron ore and pig iron and in metallurgy (as in the Krompachy Ironworks). In Transylvania and Banat, as well as in Croatia, many plants had been established for the production of raw materials and for some secondary lines of processing. By 1910 there were in Hungary some 4,241 plants with over 20 employees; the total number of persons employed was 392,000. Some 2,029 plants with a

[3] Friedrich von Fellner, "Die Volkswirtschaftliche Entwicklung Ungarns unter der verfassungsmässigen Regierung Franz Josephs I (1867–1916)," in *Ungarische Jahrbücher*, Vol. 7 (Berlin, 1927), p. 190.

total of 221,000 workers were located in the settled Magyar area; the remainder were located mostly in Slovakia, Transylvania, and Banat.[4]

The railway network developed in Hungary before this turn to more complex manufacturing. Between 1867 and 1891 the length of railroad track increased from 2,285 kilometers to 19,200; it then grew more slowly, reaching 21,400 kilometers in 1913. The railroads were centered in Budapest and branched out in direct lines toward the provinces, without connections between the lines. This arrangement brought about a serious dislocation of the transportation system immediately after World War I.

The three very small countries of the area, the Rumanian principalities (called the Rumanian Kingdom after 1881), Serbia, and Bulgaria, developed essentially as food producing and food exporting countries. Their processing facilities were extremely limited. Rumania started her industrialization policy around 1886 and had made modest progress by 1913. In 1886 she had only 83 plants with more than 25 workers each; by 1910 there were 847 such plants, with a total of 58,000 industrial workers. More significant progress was made in the exploitation of raw materials: Rumania's oil output increased from some 100,000 tons in 1897 to nearly 2 million tons in 1913, and the country became an important oil producer in that part of Europe. The building of a railroad network started in 1868. It grew slowly, in pace with industry, reaching some 3,500 kilometers of track by 1913.

Serbia—the core of interwar Yugoslavia—developed after 1878 as a satellite of Austria-Hungary and was entirely dominated by its foreign-trade interests. This situation changed after 1903, bringing with it an increase in the pace of Serbian industrial growth. By 1910 there were perhaps 170 manufacturing plants of some significance in Serbia. The development in the other south Slav lands was, as already stated, much more marked. Tiny Slovenia alone counted some 370 manufacturing plants in 1910; Croatia-Slavonia and the Vojvodina were also well ahead of Serbia. The building of railroads in the whole south Slav area progressed from north to south, from 1846 on.[5] The axis of the system was the network of lines crossing Slovenia and Croatia-Slavonia and connecting them with the Adriatic on one side, and northern Austria-Hungary on the other. Railroad construction was most intense between 1879 and 1890. In that period the connections from central Europe

4 Cf. Ladislaus von Buday, *Dismembered Hungary* (London: Grant Richards, 1923).
5 Jozo Tomasevich, *Peasants, Politics, and Economic Change in Yugoslavia* (Stanford: Stanford University Press, 1955), p. 168.

through Serbia to Istanbul and Salonika were completed. The Serbian railroad itself, however, extended only 540 kilometers in 1891 and 976 in 1913. By 1919 Serbia had 1,500 kilometers of track as against 7,500 in all the other south Slav areas.

Bulgaria in 1879 had not more than 20 small industrial enterprises. By 1910 she had 345 plants with fewer than 16,000 workers. Her development up to that point was very similar to that of neighboring Serbia. Bulgaria's railroad lines were started during the Turkish occupation in 1863; the main axis was the line toward Istanbul. By 1913 there were only about 1,900 kilometers of track in Bulgaria.

In summary, by 1910 Eastern Europe, with the exception of the Czech lands, was heavily dependent on agriculture: some 32 percent of the total population of Bohemia, 60–65 percent of the populations of Congress Poland and Hungary, and around 80 percent of those of the other regions were dependent on agriculture. An articulated industrial center with both light and heavy industries had developed only in the Czech lands. Significant processing facilities had developed around Warsaw and Budapest, and in Slovenia. In the provincial centers of Galicia, Silesia, Slovakia, and Transylvania the growth was mostly in semimanufacturing or production of raw materials. The small countries of the area had very modest manufacturing facilities; Rumania had started to acquire new economic stature as an oil producer. Two big railroad centers had grown up in Eastern Europe: Prague and Budapest. Outside these centers the area had only a sparse network of lines, most of them linked to outside railroad centers. In foreign trade all the countries, except the Czech lands and part of Congress Poland, developed essentially as exporters of livestock, agricultural produce, and raw materials, and as importers of manufactured goods.

State Undertakings and Financing

All parts of Eastern Europe relied heavily, but with unequal success, on the inflow of foreign capital. In the Czech lands the inflow was channeled through the banks to all types of manufacturing industries. Elsewhere the inflow mostly took the form of state foreign loans and of private investments, following a colonial or semicolonial pattern and centering mainly in the mining industries.

Up to 1890 the development of the Czech lands was almost exclusively nourished by foreign capital via the Vienna banks. After 1890 the accelerated growth of the region turned Prague into the second financial center of the Empire and increased her capacities for mobilizing the financial resources of the region. Particularly notable was the rapid growth of the Czech banks such as Zivnostenska (after 1868), the Böhmische Industrialbank (after 1890), and the Czech savings and loan associations.

In German Poland the development of agriculture was sustained essentially by the credit extended by the German state for colonization. The state also was primarily responsible for the construction of railroads. On the other hand, industrial development may be credited to Polish and German private capital.

In Congress Poland the Polish State Bank survived from 1828 to 1869 and played a substantial role in various domestic investments. After the liquidation of this bank and the transformation of its Warsaw branch into the Russian State Bank, its investment activity became insignificant. Development of industry and railroads took place entirely through the direct investment of Polish or foreign capital in various enterprises. As in Galicia, the banks were small and could not compare in any way with the powerful financial organizations that were financing Central and West European manufactures.

In most of the other areas the low level of savings, as well as the traditional orientation of the available domestic financial resources toward land ownership, trade, and usury, enhanced the role of foreign capital in mining and in some incipient manufacturing industries.

In Galicia mining developed exclusively with foreign capital, and railroads with funds from the Imperial Treasury. The slight industrial development there relied both on investments of the Vienna banks and on the mobilization of local resources after the formation of local banks (e.g., the Provincial Bank of Galicia).

In Hungary, toward the end of the nineteenth century, great industrial concerns were formed as joint stock companies, the shares of which belonged to credit institutions, which in turn used credits from the Vienna banks. There were also appreciable state interests in industry, channeled through the banks, which held the shares of privately owned companies. The Hungarian state owned significant mining and manufacturing facilities in the provinces (in Slovakia the Royal Hungarian Iron and Steel Works, the Royal Hungarian Copper Works, and Royal Hungarian Salt Boiling Works), numerous silk and flax mills, flour mills, and similar enterprises. Railroads were developed by both the state and private capital, though the latter was the first to construct railroad lines in Hungary. From 1886 on, the network exploited by the state was substantially larger than that under private administration. By 1900, 85 percent of all track (17,100 kilometers) was either owned or leased by the state.

The almost total lack of domestic resources in the three smallest countries made these new states heavily dependent on foreign credit and made its price extremely onerous. All these small countries enjoyed only limited credit, which deteriorated continuously as their appeals to the foreign financial markets multiplied and as the guarantees that they were called upon to supply became greater. Thus all of them formed so-called "fiscal monopolies" (for tobacco, sugar, matches, etc.), the incomes of which were mortgaged for the payment of the foreign debt.

The numerous loans contracted by these countries during the period can be grouped as follows: (1) up to 1880, military and independence loans; (2) 1880–1910, economic loans, a large part of which went to unproductive investments; [6] (3) 1910–14, military loans.[7] During the period 1880–1910 foreign capital started to flow directly into local banks and industry. The role of the state in the development of a banking system, the railroads, and manufacturing was overwhelming during all these years. Direct participation of foreign capital became in its turn decisive in banking, mining, and manufacturing around 1900. The participation of private capital remained very limited.

Protection and Encouragement of Industry

In most East European countries attempts were made to increase the pace of industrialization by protectionist policies and direct encouragement of domestic industries. The results were extremely uneven from country to country and from one period to the next.

The industry of the Czech lands developed under the protection of the high Austrian tariffs against German competition. In this case no special laws of "encouragement" were needed to foster private investments. Capital was readily available from both outside and domestic resources, especially in the 1890's.

In the three Polish areas, protection and high tariffs often operated against the local industries. Official policy in German Poland sought

[6] Transforming backward provinces of the Russian, Austrian, and Ottoman Empires into modern states undoubtedly required strenuous efforts. In the process much energy was wasted by each of these small units in building a top-heavy bureaucracy and police and military organizations.

[7] See Mirko Lamer, "Die Wandlungen der ausländischen Kapitalanlagen auf dem Balkan," in *Weltwirtschaftliches Archiv* (Jena), Vol. 48, No. 3 (November 1938).

to transform it into a supplier of consumers' goods and raw materials for industrialized Berlin and the German West. The state therefore encouraged only industries tied to agriculture and discouraged any other attempts at industrialization. In Russian Poland the textile industry grew rapidly as the Russian market was opened to its products after 1850 and during the Crimean War. As the Russian textile industry started to develop, however, the Russian government tried by various devices to restrain the further growth of Łódź as a great textile center, in favor of Moscow.[8] After 1890 systematic protection of Russian industry deprived the Polish Kingdom of raw materials and forced whole factories to move to Russia. At the same time Russian competition grew more severe in agriculture and related industries. In Austrian Poland, an unfavorable location, the paucity of raw materials (except oil), the lack of incentives to develop a local industry since the needs of the market were met by Czech, Austrian, and some Hungarian wares, and the absence of any imperial effort to develop the backward part of the Empire combined to prevent the industrial development of Galicia.

In all the other countries, the state tried more or less methodically to foster domestic industry by a combination of tariff policies and laws to encourage manufacturing. Hungary was reluctant to break the customs union with Austria and to erect an autonomous tariff, even though some Hungarian interests voiced the opinion that the existing tariffs were protecting the dual monarchy against German manufactured products to the sole benefit of Austrian industry (notably in the Czech lands). After 1880, the Hungarian state passed a series of laws to encourage its own industries and aided them through tax exemptions, freight reductions, subventions, and preference in state purchases.

Rumania and Bulgaria were the first countries to develop an elaborate system of both tariffs and laws favoring their industries. Rumania resolutely maintained a protectionist policy after 1886. In 1887 she adopted a law to encourage the "large" national industries, defined as industrial firms employing at least 25 workers and having a capital of about 50,000 lei (10,000 gold dollars). This law provided tax exemptions, exemption of imports of raw materials from customs duties, reduction of freight rates, preference in state orders, and gratuitous allocation of land for industrial buildings. A second basic law of 1912 extended the state protection to smaller plants.

8 For example, Łódź had to pay high freight rates for coal from nearby Dąbrowa in order to improve the competitive position of the Moscow textiles, for which coal had to be brought from the Donets basin.

Serbia, as already noted, provided no protection for local industry up to 1906, when a tariff war started between that country and the dual monarchy.

Bulgaria established high tariffs as early as 1883, notably against textiles from the neighboring countries. Her tariff became more comprehensive in 1897 and was again increased in 1904. During these years a series of laws encouraged local industry. The first law, in 1894, applied only to the "big" national industries, those with "not less than 20 workers and not less than 25 thousand leva capital" (not less than 5,000 gold dollars). Thanks to these laws, Bulgaria more than trebled her industry between 1900 and 1911, but the results achieved were of extremely modest proportions.

Only in the Czech lands did development become "self-generating" after 1890. Resources, favorable location, and the interests of Vienna in developing her own industrial center in the region facilitated the process. Important industrial growth occurred also in Russian Poland, but serious obstacles appeared there in the 1890's. The integration of the Czech lands and of Congress Poland into larger multinational units was clearly beneficial to their industry during most of this period. The difference in the industrial growth of the Czech lands and of Russian Poland up to 1890, and even afterwards, can be explained by the superiority of Austro-Hungarian markets over Russian. In certain regions (e.g., German Poland) the absence of their own statehood shaped their development in accordance with the interests of the dominant powers. In most other cases the lack of any developmental policy, rather than a deliberate policy of keeping certain areas at low levels of development, was the dominant feature. This accentuated the disparity in growth between the most advanced and the most backward provinces, and between capitals and provincial centers and their "hinterlands."

The countries that were just reaching for independence and emerging slowly from the feudal system were compelled by lack of financial means to rely heavily on imported capital. Imported funds penetrated these countries in the form of state loans, which were used largely in setting up top-heavy bureaucracies, building social overhead (notably transportation), and investments of a colonial or semicolonial character. In almost the entire area the high tariffs and the various incentives for industrial development operated to attract foreign capital more than to stimulate domestic investment. The role of the state as investor through foreign loans became significant in industry, but remained modest compared to the foreign investments coming through the local or foreign banks. In 1915, for instance, out of 636 million gold lei (about $127,000,000), representing the total capital invested in Rumanian industry, roughly 83 percent was of foreign origin. The state remained dominant in railroads and in public utilities.

In the decisive formative years of the capitalistic system, only Czechoslovakia and to some extent Hungary benefited from substantial influxes of outside capital at a "reasonable price." They benefited greatly from the credit resources of the Vienna banks, which could mobilize international financial resources at comparatively cheap interest rates. Western Poland benefited from the influx of German capital, even though it was directed only toward given sectors. The small countries had to rely in these critical formative years on high-priced and strictly rationed foreign credit. Domestic financial resources were negligible.

Except in Czechoslovakia and part of Hungary, the branches of industry that developed during the period were mostly consumers' goods and raw materials; there were scarcely any facilities for the production of finished goods. Growth was too limited to relieve the increasing pressure of overpopulation in the countryside, and this factor was to become more and more decisive in the period to follow.

THE INTERWAR PERIOD

General Characteristics

The East European countries emerged from World War I in a thoroughly transformed political and economic setting. Czechoslovakia and Poland appeared as new states. Although small compared with the other countries of the area, Czechoslovakia inherited most of Austro-Hungarian industry. Poland became the largest and most populous unit between the Russian and the German masses. Although badly disorganized by war, Rumania and the united south Slav lands (combined with Serbia as Yugoslavia) emerged as tremendously enlarged states: The Rumanian territory increased by 215 percent, its population by 220 percent, and its industry by 215 percent; Yugoslavia comprised a territory 5 times as large as Serbia and a population nearly 4 times as large. No less than 62 percent of the population of Yugoslavia and 58 percent of its area had belonged to Austria and Hungary. In contrast, Hungary was reduced to some 30 percent of its area and somewhat less than 40 percent of its former population. A significant

part of its prewar industry, however, was located in the postwar territory. Finally, Bulgaria was now the smallest unit with the smallest
population and the lowest level of industrial development.

On the basis of the structure of the population, the development of
industry, the importance of agriculture, the structure of foreign trade,
and various other indicators, the countries could be classified in three
categories: (1) industrial—Czechoslovakia only; (2) agricultural countries with relatively significant processing facilities—Hungary and
Poland; and (3) agricultural countries with very limited processing
facilities—Rumania, Yugoslavia, and Bulgaria. Thus, in 1921 some
40 percent of the population of Czechoslovakia were engaged in agriculture and 33 percent depended on industry. In Hungary 56 percent
of the population were dependent on agriculture and 21 percent on
industry. In Poland about 64 percent depended on agriculture and
some 15 percent on industry. In the countries in the third category,
some 75–80 percent of the population were engaged in agriculture
and 8–10 percent in industry. The heavy pressures of overpopulation
in agriculture, especially in Poland, Rumania, and Yugoslavia, were
alleviated for a short time by wide measures for colonization of the
newly acquired territories and by land reforms. In industry there were
some 66,000 plants of all types in Czechoslovakia, with some 937,000
workers. In contrast, Bulgaria had a total of only 1,400 plants of all
types and 19,000 workers. In manufacturing plants with more than
5 or 10 workers each, there were about 384,000 industrial workers in
Poland, and between 160,000 and 180,000 in each of the other three
countries. Except for Czechoslovakia, the single factor determining the
economic position of the country each year was to be the harvest.
Foreign trade again consisted essentially of exports of agricultural
products and raw materials and imports of manufactured and semi-
manufactured goods.

Each state had to build a new organization out of the multiple segments of its new territory, within which there were vast regional
differences. Previous financial and economic ties had to be transferred
to new centers. The transportation system of each state presented formidable difficulties. All these factors facilitated a powerful expansion
of the sphere of the state. Furthermore, since almost all the states were
newly created economic entities, having to compete with established
industrial countries, and were also deeply jealous of their new independence, their exacerbated nationalism was readily expressed in high-
handed policies of "nostrification" (directed against the previously

dominant nationalities, now minorities in the new states) and in ideas of economic self-sufficiency. Here were further reasons for the expansion of the role of the state, for strong protectionist policies, for laws to encourage domestic industries, and so on.

The interwar era can be divided into two periods: the years up to the onset of the great depression in 1930; and the period from then until 1938–39, when the danger of a second World War became more and more evident.

During the first period, after a few years of reconstruction and broad reorganization, the whole area registered an expansion in capital formation, and increases and diversification of outputs. The inflow of foreign capital and a wider mobilization of domestic resources in such countries as Poland and Rumania contributed to these developments. While agricultural output tended to decline after the reorganization of the countryside and extensive land reforms, industrial output tended to grow systematically up to 1929–30. Substantial increases were achieved in such key outputs as coal, iron, steel, and cement.

In the early 1930's the flight of foreign capital from the banking channels that had nourished economic expansion in the first period, the catastrophic fall in agricultural prices, erroneous and even absurd monetary and fiscal policies, which further aggravated the downswing of the business cycle, and many other factors contributed to a sharp curtailment of output, capital formation, and employment in the area as a whole. In the less developed countries, however, industrial recovery was relatively rapid in the framework of strongly autarkic policies. In the more developed countries, like Czechoslovakia, largely dependent on world markets, recovery was slow and growth was handicapped.

If one considers economic growth over the whole interwar period, one can note a moderate increase in total output and frequent decreases in per capita output of many key industrial commodities. The period was also marked by wide reorganization, concentration, and rationalization in the industrial sphere, and by the launching of new and important industries. In transportation the prewar network of lines hardly increased at all (except for that in Poland, which linked Silesia and Gdynia), but the total rolling stock increased substantially, as did the traffic of goods and passengers. Total agricultural output increased in Bulgaria and Yugoslavia and more modestly in other countries, but it dropped below the prewar level in Rumania. As the total population dependent on agriculture increased in absolute numbers, the yields per capita fell substantially in the area as a whole. Faced with a rapidly growing population, the area showed only modest reductions in the proportion of the total population dependent on agriculture. In 1938 the proportions were as follows: 33 percent for Czechoslovakia, 52 percent for Hungary, 60 percent for Poland, 72 percent for Rumania and Yugoslavia, and 76 percent for Bulgaria. In Czechoslovakia the income from agriculture represented some 23 percent of the total; in Hungary, roughly 30 percent; in Poland, 44 percent; and in all the other countries, over 50 percent. As income in agriculture was low, total income was very low. Moreover, the increases in population reduced or nullified the increases in total income. Thus, while national income in the different countries in 1938 was from 105 to 140 percent of that in 1929, income per capita was from 90 to 127 percent of that in the last precrisis year.

Expansion of State Ownership

Following the prewar pattern, the state sphere immediately after the war encompassed large agricultural and forest domains, spas, port installations, public utilities, all the railroads, and many commercial shops, as well as numerous mining and industrial undertakings, which had either developed during the war (as the armament industry) or been taken over as former "enemy property." Also in accordance with the prewar custom, the state continued to manage as "fiscal" monopolies sales of tobacco, matches, and salt, and the state lottery.

In some countries the business sphere of the state continued to grow in the interwar period, and its role became decisive in industry, in banking (some states organized and directed the main credit institutions), and in many other aspects of business life. Poland became perhaps the most typical example of the drift toward etatism in this part of Europe, whereas Czechoslovakia was the least typical. Between them ranged the other countries, with Rumania closer to Poland and Hungary closer to Czechoslovakia.

In Czechoslovakia state ownership included the customary lists of domains, spas, fiscal monopolies (much more limited there), railways, some public utilities, some small coal mines, several nonferrous mines, and one steel mill. On the other hand, the state participated in the ownership of armament industries, particularly the Skoda Works at Plzen. The adjustment to postwar conditions was worked out, however, not through state intervention but basically through the activity of private banks and large firms, the concentration of industry, and elimination of inefficient producers.

In Poland, outside the familiar types of state enterprises, the state established many new undertakings—such as armament factories, automobile and aviation plants, and chemical industries—and developed new and important port installations, maritime transportation, and railroads. According to data available for the early 1920's, the total wealth of the Polish state at the time represented over 3 billion gold dollars. The railways accounted for 52 percent of the total, state buildings for 20 percent, and state forests (7.4 million acres of timber lands) for 15 percent. The remainder was accounted for by state enterprises of all types.[9] In the later 1930's the state undertook multipurpose industrial construction in south central Poland ("Central Industrial Region"), to consist of hydroelectric stations, iron foundries, fertilizer plants, and explosives. Only the skeleton of this project was ready when World War II started. According to data for the late 1930's, the government owned no fewer than 100 industrial establishments comprising more than 1,000 units, and held the majority of the stock of 50 corporations. It owned 20 percent of the oil refineries, 50 percent of the metal industry, 20 percent of the iron production, and 80 percent of the capital invested in the chemical industry.[10]

In Hungary, outside the familiar types of state ownership, the state owned the Machine and Locomotive Works in Budapest and the Iron and Steel Works in Diosgyor. The state enterprises were losing propositions up to the 1930's, and there were serious pressures in the country against further extension of the state sphere.[11] Only in the late 1930's were opposite tendencies manifest. In that period the state drew up a vast five-year plan—the so-called One Billion Pengo Plan—intended to remodel the economy and increase its output and productivity. The plan aimed at an investment of 200 million billion pengos per year; this would have doubled the previous rate of investment, which had been less than 6 percent of the national income. Roughly three-fifths

[9] See Casimir Grzegorzek, *Le rôle économique de la Banque de l'Économie Nationale en Pologne* (Rodez: Imprimerie G. Subervie, 1935), pp. 47–48; and Leopold Wellisz, *Foreign Capital in Poland* (London: G. Allen and Unwin, 1938), pp. 174 ff.

[10] Raymond L. Buell, *Poland: Key to Europe* (New York: Alfred A. Knopf, 1939), p. 158. According to the estimate of a Polish economist quoted by Buell, the state enterprises, with a capital of 18 billion zloty in 1931, then represented 15–25 percent of the total national wealth (*ibid.*, p. 163).

[11] A detailed note on these undertakings can be found in *Financial Reconstruction of Hungary*, Tenth Report of the Commissioner General of the League of Nations for Hungary, February 1–28 (Geneva, 1925), pp. 4 ff. See also Josef Sinz, "Die Sanierung Ungarns," in *Ungarische Jahrbücher, op. cit.*, p. 404.

of the amount were to serve the army and industry.[12] The actual results of the vast scheme are hard to assess, since territorial changes and preparation for war modified the conditions existing when the plan was launched.

In Rumania the state sphere was much larger than in Hungary and included some of the largest metallurgical works in Transylvania, river and maritime shipping, and the aviation industry.[13] In 1936 the capital of the state economic enterprises was valued at 131 million lei, as compared with 317 billion lei invested in agriculture (of which 247 billion represented the assessed value of the land), 85.6 billion lei in shares of all the stock companies of the country, and 42.5 billion lei in the manufacturing industries. Of the total, the capital of the state railways was estimated at some 55 billion lei, considerably more than the amount invested in the whole manufacturing industry of the country.[14]

In Yugoslavia the state owned, in addition to the customary enterprises, all river and maritime shipping, some coal mines, most of the iron mines (the rich mines at Lubja and Vares, and the Zenica Iron Works), some steel plants, the large lumber mills, and some other secondary processing facilities. Other mining production was in private hands and largely controlled by foreign investors.

In Bulgaria the state controlled the familiar list of enterprises and owned the coal mines (Pernik) and other mines and enterprises. As in Hungary, the state sphere tended during most of the interwar period to remain the same size as before World War I.

Foreign Capital and Mobilization of Domestic Financial Resources

Let us consider briefly the relation of the state to the inflow of foreign capital, the state efforts to build adequate credit systems and to mobilize domestic resources, the limitations imposed on general economic development by the prevailing monetary and fiscal policies of the state,

[12] See Lóránd D. Schweng, *Economic Planning in Hungary Since 1938* (New York: National Committee for a Free Europe, Mid-European Studies Center, 1951), pp. 1 ff.

[13] For a detailed study of the public enterprises, see Lucian I. Turdeanu, "Intreprinderile si avutiile Statului în România" [The Undertakings and the Wealth of the State in Rumania], in *Bulletin ul Institutului Economic Românesc* (Bucharest, 1937), pp. 362–402; see also C. G. Rommenhoeller, *La Grande Roumanie* (The Hague: Martinus Nijhoff, 1926), pp. 471 ff.

[14] Virgil Madgearu, *Evolutia Economiei Românesti după Războiul Mondial* [Evolution of the Rumanian Economy after the World War] (Bucharest, 1940), p. 360.

and also the pertinent relations of state policy to various minority groups and regions.

As already stated, immediately after the war there were numerous attempts to break loose from the control of the Vienna banks and from the Central European foreign investments. In Czechoslovakia the policy of "nostrification" changed former branches of Vienna and Budapest banks into Czech banks, but the change had no significance for industrial development. The new banks continued the traditional practice of participating heavily in the ownership and control of industry. The state tried in general to avoid increasing its indebtedness abroad, but sought and obtained some credits in the London and New York markets. Foreign capital from the allied countries entered Czechoslovakia and increased its participation in such important fields as the metallurgical industry. The necessity of adjusting the country first to its new setting and later to the depression brought about systematic efforts to eliminate the least efficient producers, which caused serious distress, notably in Slovakia. While the state was not always responsible for this, its efforts to improve the situation were not particularly noteworthy.[15]

In Poland foreign capital accrued both to the state—since it had started with a relatively low foreign indebtedness—and to the banks and industry. As in the whole area, the depression forced a sharp curtailment of the activities of banks that had foreign connections. The most distinctive feature of the financial operations of the Polish state was the increase in the role played by the state banks, such as the National Economic Bank, and other financial institutions, both before and after the depression. Credits of these banks shrank during the depression—precisely when their help was most needed—since their lending policy was predicated on the theory that credit expansion should correspond to "operations effectively carried out" and should be based on commercial paper "presenting all guarantees." [16] The state banks again increased their sphere of activity in the later 1930's. In 1937 they provided over 36 percent of all the credits granted in Poland;

[15] Macartney writes of the predepression and the depression period: "Slovakian industry undoubtedly did not receive from the Czechoslovak Government the help which it urgently needed to carry it over this difficult period. On the contrary, it was placed in many respects under quite unnecessary disadvantages."—Carlile A. Macartney, *Hungary and Her Successors: The Treaty of Trianon and Its Consequences 1919–1937* (London: Oxford University Press, 1937), p. 131.

[16] I. Goldberg, *Les Banques Polonaises dependant de l'État* (Nancy, 1935). See also Wellisz, *op. cit.*, p. 163.

if the semiofficial and related banks are included, this proportion is over 47 percent.[17] At that time all public investments were brought under the program of industrial development already mentioned.

The stabilization and monetary reconstruction of Hungary were carried out in the early 1920's with the help of foreign credits extended under the guarantee of the League of Nations. State intervention in the financial sphere became extremely limited.[18] By 1930 Hungary, along with all the other countries of the area, experienced an acute need for long-term loans and investments from abroad. Such credits were unobtainable, however. At the time Hungary had a per capita foreign debt heavier than that of any other country in Europe. During the early 1930's the direct role of the state in banking and financial operations began to increase, and it became predominant after the currency devaluation in 1936.[19]

In Rumania financing of industrial enterprises was carried by the existing banking system from 1919 to 1924. After the stabilization of the currency and the ensuing shrinkage in activity of the private banks, the state stepped in and created a special financial institution (the "Industrial Credit"), which played a notable role in financing industry. Toward foreign capital the Rumanian government had a rather unfortunate attitude, which in the 1920's made the inflow of foreign capital extremely difficult. Later, when the country badly needed this help in order to establish an agricultural mortgage credit bank, the government had to give almost incredible guarantees of its good faith.[20] After the crisis of the 1930's foreign investment and foreign credit extended to local industries declined substantially.[21] As far as domestic resources were concerned, commercial banks' rediscounts with the National Bank accounted for the largest share of industrial credits—as much as 70 percent; the remainder came from other state institutions, such as the "Industrial Credit." [22]

[17] Buell, *op. cit.*, p. 159.

[18] *Financial Reconstruction of Hungary*, Twenty-fifth (Final) Report by the Commissioner General of the League of Nations for Hungary, May 1–June 30, 1926, p. 3.

[19] See *Financial Position of Hungary in the Fourth Quarter of 1937*, Twenty-fifth and Final Report by M. Royall Tyler, Representative in Hungary of the Financial Committee, League of Nations, February 26, 1938, pp. 3 ff.

[20] N. P. Arcadian, *Industrializarea României* [Industrialization of Rumania] (2nd ed.; Bucharest, 1936), p. 363.

[21] C. V. Colocotronis, *L'Organization Bancaire des pays balkaniques et les capitaux étrangers* (Paris: Recueil Sirey, 1934), p. 158.

[22] Madgearu, *op. cit.*, p. 352.

In Yugoslavia, in the early postwar years, the banking system of the new provinces extended its network into the former Serbian kingdom, bringing about a sort of unification of the banking system of the whole country. The fact that Zagreb was then a more important banking center than Belgrade helped Austrian and Hungarian capital invested in the new provinces to remain in postwar Yugoslavia. Before 1931 some 47 percent of the total financial means of the country was concentrated in the Croatian banking system.[23] After the crisis of the 1930's the role of the state financial institutions, 4 state and semistate banks, grew rapidly. The National Bank gave a new orientation to its credit policy—extension of credit to many beneficiaries, reduction of discount rates, and so on. By 1934 the state banks had extended 7.5 billion dinar credits, as against 4.2 billion extended by 20 important private banks. The tendency of the state financial institutions to concentrate available means in Serbia in preference to the other provinces became, according to certain sources, rather systematic. This fact seems to account for the apparent decline in capital formation in the new provinces.[24]

The government banks were the largest credit institutions in Bulgaria in the early postwar period, as before World War I. The National Bank, prior to its reorganization in 1926, engaged in all types of general banking. Subsequently it gave up its commercial activity, and the privately owned banks began to dominate commercial and industrial credit, thanks in part to the influx of foreign funds. After the crisis of the 1930's the role of the private banks declined, while direct state interventions increased, paralleling developments in neighboring countries.

In summary, "nostrification" partially discouraged the influx of fresh foreign capital and often forced it to take "disguised" forms. Thus many shares previously under Austro-Hungarian or German ownership passed into the management of English or neutral banks. As the limitation of domestic resources became increasingly obvious by the middle 1920's, some of the countries again resorted to the Vienna banks for capital. Through 1929 foreign capital returned to these countries mostly as short-term banking credit. The flow of foreign capital into the private economy was far more important than its inflow in the form of state loans (negotiated essentially to stabilize the currency). Although

---

[23] See Colocotronis, *op. cit.*, pp. 169–170; also Rudolf Bičanić, *Ekonomska Podloga Hrvatskog Pitanja* [Economic Basis of the Croatian Question] (Zagreb, 1938), p. 177 and *passim*.

[24] Bičanić, *op. cit.*, pp. 180, 202 ff.

in a much stronger position than before the war, these countries again found their credit extremely poor in the world financial markets.

At the decisive moment of the depression, when the prices of agricultural goods fell and short-term capital was withdrawn by the foreign banks, the ability of these states to secure foreign loans appeared to have vanished. Efforts to mobilize domestic financial resources increased, together with efforts in some of the countries to develop better articulated banking systems. Particularly noteworthy attempts to hasten economic recovery were made by the Polish, Rumanian, and Yugoslav governments. In these countries the direct role of state banking and credit institutions increased, and the commercial banks came to depend more and more on the rediscount facilities of the central banks.

Efforts to mobilize domestic resources were, however, often thwarted by monetary and fiscal policies. Their outstanding characteristic was an almost superstitious approach to currency "stabilization" and balanced budgets, which aggravated and prolonged the depression: official policies made money scarce and taxation heavy just when opposite measures were necessary.

Protection and Encouragement of Domestic Industry

The phenomena observed before World War I—high tariffs and systematic encouragement of domestic industry—continued after the war on a far larger scale than ever before. According to various computations, the actual as well as the "potential" tariff (the tariff on goods listed on the tariff schedule regardless of whether they were actually imported) increased tremendously in 1927 and again in 1931, as compared with 1913.[25]

The 1930's saw a disruption of the traditional patterns of trade and credit. Germany came to play a more important role in the area, and increasing use was made of clearing systems, bilateral trade agreements, import and export licenses, and restrictive quotas. Embargoes were placed on imports of a wide and changing variety of goods; the policies varied according to the country of origin and the momentary interests

[25] In 1913 the average "potential" tariff level of the countries of the area, excepting partitioned Poland where the levels were far higher, ranged from about 23 to 30 percent; in 1927, from 30 percent (Czechoslovakia) to 67 percent (Bulgaria); in 1931, from 46 percent (Yugoslavia) to 96 percent (Bulgaria). Cf. Friedrich O. Hertz, *The Economic Problem of the Danubian States: A Study in Economic Nationalism* (London: V. Gollancz, 1947), pp. 71 ff.

of the government concerned. Almost all the states gave extensive legal encouragement to domestic industries and attempted to secure the full effect of their protectionist policies on the home market by eliminating competition. These states created many *ad hoc* buying and selling monopolies (for agricultural produce, sugar, etc.) and encouraged the wide cartelization of domestic industry.

In Czechoslovakia protection for agriculture was instituted in 1926 and subsequently extended to many other spheres. With respect to the encouragement and regulation of domestic industry Czechoslovakia followed her prewar tradition and made no over-all legal enactment. The dispositions in favor of industry were to be found here and there in various tax laws, in the regulations concerning electrification of the country, and in other legislative acts. For example, the 1927 law on direct taxes provided for tax reductions for enterprises of a specified legal form, and a 1926 law granted a reduction in customs duties in imports of machinery. On the other hand, the state openly subsidized industrial enterprises considered to be in the public interest. Finally, competition among private firms was gradually eliminated by cartel agreements, and by the establishment of central sales agencies for the main products of Czechoslovakian industry in both domestic and foreign trade.

In Poland the erection of high tariff walls was achieved by the usual combination of high customs duties and an extensive system of licenses, etc. From the 1930's on a complete embargo was placed on a wide range of "nonessential" manufactured and agricultural imports. For the encouragement of industry Poland also adopted numerous expedients which were not codified in a single law. Some of these concerned the whole industrial complex; some concerned specific industries or projects, e.g., industries contributing to the development of the port of Gdynia, or tax exemption for undertakings important for national defense; others concerned "large-scale industries" and were aimed at encouraging investments through tax exemption, rapid depreciation write-offs, and similar measures.

In Hungary characteristic measures concerned the encouragement of domestic industry. By legal dispositions particular undertakings were granted complete or partial exemption from industrial and construction taxes, and large reductions in railway freight rates for the transport of machinery and construction equipment. On the other hand, the law allowed direct subsidies, or credits from budgetary funds, to stimulate the export of particular products or the import of indispensable equipment.[26]

In Rumania the laws of encouragement that had been passed in the Old Kingdom, such as the law of 1912, were modified and extended to greater Rumania in 1920–21 and further extended in 1936. As previously, the new legislation allowed the protected industries to purchase publicly owned lands at reduced prices, exempted them from duties on imported machinery, and allowed them reduced freight charges. Although the extension of these laws to the newly acquired territories was intended to facilitate investment there, there were the usual complaints, as in Slovakia, against alleged discriminatory taxation procedures and direct or indirect measures favoring the development of industry in the Old Kingdom. The data available on the cartelization of industry around 1933–38 illustrate clearly the important role of the internal anticompetitive forces. Cartelized industry at that time represented 46 percent of total industrial capital and 23 percent of the value of industrial output. In certain industries such as metallurgy, cartelization affected 90 percent of the capital and 42 percent of the total value of the output.[27]

In Yugoslavia the most extensive measures of encouragement to local industries were embodied in a law adopted in 1931. It stressed the "obligation of the state and public institutions to cover their purchases from domestic sources" rather than imports. For manufactured goods produced in limited quantity, domestic offers were to be preferred to any others even if domestic prices were 10–15 percent higher.

In Bulgaria a comprehensive law for the encouragement of industrial plants over a minimum size was adopted in 1928. New industrial ventures received gratuitous cessions of state-owned lands, substantial reductions in freight charges, tax exemptions, customs exemptions, and other advantages.

In conclusion we may say that after World War I most of the countries, except Hungary and Bulgaria, came into possession of a more balanced industrial system, including facilities for producing complex manufactured goods. Throughout the interwar period, however, capital goods industries remained of secondary importance in all the countries except Czechoslovakia and, up to a certain point, Poland. Significant economic expansion occurred in the area as a whole up to the

[26] P. Lénard, *La crise industrielle et l'intervention de l'état en Hongrie.* See also Arcadian, *op. cit.,* pp. 312 ff.

[27] Madgearu, *op. cit.,* p. 180.

1930's. The state played a dual role in this process. On the one hand, it helped early postwar development through such measures as the unification of the various territories acquired into a single market and through direct investments in industry. On the other hand, it hampered a more powerful economic upsurge by implementing vexatious "nostrification" measures, a xenophobian policy in respect to foreign investments, and discriminatory measures which limited the opportunities for private investment.

During the depression and afterwards, new and complex problems confronted these states. The official "orthodox" economic policies actually aggravated the depression in the early 1930's. Later, when such broad schemes as the development of a "Central Industrial Region" in Poland and the One Billion Pengo Plan of Hungary were launched, the role of the state gained in both scope and depth. World War II interrupted these projects, however, and the results are now somewhat difficult to assess.

For the whole interwar period, economic growth measured in aggregated terms was modest. Various industrial branches were characterized by either outright stagnation or very slow progress. These characteristics were aggravated in some of the newly acquired territories. Nevertheless, the period witnessed substantial progress in particular fields, such as textiles and machinery construction.

CENTRALIZED PLANNING SINCE 1947

General Characteristics

World War II brought about wide population changes, boundary displacements, and shifts in the political and economic relationships among the various groups of the society. In terms of population and boundary changes the greatest transformation took place in Poland. That country lost about 50 percent of its prewar territory to Russia, and acquired from Germany new territories amounting to more than 30 percent of the prewar territory. The Germans were expelled from the western territories, and these were settled by Poles transferred from the eastern territories. Thus, through displacement toward the west, Poland emerged as a new entity with a changed population and a different endowment of factors. Significant changes also occurred in the other countries. Czechoslovakia lost some 10 percent of her territory and 20 percent of her population; Rumania, close to 20 percent of her interwar territories and 15 percent of her population. On the other hand, Yugoslavia's and Bulgaria's territorial gains represented respectively over 3 and 7 percent of their prewar areas, whereas Hungary was the only country that retained her prewar boundaries. All the countries were badly disorganized by the war and faced formidable problems of reconstruction. With respect to the structure of the population, the development of industry, the importance of agriculture in the economy, and the structure of foreign trade, the countries could still be classified in the same three broad groups as after World War I. The only difference was that Poland's industrial capacity had increased significantly and its level of development was slightly higher than that of Hungary and nearer that of Czechoslovakia than ever before.

Whereas many of the interwar economic changes had been carried out under the slogan of "nostrification," many changes after World War II were carried out under slogans of "industrialization" and "transformation of the social structure." Wide nationalization of industry took place in the former allied countries (Czechoslovakia, Poland, and Yugoslavia) immediately after the war and in the ex-enemy countries (Hungary, Rumania, and Bulgaria) a few years later.

Political factors—the presence of Soviet troops and the newly acquired power of the Communist parties—served to emphasize the idea of centralized planning in each country immediately after the war. By January 1947, each country was organizing its reconstruction along the lines of an "over-all plan" of one to three years' duration. Notwithstanding the adoption of the Soviet method of centralized planning, some of the countries tried to develop a "three sectors economy" (state, cooperative, private) with, of course, differential rates of growth. This policy was soon abandoned in favor of development of the state sector only; the private sectors outside agriculture—in small industry, crafts, and distribution—were rapidly liquidated.

By the end of 1948 the reconstruction period could be considered closed; each country was then engaged in "long-term" planning, generally of five years' duration. These first plans were launched at various times and completed between 1953 and 1955; they were drawn on a similar pattern and conditioned development along parallel lines. The liquidation of private agriculture was attempted but with limited success because of the very stern opposition of the peasantry. By the turn of 1956 all the countries except Bulgaria simultaneously launched their second long-term plans, coincident with the launching of the sixth Five-Year Plan in the Soviet Union.

Each country patterned its reconstruction program and its long-term plans on the Soviet model. The emphasis was placed squarely on industry as against agriculture; in the producers' goods group, on the metalworking branch; in the metalworking branch, on heavy machinery. To accelerate industrialization the share of investment in the national income was increased to between 20 and 25 percent, or 4 to 5 times the prewar level. The level of private consumption was in turn sharply depressed. Following the scheduled plan of development, half of the available investment was allocated to industry, with the overwhelming share going to capital goods industries; half was allocated to the other economic sectors, with agriculture receiving lowest priority.

Having pledged themselves to concentrate on the development of a "heavy industrial base," all the countries succeeded in increasing appreciably their output of coal, steel, iron, and cement by the end of their first long-term plans. Furthermore, they substantially increased capital formation in heavy industry. But the negative aspects of these achievements were multiple. The increases in key outputs and in capital formation were accompanied by wide and dangerous economic imbalances between high-cost, expanding heavy industry and lagging light industry; between industry as a whole and stagnant agriculture; between increased productive capacity and the limited supply of raw materials; between quantity and quality of output; and between the growth in total product and in levels of living. This last imbalance caused serious social dislocation in nearly all the East European countries. To halt this tendency new policies were devised in 1953 and again in 1956. On both occasions it was strongly urged that the pace of investment should be reduced and the allocation of investments changed; this would obviously have involved a departure from the Soviet model of industrialization. The enormous popular pressures for such changes were clearly underscored by open revolts in the satellite areas. The necessity for revising the second five-year plans and scaling down many of their ambitious goals thus became urgent scarcely a few months after the plans had been launched. It appears that an impasse has been reached in Eastern Europe and that further growth can hardly be achieved by mechanical imitation of the Soviet model. It seems unlikely that the developments scheduled by the second five-year plans will be carried out even in the key sectors.

The slow increases in the output of light industries up to 1956, the efforts to shift agriculture from subsistence to money crops, the suppression of the demand for housing—all in a period of industrialization and urbanization—have depressed levels of consumption enormously.

Economic growth, carried out through an unprecedented mobilization of domestic resources, has been paid for by terrific and finally unbearable strain.

Expansion of State Ownership

The faster pace of nationalization in the three former allied countries than in the three ex-enemy countries was broadly due to the following factors: The former countries had been occupied by the Germans; both the occupation and the liberation shattered the social fabric of the countries and left the door open for a large extension of the state sphere through nationalization and confiscation of ex-enemy properties. In contrast, the social structures were better preserved in the ex-enemy countries, especially in Rumania and Bulgaria. No "international" obstacles prevented the nationalization processes in the allied countries, whereas the ex-enemy group had multiple Soviet mortgages placed on them so that a period of adjustment was necessary before state property could be expanded. Moreover, these countries were trying to return to the international scene under the best possible conditions and did not feel free in their movements, at least up to the signing of the peace treaty in 1947.

By the turn of 1948, when the "three sectors" theory was abandoned, nationalization in each of the countries of the allied group had encompassed almost all the nonagricultural sectors. The nationalized sector in industry accounted for 85–100 percent of gross industrial output, 100 percent of bank turnover, 75–80 percent of wholesale trade turnover, and 30–100 percent of retail trade turnover. The nationalization drive had started in agriculture, where the state and "producers' cooperative" properties included 7–20 percent of the arable land.

The extension of state ownership followed the same pattern in each country. It moved from the key sectors—the large capitalistic enterprises—toward the secondary sectors, or "small commodity" enterprises. The first nationalizations affected large industrial concerns, banks, transport industries, and large distribution firms. The second wave extended state property to medium-size and small-scale industry, crafts, and retail trade. Finally, the state turned its forces toward agriculture, dominated by small-scale peasant farming.

The process of nationalization is scheduled to continue up to 1970, that is, to the time when the whole agricultural sector will in its turn be swallowed by the state and the "producers' cooperatives," and will be organized on the basis of large-scale exploitation.

To summarize, the extension of the sphere of the state has had a different rationale in each of the periods considered. Before 1914 the expansion of economic activity by the state was often conceived as a reaction against real or presumed deficiencies of private capital. The state interventionists considered private capital incapable of, or reticent about, financing large investments in "necessary" projects, and viewed state intervention as prerequisite for the subsequent expansion of private investment.

In the early interwar period, the increases in state economic activities were prompted by the wide territorial changes caused by the war, and nourished by nationalistic attitudes and opinions. In many situations various opportunities for the display of private initiative of both foreign and domestic origin were deliberately closed. In the late 1930's new factors, such as the aftermath of the depression and the impending danger of war, facilitated expansion of the state's activities. Through the implementation of ambitious investment schemes, resolute emphasis on industry, and systematic autarkic tendencies, state intervention in each country acquired a depth and breadth previously unknown.

After World War II, the state sphere again expanded as a function of social and territorial upheavals caused by war, but this time also as a consequence of the powerful new Soviet and socialist influences pervading each society. In accordance with the official theories prevailing at the time, this expansion was meant neither to prevent a "properly guided," limited growth of the private and cooperative sectors, nor to cut off a "usefully" channeled inflow of capital from the West. Finally, the enormous expansion of the state sphere after 1948–49 was evidently intended to annihilate any further possibility of significant capital accumulation in private hands. In this respect, there is clearly a substantive difference between this expansion and any that preceded it. Nevertheless, the launching of a centrally devised plan, the emphasis on industry, and the encouragement of autarkic tendencies indicate a certain continuity in official thinking on the role of the state.

Protection and Encouragement of Domestic Industry

The methods of extending protection to domestic industries before World War II included attempts to increase tariff rates, impose license requirements and restrictive quotas, introduce currency controls, and so on. In the postwar period foreign trade, transformed into a state monopoly, has been reduced to a "servant" of the domestic plan and implicitly to a servant of domestic industry and its plans and capacities for expansion. In these conditions any possible competition from the outside has been eliminated, and a premium has been extended to industry as a whole, including the least efficient producers.

Having shut off the economy from any outside competitive pressures, the planners increased the share of investment in national income and the share of industry in total investment, as already noted. The basic sources of the planned investment were set as follows: (1) the unified state budget—now covering both the national economy and the government—nourished by a turnover tax and the profits from state undertakings; (2) sinking funds (used specifically to cover renewals and capital repairs); (3) bank deposits; (4) planned decreases in cost, due to increases in productivity; (5) loans; and (6) internal reserves of the various undertakings. Taxes, duties, and excises accounted for 65 to 90 percent of state revenue in the prewar East European budgets. The turnover taxes (sales taxes) accounted for 0.5 to 23.5 percent. In the postwar period the turnover tax increased to 50–70 percent of total budget receipts, for budgets covering, as indicated, a far broader scope than in the prewar period. In the period of greatest expansion before World War II, the profits from state enterprises accounted for from 0 to 11 percent of the state revenues; in the postwar period, for between 20 and 33 percent.

During the reconstruction period the percentage of investment in national income was about 10 percent in Bulgaria and Hungary and about 20 percent in the other countries. During the first long-term plan the share of investment was increased in each country to between 20 and 25 percent of national income; early in 1956 the same rates were scheduled for the second quinquennium. During the reconstruction plans the share of industry and building in total investment was between 32 and 47 percent, and that of agriculture between 6 and 13 percent; during the first long-term plan the share of industry increased to between 40 and 53 percent, that of agriculture only to between 8 and 15 percent, and that of transportation and communication decreased. In the early drafts of the second plans the priority of industry was to be maintained, while agriculture was to improve its position only slightly.

Up to 1956 all the countries followed a similar pattern of allocation of their domestic means. If one could speak of the "waste" engendered in the area before the war by the protectionist policies and exaggerated national emotions of these small national units, the waste engendered by the systematic multiplication of the same types of facilities in each during the first quinquennial period is even more obvious. At its end each country boasted a national "heavy industrial base." This has not, however, diminished the variation in levels of economic development among the countries. In terms of per capita output of steel, for instance, Czechoslovakia is in a peak class by itself. In terms of income (net material product) in 1954, Czechoslovakia led with an estimated $520 per capita, followed by Hungary with $387, Poland with $368, and Rumania with $315. This "industrial base," moreover, was often developed through strict dependence on imports of raw materials under the worst conditions: e.g., the whole Hungarian "steel complex" of Sztalinvaros (Dunapentele) rested on imports of both coal and iron from distant sources.

Toward the end of their first long-term plans the Communist regimes perceived some of the most glaring absurdities of this pattern of development, and new tendencies appeared in their second plans. Thus, instead of subordinating foreign trade to the requirements of each country's output plan, the regimes attempted to draw up output plans according to the requirements of foreign trade. Instead of launching their plans separately and multiplying the processing facilities available, all the countries except Bulgaria initiated their plans simultaneously, and for the first time implemented a division of labor in certain fields (as in heavy steel sections, some machine tools, development of specific raw and semifinished materials by particular countries according to their budgets of resources). Instead of rigid bilateral channels of trade, a tendency toward an eventual multilateralization appeared. These were only incipient tendencies, however: the plans still set ambitious goals for each country in the production of producers' goods, and were still conceived within the framework of autarkic policies. The simultaneous launching of the plans did not imply any widespread coordination among the various countries and did not preclude the displacement of the plans of the weaker by the requests of the stronger.

This type of concentration of resources and savings in the hands of the state carries with it tremendous power. As long as the system holds together it is undoubtedly possible to increase capital formation over a given span of time, and to achieve economic growth in the sectors that have been assigned priority by the planners. But, as already stated, the achievement has been paid for by sharp reductions in private consumption, has given rise to enormous imbalances and pent-up pressures, and has generated deep processes of dislocation which could lead to the complete disintegration of the system itself. The deterioration of the level of living, notwithstanding the growth in total product, the development of an increasingly cumbersome and inflexible planning machinery, the disintegration of the system of incentives, and the corrosion of the will to work in wide strata of the society have created decisive obstacles to further growth at the rates achieved so far. The recent reduction of the share of investment in total product, the shift in its pattern, the decentralization in certain industrial outputs, and the liberty granted to craftsmen, small tradesmen, and peasants to produce and to trade—all these measures have been adopted to check the processes of dislocation. It would seem that the regimes must return at least partially to some of the orientations followed before 1948, and relinquish some of the powers to direct the economy according to a rigidly drawn, all-embracing central plan. What success can be secured by the renewal of the "three sector" economy—i.e., by the official reacceptance of limited growth of the private and cooperative sectors, by decentralization, and by the other measures envisaged—remains to be seen. It is already clear, however, that the economic growth of the area over the next five to ten years cannot be scheduled except at substantially lower rates than the ones claimed to have been secured during the first five-year planning period.

Concluding Comments

1. Over the whole period considered there has been a substantial increase in the sphere of state ownership, government expenditure, and government control in Eastern Europe. National income and output have increased in the area as a whole. The two trends are related, but their relationship is not necessarily one of cause and effect. Each period of emergency, such as war and depression, has led to the expansion of state activity; but in other periods contrary tendencies have manifested themselves. Furthermore, the all-embracing extension of state activity in the area since World War II cannot be considered as the "organic growth" of past processes. It evidently has its origin in exogenous factors.

2. State activity tends to be overwhelming in the first stages of economic growth. As the economy develops and conditions are created for an increase of saving and investment in the private sector, the importance of private investment evidently tends to grow. While the role of the state remains decisive in this second phase of development, in a subsequent period the ratio between private and public investment

might tend to shift in favor of the private sector. In East Central Europe it has happened otherwise: the ratio has shifted in favor of the state. This can be attributed to factors superimposed on the process —such as the depression and its aftermath, and the conditions arising from Soviet expansion after World War II.

3. The methods employed by all the countries to foster growth before World War I and in the interwar period consisted broadly either of extending the sphere of the state wherever private capital was failing to take the initiative, or of protecting domestic industries by such means as high tariffs, encouragement laws, and subsidies. In the period of centralized planning, these same methods have been pushed to their final consequences, to the point where one can speak of a change of substance. State ownership has engulfed almost all the "means of production," and foreign trade has become a state monopoly; encouragement to industry has become the law of the state, which is now the claimant to all "savings" available.

4. The objectives of the state in respect to economic growth are sharply changed by the redistribution of power among classes within the state. The shift from a market economy to a centrally planned economy, controlled by Communist parties, implies clearly the concentration of most of the means available in "critical-growth" sectors— such as heavy industry, steel, coal, iron, and cement—and the sacrifice of the consumer's interests. Up to now this concentration of means in the key sectors has obviously corresponded to dogma rather than to an accurate evaluation of the resource budget of each country.

5. To use the characterizations of growth suggested by Hoselitz, the development of all these countries might be described as originally nondominant or in need of outside assistance, as opposed to the development of well-settled countries where economic growth has depended from the beginning on domestic resources. All the East European countries developed economically, whether as parts of larger units or as independent states, thanks to the continuous inflow of foreign capital in various forms, especially up to 1930. Their dependence on foreign capital has since decreased, and the process of growth from the late 1930's on might be called self-generating. This development has been essentially nonautonomous; it has depended in the critical years of growth on the resources of larger areas, and will continue to do so. Czechoslovakia developed within the framework of the Austro-Hungarian Empire at a far greater speed than the small "independent" countries of the Balkans. Early development in Poland and Hungary

was strictly contingent on their belonging to a wider economic area. The interwar efforts to render development "autonomous," especially after 1930, did not have impressive results in terms of either rates of growth or balanced growth. Since World War II all the countries of the area have tended to rely on their own saving and investment capacities. A bottleneck seems to have been reached in this respect, and further expansion seems possible only within the framework of a far greater dependence on the resources and trade of other countries. The tendencies toward a division of labor in the Soviet orbit and the moves toward eventual multilateral trade point in that direction.

6. The growth process in the area can be characterized on the whole as induced, or essentially carried out by the state. This is true for most of the countries, but not for all of them, in the first stages of development. It remains true in the present stage.

11 THE ROLE OF THE STATE

IN ECONOMIC GROWTH:

CONTENTS OF THE STATE AREA

Richard Hartshorne

The function of this paper is to identify and analyze the factors within the area of the state through which it must work, if it assumes some degree of responsibility for promoting or guiding economic growth. This assignment is as wide as the world and involves consideration of most of its contents, and to the best of our knowledge has not been attempted before. Until many more case studies of individual countries are available, one cannot do more than outline a method of study and a few tentative hypotheses.[1]

Conceivably the relationship between economic growth and the territory of a state could be one of cause and effect in either direction. In theory, a given state might determine what territory it should seek to control in order to deal with its needs for economic development. Actual instances in which specific territories have been added to states in accordance with such economic planning are very rare. More difficult to determine is the degree to which particular states, without conscious planning, have been motivated primarily by economic considerations in striving to obtain or hold particular portions of territory, or have endeavored to bring under one domain contiguous regions forming a well-rounded area for economic development.

This is not the place to test the validity of any such hypothesis by analyzing the evolution of state territories, for this paper is written under an opposite assumption. Economic development has always been one of the concerns of government, if only as a means of increasing

---

[1] For this reason, no attempt has been made to document sources of ideas. I have drawn freely on recent writings of Simon Kuznets and Bert F. Hoselitz and have been aided by criticisms of the previous draft of this paper, which were expressed at the conference, especially those by Edgar M. Hoover, and by criticisms sent me by John Borchert, Theodore Morgan, and Norton Ginsburg, as well as by the latter's paper on "Natural Resources and Economic Development," prepared for the Institute for Economic Development at Vanderbilt University in July 1956.

the internal and external power of the state, but that concern is almost always subordinated to other more pressing concerns of the state. Higher priority is usually given to the attainment of power in comparison with other states. The simplest method of securing greater relative power is the addition of territory and exclusion of other states from it. All states have tended to use this method; but small states sometimes have had to recognize that expansion was not possible for them, and others sometimes have found it politically undesirable. This paper assumes, therefore, that the particular territory included within each state is a factor in its economic growth but one largely independent of its economic needs. It is one of the unalterable circumstances that most states must accept and work with; where territorial change is possible, such change will be determined largely independently of the needs of economic growth.

By "economic growth" we mean increase in production per capita resulting from use of more knowledge about resources and more effective technology. Thus this definition does not include absolute increases in production resulting merely from addition of territory, or from increases in population.

To measure economic growth, we relate data and estimates of total national product, or total national income—commonly assumed to be the same—to the population. In computing rates of growth for particular countries, it may be assumed that many of the uncertainties involved in such calculations cancel. This is far from true, however, in comparing the level of economic growth in different countries at any one time. It may therefore be useful in considering differences in such levels to take account of a characteristic closely related to advanced economic development, namely, the degree of diversification of the economy of a country.

DIVERSIFICATION AND ECONOMIC GROWTH

Most of the labor force of the world is engaged in agricultural production. Modern technology offers relatively restricted opportunity for increase in such production by the same labor force because of the limited extent of arable land. Without much unused arable land to permit large-scale migration, world economic growth requires expanding nonagricultural forms of production, to draw increasingly from the labor force employed in agriculture. To enable a lesser labor force to produce an equal or greater amount of agricultural products, industries and services are necessary to supply more specialized and more efficient techniques of agricultural production.

The advanced economic areas of the world show relatively great diversification of employment among agriculture, manufacturing, commerce and other services, whereas the labor force of the areas that are least developed in terms of per capita production is overwhelmingly employed in agriculture. The proportion of the labor force engaged in nonagricultural pursuits ranges from 88 percent in the United States [2] to 15 percent in some tropical countries. High diversification of employment is not limited to those countries generally recognized as primarily industrial. Three fourths of Denmark's labor force is employed outside agriculture, and much the same is true in predominantly agricultural portions of other advanced industrial countries. Two thirds of the labor force of Iowa, for example, is employed outside agriculture.

All areas are at least somewhat diversified in production; no country or people is "purely agricultural." In areas of "subsistence agriculture," the working population is engaged not only in farming but also, it may be, in fishing or forestry, and always in local transport and processing (manufacturing) of goods produced and used, and to some extent in trade. But since all these activities are carried on with minimum specialization and on the smallest scale, production per capita is at a minimum.

The introduction of commercialization into areas that have had predominantly subsistence economies may cause the rural population to concentrate more on agriculture and to depend on outside areas for processing of products. Such commercialization of agriculture not only develops needs for workers specializing in transport and trade, but for several reasons should lead also to development of manufacturing: Certain industries operate more efficiently if located close to the source of the argicultural raw materials they process; butter and cheese factories, canneries, meat-packing establishments, and sugar mills are examples. The same is true of certain industries that process forest and mineral products. On the other hand, a much greater variety of industries, notably those converting crude or semifinished manufactures into finished products, operate more efficiently if located near their

2 The United States is assumed to be at least self-sufficient in over-all agricultural production. This is certainly not true of the United Kingdom, which shows an even higher proportion of the labor force in nonagricultural occupations (95 percent), and of certain other countries which have nearly as high a ratio.

consumers; bakeries, machine shops, vehicle and clothing factories are examples. Insofar as agricultural production per capita is increased in any area by commercialization and the gain is reflected in increased income per capita, agricultural workers represent a growing consumer market that will stimulate the local development of such industries. Finally, where both factors are combined, i.e., where finished goods are to be consumed in the same area that produces the major raw materials, manufacturing of most types is more efficiently carried on within the area, even though other requirements, such as power, must be imported.

Thus, increased commercialization of the primary industries of an area—farming, mining, forestry, etc.—provides opportunity for the development of a variety of manufacturing industries. Such development, if it takes place, increases the level of living by providing manufactured products at lower cost than either subsistence production or imports, and by attracting labor from the farm increases both the commercial market for farm products and the need for labor-saving devices in agriculture.

These elementary theoretical considerations might suggest that a world that has been tending to become One World in commercial intercourse would show a notable degree of uniformity in economic growth. On the contrary, however, comparison of the various countries of the world reveals a wider range in levels of economic development than could have been found at any previous time in history.

In considering what elements within areas are significant for their economic growth, it will be helpful to classify the individual states according to several common statistical measures of economic development, which indicate a geographic pattern of economic levels throughout the world.

World Pattern of Economic Levels

Our consideration will be more meaningful if we first eliminate the large areas of the world that, regardless of technological level, are essentially *undeveloped* (in contrast to both *developed* and to *underdeveloped*). These are the essentially unpopulated areas, whether dry deserts, subarctic and arctic lands, areas of tropical rain forest or savannah, or high mountains. Roughly speaking, in areas with a population density of less than 25 persons per square mile, most of the land is not in continuous economic use. In this study we are concerned with the *developed* or *settled* areas of the world, measured roughly by a population density of over 25 per square mile.[3]

While per capita income may be considered the single most reliable measure of the relative economic level of different countries, the well-known uncertainty and unreliability of data on per capita income make it desirable to utilize other measures in depicting the world pattern. We have already noted the significance of diversification of the labor force, as measured by the percentage employed outside of agriculture.

A third measure is offered by data on the per capita use of all commercial sources of fuel and power, even though a considerable amount of fuel is obtained from noncommercial sources (such as firewood and agricultural wastes). It has been estimated that in 1949 these provided nearly one fifth of the total fuel and power consumed in the world, but the greater part was used in underdeveloped countries and primarily for domestic heating and cooking. Much commercial fuel and power in developed countries are also used for such nonindustrial purposes, and the amount needed to yield the same results varies greatly with climate. Despite these qualifications, per capita use of fuel and power provides a convenient index of economic development. In preparing our estimates, the countries of the world were rated in accordance with three different measures: total consumption of energy from all sources by inland transport and industry in 1937 (the latest year for which such data are available); total inland consumption of energy from all sources in 1949; and total inland consumption of energy from *commercial* sources in 1950. Whichever measure was used, the groupings of countries for the purpose of this study varied in only three or four cases. For more precise determination of comparative positions of different countries, it might be important to determine which measure was most appropriate, but here it makes little difference. The third measure named, as the most recent, is given in Table 1, along with measures of per capita income and nonagricultural labor force.

We may distinguish, with a relatively high degree of reliability, three main groups of countries: those well advanced in modern economy, those so little developed as to be considered definitely under-

[3] This figure is based on European agricultural practice and appears to be suitable for most areas of the world, but in those with a notably high level of mechanized agriculture—western United States and Canada, Australia, and New Zealand—the appropriate figure would be considerably lower.

TABLE 1. POPULATION AND ECONOMIC DEVELOPMENT OF THE COUNTRIES OF THE WORLD, CLASSIFIED ON THE BASIS OF SELECTED MEASURES

	Popula-tion in millions, 1955	Per capita		Percent of labor force in nonagricul-tural employ-ment, 1955
		Income,* 1955	Energy consumption,† 1950	
Advanced Countries				
Minimum criteria		750	2.0	70
United States	165	2,343	7.5	88
Canada	16	1,667	6.5	81
Australia	9	1,215	3.1	84
New Zealand	2	1,249	2.4	82
United Kingdom	51	998	4.4	95
France	43	1,046	2.0	63
Switzerland	5	1,229	2.1	83
Belgium-Luxembourg	9	1,015	3.5	87
Netherlands	11	708	2.0	80
Germany, West	52	762	2.6	77
Germany, East	20		2.6	71
Denmark	4	913	2.1	76
Norway	3	969	4.4	74
Sweden	7	1,165	3.2	80
Intermediate Countries				
Minimum criteria		350	.5	50
Eire	3	509	1.1	50
Austria	7	532	1.5	68
Czechoslovakia	12		3.0	63
Hungary	10		1.0	50 (est.)
Poland	27		2.5	
Finland	4	941	1.2	64
Soviet Union	220	682‡	1.8	
Italy	50	442	.6	59
Spain	29	254	.6	51

Sources: International Cooperation Administration, Office of Statistics and Reports; United Nations Statistical Office, *World Energy Supplies in Selected Years, 1929–1950*, Statistical Papers Series J, No. 1 (September 1952); *Energy Resources of the World*, U. S. Department of State Publication 3428 (June 1949); Simon Kuznets, "Quantitative Aspects of the Economic Growth of Nations: II. Industrial Distribution of National Product and Labor Force," in *Economic Development and Cultural Change*, Vol. 5, Supplement (July 1957).

* Converted into dollars at official exchange rates. The purchasing power per dollar is considerably higher in most foreign countries, but not to the same degree.
† In the equivalent of metric tons of coal.
‡ Assumed to be too high because of unrealistic official exchange rate.

TABLE 1—*Continued*

	Popula-tion in millions, 1955	Per capita		Percent of labor force in nonagricul-tural employ-ment, 1955
		Income,* 1955	Energy consumption,† 1950	
Argentina	19	374	.8	75
Uruguay	3	569	.6	
Chile	7	180	.8	70
Venezuela	6	762§	.8	59
Cuba	6	361	.6	58
Puerto Rico	2		.5	63
Union of South Africa	14	381	1.8	52
Israel	2	540	.8	88
Japan	89	240	.8	52
Underdeveloped Countries *Upper Group:*				
Minimum criteria		130	.10	30
Portugal	9	201	.12	52–62
Yugoslavia	17	209	.41	33
Rumania	16		.46	
Bulgaria	7		.30	
Greece	8	239	.22	40
Turkey	23	276	.26	14
French No. Africa	23	131–176	.13–.16	
Egypt	23	133	.15	25–40
Lebanon	1	269	.35	50
Saudi Arabia	7	166	.12	
Iraq	5	195	.18	
Mexico	30	187	.60	42
Central America	10	179–307	.09–.16	
West Indies ‖	4			
Colombia	13	330	.27	23
Ecuador	4	204	.12	51
Peru	9	140	.19	37
Brazil	58	262	.22	39
Malaya	7	298	.28	
Philippines	22	201	.10	29

* Converted into dollars at official exchange rates. The purchasing power per dollar is considerably higher in most foreign countries, but not to the same degree.
† In the equivalent of metric tons of coal.
§ Assumed to be too high because of known inflation; the purchasing power per dollar is less than in the United States.
‖ Other than Cuba, Puerto Rico, and Haiti.

TABLE 1—*Continued*

	Popula-tion in millions, 1955	Per capita		Percent of labor force in nonagricul-tural employ-ment, 1955
		Income,* 1955	Energy consumption,† 1950	
Formosa #	16	102	.25	
Korea, South #	22		.11	
Manchuria #	45			
Gold Coast	5	135	.09	
Central African Fed.	7	134	.50	
Lower Group:				
Indonesia	82	127	.06	29
India	380	72	.10	29
Pakistan	82	56	.04	23
China (excl. Manch.)	580	45 (est.)	.05 (est.)	
Other Far East **	90	40–133	0–.08	15–47
Other tropical Africa ††	141	54–103	0–.09	
Other Middle East‡‡	46	54–111	0–.10	
Other tropical America §§	9	75–108	.02–.09	
Other Oceania‖‖	2		.01–.02	

* Converted into dollars at official exchange rates. The purchasing power per dollar is considerably higher in most foreign countries, but not to the same degree.
† In the equivalent of metric tons of coal.
# Included in this group on the basis of prewar data.
** Includes former French Indo-China, Thailand, Burma, Ceylon, and Nepal.
†† Includes all except the Central African Federation and Gold Coast.
‡‡ Includes Libya, Syria, Jordan, Iran, and Afghanistan.
§§ Includes Haiti, Bolivia, and Paraguay.
‖‖ New Guinea and Solomon Islands.

developed, and an intermediate group of countries which show various degrees of and inconsistencies in development.

The countries in the first group include less than one sixth of the population of the world. They are limited to areas of northwest European culture, whether in Europe or overseas. The overseas areas—the United States and Canada, Australia and New Zealand—in general show the higher indexes. Especially notable are their high indexes of diversification, since all of them produce large agricultural surpluses. Energy consumption per capita is also high, either in absolute terms, as in Anglo-America, or in relation to the amount of heavy industrial development, as in Australia and New Zealand. The European area includes not only the countries of heavy industry but also neighboring countries, notably in Scandinavia, but does not include Eire. The income figure for France appears unduly high in comparison with 1949 data and with the country's energy consumption (which is relatively low for a major producer of coal and steel), and in view of the markedly low level of diversification. There is reason to believe that much of southern France belongs in a lower category. The income figure for the Netherlands on the other hand appears unduly low in comparison with its neighbors.

The intermediate group consists largely of countries in southern and eastern Europe, including the Soviet Union, but excluding Portugal and the Balkans. In the same category are overseas countries of southern European culture in temperate South America, together with Venezuela, Cuba, and Puerto Rico; and three scattered areas, Japan, Israel, and the Union of South Africa, each of which is in marked contrast to surrounding countries. The countries in this category contain a little more than one sixth of the world's population. That they are not merely intermediate but transitional in economic development is suggested by the numerous cases of lack of correspondence among the three criteria. Czechoslovakia, Poland, the Soviet Union, and the Union of South Africa are relatively high in energy consumption, in comparison with the other indexes, in part no doubt because of the relatively large development of mining and heavy industry. In the absence of more recent income data for Czechoslovakia, Hungary, and Poland, those countries are placed in this category partly on the basis of their comparative standing in 1949. It is possible that western Czechoslovakia should be considered part of northwestern Europe. In the Soviet Union hardly more than 60 percent of the labor force is assumed to be in nonagricultural employment, and the per capita income figure is considered unduly high in terms of real income.

No doubt other instances of geographic transition from areas of more advanced economy to those of much lower could be found in this group. A regional breakdown for Italy, in particular, might show that northern Italy could be classified with northwest Europe, whereas southern Italy should be rated as definitely underdeveloped. Certainly the east coastal portion of the Union of South Africa, overwhelmingly native in population, cannot be considered intermediate in economic level.

Finland and Venezuela could be classified as relatively advanced countries on the basis of the figures for income per capita, but not on the basis of other indexes.

Japan, Spain, and Chile show income levels much lower than would be expected in view of other criteria, including the availability and use of modern transportation. In the case of Japan, in particular, one wonders whether the monetary values of income correctly reflect comparative levels of real income.

The remainder of the world, including two thirds of its population, must be classified as underdeveloped. For countries of largely subsistence production, the indexes are necessarily based more on estimates; revision on the basis of calculated real income might produce relatively large changes in apparent national income. There may therefore be little meaning in dividing this group into several categories. From examination of all the criteria, however, we can recognize certain countries in which considerable progress has been made toward income levels higher than subsistence. These countries, containing about 15 percent of the world's population, are widely scattered. They include Portugal and the Balkans; French North Africa and a number of countries in the Middle East; most of tropical America; some smaller countries in the Far East, including on the basis of prewar data the former Japanese colonies; and two countries in tropical Africa. Brazil may fall in this group because of mere statistical averages of data for major regions that differ greatly in development and are but little interrelated. A regional breakdown of that country might show that its southeastern portion ranked with the intermediate countries and that other parts belonged in the lowest category.

The remaining countries, which comprise this lowest category, contain over half the world's population. They are primarily in eastern and southern Asia, but also include most of tropical Africa, and the poorer countries of the Middle East and of tropical America. There is still a wide range of economic levels within this group; and if we had regional data for such countries as India or Indonesia, we might find that areas as large as many independent countries could be classified in the upper group of underdeveloped countries. On the other hand, per capita incomes in China, Pakistan, and much of tropical Africa appear to be less than half as great as the minimum in the upper group; productivity per capita in these countries is less than one twentieth of that in the more advanced countries of western Europe.

FACTORS IN DIVERSIFICATION

Many of the countries in the lowest economic category, including notably Indonesia, Thailand, and India, have experienced considerable increase in commercialization of primary production during the past century. Yet their economies have developed relatively little diversification. The theoretical process by which commercialization may be expected to lead to industrialization and diversification of the economy is evidently far from automatic. This paper attempts to analyze the extent to which this development depends on the contents and location of the particular country.

Such an analysis must consider the following factors: entrepreneurship, money capital, capital goods, transport facilities, sources of mechanical power, raw materials, labor, and consumer markets. To the extent that a state includes these factors or can develop them from internal sources, its economic growth depends primarily on organization, including that of government. If any of these factors is lacking, the possibility and cost of importing it must be considered. These depend not merely on material factors but also on the freedom of trade, over which the government of the importing state has a large, though not exclusive, measure of control. A requirement for imports (other than those in the nature of grants) is the capacity to pay for them in exports, through surplus production, present or future, of goods or services. Of the eight factors, four are material—transport facilities, capital goods, power resources, and raw materials; the remainder are nonmaterial or "human elements." We shall examine them in that order.

Transport Facilities

In terms of the over-all economy of a state, transport facilities form a part of its total capital goods, but for any individual producer these facilities constitute a condition that he can do little to control or develop. Because of the great amount of capital required in proportion to short-term use, they are generally constructed only by the state or semipublic agencies aided by the state. Once completed, however, transport facilities become a part of the physical heritage of the area.

Some countries possess useful routes of internal transport that required little or no effort by man, coastal waters, for example, and navigable streams or lakes. These were of great advantage to particular countries in earlier stages of the modern era and still function advantageously. But a relatively small part of the developed areas of the world today can be satisfactorily served by water transport alone.

Far more important for most areas are the facilities man has created in railways and highways. Construction and operation of such routes is possible in all habitable lands, although the costs are notably increased by particular conditions, as in the high Andean countries or in tropical rain forests. A more serious deterrent is the lack of traffic in areas of sparse population or little commercial development.

With noteworthy exceptions, all the developed areas of the world have railways connecting important urban centers. Major exceptions include China, Iran, and the countries of the Indo-Chinese peninsula. In many other countries, however, the rail system is far from adequate in rural areas, so that local transport to and from farming villages remains costly. This is the case in highland tropical America from Mexico to Bolivia, northeastern Brazil, the developed areas of tropical Africa, Turkey and the Middle East in general, peninsular India, much of Spain and the Balkans, and even in the well-settled portions of the Soviet Union.

In most parts of the world where settled lands border on undeveloped areas, rail lines traverse long stretches of territory beyond the frontier of settlement, but settlement is not expanding. Few if any areas of the world today offer the likelihood of rapid expansion of settlement following the rails, comparable with the process during the past century in the new lands of western North America, Australia, Siberia, and Manchuria. Less spectacular developments, however, may be possible in the interior of southern Brazil and along the dry margins of interior China and Siberia. Also, potentially valuable mineral resources may be opened for development by new rail lines in what are now economically inaccessible regions.

Adequate coverage of rural areas with paved roads suitable for motor transport is largely limited to Anglo-America and northwestern Europe. The absence of all-weather roads is a particular handicap in countries where many farm villages are more than 10 miles from rail lines—as in Eastern Europe, the Soviet Union, and China.

External transport, other than between neighboring states, depends in most areas on sea routes. Thanks to the universal utility of the open seas for transport, all countries with economical access to the sea may engage in trade with each other. Lack of political control of access to the sea, however important in international political relations or in time of war, is normally little handicap in economic growth—as is demonstrated by Switzerland and Czechoslovakia. On the other hand, economic development requiring foreign trade may be restricted where the cost of transport to the sea is high, whether because of distance, as in the remote interiors of the United States, Canada, and the Soviet Union, or because of difficult terrain, as in the high Andean countries.

Capital Goods

In the development of industry the first material problem after establishment of transport facilities is to secure capital goods—buildings, machinery, and so on. Their production requires large amounts of steel and coal and consequently tends to be concentrated in the relatively few areas that are specially rich in coal and iron ore. Machine-building industries also require advanced technical skills. Capital goods therefore constitute a relatively large part of international trade; areas of new industrial development are largely dependent on areas already developed.

For rapid construction or expansion of industrial plants, the ability of a country to produce its own capital goods is undoubtedly a great asset. (The great expansion of industry in the United States during World War II was concentrated mainly in established industrial areas.) In the long run, however, it seems doubtful that this factor is a serious handicap to industrial development in new areas. The textile industries of Japan and India were supplied with machinery from Great Britain and later undercut British markets in the Far East, just as Massachusetts machine factories furnished the Southeast with the means of undermining the prosperity of the New England cotton industry.

In view of the long-term use of capital goods the transport costs involved would appear to be of minor importance. Whether capital goods are produced domestically or imported may make little difference in their cost, although imports of capital goods may raise problems in the balance of foreign trade (see pages 318 ff. infra). Dependence on imported equipment does have some indirect disadvantages; if it comes from distant countries, there may be difficulty in obtaining prompt servicing and spare parts, and consequent risk of long shutdowns. Modifications of design needed to fit particular local conditions may be difficult to secure. Finally, a country that does not have its own equipment industry lacks one of the major elements in the development of a trained labor force (cf. pages 313–314 infra).

Power Resources [4]

We have noted the characteristically high per capita use of mechanical energy in countries of advanced economic growth. Insofar as the

[4] The data in this section are derived primarily from two of the sources cited for Table 1: *Energy Resources of the World,* and *World Energy Supplies in Selected Years, 1929–1950.* Of the world's consumption of commercial energy in 1937, industry

use of mechanical energy is correlated with the level of economic development, is this a relationship of cause or effect? Is the occurrence of sources of mechanical energy within the state necessary for its economic growth?

A strongly affirmative answer to the latter question is indicated by marked correspondence of the countries of major industrial development with (1) those of advanced economic growth, and (2) those of maximum power production. But the economic growth of countries that produce the greatest energy is by no means confined to those portions that produce the energy materials; whatever the relationship between production of those materials and economic growth, it evidently extends considerable distances from their sources. This extension, furthermore, is not limited by international boundaries. Countries like Denmark, almost completely lacking internal sources of power, may participate in industrial development and economic growth. Hence the conditions that determine the feasibility of dependence on external sources of mechanical energy must be examined.

Sources of Mechanical Energy. Of the various sources of fuel and power, coal is still by far the most important, as it has been throughout the development of modern economy. It has been estimated that in 1949 coal provided nearly half the world's supply of mechanical energy, and nearly 60 percent of that from commercial sources. In most underdeveloped countries, noncommercial sources—firewood, peat, and agricultural wastes—are of first importance. These are used chiefly for domestic heating and cooking, but they also furnish (or did furnish as late as 1937) a considerable part of the fuel for transport and industry in certain areas, notably Finland and similar regions of the Soviet Union, and tropical countries of America and Africa.

Petroleum, which provided one fifth of the world's supply of energy in 1949, or one fourth of the commercial supply, was more important than coal in most oil-producing regions and also generally throughout Latin America, in most of Africa north of Rhodesia, and in most of Southeast Asia.[5]

---

required approximately half; domestic uses, one fourth; railway and domestic steamship transport, 15 percent; and automotive vehicles, 7 percent (nearly twice that figure in the United States, and less than half that in the rest of the world). Most of the small remainder was used for fuel in international sea trade.

[5] Petroleum has exceeded coal in the total consumption of energy in the United States since 1953, but most of the petroleum is used for transportation; in industry, coal remains far more important.

Hydroelectric power, which provided 7.5 percent of the energy from commercial sources in 1949, is of first importance only in the mountainous countries of Norway, Sweden, Switzerland, Italy, and New Zealand, and in Finland—all of which are deficient in coal and oil.

Natural gas supplies a slightly larger amount of energy, but is limited chiefly to the United States, which produces and consumes nearly 90 percent of the world's total and secures therefrom about one fifth of its own supply of commercial energy. Natural gas is relatively important also in a few countries where it is produced locally and the over-all consumption of energy is low, as in Venezuela, Mexico, Trinidad, Rumania, and Indonesia.

Use of both water power and natural gas until recently has been limited to the vicinity of their production, and these sources of energy are generally insignificant in international movement. In 1937 the largest international transfer of hydroelectric power was from Switzerland and Austria to neighboring areas of Germany, France, and Italy; this was the equivalent of more than one million tons of coal, but provided less than 0.5 percent of the total energy consumption of each of the importing countries. In 1950 this movement was considerably less. Natural gas does not appear in international trade, except for exports of less than 1 percent of the United States' production to Canada and especially to Mexico, where the imported gas provides some 6 percent of the commercial energy consumed. Recent developments in pipeline movement of natural gas may greatly aid the overland expansion of its market, but in view of the premium value of natural gas for heating, large shipments of it are unlikely to be used in industry or transportation. Hydroelectric power and natural gas, we conclude, are valuable assets for industry within close proximity to their production, but countries lacking such resources must look to other forms of mechanical energy—primarily coal and oil.

During the century prior to World War II, fuel and power for industry were supplied very largely from coal. Despite increasing use of other sources, coal still supplied 75 percent of the world's industrial consumption in 1937, and 80 percent of industrial consumption outside the United States. The importance of the location of energy sources for industrial development in the past may be examined, therefore, primarily with reference to coal.

World Situation in Coal Production and Trade. The major features of coal production and trade throughout the world were established long before World War I. The greatest change since then has been the rise of production in the Soviet Union to one sixth of the world's total. This increase was planned solely for internal consumption and has had no important effect on international trade. In most of the world the coal situation has been dominated by the ability of the two areas of greatest production and consumption, located on either side of the North Atlantic Ocean, to produce coal in much greater amounts than those required for local consumption. Thanks to this excess production and to the cheapness and flexibility with which coal could be transported by sea, the market for coal was highly competitive in most seaports of the world. Very little coal, however, was shipped from the North Atlantic countries to those bordering the Indian Ocean and the Western Pacific. Japan, China, India, Australia, and the Union of South Africa were each self-sufficient and supplied small surpluses to other Far Eastern countries, with the exception that after 1928 Japanese imports of coal from Manchuria exceeded her exports.

American coal producers supplied Canadian requirements and the small market in the Caribbean, but were normally not able to compete with British producers in overseas areas. That the American producers had the capacity to supply the requirements of these areas, too, though at somewhat increased cost, has been repeatedly demonstrated. Whereas overseas exports normally were less than one million tons of coal, in 1920 and again in 1926 the United States exported nearly 20 million tons; and after World War II, under foreign aid programs, exports have been as high as 50 million tons in a year. At least since World War I, the coal industry of the United States has had the capacity to produce 100–200 million tons more per year than is normally required for consumption in the United States and Canada—an amount well in excess of the total requirements of world trade.

While the United States therefore has long been a major potential factor, the actual trade in coal before World War II was largely within or from northwestern Europe. The chief coal fields involved form a discontinuous belt from Great Britain across northern France, the Low Countries, Germany, and Czechoslovakia to Upper Silesia (divided, in the interwar period, among the latter two countries and Poland). The entire area, as determined by the political limits of those states, produced nearly half the world's total in 1937, or over 600 million tons. Several of the fields overlapped international boundaries, and all are relatively close to neighboring states. In consequence nearly one tenth of the total production was exchanged among the producing states, over relatively short distances by rail or inland waterway, or across the

Channel and North Sea from Great Britain to France, the Low Countries, and Germany. All told, 90 percent of the production was consumed within the producing group. (See Table 2.)

TABLE 2. COAL PRODUCTION AND INTERNATIONAL TRADE, COUNTRIES OF NORTHWESTERN EUROPE, 1937

	Million tons of coal			Energy consumption in tons per capita
	Produced	Exported	Imported	
United Kingdom	244	43.7	.1	4.28
France	45	.9	29.1	2.12
Belgium-Luxembourg	30	5.8	9.1	4.02
Netherlands	14	6.4	9.0	1.79
Germany	234	46.2	5.6	3.02
Czechoslovakia	29	4.4	1.4	1.78
Poland	36	10.2	.9	.75
Total	633	117.5	55.3	

The notable differences in per capita consumption of energy among these countries reflect not only differences in the over-all economic level but more particularly differences in the development of heavy industry. Since the steel industry uses large amounts of coking coal and is closely tied to that source, countries producing such coal may be expected to have a high per capita consumption. On this basis the indexes for Czechoslovakia and particularly for Poland were low in 1937. Had these approximated the index for Germany, those countries would have had no surplus of coal for export, unless they achieved much greater production in their sectors of the Upper Silesian field. Such increase was entirely possible, as was demonstrated during World War II when the area was rapidly developed to supply German war needs.

Beyond the requirements within northwestern Europe, the region produced the major surplus of coal for countries deficient in its production. Before 1914 this surplus exceeded 100 million tons, nearly three fourths of which was from coal fields in Great Britain, which dominated the coastal and overseas trade. Germany supplied continental markets, chiefly from the Ruhr but to a lesser extent from the Saar and Upper Silesia. Subsequently the decline in coal for bunkers and the increased use of hydroelectric power caused the export market to decrease and become increasingly competitive. Poland, from the Upper Silesian field, and Germany, from the Ruhr, competed vigor-

●usly in Scandinavia and the Baltic, and by rail in Italy, but the overseas market remained under British domination.

It is instructive to examine the amounts of coal imported by different countries in 1937, in relation to the distances involved and per capita needs for economic development. While nearly four fifths of the surplus of northwestern Europe (about 50 million tons) were taken by other countries of Europe and the Mediterranean, the amounts taken by the several sectors of this market were not in proportion to distance (see Table 3). In general the largest per capita imports of coal go to countries that without those imports would have a relatively high per capita consumption of energy from domestic coal and water-power resources. Denmark is a notable exception. Particularly striking are the contrasts between Switzerland and Italy, or between Finland and Portugal.

If we may judge by movements of coal within the United States, east central Europe from Finland to Greece was within range of economical coal shipments from Upper Silesia. From there to the Baltic is a somewhat shorter distance than from the Middle Appalachian coal field to Hampton Roads; to the Adriatic at Trieste, a little farther. British coal can be sent to Portuguese and Spanish ports for little more than to Scandinavian ports.

The only long-distance transport of large amounts of coal was to the South Atlantic coast of South America—5 million tons to Argentina, Brazil, and Uruguay, and nearly all from western Europe. The imports of Argentina presumably would have been much larger were it not that local petroleum and natural gas supplied two thirds of the power and fuel used in its industries. With increased importation of oil from the Caribbean, coal shipments to southern South America have tended to decline. Relatively few countries of the world, it should be noted, are farther from Great Britain than this area of large coal imports.

The world pattern of production and distribution of the material resources of mechanical power suggests that, whereas possession of such resources within a state is not essential to industrialization and economic development, such development has been limited largely to areas close to large power production. But the relationship is by no means consistent, nor is it clearly one of cause and effect. If proximity is a direct cause, it must be so in terms of transport costs. Most of the well-settled areas of the world are within economic reach of coal by sea transport. Coal can be shipped 5,000 miles by sea at about the same cost as 350 miles by rail. During the greater part of the century before

TABLE 3. IMPORTS OF COAL FOR DOMESTIC CONSUMPTION, IN COMPARISON WITH TOTAL
CONSUMPTION OF COMMERCIAL SOURCES OF ENERGY, 1937

	Retained imports *		Total energy consumption in tons per capita
	Million tons	Tons per capita	
Eire	2.6	.89	1.10
Denmark	5.4	1.54	1.71
Norway	3.0	.75	3.44
Sweden	8.6	1.36	2.50
Finland	2.2	.60	1.03
Baltic States	1.0	.18	.23
Switzerland	3.3	.79	1.81
Austria	3.2	.48	1.04
Italy	12.8	.29	.66
Portugal	1.3	.17	.24
Spain (1935)	1.1	.04	.50
Hungary	.4	.04	.72
Yugoslavia	.3	.02	.25
Rumania	.1	—	.37
Bulgaria	—	—	.14
Greece	1.0	.14	.18
Turkey	—	—	.13
Levant	.1	—	—
Egypt	1.3	.08	.13
French North Africa	.8	.05	.12
Tropical Africa	1.2	—	<.10
West Indies	.9	.04	.10–.35
Brazil	1.6	.04	.13
Uruguay	.3	.14	.50
Argentina	3.1	.24	.65

* Net imports less coal used in foreign bunkers. The latter totaled some 2 million
tons in the Mediterranean, but was of minor importance elsewhere.

1937 the major coal fields of northwestern Europe, close to the sea, had
been seeking export markets for their surplus production. Thus, whatever political and financial problems arise in international trade, in contrast to domestic, are presumably independent of distance.

Dependence on imported power materials necessitates a continuous
export of other goods or services of equal value from the purchasing
state. But the countries whose fuel imports represent a relatively large
percentage of the value of all their merchandise exports include coun-

tries in northwestern Europe, close to coal fields, as shown by these percentages:

Country	Value of fuel imports as percent of value of all merchandise exports, 1937
France	35
Portugal	26
Italy	26
Eire	23
Uruguay	20
Denmark	17
Norway	17
Japan	17
Sweden	17
Switzerland	15
Greece	14
Austria	12
Brazil	10

Conceivably countries farther from Europe run greater risk of being cut off from normal coal supplies in time of war. At such time, however, American coal fields have stepped into the breach. Production in the Middle Appalachian coal field has long been limited only by the demand. Because of the rail haul to Norfolk, coal from West Virginia normally cannot compete in South America with British coal. If the latter is not available, however, the difference in cost of American coal is not great enough to be a serious limitation on industrial development in Argentina.

The over-all development of the coal industry of the world since 1913 indicates that in general coal production and trade are limited by the level of economic development rather than the reverse. Most of the coal fields were known and partly developed before World War I. Since then the total production in relatively normal years has increased but little outside the Soviet Union, although the potential capacity has been greatly increased, as demonstrated in particular years. In the well-developed countries of northwestern Europe and Anglo-America, increased industrial demand for coal has hardly kept pace with the decrease in other demands, so that total consumption and production are about the same as then. Only in Great Britain since World War II has there been serious and continued difficulty in supplying the demand. Elsewhere, coal production has increased directly in proportion to the increase in industry and transport, most notably in the Soviet Union, but also in Japan, Manchuria, India, Australia, and east central Europe (Upper Silesia). In comparison with the available resources, the increase has been small in such countries as China and Indo-China. Of the countries of rising industrial development named, only Japan was unable to produce adequate amounts of coal, and it obtained from Manchuria the relatively minor imports required.

These facts are consistent with the general proposition that in the total complex of modern economic development the production of coal constitutes a relatively minor step—in terms of requirements of capital, labor, technology, and organization. If these are lacking, coal resources are of little or no value in stimulating industry. If the former are present, coal resources are an additional asset, but if they are lacking, outside fields can readily increase production to meet the need.

The technological changes in production of energy from sources other than coal, whether recent or foreseen for the near future, would appear to lessen the disadvantage of distance from coal fields. Oil competes with coal for industrial purposes only in areas remote from coal fields, because of lower costs of transport per unit of energy supplied, i.e., the use of oil reduces the handicap of remoteness from energy sources. Furthermore, the economy in use of oil for transportation reduces the imports necessary for that purpose, freeing exchange for imports for industrial purposes. Whereas hydroelectric power is more restricted than coal in respect to transport, water power is much more widely distributed over the world. Even if a country lacks water power, its competitive situation is hardly different from before the development of such power, since hydroelectric production in coal-producing areas is not more economical for industry than power from coal.

Commercial development of nuclear energy or of solar energy may well cause changes difficult to predict. It appears likely, however, that either form of development would tend to lessen rather than increase the importance of the power factor in the location of industry.

More detailed analyses of problems only touched on in this discussion would be required before general conclusions could be drawn, but two specific conclusions are clear and important: (1) In countries dependent on overseas sources for power, areas remote from the sea are seriously handicapped. (2) The enormous quantities of coal required in the basic processes of metallurgical industries, notably iron and steel, tend to limit those industries to areas close to districts producing coking coal —with the exception of the even more limited number of areas that are close to iron mining or between iron- and coal-producing districts.

Whether the fields supplying coking coal are within the state or just beyond its borders is of minor importance. Although the iron and steel industry is a necessary basis for modern economic development, its presence within any state is not essential for advanced economic development of that state. For many industrial developments based on imported steel, lack of coal within a country is no major handicap, and it is not clear that any countries accessible by sea are seriously handicapped in economic growth because of remoteness from sources of mechanical energy.

Raw Materials

Possession of raw materials is much less critical for the development of manufacturing in a state than is its possession of power resources. Industries for which proximity to raw materials is economically important are relatively few and minor. The major industrial areas of the world obtain most of their raw materials from far distant places, and in good part through international trade. The particular raw materials are often available from many different countries in each of which production could readily be expanded with increased demand. Colonial development has been important in increasing the world's total supply of raw materials, on which all countries possessing purchasing power have been able to draw.

The most critically important raw materials for modern industry are iron and steel in crude and semifinished forms. As in the case of coal, northwestern Europe and eastern United States have long been capable of producing more than enough iron and steel to supply demands elsewhere. The problems of cost and reliability are similar to those pertaining to coal. Numerous countries in northwestern Europe depend entirely on imports of steel for fabricating, just as major industrial areas in the United States depend on shipments from steel-producing areas.

The necessity of importing steel commonly establishes a state's dependence—in the case of Argentina, for example, amounting to one tenth the value of its total exports—on the same foreign state or states on which the importing country depends for its coal supply. The effect is to concentrate dependence in foreign trade; but the consequences appear to be political rather than economic in character.

Entrepreneurship

Of the human factors essential for economic development, the most difficult to measure is entrepreneurship. It is not to be assumed that any society is deficient in numbers of individuals possessing the innate characteristics needed to undertake enterprises and manage others. In many cultures, however, social mores restrict opportunities for such undertakings to members of small classes; countless numbers of potential entrepreneurs are never discovered. Furthermore, the efforts of those who can function as entrepreneurs are directed or confined to land ownership and management, or to political or military adventures. The elements determining such cultural viewpoints may be quite independent of the physical resources of a state; but the viewpoints are deeply entrenched and if supported by religious attitudes and well-established social values may be long enduring. The importance of such a system of values has long been recognized by students of Latin America; somewhat similar situations exist in other areas.

The growth of entrepreneurship in a country is to some extent the product, as well as a cause, of economic development. But among countries that have only recently provided opportunity for entrepreneurs, there are notable differences in the speed with which such classes arise and are given social recognition. It is generally recognized that Chinese culture, and presumably Japanese, is more favorable to the production of entrepreneurs, small and large, than that of most Far Eastern countries—perhaps more so than Spanish American culture.

Every country that has had any opportunity for modern economic development has produced its few large entrepreneurs, and in many the state itself endeavors to meet the need. However, the economic growth of the more advanced countries of the world has resulted from the efforts of numerous individual entrepreneurs, most of whom operate at any one time on a relatively small scale. The experience of northwestern Europe and the United States indicates that to produce entrepreneurs in such numbers it must be possible for them to come from all economic classes. The critical question for any state therefore is: To what extent does its social and economic structure and educational system permit the emergence of large numbers of individuals with the capacity of entrepreneurs?

If a state does not produce its own entrepreneurs, can it secure them from outside? Large-scale entrepreneurs, the great corporations, are ready to move into practically any area that offers opportunity for great profit. But these few supply but a small part of the need for entrepreneurship, and at high cost. Small entrepreneurs operate commonly in their home localities, or in places to which they migrated originally as workers. A country that is unable to attract large numbers of skilled workers has less opportunity of securing entrepreneurs by immigration. Even where the distance involved is minor, small entrepreneurs are least likely of all the factors under consideration to move across international boundaries, except where social conditions, legal systems, and currencies are similar—as between the United States and Canada, or France and Belgium. In contrast, the nineteenth-century boundary between Germany and Russian Poland was a veritable Chinese wall, surmounted only by such major planned developments as the textile industry of Łódź.

In areas of colonial imperialism—as distinct from colonial settlements—entrepreneurs are commonly supplied by the outside ruling state. As long as the colony depends on such imports, the number is inevitably small and the cost relatively high. Certain cultural areas have produced a surplus of small entrepreneurs who have migrated into both colonial areas and independent states. The largest in number, no doubt, are the Chinese in many areas of the Far East; similar are Hindus, Greeks, Jews, Armenians, and Portuguese scattered in various parts of Africa and tropical America. In both types of entrepreneurship, the critical question is whether these alien groups of temporary or permanent immigrants stimulate the development of entrepreneurship among native peoples, as appears to have been the case in the Gold Coast, or by monopolization of enterprise, either through political control or social segregation, actually retard such development among the indigenous population, even though they themselves can supply only a small part of the potential need.

If it can be assumed that an economy that provides maximum opportunity for many small, independently directed enterprises stimulates the efforts of many entrepreneurs, it cannot be taken for granted that similar development may not occur under large corporations, private or public. Conceivably the large corporation, concerned with increasing the volume and diversity of its production, can encourage junior officials or plant foremen to undertake new ventures with less risk to the individual than in the case of the independent operator. The difficulties resulting from great size and concentration of over-all control in a few hands are obvious but not necessarily insurmountable. State ownership and control undoubtedly imposes even more difficult obstacles, but it cannot be assumed that these cannot be overcome.

Whatever the system, the essential question concerns the freedom of individuals to function as entrepreneurs if they possess the abilities and inclinations, either at home or in countries of opportunity to which they may migrate. Freedom of movement of persons may be no less important than freedom of movement of commodities.

Money Capital

The situation of finance capital is similar to that of entrepreneurship, and the two are rather closely interconnected.

The capacity of a state to produce capital internally depends on the extent of commercial production that yields money income, and the degree to which it is available for investment. An agricultural economy that functions predominantly on a subsistence basis, as in Mexico, produces relatively little money income, whereas one on a highly commercial basis, as in Argentina, may yield a high proportion of cash income. In many countries of backward economic development, resources permitting commercial lumbering, fishing, or mining have been a primary stimulus toward commercialization. Trade in general has been the major source of investment funds for the earlier stages of manufacturing.

For an over-all picture of economic development under a capitalist system, the ultimate effect of money income from commercial enterprises might be examined in terms of well-known generalizations concerning distribution of income among classes of recipients and their different uses of income, based on needs, customs, and attitudes; but we are here concerned with the *location* of such new investments, and the relationships are much more complex. For example, a foreign corporation from a remote state may develop a major enterprise that requires large capital investment in proportion to labor costs in a country otherwise economically backward. The funds expended by the corporation for labor and local supplies stimulate some local economic growth, but much of the income, in the form of interest and dividends and salaries, never enters the country of production. Whether this income is spent or invested, it is not likely to produce available funds for small-scale enterprises within that country. It does not "lose," no money "goes out of the country," but much of the stimulus to economic growth takes effect elsewhere, notably in the country supplying the original capital.

The situation described is not true of foreign investments simply because they are foreign. Familiarity based on proximity may be a more important factor. German investors in one industry in Switzerland may be glad to reinvest their profits in other Swiss industries, whereas New York investors in large steel companies mining iron in Minnesota may hesitate to reinvest their earnings in new independent enterprises in that state.

In most cases a major part of the gross income of commercial enterprises remains in the country of production, but whether this will produce significant amounts of investment saving depends on social customs and attitudes, which vary greatly among countries, independently of opportunities for investment.

In most underdeveloped countries, economic growth requires importation of capital. Surplus capital has long been available in the world, but primarily from economically advanced countries where internal opportunities compete with external. Enterprises in less advanced countries, which lack a local supply of savings, must pay higher interest costs than those in advanced countries. Possible minor exceptions may be found among machine-producing companies, which in order to sell products having limited markets may themselves finance their sales to less developed areas, in effect supplying both finance capital and capital goods.

Whereas transport costs of capital are negligible, and large capital investments may be independent of distance, proximity to a source of foreign capital may be a distinct advantage for small enterprises. Far more important than distance in increasing the cost of imported capital are the economic and political conditions of a state that determine the reliability of investments within it. Increases in cost based on these conditions are far wider in range than the differences in cost between domestic and foreign capital in well-developed and stable states. In many underdeveloped countries the cost of foreign capital becomes prohibitive unless the state guarantees the investment or itself functions as the entrepreneur.

The world map of economic development suggests that there is a significant mutual relationship among the factors of entrepreneurship, habits of capital investment, and political stability; and that all these depend on characteristics of culture areas which extend over groups of states. These include primarily the countries of northwestern Europe, which were most affected by the Renaissance and Reformation—whether now predominantly Protestant or Roman Catholic—and the overseas areas populated by migrants from those countries.

Labor

One of the requirements for economic growth—human labor—may be assumed to be generally available in increasing supply in all settled areas. The problem of economic growth is then, by definition, that of more efficient utilization of a universally available resource that economic growth itself causes to increase.

In order, however, to use an existing labor surplus in the commercial and industrial processes essential to economic growth, the surplus must be relocated and transformed in attitudes and skills. Furthermore, to the extent that industrialization is successful, total population may increase more rapidly than primary production of the necessities of life, creating a dependence on imports, particularly of food materials.

The increase in labor supply for commerce and industry is generally produced in rural areas; economic growth involves continuous migration from farms to towns and cities. This necessitates not only major changes in manner of life and in family and community relationships, but also the construction of much more complex living facilities than are required for rural living. In our culture these factors appear not to hinder the "drift to the cities," but this may not be the case in different cultures. Many thousands of workers in industries in the larger cities of India live most of the week, or for months at a time, away from their families—perhaps hundreds of miles away. Whether delayed development of necessary social overhead—adequate housing, and so on—or social mores resistant to urbanization account for this phenomenon, it inevitably constitutes a drag on economic growth.

The problem of adapting the attitudes and practices of workers accustomed to variable and irregular farming operations, producing goods for direct consumption, to the requirements of more monotonous, regular, and not immediately purposeful work for monetary gain in industry is probably more important and difficult. The degree of difficulty varies greatly among peoples of different cultures. Efficiency in commercial production of all kinds, agricultural as well as industrial, depends increasingly on ability to read and follow printed directions. Adult literacy varies in the countries of the world from approximately 100 percent to nearly zero. In colonial or recently colonial territories, even those that are long-established and in which material economic resources are well developed, mass education has hardly begun. Much the same is true in many independent but economically underdeveloped countries, other than the Soviet Union.

Particularly critical for economic development is the supply of workers trained and skilled in machine technology and capable of directing unskilled workers in its processes. This supply is one of the great assets of countries well started in modern economic development.

A particular advantage of such countries as the United States and Switzerland is the familiarity of rural-urban migrants with machine techniques. In contrast, in countries where cultural attitudes classify all physical work at a low social level, the development of an adequate supply of technologically trained foremen and directors is difficult. An additional advantage of highly industrial countries stems specifically from equipment manufacturing, as noted earlier. This industry plays a strategic role in the training of a skilled labor force, which has a cumulative effect on the long-run supply of labor skills.

Immigration of trained workers, engineers, and managers from highly developed countries has been significant in relatively few areas of the world, and is possible today in still fewer. The United States and the British settlement colonies gained greatly from such immigration in earlier periods, as did Manchuria to some extent while under Japanese control. But Europeans, Americans, and Japanese are generally unwilling to settle permanently in areas that are already densely populated by peoples of different culture. The few exceptions —in coastal Algeria, parts of South Africa and Rhodesia, and Israel— are areas in which the original immigrant minority expected to control political and social conditions, as well as the economy.

Temporary importation of skilled workers and engineers for a few years or for a lifetime, but not for permanent settlement, is possible in any country, but it is expensive and usually undertaken only by large enterprises. Its ultimate value for general economic growth probably depends less on the success of the particular enterprises than on indirect gains from instruction of indigenous technical workers.

Markets for Finished Products

Commercial production is meaningless unless there is both human desire for the products and income with which to pay for them. With few exceptions, the products of economic enterprises are desired by the people of the world, or would be desired if placed before them, in far greater quantities than are now available. Furthermore, every newly invented product creates both a new desire and the need for other new products, for which there may be no ceiling. These sweeping statements are true for the world as a whole, but are not necessarily true if both production and desire are confined to a single country. Argentina produces normally more corn, wheat, and beef than its people would consume even if all ate all they wanted; American industry no doubt could produce more sewing machines than American consumers would want even if the machines were sold for a dollar each. But no country produces a surfeit of the total variety of goods desired by its consumers.

Domestic Markets. The population of every well-settled country constitutes a potential consumers' market for many products whose total is limited only by the country's productive capacity. Since the maximum productive capacity possible under modern technology far exceeds that achieved in even the most highly developed countries, and is increased continually by new machines and techniques, there is no limit to the potential domestic market of any country. Even in existing conditions the range in productivity, and therefore income, per capita among the countries of the world is so great—in the order of 50 to 1— that the following conclusion applies to all but a few countries: increasing efficiency of a country's production, approaching the level already reached in the most advanced countries, could double, triple, or even further multiply the country's domestic market for goods and services.

The conversion of consumer desire to consumer demand depends on increasing the efficiency of production in both primary and secondary industries. Increase in human efficiency in agricultural production is of fundamental importance not only because the largest part of the population in underdeveloped countries is engaged in agriculture, but also because agriculture at the subsistence level is the one industry by which men can live without producing a market for consumers' goods. In this respect the critical factor in agriculture is the ratio of the population directly supported by agriculture to productive land—the ratio of farm population to farm land. While gross agricultural production is increased with increasing inputs of labor, beyond a certain point—varying with different crops, animals, and conditions of land— the gross increase is less proportionately than the increase in labor, which therefore consumes directly an increasing proportion of the product. Increased use of superior techniques and better tools and machines, even if economically possible, can offset this effect only in part because land itself is a limiting factor. Such improved practices may not be economically feasible because of the low net surplus of production after consumption on the farms.

In well-settled countries, where the agricultural labor force is at least adequate for cultivation of the available arable land under existing conditions of technology, more efficient production would call for a smaller labor force on the farms. But in most economically well-developed countries natural increase in population long ago produced an excessive farm labor force, even in terms of earlier technology. Economic growth in such countries therefore requires major changes in the distribution of the labor force.

In many countries, however, agriculture is not only an occupation for large segments of the population, but also the only way of life to which they are accustomed. The entire social, economic, and political system of such countries may be so tied to agriculture and land ownership as to have created customs and vested interests that will resist changes necessary to increase the per capita production of agriculture. If such social barriers to change are overcome, surplus manpower flows from farm to nonfarm employment, available at low labor costs, and the immediate effects are increased production per man and increased per capita income on the farms. Industry is provided with both cheap labor and an increasing market. The resultant commercial and industrial expansion creates new increments of consumer markets. Industries based on cheap labor therefore may constitute a step in the economic growth of underdeveloped countries.

Farm income per capita, however, can hardly rise far above that of labor income per capita in industry, for in that event surplus labor would remain on the farm, retarding the rise in per capita production and the increase in surplus production on which farm income depends, and hence restricting the increase in total consumer markets. The potential demand of the total domestic market depends on continued increases in farm surpluses, in productivity and income of the mass of urban dwellers—including the rise of a large middle class and of still larger numbers of workers enjoying an income well above subsistence. This cannot be expected to take place, however, if agricultural production per capita remains so low and labor for industry so cheap that there is little incentive for investment in labor-saving machinery. The effect of low agricultural productivity in retarding the development of industry is illustrated by the relatively slow development of consumer industries in the southeastern United States, in spite of the surplus production of coal and other favorable factors. Study of comparable effects in the later stages of economic growth in Japan might yield significant results.

The difficulties encountered by countries where agriculture had reached a relatively mature level of development prior to modern technology emphasize the advantages of countries—e.g., the United

States, Canada, Australia, and New Zealand—whose agricultural economies have been expanding into previously unused land at a time of technological progress. That the countries of temperate South America have had a somewhat similar expansion of agricultural settlement with much less economic growth may reflect the retarding effect of a land ownership system that maintains low productivity per unit of farm population.

These examples remind us that economic expansion into new areas is not economic growth, as defined in this paper, nor in itself stimulating to economic growth. To the extent that settlers in new lands can utilize techniques producing greater outputs per man than in the areas they left, increased commerce is possible, stimulating further economic growth of industries in the country as a whole. Also, the withdrawal of excess farm population from older areas may permit some increase in surplus farm production in those areas. No doubt a major result is the disrupting effect on entrenched attitudes and methods of production, opening the opportunity for essential economic change. As a test case, it would be significant to study the degree to which the expansion of settlement in western Siberia contributed, or failed to contribute, to economic growth in Russia as a whole, either before 1914 or since.

Few if any countries today can hope for expansion into unused lands so ready for exploitation as those settled in recent centuries. Nevertheless, solution of critical problems in the permanent cultivation of tropical lands might create another "new world," into which many countries of South America, Indonesia, and tropical Africa could expand their economies rapidly. The effect on economic growth in the home countries, or elsewhere, would vary with the level of productivity per capita developed in the settlements.

Expansion of agricultural land is not limited to new lands. Even in well-developed countries there is considerable unused land which modern techniques of reclamation may make usable. Countries in northern Europe have been able to increase their agricultural land significantly in the past two centuries, Denmark perhaps most notably in proportion to its size. Modern irrigation in India and in Egypt greatly increased their areas of cultivated land, particularly that used for commercial production. This should have stimulated economic growth, but since new lands were rapidly crowded with more farm families than were needed, the effect on economic growth was minor.

Foreign Markets. With relatively few exceptions, the over-all economic production of any country is consumed predominantly in the domestic market. Even for the United Kingdom, such an expression as "workshop for the world" is misleading; the greater part of its industrial production always has been consumed within the British Isles. Nevertheless, foreign markets are critically important to the economic growth of a state for two reasons: (1) When any of the seven elements previously discussed cannot be produced internally, imports are essential; but they are possible only to the extent that foreign markets purchase the balancing exports. (2) The particular lines of production in which a country develops maximum comparative efficiency, whether because of material resources or developed skills, can be exploited beyond the domestic demand (or even desires) only by serving foreign markets.

A relatively high degree of dependence on foreign markets may result in a disadvantage independent of political consequences. If greater efficiency of production results generally in increased income for both producers and consumers, when industries serve domestic markets such increased income accrues wholly to the producing country, whereas when industries serve foreign markets the increased income of foreign consumers may be widely dissipated in world markets with little advantage to the producing country.

On the other hand, if the countries involved are trading a wide variety of products among themselves, the total stimulus to economic growth may apply to all. In other words, such a group of countries may be functioning largely as a single area of production and marketing. The distinction between "domestic" and "foreign," dictated by statistical sources and political considerations, is much too simple. Some areas are "less foreign" than others, and the difference may be greater than that between domestic and "slightly foreign." This concept arises from consideration of actual conditions of international trade prior to World War II. The greater part of the international trade of each country in northwestern Europe was with the other countries of that group; in many cases the trade was overlapping, reflecting a normal situation of interregional trade which is largely independent of political limits. The Schuman Plan is not a revolutionary economic project but an attempt to facilitate and strengthen what has long existed to some extent—a single economic unit over northwestern Europe.

Canada and the United States likewise form in many respects a single economic unit of production and consumption, in which the economies of several regions of the one are more closely interrelated with the economies of neighboring regions of the other than with more remote areas of the home country.

These two major world areas, northwestern Europe and Anglo-America, are also more closely related to each other than either is to any other part of the world. Consequently, the commercial expansion into new areas of Anglo-America in the nineteenth century was a major asset in economic growth, not only for the older settled areas on its Atlantic seaboard, but also for all northwestern Europe. That such a relationship is not determined merely by the short distance across the North Atlantic is demonstrated by the similar importance, for the United Kingdom at least, of the settlement and growth of Australia and New Zealand. The relationship is not necessarily dependent on the political connection of empire, however, for the United States and the United Kingdom have been more effective as mutual markets stimulating mutual economic growth than India and the United Kingdom have been.

Economic expansion into new areas in the foreseeable future apparently will be limited largely to tropical areas where new or increasing populations will consist predominantly of peoples of non-European (or non-American) culture, accustomed at present to low incomes and standards of living. The extent to which such expansion can provide continued increases in foreign markets for other countries depends on the degree to which it is based on labor-saving technology rather than merely on more utilization of cheap labor.

When "foreign" markets are at a distance, transport costs may be a serious handicap. For the great majority of manufactured products, particularly those finished goods for which the value added by manufacturing is high in comparison with the value of the materials, transport costs increase with the degree of finished production. On a competitive basis within the same industry, it is not, as often stated, the ratio of cost to the value of the material transported that is significant, but the absolute costs of shipment of a certain amount of finished products in comparison with that of the materials necessary to produce that amount of products. Only the few countries that have unusually favorable combinations of natural and human resources for industry can expect to base their over-all industrial development on foreign markets for industrial products.

The domestic economy of many underdeveloped countries depends critically on the export of but one, two, or three commodities of primary production. Even though the exports constitute a small part of the total national production, the situation is precarious to the degree that such production requires imports. The world market for a particular commodity does not necessarily vary with over-all market conditions. Furthermore, as long as most of the world produces surpluses of primary products, and only a few areas produce surpluses of industrial products, countries of predominantly primary production must sell in a buyer's market and buy in a seller's market. If to these normal vicissitudes there is added the disruption that war brings to international trade, the relative importance of domestic and nearby assured foreign markets is even greater in comparison with remote foreign markets. The few exceptions apply to exceptional minerals—notably gold and petroleum—which in the present world situation appear to have a reliable market whatever the production. Countries depending primarily on these, however, have the opposite risk of exhaustion of a nonreplenishable resource.

RELATIVE IMPORTANCE OF THE ELEMENTS OF ECONOMIC GROWTH

The eight elements just analyzed are in many respects not commensurable, but certain summary comparisons may be made.

Every settled country contains some significant resources or it would not be settled. A well-settled country contains a labor force adequate to exploit its agricultural resources. Economic growth may result simply from the use of techniques permitting increased production per man, without decrease in over-all production, releasing part of the labor force for new forms of production. This is possible even though the country may contain no additional natural resources. Capital goods, whether for transport or for particular commercial and industrial enterprises, raw materials for processing, and fuel for mechanical energy can all be imported. For each of these material requirements there are producers in other countries who are able and anxious to expand production. Transport costs for such materials, with the possible exception of mechanical energy, are not a serious hindrance, unless remote interior locations or other places extraordinarily difficult to reach are involved.

For economic growth it clearly is not necessary that a state contain power resources, but it is advantageous if such resources are within or near (in terms of transport costs) its well-populated regions. Whether remoteness from energy resources is an important retarding factor if the distance is largely over sea is not clear.

The *character* of economic development in any country is highly dependent on its ability to secure certain materials at minimum transportation cost—particularly coal and iron ore required for iron and steel industries. The inclusion of such industries within a state, however, is not essential to its economic growth.

The nonmaterial or human elements are far more critical for economic growth, in spite of the demonstrably similar innate abilities of human beings everywhere. The technology of modern economic growth, western technology, is highly mobile; it is cheap, readily available, and can be acquired by all literate peoples. One may therefore anticipate a time when all countries may possess the human requirements for economic growth. The process of transfer, however, may be very slow, not only because of illiteracy, but also because of the retarding effects of cultural attitudes, types of political organization, and so on. For a long time to come, the differences among the well-settled countries of the world in the essential human requirements for economic growth will doubtless be much more important than those in material resources.

The four nonmaterial factors are closely and intricately related to cultural characteristics. Social mobility and mass education, the development of skilled labor, the extent of the spirit of entrepreneurship, habits of saving for investment, and the depth of the consumer market vary together in relation to culture areas, which are generally larger than individual states and tend to expand into neighboring areas. They have expanded in the past into overseas areas, but only where the migrants could dominate the culture of the area into which they migrated.

Location of a state within a culture area favorable to the development of the social characteristics enumerated may perhaps be the most important single factor for its economic growth.

Because the relationships between economic growth and the many cultural factors involved hold true only in general, many intermediate gradations may be found in countries over the world. Nonetheless the over-all pattern is striking in its major contrasts. Unfortunately for the purpose of controlled observation, all the countries in which there is the most advantageous development of the human factors also command coal resources for mechanical energy, either within their confines or close at hand. This is also true, however, of many other countries that are relatively backward in economic development.

CONCLUSIONS AS TO CATEGORIES OF COUNTRIES

Of the three dichotomies proposed by Hoselitz two are largely determined for the state by its circumstances, independent of government decision: that between expansionist and intrinsic, and that between dominant and nondominant. Our analysis of the individual factors determining economic growth permits certain conclusions concerning these two contrasts.

Expansionist versus Intrinsic

Expansion of primary production, particularly through new agricultural settlement in previously undeveloped areas of a state, stimulates economic growth to the extent that the expanding economy is commercial. Abundance of land and the absence of antiquated equipment favor utilization of techniques producing the maximum output per unit of labor; and scarcity of labor is a strong stimulus to develop new labor-saving techniques. The newly created consumer market is consequently richer per capita than that in older portions of the country, but stimulates their commerce and industry. Emigration from the older areas may decrease, or at least lead to a slower rate of increase, in the ratio of farm population to farmland in those areas, and also in the corresponding ratio of labor force to job opportunities in urban areas. The commerce generated in the areas of new settlement may be many times greater per capita than that in older areas of more largely subsistence production. This increase in commerce creates new capital and promotes new entrepreneurs both in the new and older settled areas. The stimulating effects of such expansion into new lands are not limited to the country that includes them, but extend in lesser degree to countries with which it is closely related in international trade, migration, and investment.

Significant expansion into formerly unused lands may take the form of reclamation of districts within older settlements. And similar effects may result from the introduction of new techniques in areas long cultivated, if such techniques make possible increased production both per man and per acre.

Expansion of this kind is less dramatic than the settlement of new lands in previous centuries, but such revolutionary developments are unlikely, save possibly in tropical countries. For the future, more limited and gradual forms of expansion may be more important. In this respect the states of the world can hardly be classified in two contrasting groups; they range from countries undergoing little or no expansion to those in process of moderate expansion of settlement, and the relative positions of the different countries as measured by degree of expansion would vary from decade to decade.

Dominant versus Nondominant

Every country is dependent on others for one or more of the eight factors in economic growth. Every such international economic relation involves dependence in each direction. The degree to which such dependence may restrict or hamper economic growth is not to be measured either by the total quantity of trade involved or by the need for specific items imported; on that basis the United Kingdom would rate as the least independent of all the countries of the world.

Since all eight elements are essential for economic growth, the relative importance of different kinds of dependence is determined by the need for and difficulty of importing the respective elements. The greatest degree of dependence—that is, the situation in which a country is most subject to outside economic control—is that of a country dependent on imports of entrepreneurs, engineers, skilled labor, and capital. Obtaining these from a single foreign state may make an importing country, though politically independent, little more than an economic colony of the outside state.

If the economy of a country depends heavily on foreign markets, the degree to which this constitutes control of its economy varies with the character and variety of the exports. Exporters of primary products, generally speaking, are in a weaker economic position than are exporters of manufactured products. Countries that export only a very few commodities are in the weakest position, but even this generalization has notable exceptions.

For all countries, economic growth necessitates increased dependence on outside countries. The dichotomy between dominant and nondominant is not only a continuum of gradations, but one that cannot be measured by a single index. Whether a state's foreign trade is fairly well distributed among a number of countries, or confined largely to two countries, or overwhelmingly with one country—as illustrated by Switzerland, Canada, and Australia, respectively—is more important politically than economically.

The concept suggested by the term "satellite" seems misleading in the cases of such states as Switzerland and Denmark. These are integral if minor members of the economic community of industrial northwestern Europe; the term may better apply to Eire and Cuba, as predominantly agricultural appendages of neighboring industrial states.

In terms of significance for economic growth, the measure of dependency of greatest importance is not to be found in the statistics of commodity trade, but in respect to elements for which data are generally lacking—dependence on foreign entrepreneurs, labor (including professional labor), and capital.

12 ECONOMIC POLICY

AND ECONOMIC DEVELOPMENT

Bert F. Hoselitz *

It has become almost axiomatic that governmental influence is one of the most important factors in economic growth. Reference is sometimes made to the liberalistic policies of the mid-nineteenth century, but the experience with them either is regarded as a passing episode or is belittled by the assertion that governmental influence operated extensively "behind the scenes," even though it was little visible. This paper will examine the forms and conditions of governmental impact on economic growth in general, and seek to determine both the amount of this impact and the mechanism by which it is exercised.

DIFFERENTIATION OF SOCIAL AND ECONOMIC POLICY

The kinds of policies and decisions to be discussed must be delimited explicitly, for two reasons: (1) If we conceive of the economy of a society as a dynamic system, any governmental act that may impinge directly or indirectly upon the level of economic performance may be interpreted as influencing the (positive or negative) growth of the economy. Analysis of the role of the state in economic growth then becomes commensurate with analysis of any conceivable economic policy, which is clearly far beyond the scope of this paper. (2) As has been observed by many participants in technical assistance to underdeveloped countries, distinctions between economic and social or political policies often become blurred. A governmental health program is an instrument of "social policy," but its impact on the actual or potential economic growth of a society may be far-reaching. Again, analysis of such policies and programs would take us far beyond the limits imposed on this paper.

In a widely accepted view (which was explicitly adopted for the conference) economic growth is associated with an increase of real product

* I wish to acknowledge gratefully extensive critical comments made on an earlier version of this paper by Richard Hartshorne, Simon Kuznets, Henry Rosovsky, and Neil Smelser. These comments have led to numerous improvements of the earlier draft. None of these gentlemen, of course, is responsible for any blunders that remain.

per worker, or even per capita: that is, economic growth implies an increase in the productivity of labor. This may be achieved along three lines: (1) If the average quality of labor is improved, this will enhance, *ceteris paribus,* average productivity. (2) If labor of a given quality is combined more efficiently, the average productivity of labor will be enhanced. (3) If labor of a given quality is combined with more or better capital goods, the average productivity of labor will be increased. In practice, it will often be impossible to combine labor of a given quality with more or better capital, and a change in the quality or quantity of one input usually will entail a complementary qualitative improvement of the other. But this only strengthens the first argument, for if the average productivity of labor increases when there is no change in its quality but there is a quantitative or qualitative improvement of capital inputs, productivity will increase all the more if some such change gives rise to a complementary qualitative improvement in labor inputs.

In terms of practical socioeconomic policies, a government can attempt to increase average productivity of labor along any one or any combination of the three lines. Which of numerous possible courses will be chosen will depend on such "extraneous" data as availability and kinds of resources, type of culture and social structure, and form of political organization, and such "intrinsic" data as quantity and kind of productive factors available and patterns of demand within and outside the society undergoing change. In other words, on this level of generality no useful propositions about the role of the state in economic growth can be made.

Closer inspection of the three lines along which productivity of labor may be increased shows that the first implies mainly the "creation of human capital." This problem may be subdivided into two subproblems. One has to do with the actual improvement of skills or physique of laborers. If governmental measures are required to bring about such improvement, these measures are largely in the field of "social policy," e.g., education on all levels, improvement of health, and the institutionalization or internalization of work practices appropriate to the new tasks faced by a society.[1] The second subproblem has to do with the size of a society's population and the government's possible influence on population size. This is essentially the field of population

---

[1] These points are discussed by Melville Herskovits, "The Problem of Adapting Societies to New Tasks," in Bert F. Hoselitz, ed. *The Progress of Underdeveloped Areas* (Chicago: University of Chicago Press, 1952), pp. 89–112; and Ralph Linton, "Cultural and Personality Factors Affecting Economic Growth," *ibid.,* pp. 73–78.

policy, which has been widely discussed in the pertinent literature. Although the degree of effectiveness of governmental action in this field is disputed, it is generally acknowledged that the state may influence the magnitude and perhaps the over-all rate of growth of the population.[2] Since so-called social and population policies comprise a rather distinct class of public policy, and have their own specialized treatment in the literature, further discussion is not necessary here. Occasional reference will be made to them, however, since they often interact with public policies in other fields.

Two paths of increasing average productivity of labor are left for our consideration: the creation and accumulation of capital, and the development of new forms of productive organization. This paper is concerned chiefly with the role of government policies in these two fields.

Although capital investment and restructuring of productive organization are different types of action and it is often useful to distinguish them analytically, for our purposes we may lump them together. A sizable investment of new capital is normally impossible without restructuring of productive organization; and a thorough reorganization of production in an industry usually requires considerable quantities of capital. Moreover, either of the two procedures or their combination results in an alteration of production functions, owing particularly to changes in inputs of the nonhuman factors of production. Thus our major concern is with the role that a government can play in introducing innovations that tend to bring about these changes. Even when our problem is stated in this relatively narrow form, we are still confronted with a multitude of economic policies, which all directly or indirectly affect the rate of introduction of innovations in nonhuman productive factors. These economic policies can be classified in various ways.

Autonomous and Induced Economic Growth

In order to evaluate the general attitude of governments concerning the degree of regulation and constraint actually employed in economic policy, I have proposed the dichotomy between an autonomous and an induced pattern of development.[3] The concepts of autonomous

[2] See Joseph J. Spengler, "Some Economic Aspects of the Subsidization by the State of the Formation of 'Human Capital,'" *Kyklos*, 4(4):316–343 (1950), and the literature cited there, especially in notes 2, 3, 6, and 7.

[3] See Bert F. Hoselitz, "Patterns of Economic Growth," *Canadian Journal of Economics and Political Science*, 21:423–426 (November 1955).

and induced patterns refer to ideal-typical situations, whereas actual attitudes and policies of governments include some mixture of the two extremes. Since our problem here is posed in narrower form than in the paper in which I first stated the dichotomy, the two ideal-typical situations must be defined in the framework of this paper. With reference to the role of government in introducing innovations that significantly change the production functions employed in an economy, an autonomous pattern of development is one in which ideally all decisions to introduce such innovations are made by private individuals in pursuit of their self-oriented goals or motives. An induced pattern, on the other hand, is one in which all decisions to introduce such innovations are made by government in pursuit of some explicit or implicit objectives. The expected result of an innovation in either case is a change that will lead to an increased average product per worker. Thus the over-all result of autonomous and induced patterns of development is the same, in direction if not in magnitude. Whether a given measure is part of an autonomous or an induced pattern, or the extent to which it is part of either pattern, can be determined by observing whether the decision to introduce the measure was made in pursuit of goals or objectives of public policy or in pursuit of self-oriented ends or motives of private individuals.

The principal advantage of the dichotomy is that it provides a criterion for classifying each decision to introduce innovations. Although in extreme cases a single such decision may have far-reaching effects on growth potential or even on the actual growth of an economy, usually only a set of decisions have such effects. Thus each pattern of growth, autonomous or induced, is assumed to be composed of a set of measures, or decisions to innovate, which together form an intelligible structured system. The various measures or policies included in any such system may have very different positions on a continuum extending from extreme autonomy to extreme constraint.

Various fields of public policy have been examined by Dahl and Lindblom in terms of such continua. They find that the roles played by modern governments in regulating the economies of their countries range from one extreme to the other; [4] but they give examples only of the possibility and indeed the fact that a set of public policies may

[4] See Robert A. Dahl and Charles E. Lindblom, *Politics, Economics, and Welfare* (New York: Harper & Brothers, 1953), pp. 9–18, especially diagrams 1 and 3, pp. 10, 14.

include measures that fall over the whole range. They do not state any-thing about the frequency with which any particular measure is em-ployed, nor appraise the effectiveness of any policy in attaining its objectives. Yet it would be of great importance to know whether measures close to one end of the continuum occur much more often than those close to the other, and whether the over-all effect of one set of measures is significantly greater than that of another. For example, even under a highly liberal system of economic policy, enterprises such as a post office department may exist and be run like any other govern-mental agency. In this case some decisions to introduce innovations in the field of communications are almost routine governmental decisions, at the same time that the absence of governmental regulation of in-dustry in general constitutes a system whose pattern of growth has been predominantly autonomous. On the other hand, the presence of some private small traders or retail cooperatives in a system in which all other industry is government-owned would not weaken the fact that the pattern of growth in that system is predominantly induced. In other words, a list of the points at which various governmental policies may fall on a continuum ranging from full autonomy to full constraint is not enough: we need some indication of the relative weights of each of these policies in the total impact of government on economic growth.

In order to distinguish between autonomous and induced systems (or systems with different degrees of autonomy and constraint), we must first eliminate all aspects of government action that are common to all systems and hence not discriminatory. One such aspect derives from the concept of government as such, i.e., the proposition that government in all systems has a monopoly of power—that only the government (or persons or groups to which it delegates specific powers) has authority to make and enforce generally binding rules. Thus no measure designed to ensure the permanence of this authority, even though the measure may have economic consequences, can be used to discriminate between autonomous or induced systems. In other words, we must distinguish between the content of governmental actions affect-ing the economy and the normal prerogatives and powers that govern-ments share with no one. This distinction is important, since it is often assumed that a "strong" government—one that has abrogated to itself many political powers—also tends to engage in widespread regu-lation of economic affairs. Hence, induced patterns of growth are often assumed to be associated with governments that exercise extensive political powers, and autonomous patterns with governments that, in the words of Ferdinand Lassalle, only perform the roles of night watchmen.

Such a correlation between "strong" governments and induced change, on the one hand, and "weak" governments and autonomous change, on the other, is too simplistic. The amount of governmental interference in the economic process is not correlated with the capacity of an economy to grow, nor with the over-all strength of the government. For example, the mercantilist governments of seventeenth-century Spain ubiquitously regulated the economy, but they were weak governments and little capable of fostering economic growth. On the other hand, the British government in the mid-nineteenth century was both strong and able by its policy of far-reaching laissez faire to promote effectively the growth of the economy. Thus the rate of economic growth is not a simple function of either the strength or the regulatory activity of the government; under appropriate circumstances the best positive contribution a government may make toward economic growth is a negative attitude, i.e., self-denial of economic regulation.

This proposition may be restated as follows: it is wrong to equate "socialism" (extensive economic regulation) with "serfdom" (political authoritarianism), and equating them indicates a lack of historical and analytical sophistication. This means that induced and autonomous patterns of growth cannot be distinguished simply in terms of the over-all degree of political constraint or consensus present in a system. Although it is granted that in autonomous systems there is often a relative preponderance of consensus in the political area, and that induced systems normally are associated with a relatively high degree of political constraint, there are too many exceptions to permit the use of forms of political relations to measure the degree of autonomy or its absence in an economic system.

PATTERNS OF GROWTH RELATED TO DIFFERENCES IN SOCIAL STRUCTURE

Since a set of general propositions regarding the conditions under which autonomous or induced patterns of growth may be expected to prevail cannot be derived by classifying forms of political organization, an attempt to solve this problem may be made by analysis of social structure. I shall present, therefore, in simplified form a model for the analysis of structural-functional properties of social systems and apply it to this problem.[5]

The underlying proposition on which this model is built is that any social system experiences systemic needs or problems, which may be classified in four general categories: (1) Perhaps most fundamental are the problems associated with the maintenance of the prevailing structure and hierarchy of social and cultural values. (2) Next is the need for integration of persons and groups within a society, and for determination of criteria for membership in the society as a whole and in different groups within it. Associated with this is the need for defining the mutual relations arising in the interaction of members of the society or of its subgroups. (3) The need to attain the goals of the social system comprises the third category. These goals are not identical with the sum of goals of the members of the society; in fact, certain private goals of individuals often may conflict with the systemic goals. (4) Finally there is the society's problem of adapting to its environmental conditions. These conditions include the physical, natural environment, the geographical space occupied by a society, and the surrounding social groups with which it interacts. In a crude and superficial way each of the four classes of systemic needs or problems may be related to a special field of analysis. The maintenance of cultural patterns is related to the study of culture; integration is related to the study of solidarity; goal attainment is related to the study of the polity; and the problem of adaptation is related to study of the economy.

If this classification of systemic problems is accepted, we must next clarify the interrelations between institutions and forms of social action that may be taken in dealing with the various problems. Although all societies are constantly under compulsion to solve all four types of problems, different extraneous conditions and differences in the internal structure of a society make the solution of some problems more crucial at certain times than that of others. In other words, as societies develop they face changing overriding needs, though none of the four

[5] This model was elaborated by Talcott Parsons and his associates. It is presented in its most highly developed form in Talcott Parsons, Robert F. Bales, and Edward A. Shils, *Working Papers in the Theory of Action* (Glencoe: Free Press, 1953), Chapter 5; and it is applied to an analysis of the relations between economic activity and social organization in Talcott Parsons and Neil Smelser, *Economy and Society* (Glencoe: Free Press, 1956). An alternative model which could be adapted to our purposes is presented by Marion J. Levy, Jr., *The Structure of Society* (Princeton: Princeton University Press, 1952), especially Chapters 3–4.

categories of systemic problems ever disappears. At times certain needs of a society are so urgent that social action concerning them initiates changes that induce supplementary responses in other fields of social action. For example, the integrative or solidarity problems of a society may become so paramount at some point of its historical development that action designed to meet adaptive needs will respond to attempts to insure solidarity.

Our concern with the role of governments in economic growth makes us especially interested in the mutual relations of the adaptive and the goal-attainment sectors of action of a society. In general, if problems of goal attainment are predominant, the economy will be subjected to extensive regulation to insure meeting the systemic goals more adequately. In case the attainment of systemic goals does not present particular complexities at a certain stage in the development of a society, its adaptive or integrative problems may be dominant. The forms of social action required to meet systemic goals, on the one hand, and to meet integrative or adaptive needs, on the other, are different. In other words, the involvement of the government in social action in a situation in which political goals are paramount differs from its involvement when economic or solidarity problems are to the fore. The attainment of systemic goals, by definition, must be implemented by some person or group representing the society as a whole. This agent is normally the government. Systemic goals often coincide with private goals of members of a society; and the whole problem of governmental constraint versus popular consensus centers around the degree of coincidence between the two types of goals and the relative involvement of private action in defining systemic goals.

In meeting the adaptive and integrative problems of a society there is normally much wider scope for private action. Particularly in meeting the adaptive needs of a society, optimum effects often may be attained by pursuit of private rather than systemic goals; and the over-all scope of private action will depend on a number of circumstances. Chief among these are probably the magnitude of the systemic goals of the society, the time it has, or believes it has, to reach them, and the resources it commands.[6]

Although mention was made of four categories of systemic needs, or

[6] Alexander Eckstein has presented an exposition of these characteristics with special reference to economic growth in "Individualism and the Role of the State in Economic Growth," *Economic Development and Cultural Change,* 6 (2):81–87 (January 1958).

sectors of social action, I shall not discuss the interrelations of the fourth sector, the problems of maintaining the pattern of cultural values, with the other three sectors because the objectives of this essay do not require it and too many complex problems would be involved.

The differences between the forms and agents in each of the integrative, adaptive, and goal-attainment sectors of social action can perhaps be seen most clearly if we examine the systemic problems of an anarchist society. We cannot base this analysis on actual experiences since, apart from the alleged "anarchy" of certain primitive peoples, no anarchistic society has developed. Moreover, the proponents of theories of anarchism make the implicit or explicit assumption that a main condition for the realization of an anarchist society is a high level of economic and technological development. In such a society, then, the problem of attainment or maintenance of systemic goals is essentially absent. An anarchist society dispenses with a polity and political problems. But the various experiments of communal cooperatives—Icaria, Brook Farm, New Harmony, etc.—that in conception have approximated an anarchist society have shown the problem of solidarity to be of paramount importance, and the adaptive problem in second place. In other words, creating an anarchist society depends primarily on meeting the integrative requisites of the society; once this problem is solved more or less permanently, the adaptive problem of how best to meet the private economic goals of members of the society becomes paramount. Clearly, then, in an anarchist society economic growth would be fully autonomous.

We shall now apply the definitions expounded in the preceding paragraphs to the problem of economic policy with respect to growth. We must try first to identify the conditions under which certain systemic problems will take primacy over others, and then to relate concrete economic policies, or fields of economic policy, to a sequence of dominant problems and the means by which they are met.

ECONOMIC GROWTH AND PHASES OF SOCIAL ACTION

As a first approximation or hypothesis let us take the proposition, which I cannot substantiate empirically and which may have only heuristic value, that a society or "civilization" in the course of its historical development passes through several phases of secular evolution: First it is confronted as a major requisite with problems of solidarity, then with those of goal attainment, and finally with those of adaptation. In other words, a newly developing society must first determine who are its members and define their relations to each other, the groups and subgroups they form, the membership of these various bodies, and their respective interrelations. Economic and political (i.e., adaptive and goal attainment) concerns as separate systemic problems are on the whole subordinated to the task of integration. Once the internal "balance" of social interaction and the criteria for membership are stabilized, the society is confronted with the need for explicitly meeting its systemic goals. Economic activity is subordinated to this task, and insofar as the attainment of systemic goals requires the use of economic means, the economy becomes an instrument for attaining the over-all societal goals. Thus whatever economic growth occurs in this phase of development is induced largely by the primary requisite of supporting attainment of the social system's goals. Later, their attainment may become a routine operation, and the attainment of private goals, associated with a predominance of the adaptive sector of the social system, may become paramount. In this phase of societal development, whatever economic growth occurs is autonomous, in that the attainment of systemic goals is routinized and hence less significant than the solution of adaptive problems of the society.

To avoid misunderstanding this schema, it should be emphasized again that all four types of systemic problems are constantly present as a society passes through these phases, which refer merely to the *predominance* of some aspect of social action. In practice this relative primacy of one type of systemic problem manifests itself in the form of social institutions that are being developed in a society and the changing meaning that is attributed to a given institution at different times or in different phases. This may be illustrated by the institution of public office. When a society's goal-attainment needs predominate, public offices are normally under rigorous centralized control and are frequently an important avenue of social advancement—as exemplified in different periods of Chinese history, in the bureaucracies of the early Roman Empire or of the Byzantine Empire at the height of its power, and in the struggle of the French Crown against the *parlements* in the sixteenth and seventeenth centuries and the gradual building up of a staff of *intendants*. Under feudalism, on the other hand, integrative needs appeared predominant, and the holding of public office was a function of the solidarity structure. A public office was held, at least ideally, as a fief; it was exercised in the particularist interest of its holder, and through this interest his integration into the solidarity structure was assured. In a society in which adaptive needs predominate, the interpretation of the function of public office changes, and emphasis is placed on its resemblance to performance in the adaptive sector. In other words, criteria normally applied to business performance become the standard of performance of public services. Thus the content and meaning of public office vary immensely among societies in different phases of social development.

Analysis of the preponderant orientation of different institutions is one of the most reliable empirical indicators of the phase in which a society finds itself. If we examine a number of social institutions that are, in terms of their objective characteristics and perhaps also in terms of their historical origins, instrumentalities of one sector of social action, and if we find that they have important or primary functions in another sector, we may conclude that it predominates, rather than the first. For example, if analysis of institutions that "objectively" have their primary locus in the adaptive sector shows that all or most of them have been "perverted" to serve primarily the attainment of the systemic goals, this finding is strong evidence that the latter sector of social action predominates over the adaptive sector. If a similar relationship is also found between social institutions in the integrative sector and goal attainment, this is even stronger evidence of the dominating position of goal-attainment needs.

Different societies—and the same society in successive phases of its evolution—establish and develop different institutions. The relative predominance of any of the three sectors of social action may be assessed by comparative analysis of a society's institutions. Their total number, the number of new institutions, the relative social significance attributed to various institutions, and the interpretation of their primary functions by members of the society may be used in combination as an "index" of the relative predominance of sectors, although such an index cannot be expressed in a rigorous numerical fashion. Determination of an index must depend on use of the historians' techniques of evaluative analysis of a complex of social institutions. In other words, the test proposed here is not easy, but it should yield as good results as can be obtained at the present time, when quantitative measures of the significance of social institutions are lacking. If several "crucial" periods in the social history of various peoples were analyzed in this way, we might perhaps obtain a basic framework, in terms of which the comparative analysis of social institutions would be an important tool for the over-all evaluation of social dynamics.[7]

---

[7] Social science literature shows that many attempts have been made to come to grips with the comparative study of institutions: The writings on economic stages derive mainly from the German Historical School of economics. The recent flood of

Our proposition that every society passes through several phases, in each of which one particular set of problems—of solidarity, goal attainment, or adaptation—predominates, has certain rough parallels with the schema proposed by Toynbee.[8] The integrative phase corresponds to the initial organizing phase of a new civilization. The goal-attainment phase is that in which the society is working out ways of "responding" to the challenge with which it is confronted. The adaptive phase is that of quiescence, in which the main challenge has been met and the wealth of cultural invention and adaptive imagination available to a civilization can be displayed. But whereas Toynbee's schema is confined largely to tracing the rise and fall of civilizations, no such single line of development is implied in our "model." The transition from an integrative to a goal-attainment to an adaptive phase is merely one general trend, which I believe to be discernible in the secular evolution of societies, although I cannot find that it is theoretically necessary. This trend can be interrupted at any time by extraneous events, which may change the order of primacy of systemic problems, so that a society may return to a condition corresponding to an earlier phase in its development. For example, a society in the adaptive phase may be confronted by a crisis in which integrative or goal-attainment problems again become predominant. In such an event the over-all growth of the society will conform to an induced rather than an autonomous pattern. But the kinds of economic policies selected and applied to induce economic growth in the more "mature" phase will differ from those employed in the less advanced phase, and the differences may be accounted for by the intervening phase during which adaptive problems were dominant.

EXAMPLES FROM THE HISTORY OF WESTERN CIVILIZATION

Our model may be clarified by a few examples from the history of western European civilization. First we shall trace the development of western civilization as a whole, and then consider some special problems raised by the rise and fall of certain nations.

---

publications in comparative history is exemplified by Rushton Coulborn, ed. *Feudalism in History* (Princeton: Princeton University Press, 1956), or the series of *Receuils* published since 1936 by the *Société Jean Bodin pour l'histoire comparée* at Brussels. Since all these efforts lack an adequate basis in sociostructural theory, they fall short of the objective of this essay.

[8] See Arnold Toynbee, *A Study of History* (5th ed.; London: Oxford University Press, 1951), Vol. 1, pp. 271 ff.

Secular Development of Economic Policy

When western European society emerged from the chaos created by the destruction of the Roman Empire and the struggles of the barbarian kingdoms, its main problem was the creation of a new system of solidarity. This was achieved by the gradual evolution of the feudal system between the ninth and eleventh centuries. The feudal system, by imposing a strong personal bond between lord and vassal (a bond adapted from earlier forms of kinship relations) typified solidarity. The economy became completely subordinated to the integrative needs of the system, i.e., the distribution of economic roles conformed, at least ideally, with the status relations created by the feudal hierarchy. However, there were groups outside this hierarchy, and as time went on these extraneous groups—especially the urban communities—increased in size and power. The gradual decline of the system and the replacement of the feudal bond by a bond based on membership in a national state forms the first (integrative) phase of this secular development.

With the rise of national states that competed with one another, the problem of attainment of systemic goals became paramount. This was the period of benevolent despotism or of mercantilism. Schmoller, for example, pointed out that mercantilism

... in its innermost kernel ... is nothing but state making—not state making in a narrow sense, but state making and national-economy making at the same time; state making in the modern sense, which creates out of the political community an economic community, and so gives it a heightened meaning. The essence of the system lies not in some doctrine of money, or of the balance of trade; not in tariff barriers, protective duties, or navigation laws; but in something far greater:—namely, in the total transformation of society and its organisation, as well as of the state and its institutions, in the replacing of a local and territorial economic policy by that of the national state.[9]

Schmoller's interpretation is supported by that of Heckscher, who described mercantilism as a policy aimed at substituting unification of the state for the medieval combination of cosmopolitan universalism and local particularism, and at promoting the power of the state in relation to other states.[10] These interpretations of the political and economic policies of European societies from the sixteenth to the late

[9] Gustav Schmoller, *The Mercantile System* (New York: Macmillan Company, 1896), pp. 50–51.

[10] Eli F. Heckscher, *Mercantilism* (rev. 2nd ed.; London: G. Allen and Unwin, 1935), especially Vol. 2, pp. 16 ff.

eighteenth century have not been disputed in essence. The general conclusion is that considerations of power (attainment of systemic goals in the political field) were paramount, and that economic policies were fashioned to support the states' aspirations for power. But, as Schmoller recognized, these considerations of power were "no mere fancy of the rulers," but the "innermost need of the higher civilization itself that ... enlarged and strengthened forms of social and economic community should come into existence." [11] In other words, the policies of the mercantilist rulers were in conformity with more and less clearly recognized needs of attaining systemic goals, the paramount task of social action.

By the end of the Napoleonic wars the balance of power had become stabilized, at least temporarily. Goal attainment and social action toward that end became routinized, and the society entered the phase of secular evolution in which adaptive needs and the problems of meeting private goals became paramount. Although he has disputed the accuracy of this view, Viner interpreted Heckscher as holding that "for mercantilism wealth was desirable . . . as a means to power, whereas for the latter period [the nineteenth century] power was sought as a means to wealth." At the same time Viner asked, "If in nineteenth-century England and Holland there was less talk of power and more of wealth, may this not have been due to the fact that England then felt herself assured of all the power she felt any occasion to use while Holland recognised that power was unattainable for her no matter how much she pursued it?" [12] The problems of goal attainment in both countries, powerful and weak, apparently had become reduced to routine forms of social action. Diplomacy and international intrigue were practiced and occasional conflicts resulted in wars, but these occurrences did not disturb the essential equilibrium that had been established. Hence, whether we interpret the interrelation between economic and political policies in the nineteenth century as the effect of the conscious subordination of power objectives to welfare objectives, or as the effect of the temporary stabilization of power relations and the routinization of social action toward the attainment of systemic goals, adaptive problems had become dominant.

The beginning of the twentieth century and the era of world wars disturbed this balance. Societies found themselves in crisis, and with

[11] Schmoller, *op. cit.*, p. 49.

[12] Jacob Viner, "Review of Eli F. Heckscher's *Mercantilism*," *Economic History Review*, 6(1):100–101 (October 1935).

the end of World War I a new period was inaugurated in which integrative problems were foremost in some societies and goal-attainment problems in others. Economic measures again were adapted to meet these problems, and a new period of induced growth—wherever growth occurred at all—set in. In the last 30 years, however, two events have tended to blur the distinction between goal-attainment and adaptive needs of western societies, and societies aspiring to imitate and equal them in power and wealth. One was the great depression of the 1930's, and the other was the rise of new states with aspirations for higher levels of economic welfare after World War II. Both involved economic problems, which are met essentially by action in the adaptive sector of society. But the need to overcome the depression and the need for latecomers in the process of economic development to catch up with those on a higher level of economic advancement became objectives of society as a whole, i.e., systemic goals to be attained. The power, stability, and indeed survival of the societies affected by these needs came to depend on the solution of problems of economic growth. The process of economic growth in this phase of secular development, the manipulation of the adaptive sector as a whole, became one of the instrumentalities for meeting the systemic goals of society.

Formation of National States

The preceding description of events in the last few decades indicates that the integrative, goal-attainment, and adaptive phases vary in duration from one society to another, and their dates of incidence depend on the external conditions under which a new society emerges and develops. If an old empire breaks apart and several of its parts form separate states, the first important problem each has to face is that of integration. Each must define its own sovereign area, and prescribe rules for those persons who have become its members.[13]

Problems of integration also appear prominently when new states are formed through combination of parts, or annexation of new territory. For example, such problems clearly predominated in Germany and Italy during most of the early nineteenth century, when those states were undergoing national unification. The dispute over whether Austria-Hungary should be included in or excluded from a greater

[13] For a more detailed discussion of this subject, see Bert F. Hoselitz, "Nationalism, Economic Development and Democracy," *Annals of the American Academy of Political and Social Science*, 305:1–11 (May 1956).

German *Reich* and the gradual process of Germany's unification, first through mutual customs arrangements, later through the formation of the *Norddeutscher Bund,* and finally through the founding of the German Empire and the annexation of Alsace-Lorraine, indicate how new complexities were presented by the problem of integration as some old ones were eliminated. Even with the formation of the German Empire in 1871 the integrative problem was not solved, since Germany continued to be plagued by questions of local autonomy, anticentralist sentiment, and centrifugal political tendencies. But unification did make possible much greater concentration on the attainment of systemic goals, and only the effective resolution of the integrative phase permitted imperial Germany to enter its expansionist phase, in which primary rank was given to meeting the political goals of the society. This changing pattern is clearly exhibited in the policies of Bismarck, especially in what many historians consider the great change in his political views during the 1870's, which was the outward expression of the dimly perceived fact that the society's integrative problems were relatively resolved and that a more concerted attack could be made on the gratification of systemic goals.[14] Italy experienced a similar change in phase at about the same time. France and England also went through the successive stages of integration, goal attainment, and adaptation. Their integrative processes, culminating in the formation of national states, began considerably earlier than those in Germany and Italy and were substantially completed by the beginning of the seventeenth century.[15]

The closer we inspect the patterns of evolution of these and other societies the clearer the differences become, especially in the institutions that developed in each society to implement the needs in each phase, and in the "overlap" between different sectors of social action. For example, in almost no period of the development of Spanish society during the Middle Ages and early modern era were the needs of its solidarity system clearly paramount. Although the struggle to achieve

[14] On Bismarck's political activities see the excellent study by Erich Eyck, *Bismarck and the German Empire* (London: Allen and Unwin, 1950), especially pp. 223 ff.

[15] This process of integration in European societies is well described by Jan Huizinga, "Uit de voorgeschiedenis van ons nationaal besef," *Verzamelde Werken* (Haarlem, 1948), Vol. 2, pp. 97–160, and "Patriotisme en nationalisme in de Europeesche geschiedenis tot het einde der 19e eeuw," *ibid.*, Vol. 4, pp. 497–554, especially pp. 497–516. Cf. also his "L'état bourguignon, ses rapports avec la France, et les origines d'une nationalité néerlandaise," and "How Holland Became a Nation," *ibid.*, Vol. 2, pp. 161–215, 266–283.

unity and settled relations among the Christian countries during the six centuries preceding the fall of Granada may be considered as one aspect of the attempt to resolve the need for integration, this objective was always overshadowed by the more powerful need to attain the goal shared by all non-Muslim powers on the peninsula—reconquest. Thus when integration was achieved, it was impressed on the society from above, as it were, rather than produced integrally out of its conditions of existence. Whether this fact had bearing on the spectacular failure of Spain to exploit its role of political leadership in Europe when it attained its "golden age" is a difficult question to answer. It may be relevant, however, to ask whether the "decadence" of Spain in the seventeenth century had its origins in the imperfect social integration of Spanish society during the Middle Ages.[16]

This discussion suggests that the integration, adaptation, goal-attainment schema can be applied on various levels, and that, depending on the level of application, phases of different magnitude in time and intensity may be indicated. The national state is not the smallest social entity to which the schema can be applied. The social change experienced by an occupational group, a social class, or even a particular locality can be described in terms of the schema.

Evolution of Entrepreneurship

This may be illustrated by a brief discussion of the role of entrepreneurial groups, especially since entrepeneurs have been considered so important as promoters of economic change and advancement. In his study of the stages in the development of capitalism, Pirenne drew attention to the recurring waves of entrepreneurial vigor in European economic history, and derived several generalizations from his findings.[17] Although Pirenne writes about "capitalism," it is clear that he does not have in mind a social system but a group of men, "capitalists,"

---

[16] The voluminous literature on the decadence that afflicted Spain under the later Hapsburg kings lends some force to this interpretation. See, for example, the impressionistic but brilliant exposition by José Ortega y Gasset, *España Invertebrada* (9th ed.; Madrid: Calpe, 1955), pp. 133 ff.; for a factual discussion of the same point, see Maurice Schwarzmann, "Background Factors in Spanish Economic Decline," *Explorations in Entrepreneurial History*, 3(4):221–223 (April 1951).

[17] See Henri Pirenne, "The Stages in the Social History of Capitalism," *American Historical Review*, 19:494–515 (April 1914). I am grateful to Neil Smelser for suggesting that this essay attempted to deal with this problem on a somewhat different level.

or persons who would be designated today as business leaders or entrepreneurs. Thus at the outset he says that "for each period into which our economic history may be divided, there is a distinct and separate group of capitalists," and later he speaks of *"homo capitalisticus."* In general, the entire essay is concerned with the persons who perform "capitalist" actions, rather than with the components that make up a social system.[18] Pirenne concluded that entrepreneurship developed in Western society in a series of spurts, interrupted by periods of quiescence and even crisis; that the periods of spurt were characterized by the prevalence of relative economic freedom, or at least freedom for entrepreneurial activity, and that each period of economic freedom was replaced by one of regulation and control; and that the descendants of business leaders who rose to the top while freedom prevailed tended to lose their innovating and progressive spirit and to become conservative, so that the rising entrepreneurs in the next period came from a new group of "parvenus, brought into action by the transformations of society, embarrassed neither by custom nor by routine, having nothing to lose and therefore the bolder in their race toward profit." [19]

The particular periods during which entrepreneurship of the kind described by Pirenne throve were the twelfth and thirteenth, sixteenth, and the late eighteenth and early nineteenth centuries. The first period coincides with the beginnings of the urban revolution in Europe, the second with the Renaissance and the aftereffects of the discoveries, and the third with the industrial revolution and the rise of European liberalism. In the first period entrepreneurial development was centered in northern Italy and the Low Countries; in the second, in parts of Germany, France, the British Isles, and some Italian republics; and in the third, it spread gradually from Great Britain over the continent. The chief form of entrepreneurship in the first period was long-distance commerce; in the second, international trade combined with colonial exploitation and financial transactions, usually through various kinds of financial operations with governments; and in the third, the development of manufacturing and tertiary industries.

However valuable Pirenne's exposition may be, it does not fully explain the similarities and differences of these phases in the history of entrepreneurship and of entrepreneurs as a social class. Pirenne could not explain, except very superficially, why the first and second phases did not lead to any sizable industrialization, nor why the spread of

[18] *Ibid.*, pp. 494, 504, and *passim.*
[19] *Ibid.*, pp. 514–515.

vigorous entrepreneurial groups remained limited to particular geographical regions. I believe that use of the schema presented in this paper may throw more light on these problems, and also on the effects of freedom and regulation as forms of economic policy.

Each of the periods of entrepreneurial vigor observed by Pirenne coincided with a specific phase in which some systemic problem was paramount in Western society. The first wave of entrepreneurs developed in regions where the integrative system of feudalism was relatively weakest. In northern Italy where the conflicting claims of three overlords—emperor, pope, and Byzantine monarch—clashed, a viable system of feudalism did not develop. Similarly, in the coastal areas of the Low Countries, emanating from Frisia and the Dietmarschen as a center, a nonfeudal stronghold persisted throughout the early Middle Ages. Moreover, the coast of present-day Belgium and the Netherlands was more exposed to the invasion of the Normans than were most other parts of northern and western Europe. Hence the degree of feudal integration in these portions of Europe was relatively weak, and this weakness was enhanced by the somewhat controversial status of the Low Countries between French and Imperial overlordship.[20] The different form of social development in these interstices of the feudal system of social integration appears, therefore, as a phenomenon explicable in terms of strong environmental and internal social-structural conditions.

Thus the early commercial cities developed, on the whole, in regions where feudalism had failed in the task of social integration. At first these early cities were antifeudal institutions, creating their own integrative ties and criteria for membership. Once these independent entities had come into existence, however, and had begun to play a role of their own, even feudal overlords founded fortified urban places, to which they granted special privileges, as a means of supporting their own policies of goal attainment.[21] With the development of more vigorous internal structures in the "free" cities, on the one hand, and the use of cities as a means of pursuing political goals, on the other, regulation of the internal and external economic (and political) relations of the citizens became increasingly imperative for those who controlled

---

[20] On the regional distribution of feudal institutions and their greater and lesser strength in various parts of medieval Europe, see Marc Bloch, *La société féodale* (Paris: A Michel, 1939), Vol. 1, pp. 271 ff.

[21] On this point with reference to lower Germany, see Gisela Vollmer, *Die Stadtentstehung am unteren Niederrhein* (Bonn: Ludwig Röhrscheid, 1952), pp. 5–6.

elite positions in the cities. The original freedom of movement and of enterprise was curtailed by measures of control and regulation, with the consequences that Pirenne has so eloquently described. In other words, in the early stages of commercial development in twelfth-century Europe the adaptive goals of private merchants had ample room for free play, but they were gradually subordinated to the integrative and goal-attainment needs of the ruling groups in the cities; this fact is illustrated by the regulation of economic activity in the interest of "higher" political or integrative goals.

In the second phase of entrepreneurial vigor (in the sixteenth century), as in the period that followed the cessation of Norman and Magyar invasions, a series of incidents particularly favored the prominence of certain adaptive needs. New trade routes and, indeed, an entirely new world were opened and became accessible to the entrepreneurs of west European countries. Most directly affected by these developments were Spain, France, and England, and the European provinces or cities that may be regarded as their economic and political satellites. Thus the financial magnates of southern Germany, the Low Countries, and the cities of northern Italy—particularly Genoa—were completely dependent on the changing fortunes of Spain.[22] Spain and England were then preoccupied with problems of goal attainment. National unification had been attained, and religious unity, although somewhat disturbed in England, was never seriously threatened. In France, also, national unification had been attained, notably after the incorporation of Burgundy, but the religious wars brought integrative problems to the fore, at least temporarily. It seems clear that in all three countries entrepreneurs had relative freedom of activity in only two fields: in overseas trade and exploration, or in financial and other economic operations that were designed ultimately to support the goal-attainment needs of the political leadership. That the area of free entrepreneurial activity should be circumscribed by the goal-attainment needs of the political rulers was not questioned; and the total amount of regimentation attempted by means of patents, privileges, tariffs, duties, subsidies, prohibitions, and other forms of control was similar in the three countries. If in the long run economic regulation was less comprehensively enforced in England than in France, this was not because of

---

[22] See Rámon Carande, *Carlos V y sus banqueros: la Hacienda real de Castilla* (Madrid: Revista de Occidente, 1949), *passim;* Fernand Braudel, *La Méditerranée et le monde méditerranéen a l'epóque de Philippe II* (Paris: Colin, 1949), pp. 535–536, 784 ff.

any lack of ambition on the part of British monarchs and their ministers, compared with their French counterparts, but because of the different pattern of social and political integration in the two countries. In France the political and administrative unification of the country was based ultimately on the development of the office of *intendants* and the gradual loss of power by the local *parlements, baillis,* and other officers. In England far-reaching local autonomy remained the basis of political and administrative unification, and hence the enforcement of economic regulations met with greater obstacles and was thwarted more often than in France.[23]

The third and doubtless most important entrepreneurial revival, in the late eighteenth and early nineteenth centuries, falls in the period in which we have found great emphasis on adaptive needs in Western civilization. The variety of entrepreneurial action was larger than in the two previous periods of entrepreneurial vigor. Whereas the emphasis had been on long-distance trade and the financing of large-scale operations, usually affecting the financial needs of governments, entrepreneurs in this last phase concentrated on industrialization, trade, and other services of greater local significance. Instead of filling interstices in a social system, adaptive behavior tended to impinge on other forms of social action, and the performance in these other fields was judged often in terms of norms established in the adaptive sector of society. The developing crisis in the twentieth century altered this relationship between adaptive problems and those of goal attainment so that the phase of unfettered entrepreneurship was followed by another period of regulation and control of enterprise.

It would be difficult to say that this change has led to any significant decrease in the growth potential of those societies that have already passed through a phase of liberalistic entrepreneurship. The empirical findings available suggest that rates of secular growth in several Western countries were higher in the period preceding World War I than afterward.[24] It is not clear, however, whether the differences in magnitude of the rates are due to regulatory practices or to the widespread political and economic instability of the period. Some countries that experienced a relatively high degree of control, e.g., Russia, Italy, and to

[23] See John U. Nef, *Industry and Government in France and England, 1540–1640* (Philadelphia: American Philosophical Society, 1940), Chapter 2, especially pp. 35–57.

[24] See Simon Kuznets, "Quantitative Aspects of the Economic Growth of Nations: I. Levels and Variability of Rates of Growth," *Economic Development and Cultural Change,* 5(1):15 (October 1956).

some extent Sweden, show higher rates of growth in the twentieth century than in the period before World War I.

An important conclusion may be drawn from this analysis of entre-preneurship as a social institution at different periods in the historical development of the Western world, particularly if we scrutinize the re-lation between governmental control of entrepreneurial activity and capacity for economic growth. In all periods entrepreneurship and the unfettered pursuit of adaptive needs exerted a marked effect on eco-nomic growth. But in the earlier periods entrepreneurial activity was confined to special geographical or functional areas, and as soon as integrative or goal-attainment needs tended to become paramount in these areas, entrepreneurship tended to become routinized and weak, and economic growth was seriously slowed or halted altogether. Where it continued, it had to adapt itself to the integrative or goal-attainment needs that were now predominant. In the third period of entrepre-neurial vigor, adaptive needs in most west European societies became so strong that they contributed to the formation of an integrated pattern of social action embracing all the sectors of the system, so that even when goal-attainment or integrative needs ultimately became paramount, the adaptive institutions that had been created were more adaptable to meeting these needs than before. Principles of action that had been developed in the adaptive sector could be transferred to goal attainment without loss in meaning or effectiveness; and the objectives of existing institutions, originally predominantly adaptive, could be deflected to serve goal attainment. The transition in capitalist countries from a system in which ultimate control was exercised by entrepreneurs to one in which it is exercised by managers is a case in point.[25]

FORMS OF INDUCED GROWTH: HORIZONTAL VERSUS VERTICAL PLANNING

The development of modern planning techniques and the recent proliferation of attempts to promote induced economic growth provide another illustration. At the present time, as in the mercantilist period, economic growth tends to have strong induced features. The economic policies of both periods may crudely be called "planning," simply as a succinct term for a general set of economic policies emanating

[25] For further illustration see Talcott Parsons and Neil J. Smelser, "A Sociological Model for Economic Development," *Explorations in Entrepreneurial History*, 8(4): 191–193 (April 1956); but see also the criticism by Hugh G. J. Aitken, "Professor Parsons' Puzzle," *ibid.*, 9(2):99–103 (December 1956).

from a situation in which a pattern of induced rather than autonomous growth predominates. To distinguish mercantilist and modern planning, I call the former "horizontal" planning, and the latter, "vertical" planning. Alternative designations are "comprehensive" planning, or planning in breadth, for "horizontal" planning; and "selective" planning, or planning in depth, for "vertical" planning. I shall use these terms interchangeably.

Horizontal planning designates an economic policy under which regulatory activity embraces a mass of specific rules for many minute transactions and forms of economic behavior. A good example is an economic plan that makes detailed provisions for the outputs of various industries and plants, sets up an extensive system of priorities and allocations of materials, and minutely prescribes prices and conditions of exchange. The early plans of the Soviet Union and its satellites approximate this type of planning. Another example is the characteristic economic policy of a mercantilist state, which often minutely regulates conditions of production, consumption, and exchange. Tolls, sumptuary laws, guild regulations, rules for state enterprises, premiums, prohibitions, tariffs, exchange controls, staples, patent rights, monopoly privileges, and many other regulatory features characterize this system. The usual outcome is that such a system is overdetermined, regardless of whether it is a "rational" plan or more *ad hoc*. Thus a working economy is possible only if the regulations are disobeyed when necessary, or if the system is allowed to break down at some points. Examples of such breakdowns in the Soviet production plans are the many cases of underfulfillment; in the mercantilist system, the frequency of smuggling and other ways of circumventing prohibitions.

Vertical planning designates an economic policy under which regulatory activity is concentrated in a limited number of spots that have crucial significance for a wide range of economic action. Examples of vertical planning are the system of functional finance proposed by Lerner, and the socialist planning of a "market economy" type proposed by Lange.[26] In general, policies of price control and direct allocation are characteristics of horizontal planning; and monetary and fiscal policies, of vertical planning. Many regulatory systems even in the most advanced countries, which rely primarily on planning in depth, often

---

[26] See Abba P. Lerner, *The Economics of Control* (New York: Macmillan Company, 1944), Chapter 24; and Oscar Lange, *On the Economic Theory of Socialism* (Minneapolis: University of Minnesota Press, 1938), pp. 72 ff.

include elements typical of horizontal planning; and *vice versa,* in some systems of horizontal planning, elements characteristic of vertical planning may be encountered. Vertical or selective planning is more resistant to breakdown or evasion than is horizontal or comprehensive planning, although they may be equally efficient in their ultimate regulatory impact.

It would be wrong, however, to charge the mercantilist policy makers for not having devised vertical planning. The introduction of such a system is contingent upon completion of an adaptive phase, or at least upon acceptance of the policies from an outside society that has passed through such a phase. The basic difference between a characteristic measure of horizontal planning and one of vertical planning lies in the former's normally rigorous prescription of kinds of action, and the latter's imposition of limits within which the individual is free to pursue maximization of his private goals. A crude example of this difference, from the field of commercial policy, is the contrast between an import license and an import tariff. The recipient of a license is told precisely what he may do: he may import a specific quantity of a particular commodity from a given source under certain conditions at a given time for a given price. The importer confronted with a tariff can act freely in pursuit of his own private goals, provided that in pursuing them he observes the existing tariff regulations. The net effect of both policies in terms of total imports of a given commodity in a given year may be the same. The difference between the two methods does not lie in their effects,[27] but in the fact that vertical planning consciously sets conditions in which the adaptive system can operate to maximize its support of systemic goals. Under horizontal planning the adaptive sector is directly placed in a position of subservience to the attainment of systemic goals.

[27] I do not imply that the ultimate effects of horizontal and vertical planning will not differ under any conceivable conditions. Situations may exist, such as the famous instance of the beleaguered city, in which the only effective policy measures are methods of horizontal planning, i.e., direct allocation. Probably one could list many situations less artificial than the beleaguered city in which horizontal and vertical planning would lead to different results, or in which only one type of policy would be possible; but this is not an issue here. What particular measures of economic policy can or should be adopted in a particular situation will depend on a number of factors, chief among them the primary goals sought, the means and resources available, and the political and social relations prevailing in the society. Our discussion is concerned primarily with the differences in social structure that are related to differences in economic policy, i.e., in forms of planning.

SUMMARY AND CONCLUSIONS

The core problem of this paper was to examine the distinction between autonomous and induced growth patterns, elaborated in an earlier paper, and the conditions in which each pattern develops. Since governmental policies may be brought to bear on the quality and quantity of both human and nonhuman resources available to an economy, and since determination of the supply of the human factor involves a number of difficult but separable problems, analysis of the contrast between autonomous and induced growth was confined to the role played by government in fields of public policy that impinge on the supply or use of nonhuman resources.

Using this restricted connotation of the concepts of induced and autonomous growth, I have tried to relate them to differences in political organization and social structure, and have found certain empirical correlations between changes in structural-functional relations experienced by a society in its secular development and changes in patterns of economic growth. Although it was not possible to develop a theoretical model to explain fully the phases through which a society passes, it was possible to show, on theoretical grounds, why an induced pattern of economic growth is correlated with a phase in which problems of goal attainment predominate, and why an autonomous pattern of growth is correlated with a phase in which adaptive problems predominate. The reasons for this correlation were found in the positions of the goal-attainment and the adaptive sectors of action in relation to one another in different phases, and in the necessary consequences of this changing relation of the two sectors for economic policy, especially economic policy that affects the supply of capital and the form of productive organization.

Although a correspondence between patterns of economic growth and phases in the secular societal development can be established, the secular development of societies does not follow an invariant trend. In the most general model I argued that there are reasons to expect the predominance of the integrative phase to be followed by that of the goal-attainment phase, and this in turn by the predominance of the adaptive phase; but we found that this process may be interrupted at any point through the intervention of "extraneous" factors, and that such intervention may alter the relative hierarchy of systemic problems. Among the possible changes, the one of greatest interest was the reappearance of a crisis situation in Western society in the last 40 years, which has made goal-attainment needs again predominant—after a phase in which adaptive problems and the need to meet private goals had predominated in most west European countries. During that phase the degree of prominence of the adaptive sector varied in relation to the degree of effectiveness with which goal-attainment problems could be routinized in different countries. For example, in Great Britain, the Netherlands, and the United States, where these problems were relatively successfully routinized, the predominance of adaptive needs was clearer than in Germany, where the process of national unification was a systemic problem of overwhelming importance during most of the nineteenth century. In central Europe the emancipation of adaptive action from goal-attainment needs never became as clear-cut as in Great Britain or the United States, and economic growth was never as clearly autonomous in Germany as in those two countries. Nevertheless, even in Germany adaptive problems played a very prominent role.

The temporary dominance of adaptive problems and of private goal-attainment as a social value of high status had the effect of changing the forms and techniques of economic policy, when systemic goal-attainment once again occupied a position of primacy in western societies. Instead of systems of horizontal planning, which had characterized earlier phases of development, systems of vertical planning could now be adopted. Since these systems flow out of a society in which adaptive needs occupy a high place and can be operated efficiently only in an economy that is itself highly complex, functionally specialized, and relatively highly productive, their introduction is contingent upon these conditions. Individual measures characteristic of vertical planning may be employed at almost any level of economic advancement, but a whole system of vertical planning is effective only in a society with highly specialized and complex economic institutions. For this reason the transfer of vertical planning systems to societies that are only beginning a process of industrialization and modernization encounters many obstacles and difficulties. We find, therefore, that insofar as latecomers in industrialization undertake developmental planning (i.e., induced patterns of growth), they employ either horizontal systems or, at best, systems in which measures characteristic of both horizontal and vertical planning are combined.

On the basis of this analysis we may conclude that autonomous patterns of growth are rather rare. They develop only in societies in which the integrative and goal-attainment problems have been reduced to the point where they require more or less routinized action. In other terms, autonomous growth takes place only in societies in which a fairly high degree of internal sociostructural equilibrium has been achieved, and in which the distribution of political power throughout the social structure and the power relations between the society as a unit and similar surrounding units have reached rather high degrees of stability. This situation is not likely to occur often, and only a few genuine cases of autonomous growth are on record. Most of them took place in Europe and overseas countries inhabited chiefly by European populations, and were confined to a period that began not much earlier than the eighteenth century and ended with the great world conflicts in the twentieth century. Our records of the economic history and forms of economic growth in earlier societies are too incomplete to permit any sure recognition of periods of autonomous economic growth in other civilizations than the modern Western world.

Induced patterns therefore must be regarded as the more typical form of economic growth. But we may distinguish two contrasting types of induced growth. One type is characteristic of relatively poor societies in which the government either directly participates in the allocation of nonhuman (and often also human) resources, or regulates and controls a large mass of often minute actions in the economic field. The other and more "modern" type of induced growth is characterized by vertical planning or planning in depth, i.e., the manipulation of a few strategic factors so that within more or less narrow limits private behavior directed toward the gratification of private goals is possible and, indeed, expected. This type of economic policy can function effectively only in an economy with highly specialized institutions, capable of a relatively high level of productivity.

The techniques of this type of economic policy form a body of organizational and administrative tools, which can be taken over by societies whose economies have not reached the required levels of productivity and functional specialization. Vertical planning normally will not function too efficiently in these societies, and their actual patterns of induced growth will be based on a mixture of policy measures drawn from the more modern and the more "antiquated" systems of economic policy. As these latecomers in economic modernization gradually develop more specialized institutions and patterns of action, and as their average level of productivity rises, they will be able to "modernize" their economic policies.

If the current political crisis of the mid-twentieth century can be overcome, goal-attainment problems may again recede in importance and perhaps even become routinized, and adaptive problems again assume predominant significance. In this event even the latecomers in economic modernization may experience a phase of autonomous economic growth. It is perhaps too optimistic to expect these developments to take place. In their absence we must expect future economic development in all parts of the world to follow at best induced patterns of growth of the vertical, selective planning type.

13 THE STATE AND ECONOMIC GROWTH: SUMMARY AND INTERPRETATION

Joseph J. Spengler

Sacrifice on behalf of the individuality of the state is the substantial tie between the state and all its members and so is a universal duty.—George W. F. Hegel, *Philosophy of Right* (1833).

State power has an unbroken record of inability to do anything efficiently, economically, disinterestedly or honestly.—Albert J. Nock, *Our Enemy, The State* (1935).

In this essay I shall attempt to summarize the papers included in this volume, and to provide an account of some of the issues that arose at the conference. Salient points are noted in the several summaries below, but not the supporting evidence. Comments and interpretation are introduced where relevant, but principally toward the close.

It will be recalled that the countries dealt with were classified in terms of three criteria: whether economic growth had been principally *expansionist,* through exploitation of unutilized resources, or *intrinsic,* through more intensive utilization of resources already in use; whether the economy was essentially self-contained and hence *dominant,* or highly dependent on foreign markets and resources and hence *nondominant* or *satellitic;* and whether economic growth was *autonomous* as a result of decisions by private agencies in pursuit of private goals, or *induced* as a result of decisions by the same agencies that made political decisions. It was further assumed that a country's position on any one of the three continua was independent of its position on each of the other two, so that eight types of growth were possible: (1) expansionist, dominant, autonomous; (2) expansionist, dominant, induced; (3) expansionist, nondominant, autonomous; (4) expansionist, nondominant, induced; (5) intrinsic, dominant, autonomous; (6) intrinsic, dominant, induced; (7) intrinsic, nondominant, autonomous; (8) intrinsic, nondominant, induced. The number would be fewer if a country's position on one continuum were correlated with its position on another. It was supposed that countries illustrative of each of the eight types could be found. Classification in any given cell was recog-

353

nized as time-bound, however, since a country tends to pass from an expansionist to an intrinsic stage, may show change over time in degree of state intervention, and may pass from a nondominant to a dominant stage.

DETERMINANTS OF ECONOMIC GROWTH—
UNITED STATES, CANADA, AUSTRALIA

This section summarizes the general paper by Hartshorne and the papers by Broude, Aitken, and Butlin. Hartshorne argues that a country's growth potential depends on material and nonmaterial conditions. Its actual growth, as compared with its potential, depends in part on whether interest in economic development is subordinated, by those who control the apparatus of state, to power considerations, attempts to extend a state's territorial sway, etc. His argument suggests that a ceiling is put on a country's growth potential by its material conditions, and that, however effectively a country uses its resources, its industrial structure will reflect its material plenty and shortages. Much more significant is his argument that in various ways, but especially through commerce, a country may surmount deficiencies in at least three of the four main material conditions (i.e., transport facilities, physical capital equipment, raw materials) on which growth depends. He remarks that it may be very difficult to surmount a shortage of energy sources; if suitable coal is not economically available, development of an iron and steel industry is greatly restricted; furthermore, industrial development in general is handicapped in places far from the sea but dependent on overseas sources for power. Of the four strategic nonmaterial factors —entrepreneurship, capacity to finance capital formation, skill of labor force, and accessibility to suitable markets—the first two are highly intercorrelated and all four tend to develop together. Accessibility to foreign as well as to domestic markets is crucial when a country is dependent on foreign sources for raw materials, capital equipment, etc. The capacity of a state to affect the course of economic growth thus ultimately depends on its capacity to modify one or more of the nonmaterial conditions on which such growth depends, to increase the efficiency with which it exploits its resources, and to overcome deficiencies in material conditions.

Although Hartshorne emphasizes the nonmaterial determinants of economic growth, he does not anticipate that the underdeveloped parts of the world (embracing about two thirds of the world's population, of which perhaps nearly one fourth are now making progress) will soon attain anything like the degree of development found in already developed parts (inhabited by close to one sixth of the world's population). He does not foresee much expansion into new areas outside the tropics; but he indicates the possibility of some expansionist development even in countries that are already well-settled, and of even greater expansionist development in countries with relatively low population density (roughly below 25 per square mile) or still amenable to exploitation through highly mechanized agriculture.

During the periods covered, the United States resembled Canada and Australia in being both expansionist and autonomous (although much less strongly so than was formerly supposed); it differed in being dominant and perhaps also in being somewhat more autonomous. Broude's analysis of growth in the United States before 1890—expansionist and (abstracting from the influx of immigrants, capital, and know-how) dominant—reveals that decisions having to do with the formation and employment of capital were significantly affected by political agencies. More generally, economic functions performed by government at its several levels exceeded what may be considered the minimal: governments afforded protection and stimulus to capital formation and participated in a wide range of activities, although always in an economy that was predominantly laissez-faire in ideology [1] and in practice, and that became more autonomous about the middle of the century. Not only did government create a favorable climate and an optimistic state of expectations; it also assumed critical or marginal risks and, on

---

[1] Whether there was less demand for intervention by governments in the 1840's and 1850's and perhaps for a while after the Civil War than in 1820–40 has not been clearly resolved. It is to be expected that, in proportion as minimal requirements for economic growth are brought into being, whether under public or private auspices, demands for state intervention will diminish, ceteris paribus. Sidney Fine reports that after 1840 the promotional activities of the states diminished, that laissez faire predominated in academic and popular ideological writings until the close of the period Broude is treating, and that the courts made laissez faire the law of the land during this period (which was followed by a period during which state intervention greatly increased). See his Laissez Faire and the General-Welfare State (Ann Arbor: University of Michigan Press, 1956), pp. 23 ff., 47 ff., 127 ff. R. M. Havens reports, however, that whereas before the Civil War American presidents were more disposed to proclaim laissez faire than to adhere to it when confronted by concrete problems, later in the century they not only gave less unqualified approval to laissez faire but also recommended departures from it more frequently. See his "Laissez-faire Theory in Presidential Messages during the Nineteenth Century," Journal of Economic History, Vol. 1, Suppl. (1941), pp. 86–95.

occasion, gave direct and specific support to private industry. One is impressed both by the importance of the role played by government land grants—particularly in contrast with the restrictive influence of the Wakefield theory as applied in Australia and Canada [2]—in fostering economic development, and by the aggregate amount of growth stimulation from relatively minor governmental influences (e.g., psychological impact of mere presence of government, accessibility to government credit, and governmental expenditures, which were developmental in effect although not specifically identifiable as such).

One gains at least two impressions from Broude's account: (1) Conditions in the United States were such that, when the minimal requirements for growth had been met, the growth process got under way with much greater assistance than in Canada and Australia from heavy immigration (fostered by an absence of restriction and of social rigidities such as were introduced into Latin America and perhaps other areas from Europe). (2) When the minimal conditions had been met in the East and viable concerns and enterprises had been established there, these could facilitate the development of the West and thus make recourse to public aid less necessary than it otherwise would have been. Throughout most of the period, it was necessary only to turn over capital and land to profit-seeking entrepreneurs and promoters to get the growth process under way. A survey of the growth-promoting activities of state governments might reveal that the scope and form of such activities were affected, especially in newer states, by the availability of strong private enterprise in the East.[3]

Broude draws attention to three issues of great significance for the subject of this conference: the impact of expansion on autonomy; the importance of strategic sorts of governmental expenditure which break bottlenecks or otherwise start private activities when potentials are present; and the role of intersectoral relations and interregional communication of economic stimuli. On the first issue it might be argued, Broude suggests, that the westward advance of the frontier and its impact on American experience made the role of the central government smaller than it otherwise would have been. He does not, of course, have in mind the decentralization of decision making that

2 See Brinley Thomas, *Migration and Economic Growth* (Cambridge, England: Cambridge University Press, 1954), pp. 202–208.

3 I have in mind growth-promoting activities, not growth-restricting or purely regulatory activities inspired by fear of exploitation, of being reduced to "colonial status," etc.

eventually tends to accompany full development of a country's border and similar lands and the continuing increase of its per capita income. With respect to the second, barriers to development that, for economic or other reasons, often were beyond the powers of private enterprise to remove proved to be removable through small outlays by government. The cumulative impact of such intervention seems to have been considerable; yet Broude suggests that the importance of this leverage effect may have been exceeded by the allocative influence exerted by governmental policy and spending. On the third issue, in addition to the important multiplier and other stimulating effects of various governmental expenditures, both governmental and private expenditures in particular sectors produced multiplier and stimulating effects in other sectors, along lines suggested by Chipman and Duesenberry. Unfortunately the extent of this intersectoral influence has never been assessed with care. Presumably the sectors composing the American economy were much less closely interconnected before the Civil War than thereafter, with the result that intersectoral influence, which was demonstrably great after 1865, may have been much less during the first half of the century.

The histories of Canada and Australia differ notably. According to Aitken, the state (here understood to include provincial and local governments as well as the federal government established in 1867) continued to play an important role in the economic development of Canada for many decades after Lord Durham had called attention in 1839 to this accepted function of Canadian government. A developmental role was played by provincial governments, but with regional objectives in view, prior to confederation, for Canada then consisted of regions with quite diverse interests that underwent modification (particularly because of changes in American policy) but never were represented to any province's satisfaction by a British government with transcending imperial concerns. Two circumstances seem to have been largely responsible for the extent of state intervention in Canada: (1) the inability of unassisted private enterprise to carry out, in a sparsely populated and not well-integrated economy, many of the developmental projects required; and (2) growing recognition that the political and economic autonomy of Canada could not be preserved, and that the aspirations of various of the provinces could not be realized, unless the economy of the country were integrated into a national entity and guarded against competition and encroachment from the South—unless, in short, the government induced defensive expansionism. In the achievement of the latter the federal government played a leading part, just as the provincial governments had earlier played a part in the financing and development of transport, banking, etc. Underlying the content and the timing of Canadian economic policy, Aitken finds, has been pressure on the government to help producers of staples (particularly fish, fur, timber, wheat, minerals) surmount their production and distribution problems and obtain favorable prices in important foreign markets.

The pillars of Canadian national economic policy after federation were the government's support of the construction of the Canadian Pacific Railroad (not completed until 1885) and additional transcontinental lines, and the establishment in 1878 (a quarter century after demands had first been made) of a system of national tariff protection, which was intended, among other things, to attract immigrants and capital, foster industry, and thus provide traffic for the newly established but under-utilized transport system. Through these actions, not possible until after confederation, east-west arteries were established, the west was opened to exploitation, and an industrial basis was established in Ontario and elsewhere. Moreover, although private enterprise carried through the construction, the basic developmental decisions were made by governmental bodies. In the twentieth century the state continued its interventionist role, presumably to assist economic development. Among its objectives have been stabilization of the western wheat economy, together with reduction of some of the costs and risks in agriculture; facilitation of the exploitation of Canada's quasi-monopolistic position in the newsprint industry; completion of construction of the St. Lawrence Seaway and hydroelectric power sources associated with it; and, since World War II, regulation of the oil and gas industries in the light of Canada's supposed industrial requirements.

Detailed comparisons between aspects of Canadian and other American economic development probably would be illuminating. The role of the state tended to be larger in Canada (and even in Australia) than in the United States because the minimal requirements for economic development were not met so early. Undoubtedly, the role of the state in Canada would have been even larger in recent years were it not for the strength of private enterprise in the United States. Such enterprise has contributed appreciably to Canada's industrial growth, thereby saving Canada some of the initial developmental expense involved. Illustrative at the moment are the contributions being made to the development of Canada's mineral resources; without these contributions the state might have had to make considerable outlay. Again, the United States probably made interventionism less necessary by pursuing a policy of free immigration, for failure to pursue such policy must have retarded Canada's economic growth appreciably. It is probable, too, that social-structural factors affected Canada's growth as much as (if not more than) that of the United States. These factors probably account in part for the smallness of Canada's gross immigration; they account in part for interprovincial differences in economic development; they may have contributed to the strengthening of the Canadian constitution, drawn up when the dangers implicit in states' rights had just been underscored by a war to the south. Finally, Aitken's study supports the general thesis that search for national security always strengthens the economic role of the state, the validity of which was not appreciated in the United States until 1917.

Butlin's account suggests that if one abstracts from the response of the Australian colonies to the depression of the 1890's—itself partly an outcome of the policies pursued in 1860–90—the impact of government on economic development was more indirect in Australia than in Canada. Australia was not so strongly confronted by the need to transform itself into a national economy, even though federation in Australia, as in Canada, was furthered by the fact that the colonies or provinces became aware that they had many common interests. The relatively more rapid progress of urbanization in Australia, although probably facilitated by governmental expenditure, must have intensified the need for governmental investment in economic and social overhead capital in Australia as compared with Canada.

Whereas Australian governments played somewhat of a developmental role before 1860, only after that date did the role become quite significant, and then probably less significant than in Canada, at least after confederation. The developmental role played by government in Australia consisted primarily in encouraging and assisting immigration and in investing funds borrowed abroad—about one half of Australia's capital imports during the period covered—in economic and social overhead capital, including railroads. Tariffs were introduced by colonies, at first largely to provide revenue, but are not described as having contributed notably to industrial development. Even the government's assuming of responsibility for railroad construction came about somewhat accidentally, prompted by the belief that governments could borrow the needed British funds more cheaply and in larger amounts than could private enterprise—of which there apparently was a dearth.

When subsequent experience proved that governments could finance and build railroads, it was no longer urged that rail transport be developed by private enterprise.

Among the more interesting of Butlin's findings is that respecting the shorter-run retardative effect of relatively heavy expenditure by the government of funds borrowed abroad or obtained through land sales. While much of this money was expended on railroads, they were so situated and so constructed that they did not begin to pay significant social dividends until after World War I. Meanwhile, heavy government expenditure, whether for railroads or other purposes, contributed greatly to the establishment and maintenance of a sellers' market for labor, since the colonial governments did not attract or assist enough immigrants to offset increases in the demand for labor occasioned by governmental borrowing abroad and spending in Australia. Wages advanced rapidly, therefore, and a strong trade-union movement came into being; the growth of those forms of industry and agriculture in which labor played a relatively important role was impeded, and activities in which labor was relatively less important (e.g., the pastoral) were unduly favored. In consequence a sufficiently differentiated labor force did not develop. Presumably, the fact that part of the multiplier effect of government expenditures flowed abroad did not affect the economy adversely until the 1890's, when employment was no longer full, as it had been during most of the three preceding decades.[4]

As has been implied, Australia's situation differed from that of Canada in at least two respects: (1) Australia was much farther from sources of population and capital and from markets; and (2) it was free of both the advantages and the disadvantages of being situated on the borders of an economically powerful neighbor. Australia therefore must have experienced more difficulty in establishing the minimal requirements for development, although this difficulty probably was reduced somewhat by the concentration of its population. The Canadian economy appears to be freer of rigidities than the Australian, in part because labor has not been so homogenous and in such short supply and in part because of the continuing competition and example of the economy to the south. Presumably these differences are reflected in the differences between the growth roles of the Canadian and the Australian governments.

[4] L. F. Giblin did not develop his multiplier, to account for the cumulative impact of a decline in export values, until 1930. See A. L. Wright, "The Genesis of the Multiplier Theory," *Oxford Economic Papers*, 8:189–190 (1956).

MANCHURIA, RUSSIA, "PEOPLES' DEMOCRACIES"

This section summarizes two papers on countries whose growth conformed to the expansionist-induced pattern—Manchuria and Russia—and a paper on the "peoples' democracies" whose growth, although essentially intrinsic, came after 1945 to conform closely to the induced pattern that developed in Russia after 1918. Both Manchuria and Russia underwent expansionist growth during the period under survey, but their markedly induced patterns of growth were in sharp contrast with those of Northern America and Australia, and their populations were much more backward, even by early nineteenth-century standards.

Manchuria provides a unique and most interesting example of an economy in which the induced, nondominant, and expansionist growth patterns became united. Reubens has concentrated his attention on the period 1860–1931, during which British, Russian, and Japanese spheres of influence were established, and on 1931–40, during which Japan integrated Manchukuo into her empire. As long as the Chinese remained in control, Manchuria remained traditional and premodern, despite its great potentialities. The values, aspirations, and institutions of the Chinese in Manchuria were not suited to introducing Western methods and transforming and modernizing its economy; not even successful merchants showed a disposition, as emigrant Chinese merchants sometimes did in South Asia and elsewhere, to become creative industrial entrepreneurs. Only through foreign intervention, by the British, the Russians, and above all the Japanese, was the crust of custom effectively broken and consciousness of opportunity greatly increased. Economic life was commercialized and rationalized, and the capital and technology required to transform the economy were introduced. This developmental process did not become very powerful, however, until near the close of the nineteenth century, especially after the Sino-Japanese War when effective Russian and Japanese participation began, only to result in Russia's defeat by Japan and her expulsion from Southern Manchuria and Kwantung. Thereafter, Japanese penetration was rapid and on a large scale, being carried on by that remarkable joint agency of private enterprise and Japanese government, the South Manchuria Railway Company, and supplemented by private enterprise (both Japanese and Chinese, and much of it in agriculture), whose aggregate investment exceeded the direct undertakings of the SMR.

Meanwhile development was also proceeding, but more slowly, in the Russian zone of Manchuria. Under the leadership of the SMR, whose operations were both very profitable and compatible with the law of comparative advantage, a relatively skilled labor force, mostly Chinese, was created; Chinese entrepreneurship was provided with opportunity; and economic and social overhead capital (especially transport), some of which could not immediately yield satisfactory social returns, was supplied. Reubens believes that without foreign intervention, especially the governmentally assisted Japanese intervention, the great transformation that was taking place would not have got under way.

Foreign and domestic developments in the late 1920's and early 1930's brought about the establishment of a puppet state, Manchukuo. The direct and indirect roles of the state in the country's economic development increased greatly. Development, initially under a general plan and after 1937 under a Five-Year Plan, was oriented to the creation of an essentially self-sufficient empire within the complex of an East Asian "co-prosperity sphere." At first, emphasis was placed on the further development of transport, of the industrial foundation, and of the financial and banking structure; tariff protection was introduced, and resource surveys were undertaken. Subsequently, heavy industry, agriculture, and transport were favored; light industry and services, virtually ignored. Nearly all the additional capital invested came from Japan. The gradualist approach of the SMR gave place to that of the Manchurian Heavy Industry Company (financed in equal parts by the government and "new" Zaibatsu) and, more generally, to a system under which the government exercised influence through ownership, participation, and various regulations. Even so, as late as 1939, only about one third of all investment in strategic companies and somewhat less than one sixth of all company and partnership investment were held by the Manchukuo government.

Reubens points to the fact that shorter-run disequilibrium (to which private enterprise may make equilibrating response) usually accompanies even a satisfactory growth process, so that it is difficult to apply rationalist criteria of maximization. This difficulty is accentuated by extension of the time period involved, during the early part of which current outlays cannot yield satisfactory social returns, and error is likely to result if short-run criteria are employed to judge what must be assessed in terms of longer-run criteria. These difficulties are involved in attempts at assessment of the government's role in Manchuria, since its economic development was discontinuous and often attended by shorter-run and even by medium-run waste. Yet, one infers, the country's development would not have taken place in the absence of considerable foreign governmental intervention. Even more difficult of assessment is the Manchukuo era, since World War II and its aftermath prevented realization of the economic fruits of the major developmental activities undertaken in this period.

The economic condition of Russia and of the so-called "peoples' democracies" of Eastern Europe during the periods surveyed was similar to that of parts of Germany and Austria some decades earlier. With the partial exception of what became Czechoslovakia, all faced similar problems in that they were predominantly agricultural, nonindustrialized, and very short of both enterprise and savings available for investment in economic development. The economies of all the communist countries fit nicely into the induced category, therefore, even though the Russian was dominant and expansionist, whereas the others were satellitic and essentially intrinsic. The developmental history of each is divisible into two periods, the precommunist and the communist, but the latecomers to communism necessarily patterned their programs after the Russian, which had been in effect some 25 years. In Russia development under the first two five-year plans was assisted by the fact that during the czarist period considerable overhead capital (some of it in the form of transport that was not optimally located) had been constructed, and this permitted the use of resources for other purposes. Undoubtedly, the "peoples' democracies" were greatly assisted in carrying out their developmental programs by overhead and industrial capital accumulated there before 1945.

During the period 1890–1914, treated by Carson, the Russian economy experienced unprecedentedly rapid growth, especially in industry. In this period the country faced a double task, that of reorganizing its predominating activity, agriculture (not freed of serfdom until 1861), in the interest of greater efficiency, and that of facilitating or undertaking the establishment of various forms of enterprise, which unassisted private entrepreneurs seemed incapable of getting under way. Industrial capital was continuously in short supply, even though considerable amounts flowed in from abroad; this shortage was somewhat accentuated by the state's having to meet part of the expense of agricultural reform, and the overhead cost of colonizing peasants on lands to the east of those that had been under cultivation. State intervention came easily, of course, for much of Russia's land and wealth still remained under state ownership, and it had been customary for the state to participate in or undertake enterprise, at least since the time of Peter the Great. In and after the 1890's, however, major reliance was placed on protectionism (established in 1877); and the government, although ready to assist private entrepreneurs, was disposed to leave to them the operation and management of enterprises in most fields other than railroads, transportation, communications, and distilling. With the communization of the country after World War I, however, the economy became much more induced than in 1890–1913. After 1918, economic decisions regarding the use of resources and capital eventually came to be made almost entirely by agencies that made political decisions or that were responsible to political agencies.

In the "peoples' democracies" after World War II, just as earlier in the Soviet Union, responsibility for economic decisions passed to the makers of political decisions. Before 1939, however, and even before 1913, there had been much of the "induced" about economic decisions. Before 1913 their content was greatly affected by the satellitic character of the economies in Hungary, Rumania, Bulgaria, and what became Yugoslavia, and by the nonsovereign and satellitic conditions of the three areas into which Poland had been divided. The governments of these countries participated in the foundation of enterprises, established protectionism, which in turn helped to attract foreign capital, and resorted to tax exemption and other stimuli; even in Poland there was state intervention, at least until fear developed that Polish industry might become competitive with industry in the controlling countries. Greatest interest was manifested in the development of railroads and utilities. Despite the efforts of the various governments, the whole region remained heavily dependent on agriculture as late as 1913. Only in the Czech lands had industrial development become "self-generating"; elsewhere, with the partial exception of Hungary, there was little manufacture of finished goods, and industry was confined largely to supplying consumers' goods and refining raw materials. The minimal requirements of development were met in only a small part of Eastern Europe.

With the close of World War I, the reunification of Poland, the creation of Czechoslovakia, and the enlargement of Rumania and Yugoslavia, governmental intervention and participation in economic activities greatly increased, being most pronounced in Poland and least in the Czech lands, where industry was most advanced and diversified. There was recourse to state banking and to much more prohibitive protectionism than had obtained before the war; but these measures failed to attract foreign capital, for long-run foreign investment had been discouraged by xenophobic "nostrification" policies, by measures discriminatory against private investment in general, and by the depression of the 1930's. Progress during the interwar period was modest, therefore, although substantial in some industries (e.g., textiles, machinery construction). After World War II and the resulting boundary changes, state enterprise on the Russian model dominated economic development in each of the "peoples' democracies" but did not free them of their satellitic characteristics.[5]

According to Spulber, the rationale underlying state intervention changed from period to period. Before 1914 it was justified on the ground that private enterprise was incapable of financing and undertaking some of the activities deemed "necessary." In the 1920's nationalism and xenophobia served both to keep out foreign enterprise and to handicap private enterprise. In the 1930's intervention reflected both fear of war and concern, arising out of depression experiences, that private enterprise could not establish a self-sufficient economy. After World War II, in accordance with the Russian model, economic decision-making passed completely under the control of the state, and the somewhat jumbled prewar governmental interventionism gave place to methods that almost entirely excluded foreign competition, internal consumer sovereignty, and freedom of choice, and that raised capital formation to unprecedentedly high levels by greatly depressing consumption. At present, of course, plans in various countries are being changed, in part because of dissatisfaction with earlier results.

Commenting on what has taken place during the past 100 years, Spulber reports a secular upward trend in state economic activity but suggests that, at least under some conditions, achievement of a self-sustaining and expanding system favors an increase in the role of private enterprise. State intervention up to the 1940's comprised protectionist measures and the provision of capital to enterprise; only thereafter did it concentrate on the development of key heavy industries. Spulber suggests that continuation of economic development in this area, even under communist auspices, will entail departure from the unprecedented amount of autarky that has underlain communist planning until now.

[5] See Nicolas Spulber, "Factors in Eastern Europe's Intratrade and Cooperation," *Journal of International Affairs*, 11(1):20–30 (1957); David Granick, "The Pattern of Foreign Trade in Eastern Europe and Its Relation to Economic Development Policy," *Quarterly Journal of Economics*, 68:377–400 (August 1954).

GERMANY, SWITZERLAND, TURKEY

The papers dealing with Germany, with Switzerland, perhaps the most autonomous developed country in the world, and with Turkey, an economy whose internal situation resembled somewhat that of the "peoples' democracies," are summarized in this section. The experience of Germany and Turkey lends some support to Hoselitz's model, to be discussed in the next section. Goal-attainment policy dominated Prussia in the absolutist period; at a late date Bismarck's social legislation was in part a response to the resurgence of the problem of integration. Even the removal of restrictions by the Prussian bureaucracy after 1850 in response to the demands of the bourgeoisie represented a kind of goal-attaining response. In Turkey, after integration and solidarity had been achieved in 1923–33, horizontal planning was introduced to realize goals that had been generally agreed upon; these goals, like Canada's, were prompted in part by defense considerations.

Turkish economic development during the period 1933–50 may be said to have corresponded to the induced, intrinsic, and dominant patterns, particularly if a tendency to draw on foreign sources and give greater scope to private enterprise toward the close of the period is disregarded. The shift toward nation-oriented etatism in the first years was somewhat affected by anticapitalistic ideological and institutional developments elsewhere. It seems to have been prompted principally, however, by the failure of private enterprise to live up to expectations during the preceding decade, a failure attributable in part to a marked shortage of entrepreneurs because of the departure of those ethnic groups from which the commercial class had been largely recruited. The Turkish government, therefore, undertook to accelerate the development of the manufacture of consumer goods and domestically utilized goods based on local raw materials, together with the partial fabrication of abundant raw materials for both export and domestic use. In order to develop such industries two holding-company banks were created and financed by the government, which already dominated military production, transport, communications, and utilities, and existing state monopolies (in tobacco, salt, explosives, and alcohol). Only commerce and the remaining branches of industry were freely open to private enterprise. Ironically, however, while this program was being carried out, there gradually emerged a private industrial and commercial class, together with engineers and economic specialists in the public sector. These became critical of the monopolistic character of state enterprise and the failure of the state to give greater scope to private enterprise. As a result, and because of the impact of the Marshall Plan, a greater role was allowed domestic and foreign private enterprise, and more attention was given to agriculture, which up to that point had been discriminated against by the planning authorities.

The Turkish experience paralleled that of Prussia in the nineteenth century in that conditions more favorable to the conduct of private enterprise than had existed earlier were brought into being, although developments unconnected with Turkey's horizontal planning seem to have contributed markedly to the introduction of more autonomy. Kerwin believes that some of these improvements would not have been made in the absence of state intervention, the burden of which seems to have fallen on consumers, above all, on the peasant consuming class. He suggests that the country became much more conscious of power, that the commercial class was strengthened, and that a skilled working class began to develop. It is probable also, on balance, that capital formation was stepped up and transport improved. It is not clear, however, whether the resources invested in state plants were put to the best possible use, and it is evident that agriculture was adversely affected. The planning carried on proved defective in other respects; in particular, there was too little investment in health, agricultural extension service, education, and the training of technicians (e.g., there were not enough technicians to run the machines introduced).

Pounds' study of the role of the Prussian state yields two conclusions of especial interest. First, while German economic development conformed largely to the intrinsic and dominant patterns, it did not approximate the autonomous pattern until late in the nineteenth century. Earlier the Prussian state had played an important and continuing role in the development of heavy industry, largely to satisfy anticipated military requirements. It established heavy industry in Silesia and later in the Saar, supervised considerable private industry in order to insure the progressive character of its performance, and created a body of skill, technology, and experience that finally enabled private enterprise to flourish, at least where state control did not eventually deter private investment as it did in Upper Silesia before the 1870's. In consequence private industry became dominant in the closing third of the nineteenth century, after having been under considerable state control in the middle third and greatly stimulated by state action in the first third. The distribution of industrial activity was affected accordingly: with the removal of local tariffs and other barriers to the establishment of a common market in the second half of the nineteenth century, interregional competition gave play to the law of comparative advantage and some areas declined in relative or absolute importance. The second conclusion yielded by Pounds' study is that the state's major contribution did not consist in making capital available to heavy industry—capital requirements were quite small at first—but in importing the knowledge and skill required, giving these opportunity to accumulate and spread, and, more generally, giving play to the force of what Marshall called increasing return.

Parker, in his study of the role of technology and of interstate differences in interventionist procedure in Germany and France, raises a question of a different nature: how it comes about that modern industry, with its characteristic technology and processes, varies only insignificantly from one country to another, despite wide political and cultural differences. The fact that a common result is achieved implies that in each national society the diverse elements which may facilitate or hinder industrialization and growth are finally adjusted to each other so as to make rational economic progress possible. The secular state is the agency that brings about these necessary adjustments, in two principal ways. Through public education the state counteracts both hindrances to economic development and the allurement of alternatives to the acquisition of wealth. Through a suitable legal and administrative system the state puts the products of that education to their maximum use. By way of example Parker points to the roughly comparable results that were achieved in mining and smelting in French and German Lorraine between 1871 and 1914, despite the fact that French mining law was much more restrictive than the German and the French system of technological education was much more general, thorough, and exacting. It is inferrible that each system was accommodated to the realization of the same basic objective, a heavy industry complex. Pounds' study reveals, however, that in the eighteenth century the French state's efforts to encourage development of a metal industry were not as successful as the Prussian, probably because France's government was inefficient and corrupt. France's history after 1850 shows that, even when a country is well provided with capital, technical skill and knowledge, competent entrepreneurs, and industrious habits, its economic growth may be retarded, particularly by governmental policies that shunt its resources out of activities in which its comparative advantage is great into those in which it is small.[6]

[6] See Rondo E. Cameron, "Economic Growth and Stagnation in France, 1815–1914," First Newberry Library Conference on French History, Chicago, (May 11,

Bürgin's account of the development of Swiss industry indicates that an analysis of the role of the state in the economic development of Switzerland resembles *Hamlet* without the Prince of Denmark. Swiss economic growth conformed closely to the intrinsic and the autonomous patterns. It also conformed to the nondominant pattern in that foreign markets were important and that much Swiss industry originated with refugees who escaped to Switzerland, mainly from Catholic countries and in some instances from areas where territorial states swamped erstwhile commercial cities. It was unnecessary before 1800 for any Swiss government to attempt to establish industries, since private entrepreneurs had performed or were performing this function just as they were supplying capital, out of commercial and handicraft and (later) financial profits, supplemented by refugee capital and earlier the earnings of mercenaries. Swiss merchants and middlemen, because of their geographical situation and the recognition that they did not represent mercantilist economies, enjoyed a preferred position and were able to reap additional advantages when their neighbors engaged in war. While several Swiss governments on occasion sought to engage in mercantilist practices, these bore little fruit; no significant promotion of industry in the mercantilist sense ever succeeded. The economy of Switzerland thus remains the most autonomous of those dealt with in this volume, for there it is almost universally accepted now, as in the nineteenth and earlier centuries, that the economy is supposed to be the concern of private persons. As yet, acceptance of this tenet has not been undermined even by full-employment theory.

Swiss economic history lends some support to Hartshorne's argument that the presence of natural resources need not play an indispensable role in economic development. It was technological and related knowledge, most of it secured originally through immigration, that gave Swiss industry its start and kept it abreast of similar industries elsewhere. Prior to 1800 Swiss industrialists, confronted by a small domestic market and dependent on foreign markets, sought to keep their technology in the forefront and their firms small, and to get cheap, duty-free foodstuffs and raw materials from abroad. Furthermore, they increasingly specialized and differentiated their exports so as to meet both

---

1957); and on the abundance of French capital, "French Finance and Italian Unity: The Cavourian Decade," *American Historical Review,* 62:552–569 (April 1957). Whereas the papers in this volume deal only with effects of capital imports, a study of French or English economic growth might inquire whether domestic growth was checked by a greater outflow of capital than domestic potentialities warranted.

foreign competition and foreign protectionism. The availability of cheap capital, together with a high degree of labor mobility, enabled alert entrepreneurs to make adaptations as they became necessary. Although conditions were modified by the industrial revolution, Swiss industrialists continued by these methods to meet the shortages of raw material to which the country was subject. Bürgin does not inquire to what extent Switzerland's economic development was slowed in the middle of the nineteenth century by the "night watchman" character of the Swiss state, the persistence of sectional rivalries, and the absence of a banking system sufficiently developed to amass domestic and attract foreign capital.

HOSELITZ'S SCHEMA AND ANALYSES

In Hoselitz's earlier paper, outlining the schema employed in selecting countries and time periods for study in preparation for this conference, a distinction was made between induced and autonomous patterns of growth. In his paper in this volume Hoselitz again makes this distinction, using the terms in a narrower but still ideal-typical sense, and bases his main findings on it.[7] He reaches three important conclusions: (1) His analysis of periods when a relatively induced pattern of growth tends to prevail indicates that, in the course of a state's history, growth more frequently conforms to an induced than to an autonomous pattern. (2) Having distinguished between "horizontal" or comprehensive planning and systematic "vertical" or selective planning, he finds that horizontal planning tends to be encountered among underdeveloped latecomers to industrialization, whereas systematic vertical planning tends virtually to be confined to advanced societies with highly specialized and relatively complex economic institutions. (3) In the future, with the resolution of the problems that have greatly

[7] Growth conforms to the induced pattern when the government, in pursuit of objectives, makes the decisions that increase average productivity (e.g., by increasing capital per head or introducing more efficient forms of productive organization); it conforms to the autonomous pattern when the decisions are made by private individuals in pursuit of self-oriented goals or motives. In actual growth patterns, of course, both autonomous and induced elements are likely to be present. Because some functions are always performed by the state, it is essential to eliminate performance of such functions from consideration and then to determine from the nature of the elements remaining whether an actual growth pattern is predominantly induced or autonomous in character.

increased the importance of induced economic growth in the present century, an autonomous pattern may again come to prevail for a time.

Reasoning in structural-functional terms, Hoselitz identifies four somewhat interrelated categories of ever present societal needs, which sometimes can be met through routine operations and procedures but at other times can be satisfied only through intensified and suitably organized efforts. These categories of problems or needs are: the *maintenance,* concerned with preserving the prevailing structure and hierarchy of social and cultural values; the *integrative,* concerned with the absorption of individuals and groups into a society, with the determination of this society's membership criteria, and with the definition of the relations of its interacting members or subgroups; *goal attainment,* concerned with the realization of systemic goals (e.g., provision of economic and social overhead capital, technical training, etc.) as distinguished from the goals of private individuals; and *adaptive,* having to do with the adjustment of a society to its physical environment and to the surrounding social groups with which it interacts. Hoselitz believes, although he is not able to establish a theoretical basis for this belief, that historically a society, having resolved the main problem of integration, concerns itself with goal-attainment problems (cf. Toynbee's "challenge" stage), the burden of which varies greatly, i.e., with the magnitude of the systemic goals sought, the speed with which they are sought, and the resources available for their realization. Finally, when these problems have been resolved and the attainment of the systemic goals has been largely routinized, the society concerns itself with essentially private, individualistic problems and needs of the adaptive sort. Economic growth thus tends to conform to an induced pattern when goal-attainment problems predominate, and to an autonomous pattern when adaptive needs and problems predominate.

As long as a society, having resolved its integrative problems, remains primarily concerned with attainment of systemic goals, the direct and positive role of government will be great. If the realization of these goals is conditioned by the availability of a society's resources and the uses to which they are put, as is usually the case, utilization of these resources will be subjected to a great deal of governmental decision-making and control, and much of the economic growth that takes place will be induced. When, however, the systemic goals have been realized or routinized, the role of government will be relaxed; resource use and economic growth will then conform largely to the autonomous pattern.

The solution of integrative and goal-attainment problems may not be permanent and, in fact, never has been permanent. For this reason autonomous growth patterns may give place repeatedly to induced growth patterns, as Pirenne's and other studies reveal. When an old system (e.g., feudalism) dissolves, or an old state (e.g., Austria-Hungary, the Ottoman Empire) falls apart, or when a new state is being constituted (e.g., nineteenth-century Germany, or Italy), integrative problems come to the fore at once, and these are followed by goal-attainment problems. During this stage of a country's evolution, therefore, economic growth is likely to conform to the induced pattern. When, however, these problems have again been solved—as in Germany late in the nineteenth century and long before in England, France, and Holland—individuals become free to satisfy private adaptive needs as they choose, with the result that economic growth becomes autonomous and the procedures developed to meet adaptive needs may even be adjustable later to the service of goal attainment (e.g., when entrepreneurs are converted into managers). But when new crises arise, as in the present century, goal-attainment problems also come to the fore again, and growth conforms more to the induced pattern.

The nature of the planning that government decision-making involves changes as a society progresses. When economies are greatly underdeveloped, as in the heyday of mercantilism or in the early Soviet Union or in some present-day countries, many specific goals are sought, and horizontal planning tends to predominate or even to prevail, sometimes in so overdetermined a measure that the economic system breaks down unless the conditions of the plan are violated whenever necessary. It is believed that many specific activities must be undertaken at this stage because, with the economy still undeveloped, given tasks cannot be accomplished unless complementary activities are also carried out. When, however, an economy has become complex and functionally specialized and adaptive needs have come to be important, vertical planning (especially of a systematic sort), which "establishes the limits within which the individual is free" to pursue his private, self-oriented goals, tends to prevail. This type of planning will tend to replace horizontal planning in underdeveloped countries as adaptive needs become important and their economies become sufficiently complex, specialized, and productive. In time, therefore, should the crisis that interrupted autonomous growth in the present century be resolved and goal-attainment problems decline in importance, autonomous growth may again predominate.

ISSUES DISCUSSED BY THE CONFERENCE

In this section a number of issues raised at the conference are considered. Attention is given, first, to seven types of questions suggested by the papers and the discussion of them and, second, to the supposed shortcomings of the analytical and explanatory schema employed.

Specific Problems

1. The effectiveness of public decisions designed to induce growth varies greatly, just as does that of private decisions directed to the same purpose. This variation is often overlooked, however, especially by those who contrast optimum political decision-making with random private decision-making. What can be accomplished turns, *ceteris paribus*, on the skill, aspirations, capabilities, etc. of makers of political decisions. Their qualities vary greatly, just as does the manner in which decision making and provisions for its execution are organized and distributed. The bureaucracy charged with formulating and carrying out growth-oriented decisions may be lacking in integrity, skill, or drive, or it may be well endowed in these respects. Other things being equal, results tend to be bad under the former condition and good under the latter. Again, under given technological conditions and external constraints (e.g., treaty obligations), what a "state" or "government" can accomplish in economic growth is conditioned by the way in which responsibility for initiating and carrying out decisions is distributed among the several repositories of "political power" (i.e., national or provincial or departmental or state government, metropolitan or municipal corporation, county). This distribution affects what can be done at any time, how fast it can be done, the procedures that are followed, etc. Because a national government has the greatest access to funds, development programs conducted at the national level can usually accomplish much more than can those carried out at lower levels, although it may be easier to reach an activity-releasing consensus at a lower level where the population affected is more homogeneous. It is to be inferred, therefore, that some minimum of concentrated and centralized power is required for political decision-makers to get rid of initial rigidities that prevent growth, to augment the rate of involuntary saving, to mobilize sentiments behind growth, and otherwise influence economic development significantly. What this optimum degree of centralization is, however, we do not know; nor do we know

how a state's capacity to influence economic development varies with differences in degree of such concentration beyond the optimum, since increase in concentration beyond some point may involve increase in governmental difficulties.

The argument just presented is probably more applicable to a situation in which the state remains the agency of the national community, as in Western democracies, than to one in which the national community is dominated by those who control the state and its apparatus, as in the Soviet Union or Mainland China. This statement suggests that, when one is analyzing the developmental role of the state, one must distinguish between countries in which the state is the agency of the national community and countries in which the state dominates the national community. In the latter all developmental decisions and activities are formed and executed by the state, whereas in the former only certain developmental decisions are made by the state and only certain developmental activities are carried on by the state.[8]

2. Structural-functional analysis, even in a much less elaborate context than that used by Hoselitz, does suggest that a major cause of state intervention has been the failure of private enterprise, for whatever reasons, to undertake activities that enough strategically situated members of the community believed should be undertaken. Such a belief may have been badly founded, may have entailed a misuse of resources, and eventually may have been given up because of failure; but until then it led to state intervention.[9] From this statement, however, it is evident that conditions in addition to nonsatisfaction of a supposed need must be present; thus if optimizing resource use is appreciated and the support of many individuals is a precondition to intervention, it is much less likely to take place than when ignorance of optimizing rules and approval by a small minority suffice to beget action.

3. Economic growth is affected by every action of political decision-makers that influences the uses to which resources are put (e.g., whether to formation of industrial or public capital). It is thus affected both by actions that are intended to affect it and by those that are not. It is only through detailed historical study that the consequences of actions of the latter sort, and the variation of their impact over

[8] Political scientists might illuminate the problem under consideration, were they to deal with the notion of state not as a concept used in public law but as one intended to suit the needs of empirical discourse and research.

[9] On functionalism see Robert K. Merton, *Social Theory and Social Structure* (Glencoe: Free Press, 1949), Chapter 1, especially pp. 32–38, 52, 73.

time, can be estimated. It seems probable, however, that the major influence of the state on the course of economic growth is exercised through actions intended to have such effect, be they well or badly conceived. Yet some of the papers reveal that even actions intended to accelerate growth may have an adverse effect (e.g., in Australia, Turkey, France, Russia, Eastern Europe).[10]

4. As long as the state is separate from the community and functions primarily as its agent, as was the case in most of the countries dealt with, intervention by the state is likely to conform to the notion of vertical planning rather than to that of horizontal planning; and the rationale is likely to be a variant of that expressed in liberal economic and political literature and implicit in political practice before 1920 and most of that after 1940. The deliberate developmental role of the state then is confined principally to carrying out overhead activities of the sort that the state seems better able to do than private enterprise, and to intervention in situations in which, under private auspices, activities would not be carried to the point where marginal social costs and marginal social benefits became approximately equal. Among the activities in which the point of equivalence between marginal private cost and marginal private benefit did not tend to coincide with that between marginal social cost and marginal social benefit, there were usually included investments in some forms of economic and social overhead capital. In the former category are investments in transportation, communication, power, irrigation, drainage, soil conservation, and similar facilities; in the latter, investments in sanitation, education, and similar facilities.[11] Investment in such overhead facilities may not be carried far enough under purely private auspices because these facilities contribute both indirectly and directly to the generation of gross national product, and because they are lumpy, not nicely adjustable to current requirements, and often need to be built in advance of the time when they can be fully used. Moreover, if they are not carried far enough, investment in industrial and related capital, to which the indicated

[10] It is necessary, when studying the effects of different sorts of actions, to allow for biases that may be inherent in surviving empirical evidence. I have dealt with this problem in a different connection in "Laissez Faire and Intervention: A Potential Source of Historical Error," *Journal of Political Economy*, 52:438 ff. (October 1949).

[11] Housing, social welfare, and similar facilities also are forms of social overhead capital. These are not included in the present discussion, however, since under Western democratic regimes too much rather than too little of an economy's resources may be invested in these forms, given as the desideratum a high rate of economic growth.

forms of overhead capital are complementary, is slowed down. The state, therefore, usually must subsidize, help finance, or otherwise bring about investment in overhead capital. When a state, particularly an underdeveloped state, provides this capital expeditiously, there is likely to be much less need for direct planning, and obstacles to growth (e.g., institutional and social-structural resistances, a state's shortage of administrative tools, backwardness in general) are likely to be less powerful.

Historically, in countries where a laissez-faire philosophy prevailed, the state participated in economic activities of three types: (1) activities technically or otherwise more amenable to public than to private enterprise, even though roughly compatible with consumer sovereignty and freedom of choice (e.g., educational system, social security system); (2) activities considered more amenable to public than to private enterprise, although they represented the aspirations and choice of only a portion of the affected population (e.g., combination hydroelectric and flood-control system); (3) activities not likely to be undertaken on a sufficiently large scale under the auspices of private enterprise, even if quite amenable to it (e.g., establishment of a transport system). Most of the growth-oriented activities in which the state participated were of the second and third types. The state could undertake these measures because there had been surrendered to it, in varying measure and for varying periods of time, that political sovereignty and freedom of choice on the possession of which the exercise of consumer sovereignty and freedom of choice ultimately is contingent. This surrender became great and protracted in countries in which horizontal planning was resorted to (e.g., the communist states, Turkey, Manchukuo in the late 1930's). The degree of surrender becomes less, of course, as consumer tastes and demands change in a direction compatible with the state's activities, and becomes greater when change is in the opposite direction.

The state's intended actions, beyond those designed to create a general milieu (monetary, tax, fiscal, etc.) favorable to economic growth, would be directed principally to increasing the volume of inputs devoted to growth in some or all of its forms; to decreasing input per unit of output, whether by transforming factors, modifying factor combinations, or otherwise; and to diverting inputs into comparatively productive growth-generating activities or organizational forms, from situations where unemployment or underemployment prevailed, and from use in relatively unproductive industries or in consumer-oriented and other industries not favorable to growth. This diversion might be carried out so as to insure balanced growth.[12] Diversion would be accomplished directly if the state set up more or less independent agencies to transform hired inputs into goods and services favoring growth; and indirectly if the state employed private entrepreneurs to carry out these tasks, or established market and other conditions and expectations calculated to prompt entrepreneurs to undertake these tasks in the hope of profit. Since what inducements are employed in a society is of much significance, great emphasis on the distinction between induced and autonomous growth patterns may divert attention from the specific character of the inducements actually utilized.

5. Much controversy revolves around the state's double role as a producer and a user of capital. It is commonly argued that the state has played an indispensable role in making provision for various forms of economic and social overhead capital, even when this capital has long gone under-utilized, a condition more likely in a heartland country than in a maritime country in which outlay on transport tends to be lower in relation to amount of activity. Concerning the great importance of state provision for the introduction of advanced technology and the training of a skilled labor force there is no dispute. Nor is there dispute that, when a state provides overhead capital, it elevates the productivity of complementary factors and creates a disequilibrium to which enterprise must adjust and may even respond synergistically. It is admitted, furthermore, that the time horizon of private enterprise operating in underdeveloped countries is likely to be shorter than developmental programs require,[13] with the result that the state has to support activities involving relatively long time horizons.

Beneath this controversy lies, on the one hand, an awareness of the theoretical difficulties that attend determination of discount rates and capital formation rates compatible with welfare considerations (especially in the absence of effective expression of consumer sentiment) [14] and, on the other, a lack of firm information on the empirical issues.

[12] See M. Fleming, "External Economies and the Doctrine of Balanced Growth," *Economic Journal*, 65:241–256 (June 1955).

[13] The length of the time horizon varies not only with country and degree of security but, in a given country, with the type of enterprise, tending to be much longer among large corporations than among small partnerships and proprietorships. In an underdeveloped country it is probable that both internal conditions and the form of enterprise will make for relative shortness of time horizon.

[14] On some of these difficulties see J. de Graaff, *Theoretical Welfare Economics* (Cambridge, England: Cambridge University Press, 1957), pp. 99 ff.; also A. C. Pigou, *Socialism versus Capitalism* (London: Macmillan & Co., 1937), Chapter 8.

Time horizons, quality of foresight, and flexibility of invested capital are involved. It does not follow that because the state tends to be charged with tasks involving relatively long time horizons, those who make the crucial decisions will hit on the "right" time horizon. In liberal democracies politicians often are governed by short-run considerations, whereas decision makers in nondemocracies may choose, without suffering repercussions, to be governed by unusually long-run considerations. It is hardly to be supposed a priori that foresight at any given time will be less imperfect among public than among private decision-makers. The extent to which misuse of resources will arise from imperfection of foresight or incorrect selection of time horizon will be greatly affected, therefore, by how flexible overhead capital is and by the degree to which error-reporting mechanisms operate and contribute to modifying incorrect decisions. If overhead and other relevant forms of capital are flexible, improperly invested capital can be readapted at small cost to the more effective service of consumer or other relevant preferences; if not, much of the usefulness of the resources embodied in the capital will have been lost. In a market-dominated economy mistakes in capital investment are registered early, with the double result that investment is readapted when possible and, when not possible, it is written down to a value commensurate with its productivity; underinvestment, of course, produces an opposite effect. In consequence, later investment decisions are made in the light of this experience, be it favorable or unfavorable. It is to be doubted, however, that comparable error-reporting mechanisms operate in the public sector, and that public decision-makers are disposed to make necessary responses quickly, when error is disclosed. If this doubt is well-founded, resources are more likely to be misinvested in the public than in the private sector.[15] The experience of at least one communist country reveals such misinvestment.[16]

[15] Over against this must be set the argument (present in a considerable body of literature) that in the private sector there is a strong bias against carrying investment as far as equivalence at the margin requires. It is also said that "purposeful obsolescence" operates in the private sector, as does pyramid building in the public, to absorb resources that could be put to better use.

[16] In his speech at the eighth plenum of the PZPR Central Committee, October 20, 1956, the Polish premier, W. Gomulka, reported that there had been established at Zeran an automobile factory capable of producing only automobiles of an older type, and these at "disproportionately high production costs." The ex post contribution of this factory must therefore have fallen below its ex ante contribution, yet there is no evidence that its value was written down accordingly. My colleague,

6. In the statements above, conformity with the indications of consumer sovereignty and freedom of choice has been implicitly and explicitly employed as a measure of the correctness of a policy. It is not possible here to set down the qualifications to which some would subject this criterion, but in some welfare indexes it is only one of several criteria. The role of consumer sovereignty and freedom of choice has been much larger in noncommunist countries (including even Turkey and Manchukuo, where planning became essentially horizontal) than in the communist countries. It is probably correct to say that the communist approach has been possible only after the underlying population has virtually surrendered political sovereignty (and therewith consumer sovereignty and freedom of choice) to a political and managerial elite with military and police power at its command. Presumably "welfare" has been reduced. It remains to be seen, however, whether political liberty and consumer preference are necessarily incompatible with a high degree of centralization in all types of countries. Turkey's experience suggests that political liberty may co-exist with a high degree of centralization. It may also be argued that, as productivity per head rises in a nonautonomous country, consumer goods production will increase in importance, with the result that consumer preference increases in power; and that the resulting decentralization of industrial decision-making will be re-enforced by geographical decentralization, as inter-regional disparities diminish with the spread of technology, etc.

7. A number of issues merit more discussion than they received at the conference: (a) A country's size appears to be an important determinant of the kinds of problems confronting its economy and of the direction in which solutions may be sought. A large country is likely to be relatively independent of foreign sources and markets, and relatively free to maneuver technologically and economically and (even if burdened with relatively heavy transport costs) to carry out public and private programs in various ways; it is also relatively capable of

---

Calvin B. Hoover, drew my attention to this speech. Examination of the speeches of communist leaders (e.g., those of N. Khrushchev) reveals a tendency to exaggerate the prospective benefits to be derived from further investment at the expense of austerity. Presumably such exaggeration is followed by actual investment, even in the face of objections from better-informed technical personnel. Presumably, also, there is little tendency on the part of those who (probably after protracted delay) become aware of resulting errors of misinvestment or overinvestment to draw attention to them or to take corrective action (except when those struggling for power find it advantageous to encourage such action).

realizing economies of scale and balance in both public and private sectors. A small country can rarely achieve these advantages, even with freedom of trade; nor can it escape difficulties associated with dependence on imported resources, or such cumulative adverse effect on its supply of skills as may arise from dependence on imported resources. These disadvantages are greatly accentuated when a small satellitic country (e.g., a "people's democracy" in East Europe) is not free to trade with the rest of the world. A small country may also find relatively more burdensome than does a large country the business of satisfying integration and other general goals. (b) When a country's size is taken into account, it becomes easier to specify the role that nonhuman resources do or may play in its economy. (c) A distinction should be drawn between invention and innovation, on the one hand, and imitation and adaptation, on the other. It is much easier for a state to facilitate the imitation and adaptation of superior technologies that have been developed elsewhere than to generate invention and innovation in the first place. It is preferable, in fact, that the state as such play only a minimum and indirect role in the generation of invention and innovation, for effective performance of this role requires great freedom. Some of the papers indicate that states were successful in performing an imitative role (e.g., Prussia, Manchuria) but not in carrying out an innovative role.

Comments on Schema Used for the Conference

Assessment of Hoselitz's two schemes of analysis is not attempted here, but merely a presentation of comments prompted by them and of an argument to the effect that policy may constitute the best point of departure for the study of how to induce growth. The schema referred to in the Introduction has little predictive and only limited explanatory value. It does not, of course, serve purposes it was not intended to serve, such as illuminating how the growth process becomes institutionalized, identifying strategic variables, indicating when social structures are capable of changing in any one of a number of directions, facilitating analysis of the unique factors present in every growth situation. Unless detailed study discloses more correlation among the three continua than has been revealed in this volume, the schema will not permit prediction. It may be that state activity tends to be relatively great when a country is in an early expansionist stage, only to subside, in a relatively autonomous society, when private enterprise in regions initially developed (e.g., eastern United States) has become powerful enough to carry out development in less advanced regions, if sufficient resources are available.[17] Also, as an economy moves from an expansionist into an intrinsic stage, it may be able to supply its capital requirements better (since it no longer has to invest so heavily in low-turnover capital), and to become relatively less satellitic generally, particularly when its per capita income rises and therewith the relative importance of services. However, if increasing political independence is associated with movement from an expansionist to an intrinsic stage, the role of the state will tend to increase initially at least (e.g., Poland, Australia, India after 1947) because political independence entails a change in the content of the social-welfare index and thus stimulates state intervention in its behalf (e.g., transport and investment may now have to be differently distributed). It is probable, of course, that as an economy changes along one continuum, there are changes in content of activity if not of position along the other two. Thus a state is likely to be faced by different tasks in the intrinsic stage than in the expansionist.[18]

Ambiguities present in the second schema, it was alleged, reduce its predictive and its explanatory powers.[19] Systemic goals were not considered to be clearly enough demarcated from adaptive goals, nor was there sufficient specification of the conditions under which the presence of systemic goals would and would not incite action entailing induced growth. Other criticisms were to the effect that it was not made sufficiently clear when the goal-attainment phase gives place to the adaptive phase, and by what circumstances this replacement process is conditioned. The genesis and the recurrence of systemic goals were not ade-

[17] The effect of the development of new regions on that of old is of interest. Given full employment in old regions, their growth would be retarded by the diversion of resources to new regions, unless this process produced increasing returns and stimulated increasing efficiency in the old regions. However, if chronic unemployment existed in old regions, investment in the development of new regions might be accompanied by further development of the old. See the studies by Duesenberry and Chipman cited by Broude, pp. 23, 24, supra.

[18] It is always evident when there has been movement along the satellitic-dominant continuum or along the expansionist-intrinsic continuum, but whether there has been net movement along the induced-autonomous continuum is not always evident. Changes may take place simultaneously in public and in private decision-making and may offset each other, so that the position on the continuum does not change, even though superficial examination of the changes taking place might suggest a shift in position.

[19] The distinction between horizontal and vertical planning was not subjected to criticism.

quately accounted for, nor was enough consideration given to the possibility of cycles or phases in time, together with time lags. Inasmuch as individual wants of the sort stressed in the adaptive phase are always important, it seemed quite possible that changes in the character of these wants might dissipate the capacity of the state to continue to sacrifice consumer preference of systemic goals, particularly under modern conditions. It was noted that the schema did not illuminate the kinds of inducements utilized by the state, nor explain adequately when horizontal rather than vertical planning is resorted to.

The experience of advanced Western countries is of little value to underdeveloped countries, it was suggested. In the West high rates of growth were associated with highly intercorrelated conditions (i.e., democratic institutions, a strong middle class, a pluralistic power setting) that are not present and not easily introduced into most underdeveloped countries. In fact, when one does encounter a high rate of growth in such countries, it has always been associated with the pursuit, at least for a time (as in Japan), of integrated policies under the leadership of a strong central authority. What particular policies such an authority should pursue are discoverable, at least in part, through careful study of the impact of specific policies followed in the past, both within and outside the West. There has been enough repetition of particular policies to permit assessment of their impact and to infer from their impact what variables are most strategic for purposes of growth and how these variables are related, both to one another and to nonstrategic variables.

INDEX OF NAMES

INDEX OF SUBJECTS